Praise for Frances Mayes

"A poet of her world, a writer inventing the world as she moves through it, unwilling to accept anyone else's version . . . there is an immediacy combined with the sense of an ongoing traditional struggle that pushes the poem out, makes it a poem of necessity."

—*San Francisco Chronicle*

"Mayes has an urgent interest in the ways past and present converge. . . . She writes with terse magic."　　　—*Los Angeles Times*

"A poet with stylistic variety, technical skill, and—most importantly—an informing vision . . . [She] works in the manner of a fine photographer placing unlikely objects into surprising conjunctions." —*Choice*

Praise for
Under the Tuscan Sun and *Bella Tuscany*

"Frances Mayes is, before all else, a wonderful writer."

—*Chicago Tribune*

"An intense celebration of what she calls 'the voluptuousness of Italian life' . . . [Her book] seems like the kind of thing you'd tuck into a picnic basket on an August day . . . or better yet, keep handy on the bedside table in the depths of January."

—*The New York Times Book Review*

"Somehow, this is a narrative at once joyful and full of common sense, a balance that few other writers have struck so perfectly. It's as intimate as a lover's whisper, honest and true, and vividly captures a sense of place."　　　—*San Francisco Chronicle*

"A love letter to Italy written in precise and passionate language of near-poetic density . . . this is a book to treasure, as the author so clearly treasures the life she engraves on our hearts."　　—*Newsday*

THE DISCOVERY OF
POETRY

THE DISCOVERY OF
POETRY

A FIELD GUIDE
TO READING AND WRITING POEMS

FRANCES MAYES

A Harvest Original • Harcourt, Inc.

Orlando   Austin   New York   San Diego   Toronto   London

Requests for permission to make copies of any part
of the work should be mailed to the following address:
Permissions Department, Harcourt, Inc.,
6277 Sea Harbor Drive, Orlando, Florida 32887-6777.

www.HarcourtBooks.com

Earlier editions of *The Discovery of Poetry*
were published by Harcourt Brace College Publishers.

Library of Congress Cataloging-in-Publication Data
Mayes, Frances.
The discovery of poetry: a field guide to reading and writing
poems/Frances Mayes. — 1st Harvest ed.
p.   cm.
"A Harvest original."
Includes index.
ISBN 0-15-600762-2
1. Poetics. 2. English poetry—Appreciation. 3. American poetry—
Appreciation. 4. English poetry—History and criticism.
5. American poetry—History and criticism.
PN1042.M34 2001
808.1—dc21   2001024958

Text set in Electra LH
Designed by Lydia D'moch

Printed in the United States of America

First Harvest edition 2001
G I K J H F

Permissions acknowledgments begin on page 497
and constitute a continuation of the copyright page.

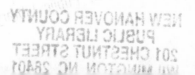

Contents

Invitation   ix

1. Sources and Approaches   1

    The Origin of a Poem   1
    The Art of Reading   5
    Poems   15

2. Words: Texture and Sound   25

    Texture of Language   25
    Choosing Words   30
    The Muscle of Language   34
    Sound Patterns   35
    The Surprise of Language   40
    The Kinship of Words   42
    Poems   50

3. Images: The Perceptual Field   66

    Three Image Poems   68
    Images and Perception   72
    Literal Images   75
    Poems   77

Figurative Images   85
Symbols   101
Poems   108

4. The Speaker: The Eye of the Poem   138

    The Invented "I"   140
    The Personal "I" Speaker   146
    The Public Voice   151
    The Invisible Speaker   153
    Poems   155

5. Rhyme and Repetition   165

    Rhyme   170
    Poems   179
    Repetition   184
    Poems   201

6. Meter: The Measured Flow   217

    What Is Meter?   219
    Scansion   221
    Iambic Pentameter   224
    More Key Meters   232
    Two Other Metrical Options   245
    Rhythm and Meaning   251
    Poems   254

7. Free Verse   267

    The Genesis of Free Verse   269
    The Free Verse Craft of the Line   272
    Voice   285
    Free Verse, the Tradition and Beyond 287
    Poems   287

8. *Traditional and Open Forms*   301

    Looking at Forms   303
    Traditional Forms   307
    Poems   328
    Open Forms   341
    Prose Poems   345
    Open Forms Poems   348

9. *Subject and Style*   363

    Types of Poems   364
    Style   374
    Poems on Four Subjects   382
    Poems   404

10. *Interpretation:*
    The Wide Response   421

    What Is Meaning?   427
    Gaps and Holes   428
    Power Sources   436
    Critical Discriminations   453
    Poems   461

11. *A Poet's Handbook*   479

    Invoking Your Muse   479
    Beginning with a White Page   481
    Suggestions for Writing and Revising   482
    Exercises   486
    Your Poems out the Door   494

Index of Titles   507

Index of Authors and Titles   512

Index of Terms and Topics   518

Invitation

Field guides always attract me. On a shelf near my desk I see volumes on birds, marshes, geology, shells, forests, and wildflowers. Leafing through my shell book, I become engrossed in the variety of sea cucumbers, corals, and anemones. The scallop shells are sometimes mottled like a rusty hinge, sometimes dawn-colored, smooth, and nacreous. When I was a child, I especially liked what I called mermaid fingernails — also known as jackknife clams. Seeing them recalls me to the beach at Fernandina, where at sunrise I rode on the back of a sea turtle as she made her way back to the sea after laying eggs in the cool sand.

A field guide is an *aide-memoire* as well as a taxonomic treasury and a source of new information. An added pleasure is simply the joy of names, a tactile discovery as real as finding shells the last high tide rolled onto the shore. Now when I go down to the beach near my house in California, I am walking on the last edge of America. My books stay at home on the shelf. No one's classifications interfere with the fresh air blown across the water from perfumed islands, with the glass-green curve of the breaking wave, with swags of foam, or with the mighty inner *release* afforded by the expanse of water. In his poem "Ocean," Czeslaw Milosz describes this endless blue as "a billion-year-old abyss," a perception that tightens the rachet of my own view. Calico clams, I say aloud, coquina, limpet, quahog, cockle, pandora, astarte. Sea pin, jingle shell, kelp crab, basket star. The words in the air come alive, like the things themselves, blending without edge into that most natural and ancient act, a walk on an early spring morning.

I would like *The Discovery of Poetry* to be a field guide to the natural pleasures of language — a happiness we were born to have. The first poems I loved were those that let me swim in sound. Sidney Lanier's "The Marshes of Glynn" thrilled me because I went to those same coastal marshes every summer. I learned long sections of the poem and, head out the car window like a dog, shouted "Gloom of the live oaks, beautiful braided and woven," as my mother drove over the low bridges to the island. The burning sulphur stink of the paper mills poured into the car. ". . . with a step I stand/On the firm-packed sand," I continued. My sisters yanked me back in the car and rolled up the window. Later, I fell into Steven Vincent Benét's great love of American names — Carquinez Straits, Little French Lick, Medicine Hat. The ending especially stirred me:

> I shall not rest quiet in Montparnasse.
> I shall not lie easy in Winchelsea.
> You may bury my body in Sussex grass,
> You may bury my tongue at Champmédy.
> I shall not be there. I shall rise and pass.
> Bury my heart at Wounded Knee.

When I went to college in Virginia, hundreds of miles north of my Georgia hometown, I was used to Deep South seasons, a subtle blend of spring into summer into fall. That first autumn startled me. The whole landscape along the James River transformed, especially the ginkgo trees, which turned gold and suddenly, all on the same day, rained their fan-shaped leaves in circles around their trunks. I observed this with no accurate words to describe my astonishment. When spring came, the enormous old weeping cherry outside my dorm bloomed as though it had invented the word. To stand under a blossoming cherry and look up through transparent petals at the sky! I was taking a poetry class. Leafing through the textbook, I came across A. E. Housman's poem:

LOVELIEST OF TREES
(A. E. Housman, 1859–1936)

Loveliest of trees, the cherry now
Is hung with bloom along the bough,
And stands about the woodland ride
Wearing white for Eastertide.

Now, of my threescore years and ten,
Twenty will not come again,
And take from seventy springs a score,
It only leaves me fifty more.

And since to look at things in bloom
Fifty springs are little room,
About the woodlands I will go
To see the cherry hung with snow.

I read the poem out loud until I knew it by heart. I liked the soft-spoken sound of the words; their lightness seemed to suit the tree. I was struck by the knowledge that I had spent nineteen years without seeing a cherry tree in bloom. Poems can change an experience by imaginatively naming or extending a feeling or thought. "Loveliest of Trees" *connected*, giving me perceptions in addition to my own. A friend and

I copied the poem and tacked it to the tree. Every day we saw people stop to read the poem and look up at the sky through the blossoms.

For years after (and perhaps still) someone placed the poem on the tree each spring. I already had notebooks full of poems clipped from magazines or copied from books, but this experience began a lifelong passion. My bookstore account soared. Yeats, Keats, Pound, Bishop, the Greek plays. I enrolled in a creative writing class and saw scrawled on my first portfolio, *what is to become of you?* My family begged me to study something practical: Get your head out of the clouds.

Too late. I already had seen that reading a fine poem makes me rediscover the bright freshness of creation. Writing a poem doubles, triples the experience or connection that initiated it. I became a teacher of poetry and wrote hundreds of poems. On nights of insomnia or on long walks, I have the poems I know as close companions. Even the back seat of my car is scattered with poetry books, in case I'm stuck in traffic. I leave my car unlocked and no one ever has stolen one. Falling in love with a book brings the same catapulting madness and zest that falling in love with a person brings.

About ten years ago, a move to Italy mysteriously propelled me into writing prose. I found that my long training in poetry migrated to the new form. In my many years of teaching, I always told students that poetry is excellent practice for the mind because it is *the* language art. Learning to *see* precisely how words work pulls you closer to what you want to write — whether it's a newspaper article, a cost estimate, a letter home, or a novel. I found the truth of that firsthand. My old habit of reading while taking a walk transferred easily to my new life in Italy. A slender volume of poems, a bottle of water, and I'm free to wander the Roman roads and Etruscan terraces all morning.

So many other joys come to mind. We look at art for clues about our lives. When you take a walk at night, lighted rooms are irresistible. You see a child setting the table, a vase of wildflowers, a stack of books on a chair. Through the open window you hear — is that Nina Simone singing "The Twelfth of Never," one of your favorites? You imagine what's cooking on the stove. All these images form a quick glimpse of how those mysterious others behind the glass live their lives. Poems give you the lives of others and then circle in on your own inner world.

Look at this private moment.

GLISTENING
(Linda Gregg, 1942–)

As I pull the bucket from the crude well,
the water changes from dark to a light
more silver than the sun. When I pour it
over my body that is standing in the dust
by the oleander bush, it sparkles easily
in the sunlight with an earnestness like
the spirit close up. The water magnifies
the sun all along the length of it.
Love is not less because of the spirit.
Delight does not make the heart childish.
We thought the blood thinned, our weight
lessened, that our substance was reduced
by simple happiness. The oleander is thick
with leaves and flowers because of spilled
water. Let the spirit marry the heart.
When I return naked to the stone porch,
there is no one to see me glistening.
But I look at the almond tree with its husks
cracking open in the heat. I look down
the whole mountain to the sea. Goats bleating
faintly and sometimes bells. I stand there
a long time with the sun and the quiet,
the earth moving slowly as I dry in the light.

So many people are denied the deep gratification of poetry. Their educations have trained them to read for information. When I told my uncle that a book of my poems had been published, he said, "Poetry is Greek to me." He did not open the pristine white covers of my first book. The same people who play the cello, pilot planes, design software, and teach astronomy assume that poetry is difficult. Or the thudding rhyme and banal haiku of the "poetry unit" assured them that poetry is irrelevant. So easy it is to forget how to play. As children, we enter the spirit of make believe and accept temporary worlds. We pretend we are pioneers or explorers; we follow our imaginations. Samuel Taylor Coleridge called this process the "willing suspension of disbelief." As adults, we sometimes abandon this talent. Yet we still enter temporary worlds when we yell at a soccer game or swim meet, cry or applaud at a play, or get carried away by a friend's story. For a while we forget the immediacy of ourselves and go *with* the witnessed experience. Like play, poetry lets us enter other territories.

Why did no one ever hand my uncle a direct poem such as Jane Kenyon's four-line "The Sandy Hole" — a brief and brutally accurate captured moment?

THE SANDY HOLE

(Jane Kenyon, 1947–1995)

The infant's coffin no bigger than a flightbag. . . .
The young father steps backward from the sandy hole,
eyes wide and dry, his hand over his mouth.
No one dares to come near him, even to touch his sleeve.

Something is named. Something is noticed. The words are spare and plain. Isolated on a white page, the poem seems to float in the white silence around it. This is how a poem comes to the border between the speakable and the unspeakable.

If no one ever handed you poems that brought you close to the art of poetry, I hope that the words in this book will invite you. As a writer, teacher, and reader, I value the link between reading poetry and writing it, so throughout the book I include suggestions for writing. When words from your own imagination, intellect, and experience flow through your pen, what you are reading in these chapters becomes generative. My suggestion to you: Acquire a new notebook and, as Billy Collins does, record the "bright, airy dictation" of your responses.

TUESDAY, JUNE 4TH, 1991
(Billy Collins, 1941–)

By the time I get myself out of bed, my wife has left
the house to take her botany final and the painter
has arrived in his van and is already painting
the columns of the front porch white and the decking gray.

It is early June, a breezy and sun-riddled Tuesday
that would quickly be forgotten were it not for my
writing these few things down as I sit here empty-headed
at the typewriter with a cup of coffee, light and sweet.

I feel like the secretary to the morning whose only
responsibility is to take down its bright, airy dictation
until it's time to go to lunch with the other girls,
all of us ordering the cottage cheese with half a pear.

This is what stenographers do in courtrooms,
alert at their dark contraptions catching every word.
When there is a silence they sit still as I do, waiting
and listening, fingers resting lightly on the keys.

This is what Samuel Pepys did too, jotting down in
private ciphers minor events that would have otherwise
slipped into the heavy, amnesiac waters of the Thames.
His vigilance paid off finally when London caught fire

as mine does when the painter comes in for coffee
and says how much he likes this slow, vocal rendition
of "You Don't Know What Love Is" and I figure I will
make him a tape when he goes back to his brushes and pails.

Under the music I can hear the rush of cars and trucks
on the highway and every so often the new kitten, Felix,
hops into my lap and watches my fingers drumming out
a running record of this particular June Tuesday

as it unrolls before my eyes, a long intricate carpet
that I am walking on slowly with my head bowed
knowing that it is leading me to the quiet shrine
of the afternoon and the melancholy candles of evening.

If I look up, I see out the window the white stars
of clematis climbing a ladder of strings, a woodpile,
a stack of faded bricks, a small green garden of herbs,
things you would expect to find outside a window,

all written down now and placed in the setting
of a stanza as unalterably as they are seated
in their chairs in the ontological rooms of the world.
Yes, this is the kind of job I could succeed in,

an unpaid but contented amanuensis whose hands
are two birds fluttering on the lettered keys,
whose eyes see sunlight splashing through the leaves,
and the bright pink asterisks of honeysuckle

and the piano at the other end of this room with
its small vase of faded flowers and its empty bench.
So convinced am I that I have found my vocation,
tomorrow I will begin my chronicling earlier, at dawn,

a time when hangmen and farmers are up and doing,
when men holding pistols stand in a field back to back.
It is the time the ancients imagined in robes, as Eos
or Aurora, who would leave her sleeping husband in bed,

not to take her botany final, but to pull the sun,
her brother, over the horizon's brilliant rim,
her four-horse chariot aimed at the zenith of the sky.
But tomorrow, dawn will come the way I picture her,

barefoot and disheveled, standing outside my window
in one of the fragile cotton dresses of the poor.
She will look in at me with her thin arms extended,
offering a handful of birdsong and a small cup of light.

"How can you teach creative writing?" many dubious, querulous
people have asked me. And more aggressively, "Who taught Shake-
speare? Did he take Creative Writing 301?" The questions both bore
and astound. No one can teach anyone to become a great anything.
If your blood is on fire with the love of language and the desire to
make something with words, you probably know that. You probably
know, too, that no matter how awkward your writing is right now,
something in you will make you a writer. The German poet, Rilke,
pinpointed this phenomenon when he wrote, "The future enters us
in order to transform us long before it happens." Working on your
craft with a good guide is a lucky move. You can save years. Many
people find an interest in writing late; their talent is just waiting to be
uncovered and developed. They're the ones Ben Jonson had in mind
when he said, "A good poet's made as well as born." Teaching in a
large urban university, I've been surprised to find that genuine talent
is not at all unusual. What is unusual is the perseverance and will it
takes to become a writer. Even without a blazing talent, almost every-
one can learn to write good poems.

The architecture of *The Discovery of Poetry* suggests a personal
course of study that the reader may pursue alone or with a group of

friends. Poetry differs from other kinds of literature in several ways. Poems, of course, are usually structured in lines rather than in margin-to-margin sentences and paragraphs. Poets often arrange words in sound and rhythm patterns to accent particular words or intensify meanings. And poetry deeply involves the imagination, both writer's and reader's. The present, a dream, a memory, a conversation — several aspects of experience may operate simultaneously. These qualities require more of us. The *way* a poem is written has everything to do with the subject. Craft and subject work symbiotically. William Butler Yeats asks:

> O body swayed to music, O brightening glance,
> How can we know the dancer from the dance?

We can't know. And why should we want to? A poem's subject, art, craft, inspiration, and sweat are as inseparable as dancer and dance. As a reader, I am all for the swaying of the music and the brightening glance — the *whole* poem, plucked like a warm, ripe peach from the tree. Still, I find that there is everything to be discovered by focusing on one aspect or another of the poem's anatomy — images, sound, rhythm, form. In *The Discovery of Poetry*, we will begin with words and images, the basic raw materials of the poet. We progress by adding more elements of the poem in a sequence that reveals how a poem supersedes its sum of parts. At the end of each chapter, I include a group of poems for further contemplation. I like the way poems from varied styles and periods can talk back to each other. Reading aloud, discussing chapters and poems with friends, going to hear poets read, writing in your notebook — this is a pleasurable way to spend a rainy winter, or a lifetime.

Sources
and Approaches

*If I feel physically as if the top of my head
were taken off, I know that is poetry.*
—EMILY DICKINSON

The Origin of a Poem

What motivates a poet to write? When Emily Dickinson said about her art, "My business is circumference," she was talking about her desire to explore experience by drawing it into a circle of her own, a world. Similarly, Wallace Stevens wanted each poem to give "a sense of the world." D. H. Lawrence thought the essence of good poetry was "stark directness." Telling or uncovering truth is the prime motive of poets like Muriel Rukeyser, who once asked, "What would happen if one woman told the truth about her life? / The world would split open." William Wordsworth valued "the spontaneous overflow of powerful feelings." When William Carlos Williams called a poem "a machine made of words," he simply meant to say that the best-formed poems function smoothly, with oiled and well-fitted parts, not far from Samuel Taylor Coleridge's ideal, "The best words in the best order."

Many poets aspire to reach "the condition of music"—some aim for the heavenly music of the spheres, while others want the words to "boogie." William Butler Yeats thought, "We make out of the quarrel with others, rhetoric, but of the quarrel with ourselves, poetry." His writing emerged from the internal fault line between conflicting thoughts and emotions. Yeats's desire to understand his human condition echoes Walt Whitman, who wanted the reader to "stand by my side and look in the mirror with me." For Matthew Arnold the impulse was external, not internal. His poetry came from "actions, human actions; possessing an inherent interest in themselves, and which are to be communicated in an interesting manner by the art of the poet." Some pull of inner necessity draws the poet to the page, whether to explore a problem, pursue a rhythm, break apart logic, express an emotion, tell a story, or simply to sing. When asked the familiar question, "Why do you write?", writers often answer, "Because I have to," (though prose writer Flannery O'Connor replied, "Because I'm good at it."). The impetus of *having to*, for the reasons named above, gives poetry its fire and urgency.

Because of all these diverse sources, no one ever has come up with a satisfactory definition of poetry, just as no one can define music or art. Those who want to proclaim what is or isn't poetry have thankless work cut out for themselves. No umbrella is wide enough to cover the myriad versions, subjects, and forms. If a poem interests you, better to just go along with Walt Whitman's assertion, "...what I assume you shall assume, / For every atom belonging to me, as good belongs to you." Reasons for reading and for writing seem almost as numerous as atoms.

Sometimes poets write to recreate an experience.

A BLESSING
(James Wright, 1927–1980)

Just off the highway to Rochester, Minnesota,
Twilight bounds softly forth on the grass.
And the eyes of those two Indian ponies
Darken with kindness.

They have come gladly out of the willows
To welcome my friend and me.
We step over the barbed wire into the pasture
Where they have been grazing all day, alone.
They ripple tensely, they can hardly contain their happiness
That we have come.
They bow shyly as wet swans. They love each other.
There is no loneliness like theirs.
At home once more,
They begin munching the young tufts of spring in the darkness.
I would like to hold the slenderer one in my arms,
For she has walked over to me
And nuzzled my left hand.
She is black and white,
Her mane falls wild on her forehead,
And the light breeze moves me to caress her long ear
That is delicate as the skin over a girl's wrist.
Suddenly I realize
That if I stepped out of my body I would break
Into blossom.

What happens at the end? After a simple, sensuous description of stepping over barbed wire into the field with the Indian ponies, the poem abruptly changes. The speaker (the "I" in the poem) stops describing external action. He shifts to the *inner* experience of his happiness. The last two lines surprise us with their bold originality. Rapport with the natural world is a common experience, but the speaker here reacts intensely. He expresses an *imaginative* level of that experience, allowing us to recognize our own feelings in a new way. If he'd ended the poem at "wrist," we could not possibly have imagined the powerful idea of the spirit transforming into blossom.

A poet may write primarily out of a delight with the sounds of language:

COUNTING-OUT RHYME
(Edna St. Vincent Millay, 1892–1950)

Silver bark of beech, and sallow
Bark of yellow birch and yellow
    Twig of willow.

Stripe of green in moosewood maple,
Colour seen in leaf of apple,
    Bark of popple.

Wood of popple pale as moonbeam,
Wood of oak for yoke and barn-beam,
    Wood of hornbeam.

Silver bark of beech, and hollow
Stem of elder, tall and yellow
    Twig of willow.

Millay plays with words, rhymes, and repeating patterns of vowels and consonants. There is nothing to understand, only something to hear and imagine. Even though it has no message, the poem evokes reactions. It sounds like a chant. You probably remember the one-potato, two-potato counting-out rhymes from childhood, and how repetition can cast a spell. Perhaps Millay's words call up images of trees in different seasons or memories of playing in a forest. I remember the passwords to a club I was part of in the fifth grade:

> Tinky toesy timbo nosey
> Hooey booey booskie
> Pin pin rickey
> Pom pom mickey
> No me oh non phooey hoo.

Who knows where such rhymes come from, except from the basic fun of making noises with words?

Sources of poems, like their subjects, approaches, and meanings, are endless. Whatever the motivation might be, the making of all art is a fundamental and instinctive impulse. More than twenty thousand years ago, at Pech Merle in France, the earliest artists painted a group of spotted horses on the damp walls of caves. Around the realistic forms are several handprints. No one who has seen them could forget these strange reminders, like signatures, of the cave painters. These are startling images of the human desire to create. Did the drawings give magic control over hunting that animal? Was the horse a religious image? Were the paintings done for entertainment on long, cold nights in the cave? Were the horses so beautiful that the painter searched for just the right spot, placing the chest of the animal over a swelling in the cave wall to get the right sense of the animal's form? Perhaps none — or all — of these possible sources were in the artist's mind. As we look at the pictures, the artist mixing paints from blood and soot and ashes seems very close. We have to resist matching our hands to the black outlines on the wall. The natural desire to make art easily spans the epochs.

Art is the real "news" source of any culture. The cave paintings are the liveliest news items from prehistory. Today, as ever, movements in art reveal more about a moment of human consciousness than the Ten O'Clock News. Art reveals a culture's values, pressures, breakdowns, new directions. Contemporary poems are comments on our time; poems from other times and places give us glimpses into other lives.

The Art of Reading

When an interviewer asked William Stafford how old he was when he started writing poems, Stafford replied, "How old were you when you stopped?" Writing poetry, he meant, is a normal function. So is reading. This is especially important to realize because many of us are overtrained to read for factual information. Overly pragmatic, we look for a result, a conclusion. In addition, Americans are particularly time-conscious.

Although poems may include useful information and conclusions, these aren't prime reasons for reading. Poems take concentration and time. Because many people assume they cannot understand poetry, they bring to it an overly serious mind-set. They fear that complex meanings must be wrung from the poem like water out of a dishrag.

The writer starts and ends elsewhere:

from AN ATLAS OF THE DIFFICULT WORLD
(Adrienne Rich, 1929–)

XIII (DEDICATIONS)

I know you are reading this poem
late, before leaving your office
of the one intense yellow lamp-spot and the darkening window
in the lassitude of a building faded to quiet
long after rush-hour. I know you are reading this poem
standing up in a bookstore far from the ocean
on a grey day of early spring, faint flakes driven
across the plains' enormous spaces around you.
I know you are reading this poem
in a room where too much has happened for you to bear
where the bedclothes lie in stagnant coils on the bed
and the open valise speaks of flight
but you cannot leave yet. I know you are reading this poem
as the underground train loses momentum and before running
    up the stairs
toward a new kind of love
your life has never allowed.
I know you are reading this poem by the light
of the television screen where soundless images jerk and slide

while you wait for the newscast from the *intifada*.
I know you are reading this poem in a waiting-room
of eyes met and unmeeting, of identity with strangers.
I know you are reading this poem by fluorescent light
in the boredom and fatigue of the young who are counted out,
count themselves out, at too early an age. I know
you are reading this poem through your failing sight, the thick
lens enlarging these letters beyond all meaning yet you read on
because even the alphabet is precious.
I know you are reading this poem as you pace beside the stove
warming milk, a crying child on your shoulder, a book in your
     hand
because life is short and you too are thirsty.
I know you are reading this poem which is not in your language
guessing at some words while others keep you reading
and I want to know which words they are.
I know you are reading this poem listening for something, torn
     between bitterness and hope
turning back once again to the task you cannot refuse.
I know you are reading this poem because there is nothing else
     left to read
there where you have landed, stripped as you are.

                                                      1990–1991

Many poems, on first reading, are as direct as this one.

The most important aspect of appreciating any poem is extensive
reading — the more the better — of poems of all kinds, and the best
reader is the one most open to the poem on the page. Novelist Henry
James said, "Be one on whom nothing is lost." Here are some guide-
lines toward that ideal:

- Poems are written in lines. The length of the line and where it
  breaks help establish the poem's rhythm. We'll read more about
  this later. For now, let the punctuation mark at the end of the line

guide you. A comma indicates a distinct pause; a period indicates a full stop. If there is no punctuation mark where the line breaks, regard that break as a very slight pause—a half-comma—that emphasizes the last word on the line. Lines are not necessarily units of sense. Often the sense flows on from line to line in a continuous sentence. If there's no period, keep reading; don't interrupt your reading of the sentence just because the line stops, as in these lines by Percy Bysshe Shelley:

> I met a traveler from an antique land
> Who said: Two vast and trunkless legs of stone
> Stand in the desert...

New lines often start with capital letters, but this does not necessarily indicate that a new sentence is starting. Understand the lines above as: "I met a traveler from an antique land who said, 'Two vast and trunkless legs of stone stand in the desert.'" Capitals along the left margin of a poem add a formality to the poem and give a slight emphasis to the opening words of the lines. Practice pausing for the line break but continuing the thought. Look, for example, at the importance of the *realize, break,* and *blossom* at the line breaks in this excerpt from James Wright's "A Blessing":

> Suddenly I realize
> That if I stepped out of my body I would break
> Into blossom.

Emphasis on *realize* signals a change in the speaker's thinking. The emphasis on *break* is tricky: for a suspenseful instant, we don't know what will come next. *Blossom* is the most important word in the poem. Coming last in the shortest line, it gets strong emphasis both visually and orally.

- Read a poem once silently, then once aloud, just listening to the sounds. With long poems, read at least a few sections aloud. Notice the action of the verbs.

- Old wisdom claims that all poems come from courting, praying, or fighting. The traditional classification of poetry is into lyric, narrative, and dramatic. A **lyric** is a songlike poem (originally played on the lyre), usually told in first person; a **narrative** is a story poem; and a **dramatic** poem demonstrates a conflict, often using the third-person voice. These categories easily blur. A narrative may have lyric passages; a lyric may be dramatic; a dramatic poem may tell a story. More useful for sharp-focusing a poem will be to pinpoint two or more basic qualities of its subject: Is it a poem of personal experience? A description? A revelation of a single moment? A poem of political or social comment? A poem of word play? A retelling of a myth? A memory? A meditation on a spiritual or religious question? A song? A sermon? An argument?

- What makes a poem effective? You gradually will build a critical vocabulary for *why* and *how* rhythm, image, and word choice work. Right now, notice your *general* responses to the poem. What is your first impression? Is the poem interesting? Does each line propel your attention down the page? What personal associations does the poem evoke? A poem usually has plural meanings; some of them are entirely personal to an individual reader.

- Who is speaking? "I"? "We"? A character, historical or invented? To whom is the poem addressed? "You"? The reader? A character, named or unnamed? A nation or group? What is the overall tone of voice of the speaker? Sincere? Ironic? Intimate? Matter of fact? Mocking? Distant? Contemplative? Frenzied? Questioning? **Tone** of voice shows the speaker's emotion and sense of the situation. Reading aloud will help you hear the speaker's tone.

- Note difficult sections. Sometimes copying these parts will clarify them. Look up unfamiliar words and **allusions,** those references to people, objects, or events outside the poem. A poem might mention Norse gods, brand names, or English spies; it might refer to a biblical story, a battle, an ancient tool — or another work of literature. Not every allusion is important to understand, and many are self-explanatory in the context of the poem. Arm yourself with a good dictionary and a book of myths. When you see a poem titled

"Leda and the Swan," you'll need to track down exactly who Leda was.

- Don't overinterpret. Meanings don't hide behind every bush. If you **paraphrase** (put what the poem says into your own words), that will be a useful prose replica of the poem, a flat rendition of what the poem says without the qualities of craft that make it a poem. Poems usually suggest much more than they actually say; some are complex, with layers of meanings that repay weeks of study. However, when someone told me that the black and white ponies in "A Blessing" symbolize good and evil, he'd gone too far. Nothing in the poem suggests this interpretation. The ponies are themselves. They suggest also the beauty of the natural world and something of its mystery—but good and evil, no.
- Some people fear that analysis takes away from enjoyment; "explain it, drain it," they say. Protracted analysis can wear you out, but good critical consideration is creative and rewarding.

Like a loaf of bread—which is somehow more than flour, yeast, salt, and water—a poem is more than words, rhythm, and lines. Samuel Taylor Coleridge once said that the pleasure of poetry comes from the "whole, consistent with a consciousness of pleasure from the component parts. . . ." In the following chapters, I will focus attention on various topics, one at a time. As much as possible, the goal always is synthesis: putting the parts together to comprehend the whole.

By way of an introduction to close reading, consider the following poems, each quite different from the next. Use the above guidelines to direct your attention.

If you have read Shakespeare's *Macbeth*, you probably remember the witches' chant (Act IV, scene i). Here is an excerpt:

> Double, double toil and trouble;
> Fire, burn; and, cauldron, bubble.
> Fillet of a fenny[1] snake,

---

[1] *fenny*: from boggy ground (a fen).

In the cauldron boil and bake;
Eye of newt, and toe of frog.
Wool of bat, and tongue of dog,
Adder's fork, and blind-worm's sting,
Lizard's leg, and owlet's wing, —
For a charm of powerful trouble,
Like a hell-broth boil and bubble.

Notice the words Shakespeare uses and take another look at Millay's "Counting-Out Rhyme" (page 4), listening to the consonants and vowel sounds in each poem.

THE SUNNE RISING
(John Donne, 1572–1631)

Busie old foole, unruly Sunne,
    Why dost thou thus,
Through windowes, and through curtaines call on us?
Must to thy motions lovers seasons run?
        Sawcy pedantique wretch, goe chide
        Late schoole boyes and sowre prentices,
    Goe tell Court-huntsmen, that the King will ride,
    Call countrey ants to harvest offices;
Love, all alike, no season knowes, nor clyme,
Nor houres, dayes, months, which are the rags of time.

        Thy beames, so reverend, and strong
        Why shouldst thou thinke?
I could eclipse and cloud them with a winke.
But that I would not lose her sight so long:
        If her eyes have not blinded thine,
        Looke, and to morrow late, tell mee,
    Whether both the India's of spice and Myne
    Be where thou leftst them, or lie here with mee.
Aske for those Kings whom thou saw'st yesterday,
And thou shalt heare, All here in one bed lay.

> She is all States, and all Princes, I,
> Nothing else is.
> Princes doe but play us; compar'd to this,
> All honor's mimique; All wealth alchimie.
> Thou sunne art halfe as happy as wee,
> In that the world's contracted thus;
> Thine age askes ease, and since thy duties bee
> To warme the world, that's done in warming us.
> Shine here to us, and thou art every where;
> This bed thy center is, these walls, thy spheare.

A lover complains extravagantly to the sun for disturbing his tryst. The lover's tone of voice is arrogant, humorous, boastful, and tender as he tells off the sun for disturbing his morning. Those in love are outside the circle of time proscribed by the sun; they know neither season nor climate. The lovers also are all-powerful. A mere wink eclipses the strong beams of the sun (line 13). But the lover hesitates to blink away the sun because he'd lose sight of his love. Midway in the poem he begins to stake out a big claim: he and his love are a world. Wildly, he tells the sun (if the sun itself hasn't been blinded by his love's fiery gaze) to come back after traveling to the Indies and see if rich spices and mines ("Myne") aren't there in the bed. The sun can expect all kings there in bed also. He goes on: She is all nations, he is all rulers.

The sun can see only with split vision: half of the world at a time. The lovers are luckier: The world they create is together, undivided. The sun is old, with one duty only, to warm the world and "... that's done in warming us," the lover proclaims. He commands the sun (after initially trying to banish it) to shine on them, make their bed the world. Such contradictions are common in Donne.

This poem introduces some hallmarks of his style: wit, paradox, allusion, boldness, sophistication, passion. His language is sharp, argumentative, intellectual. In his time, no one but Donne was irreverent enough to address the sun as "Busie old foole" and to pit his own powers against the powers of the sun.

Poems written on waking at dawn are called **aubades.** Usually a lover is leaving the bed regretfully after a night of passion.

Sometimes archaic spellings are modernized. Here they are not but often the words aren't as odd as they appear at first glance. If you read by sound, they come clear. *Sowre prentices,* for example, is "sour apprentices"; *pedantique* and *clyme* are seventeenth-century spellings of "pedantic" and "clime" (climate). "Both the India's of spice and Myne" (line 17) refers to the East and West Indies, where there are spices and gold mines. Other clues indicate when the poem was written, but in some ways it seems contemporary. Donne convinces us that the lovers are a world unto themselves.

STEPPING WESTWARD
(Denise Levertov, 1923–1997)

What is green in me
darkens, muscadine.

If woman is inconstant,
good, I am faithful to

ebb and flow, I fall
in season and now

is a time of ripening.
If her part

is to be true,
a north star,

good, I hold steady
in the black sky

and vanish by day,
yet burn there

in blue or above
quilts of cloud.

There is no savor
more sweet, more salt

than to be glad to be
what, woman,

and who, myself,
I am, a shadow

that grows longer as the sun
moves, drawn out

on a thread of wonder.
If I bear burdens

they begin to be remembered
as gifts, goods, a basket

of bread that hurts
my shoulders but closes me

in fragrance. I can
eat as I go.

I've always liked this quiet lyric of celebration, maybe because of the sound of the word *muscadine* (rhymes with *green*), a grapevine with dark purple fruit used for dense wines. The title suggests the journey toward the sunset, which suggests death. The speaker enjoys the progress of living each step of the way (the ripening from green to dark purple). The first half interprets in a positive way two contradictory ideas: Woman is inconstant, woman is steady. This woman is both, like the earth and stars. She is tidal, seasonal, yet steady as a star.

She sees herself as elemental, one with nature. The last half affirms that nothing excels an intense sense of self. Like Donne, she embraces rather than denies contraries.

I like the poem's simple, mostly one-syllable, nature words (*north star, black sky, clouds, salt, shadow, sun*), which seem to reinforce the speaker's relationship to the natural world.

Poems

In my field guide to wildflowers, the specimens are arranged by color, form, and detail. This book's chapters end with a selection of poems to read and think about or to discuss with friends. Often, these poems may "talk" to each other, by contrast or similarity, but always they will be connected to the chapter's subject.

I Wandered Lonely as a Cloud
(William Wordsworth, 1770–1850)

I wandered lonely as a cloud
That floats on high o'er vales and hills,
When all at once I saw a crowd,
A host, of golden daffodils,
Beside the lake, beneath the trees,
Fluttering and dancing in the breeze.

Continuous as the stars that shine
And twinkle on the milky way,
They stretched in never-ending line
Along the margin of a bay;
Ten thousand saw I at a glance,
Tossing their heads in sprightly dance.

The waves beside them danced, but they
Outdid the sparkling waves in glee;

A poet could not but be gay,
In such a jocund company;
I gazed — and gazed — but little thought
What wealth the show to me had brought:

For oft, when on my couch I lie
In vacant or in pensive mood,
They flash upon that inward eye
Which is the bliss of solitude;
And then my heart with pleasure fills,
And dances with the daffodils.

SPRING AND ALL
(William Carlos Williams, 1883–1963)

By the road to the contagious hospital
under the surge of the blue
mottled clouds driven from the
northeast — a cold wind. Beyond, the
waste of broad, muddy fields
brown with dried weeds, standing and fallen

patches of standing water
the scattering of tall trees

All along the road the reddish
purplish, forked, upstanding, twiggy
stuff of bushes and small trees
with dead, brown leaves under them
leafless vines —

Lifeless in appearance, sluggish
dazed spring approaches —

They enter the new world naked,
cold, uncertain of all
save that they enter. All about them
the cold, familiar wind —

Now the grass, tomorrow
the stiff curl of wildcarrot leaf
One by one objects are defined —
It quickens: clarity, outline of leaf

But now the stark dignity of
entrance — Still, the profound change
has come upon them: rooted, they
grip down and begin to awaken

CHANSON INNOCENTE[1]
(e. e. cummings, 1894–1962)

in Just-
spring   when the world is mud-
luscious the little
lame balloonman

whistles   far   and wee

and eddieandbill come
running from marbles and
piracies and it's
spring

when the world is puddle-wonderful

---

[1]*Chanson Innocente:* Innocent Song.

the queer
old balloonman whistles
far   and   wee
and bettyandisbel come dancing

from hop-scotch and jump-rope and

it's
spring
and
   the

      goat-footed

balloonMan   whistles
far
and
wee

THOSE WINTER SUNDAYS
(Robert Hayden, 1913–1980)

Sundays too my father got up early
and put his clothes on in the blueblack cold,
then with cracked hands that ached
from labor in the weekday weather made
banked fires blaze. No one ever thanked him.

I'd wake and hear the cold splintering, breaking.
When the rooms were warm, he'd call,
and slowly I would rise and dress,
fearing the chronic angers of that house,

Speaking indifferently to him,
who had driven out the cold
and polished my good shoes as well.
What did I know, what did I know
of love's austere and lonely offices?

＊

A FATHER AT HIS SON'S BAPTISM
(Amy Gerstler, 1956–)

Cutlet carved from our larger carcasses:
thus were you made — from spit and a hug.
The scratchy stuff you're lying on is wool.
You recognize the pressure of your mother's hand.
That white moon with a bluish cast is a priest's face,
frowning over a water bowl. Whatever befalls you now,
you've been blessed, in a most picturesque
and ineffective ceremony dating from the Middle Ages.
Outdoors, the church lawn radiates a lethal green.
A gas truck thunders down the street.
Why, at emotional moments, do the placid trees
and landscape look overexposed, almost ready
to bleach away, and reveal the workings
of "the Real" machine underneath?
All bundled up on such a hot day:
whose whelp, pray tell, or mutton chop are you?
— tail-less, your cloudy gaze a vague accusation,
not of the sins of my history, but ignorance
to come, future cruelty. You're getting red
in the face, blotchy, ready to wail. Good.
From now on protest and remember everything.
Your cries assail even the indigent dead,
buried in charity plots right outside,

slowly releasing their heat, while you,
born out of the blue into a wheezing spring,
watch a chaotic mosaic assemble itself.
You tune up. My love for you is half adrenaline,
half gibberish. More Latin and the priest
splatters you. He's got one good eye,
and a black patch, like a pirate.
Now, smiling as if he knows something I don't,
he hands you to me. If I drop you, loudmouth,
will you bounce or fly? You were chalky
and bloody at first, in the doctor's grip,
looking skinned and inside-out.
Boyhood, a dangling carrot. I stare at you
and experience the embarrassment of riches. I
need to loosen my tie or I'll faint.
Outside a rake scrapes, sprinklers hiss.
It might be best to set you down
in one of these squares of light on the floor,
striped by venetian blinds, and leave you safe
in that bright cage. I could go have coffee,
and come back when we can carry on
a conversation. Men and women are afraid
of each other. It's true. Whisper
and drool of my flesh, I'm terrified of you.

986[1]
(Emily Dickinson, 1830–1886)

A narrow Fellow in the Grass
Occasionally rides —

---

[1] 986: Dickinson did not title her works;
after her death, editors numbered her
poems in approximate chronological order.

You may have met Him — did you not
His notice sudden is —

The Grass divides as with a Comb —
A spotted shaft is seen —
And then it closes at your feet
And opens further on —

He likes a Boggy Acre
A Floor too cool for Corn —
Yet when a Boy, and Barefoot —
I more than once at Noon
Have passed, I thought, a Whip lash
Unbraiding in the Sun
When stooping to secure it
It wrinkled, and was gone —

Several of Nature's People
I know, and they know me —
I feel for them a transport
Of cordiality —

But never met this Fellow
Attended, or alone
Without a tighter breathing
And Zero at the Bone —

SALT
(Frances Phillips, 1951–)

I

They drag the dead pony out of the field,
wet snowflakes over the surface of her eyes.

Those slumped axhandle bones and her hair still shimmering
needles, or the wet slick in the arch of a shoe.

They drag her in her husk.
If only the hacker could lift her
before opening that slat-backed truck
spilling out its yellow dog straw.

She still smells like a sweater where kittens are born.

II

I sweep the tack room where touches of cold
dust stick to spider webs.
I cover the saddle with a carrot sack
and fold her bridle in a box
with my helmet, now too small.
In her trough, the thick cake of rusty salt
is smoothed where she polished her tongue.
It is the common objects, the shoes,
that become our pictures of grief.

Stumbling back to the house, my hands
are in my pockets
and my elbows pull me from
side to side.

I move through chores as if
this were any day.
Then, stretching the laundry
across the line;
a sudden wet mouth of sheet
wraps around my arms.

III

I watch the window where a great snail of dusk
leaves a silvery trail
across the ledge.
Inside the hot house, a ripe tomato smell.
Through the dark boards I slip
slowly into fretful sleep.

If I get out of bed I am alone
with the salt on the floor.
I sweep it into a pile
and throw blue lumps of it
out the open window.
The floor is iron gray and tilted
as if we are sailing.

INTRO TO POETRY
(Steven Bauer, 1948–)

You thought it was math that taught
the relation of time and speed
but it's farther than you knew
from that sun-lit white-walled classroom
to this darkened lounge with its couch
and overstuffed chairs. How many miles,
would you say, since you talked
as if poetry were no distorting mirror,
one-way street? But listen, sometimes
it's like this, a stranger's Ford pulls up,
and you, with no plans for the afternoon,
get in. He doesn't talk, stares at the road
and it's miles before you understand

you didn't want to travel. His lips say *no*
as you reach for the radio's knob.

In this silence you fall deeper
into yourself, and even the car
disappears, the stranger's face blurs
into faded upholstery, and all things
being equal, you're alone as though
you've wandered into a forest with night
coming on, no stars, the memory of sun
and a voice's asking *Is this my life?*

A LONG TIME MORE
(Dara Wier, 1949–)

I will say to you let's go
when we are dead together.

Let's not be dead any longer;
not there with all the already gone,

not where nothing we want we'll know,
no more I have to have this now,

no more not one time more not ever.
Back where we've come from,

back there we'll go.
We will be thirsty again together,

and find food and clothes and comfort,
and this time take time,

this time neither too fast,
this time ever more slow.

Words:
Texture and Sound

One deep feeling called by its right name names others.
—EUDORA WELTY

A poem on a stately theme often will use measured, exalted language. A poem on marlin fishing in rough seas will be lively, "salty." If the subject is jazz, the words will play a riff of their own in your ear; if they don't, the poem probably will seem "off." Whatever the subject, the writer works and plays with words to fit sounds and sound patterns to the subject.

James Joyce used 29,899 different words in his novel *Ulysses*. Obviously, writers in English have rich choices to make, and each word has layers of meaning. We bring our personal associations to a word along with our knowledge of its dictionary meanings. The dictionary defines *chocolate* or *dog*, but we have hundreds of further links to the words. Every word has **denotation** (explicit meaning) and **connotation** (suggested meaning).

Texture of Language

Equally crucial to what the poet has to say is how it is said. Words have meaning and also texture. There's more than difference in meaning between *summer smoke, cellar door* and *rot gut, mug shot.* English branched from complex Teutonic (Germanic) roots but also absorbed much of the more mellifluous Latin (Romance) languages. The texture of a one-syllable word with two or three consonants sounds harder to the ear than a word such as *mellifluous,* which seems to drift along. As you listen, you respond to texture. It is as if you could run your hand over the poem's surface. Are the words soft and flowing, or chopped and harsh? Are they worn down, heavy and flat, or light and smooth? Sound alone tells a lot about the poem.

Words are the basic building blocks of poetry. The poem is made word by word. No other choices the poet makes — subject, structure, speaker — are more important than the quality of individual words.

Sometimes a poem can mean little or nothing, yet the stimulus of words alone wins our attention. We begin to invent for ourselves. Our ears prick up for the pleasure of listening to interesting sounds. The invented and odd words in this poem from *Through the Looking-Glass* hook the ear. Our eyes also are attracted by words' textures. Poetry is partly a visual experience; the shape of the poem on the page and the look of the words claim our interest. Humpty Dumpty had no trouble explaining every word of this to Alice. He maintained he could explain all poems, even "a good many" not yet written.

JABBERWOCKY
(Lewis Carroll, 1832–1898)

'Twas brillig, and the slithy toves
    Did gyre and gimble in the wabe;
All mimsy were the borogoves,
    And the mome raths outgrabe.

"Beware the Jabberwock, my son!
    The jaws that bite, the claws that catch!

Beware the Jubjub bird, and shun
  The frumious Bandersnatch!"

He took his vorpal sword in hand:
  Long time the manxome foe he sought—
So rested he by the Tumtum tree,
  And stood awhile in thought.

And as in uffish thought he stood,
  The Jabberwock, with eyes of flame,
Came whiffling through the tulgey wood,
  And burbled as it came!

One, two! One, two! And through and through
  The vorpal blade went snicker-snack!
He left it dead, and with its head
  He went galumphing back.

"And hast thou slain the Jabberwock?
  Come to my arms, my beamish boy!
O frabjous day! Callooh! Callay!"
  He chortled in his joy.

'Twas brillig, and the slithy toves
  Did gyre and gimble in the wabe;
All mimsy were the borogoves,
  And the mome raths outgrabe.

The sentences sound real; the invented words could be real. Often, people like to hear poets read in languages they cannot understand. A woman leaving a reading by the Polish poet Czeslaw Milosz said she was glad he'd read some of his work in Polish because the language sounded exciting, like horse hooves over cobblestones. Her friend said one poem sounded like books dropped down a stairwell. Unable to hear nuances in the foreign language, they still responded to the overall texture of sound. Story writer Isak Dinesen's workers in Africa asked her to read to them because her voice sounded like falling rain. The *noise* a poem makes is part of its meaning. Sound and patterns of sound make direct connections to the senses and extend to the imagination.

Many poets begin writing out of love for the noises of language. Dylan Thomas, who wrote poems characterized by exuberant language, remembers:

> The first poems I knew were nursery rhymes, and before I could read them for myself I had come to love just the words of them, the words alone. What the words stood for, symbolized, or meant, was of very secondary importance; what mattered was the *sound* of them as I heard them for the first time on the lips of the remote and incomprehensible grownups who seemed, for some reason, to be living in my world. And these words were, to me, as the notes of bells, the sounds of musical instruments, the noise of wind, sea, and rain, the rattle of milk carts, the clopping of hooves on cobbles, the fingering of branches on a windowpane, might be to someone, deaf from birth, who has miraculously found his hearing. I did not care what the words said, overmuch, nor what happened to Jack & Jill & the Mother Goose rest of them; I cared for the shapes of sound that their names, and the words describing their actions, made in my ears; I cared for the colors the words cast on my eyes. . . . I tumbled for words at once. And when I began to read the nursery rhymes for myself, and, later, to read other verses and ballads, I knew that I had discovered the most important things, to me, that could be ever.
>
> from *Poetic Manifesto*

Thomas probably would appreciate this poem about "the naming of things into their thing," which explores the elemental pleasure of words:

SAYING THINGS
(*Marilyn Krysl, 1942–*)

Three things quickly — pineapple, sparrowgrass, whale —
and then on to asbestos. What I want to say tonight is
words, the naming of things into their thing,
yucca, brown sugar, solo, the roll of a snare drum,
say something, say anything, you'll see what I mean.
Say windmill, you feel the word fly out from under and away.
Say eye, say shearwater, alewife, apache, harpoon,
do you see what I'm saying, say celery, say Seattle,
say a whole city, say San Jose. You can feel the word
rising like a taste on the palate, say
tuning fork, angel, temperature, meadow, silver nitrate,
try carbon cycle, point lace, helium, Micronesia, quail.
Any word — say it — belladonna, screw auger, spitball,
any word goes like a gull up and on its way,
even lead lifts like a swallow from the nest
of your tongue. Say incandescence, bonnet, universal joint,
lint — oh I invite you to try it. Say cold cream,
corydalis, corset, cotillion, cosmic dust,
you are all of you a generous and patient audience,
pilaster, cashmere, mattress, Washington pie,
say vise, inclinometer, enjambment, you feel your own voice
taking off like a swift, when you say a word you feel like
a gong that's been struck, to speak is to step out of your skin,
stunned. And you're a pulsar, finally you understand light
is both particle and wave, you can see it, as in
parlour — when do you get a chance to say parlour —
and now mackinaw, toad and ham wing their way
to the heaven of their thing. Say bellows, say sledge,
say threshold, cottonmouth, Russia leather,
say ash, picot, fallow deer, saxophone, say kitchen sink.
This is a birthday party for the mouth — it's better than ice cream,

say waterlily, refrigerator, hartebeeste, Prussian blue
and the word will take you, if you let it,
the word will take you along across the air of your head
so that you're there as it settles into the thing it was made for,
adding to it a shimmer and the bird song of its sound,
sound that comes from you, the hand letting go
its dove, yours the mouth speaking the thing into existence,
this is what I'm talking about, this is called saying things.

Words *are* names, and naming is a rite. It's bad luck to rename a boat. Babies' names, once the birth certificate is filled in, are seldom changed. Once called by an unfortunate nickname like "Lard" or "Pug," a person can be stuck for life. Your own name has a sound like no other; it seems to belong to you as intrinsically as "chair" does to chair or "book" does to book.

Naming is one of the great involvements of the writer, the bonding of words as close to the subject as possible. In *Let Us Now Praise Famous Men*, James Agee wrote about Southern sharecroppers during the Great Depression. In his frustration over finding words powerful enough to make tangible the farmers' poverty, Agee said he would like to glue one of their shoes to a page of each book. He wanted the word to have the power of the actual object. Words are chosen for poems with the same passion for precision.

Choosing Words

*This morning I deleted the hyphen from "hell-hound" and made
it one word; this afternoon I redivided it and restored the hyphen.*
— Edward Arlington Robinson

Given that poets can't glue shoes on the page, how do they find the best words? Good poems use language with freshness. What is a fresh word? Some always seem new: star, biscuit, carnation, mint, foot, hair, rock, knot, cat, seed, goat, worm, ruby, salt, thorn, rooster, sock, milk. . . . The endless list of totally ordinary nouns never seems old because these **concrete words** name specific things. (**Abstract words** describe generalizations or concepts such as work, generosity, jealousy, pain.)

Shakespeare must have been thinking of concrete naming when he wrote:

> Fie, fie upon her!
> There's language in her eye, her cheek, her lip,
> Nay, her foot speaks; her wanton spirits look out
> At every joint and motive of her body.

The language *in* her eye is the point here. The words to describe her are all over her body; every part of her speaks. If Shakespeare decided to describe those eyes, chances are he would not be content to say they were dark brown. He would want the *exact* quality of the brown — say, sun on sherry in a glass; in a different mood, he'd describe her with round, bulging eyes like an old horse.

Onomatopoeia always sounds fresh. *Hiss, slap, rip, buzz, sizzle, pop*: an onomatopoeiac word is one whose sound imitates meaning. *Bang, burp, gargle, screech, gabble, croak*: onomatopoeiac words are noise words. Many words in our language have hidden onomatopoeiac connections. *Barbarian*, for instance, comes from the ancient Greek mimicking of foreign invaders' speech. The Greeks thought the invaders sounded as though they were saying, "bar, bar, bar, bar." Noise words are direct. They're used for their impact and immediacy. Writers invent onomatopoeiac words: she *shugs* through in her slippers, he *hoicks* the chair closer, a boat *thucks* across the water. Some of these inventions become part of everyday speech. This is one of the ways languages grow.

When words lose their voltage through overuse, they become **clichés.** We're familiar with clichés in ordinary speech: working like a dog, busy as a beaver, warm as toast, the fact of the matter, first and foremost, sigh of relief, short but sweet, fatal flaw. These once-strong expressions now pass — to use a cliché — in one ear and out the other.

Poetry has its own stock of phrases and words that have been used up. In certain poems perhaps a cliché can be revived, but most of these old warhorses deserve a long rest:

mirror of my mind	grim reaper
thou art true	eternal sleep
soaring spirit	veil is parted
crystal clear	shining hosts
spectral ships	on golden wings
purple twilight	dwelt
truth and beauty	O, time
drenched by light	heavenly sphere
soul-enhancing	night is falling
twinkling stars	shimmering water
sweetness and grace	alas
roaring fire	memory weaves
voice of the wind	voice of woe
dreams go with you always	threads of memory
brief years	shadow of death
radiant glow	dying embers
press your lips to mine	crimson tide
golden mist	time immemorial
enchanted realms	dewdrops
days to come	undimmed
alien lands	infinity
muted strings	dispel the clouds
your essence	endless horizon
bitter end	shaft of light
tracery	crystalline

Some of the phrases on the list were brilliant when they were first used: "crimson tide," though now a hand-me-down, was new in Shakespeare's *Richard III*. Others, however, were lazy language all along. It's hard to imagine that "grim reaper" was ever fresh.

Besides the ground-down quality of poetic clichés, they usually sound archaic. We don't say *oft, o'er,* or *yon* anymore, so the sudden appearance of such a word in a contemporary poem displaces the tone into another time. In a poem from an earlier century we accommodate our ears to the language of the era. We may still have some difficulty learning to read early poems with vocabularies quite different from our own. Those poems require us to work a little harder. Sometimes we need to learn obsolete words and figure out references to customs and past events.

Even the subject of a poem can be a cliché. Only through a sharp ear for language can a well-worn subject such as the moon be refreshed. The face and being of the beloved is certainly such a subject too. We can find rosebuds in many cheeks in English literature. We expect lavish praise and superlatives—but look at this early fifteenth-century poet's unexpected assessment of his love.

OF MY LADY
(Thomas Hoccleve [ca. 1369–1450])

Of my lady well me rejoise I may!
Hir golden forheed is full narw° and small;   narrow
Hir browes been lik to dim, reed coral;
And as the jeet° hir yën° glistren ay.   jet, eyes

Hir bowgy° cheekës been as softe as clay,   bulging
With largë jowës° and substancial;   jowls
Hir nose a pentice° is that it ne shal   penthouse
Reine in hir mouth though she uprightës lay.

Hir mouth is nothing scant with lippës gray;
Hir chin unnethë° may be seen at al;   hardly
Hir comly° body shape as a footbal,   comely
And she singeth full like a papëjay°.   parrot

The Muscle of Language

When the poet strengthens certain aspects of language, it's for particular purposes. The use of many active verbs, for instance, gives force and movement. The use of many adjectives or adverbs gives an impression of abundance, whereas an absence of modifiers pares language down. A high density of one-syllable words gives a definite, emphatic impression. Any *one* effect used over and over has an impact. In "Pied Beauty," Gerard Manley Hopkins selected fresh and surprising words such as *brinded, tackle, adazzle, fallow, fickle, rose-mole, stipple.* He uses several hyphens to get words as close together as possible. With an emphasized usage like this, the poet purposefully draws your attention to his word choice. Although the meaning of the poem is simple — praising God for creating dappled beauty — many of the packed-tight words may need to be thought through or looked up in the dictionary.

 In Your Notebook:

Leaf through several books or spend an hour with a dictionary. Make a list of your one hundred favorite words. Pick what your eyes, ears, and imagination particularly respond to. This will sharpen your ear for the use of words in the poems that follow. After you've made the list, look at it as a whole. What do your words have in common? Are they vivid? Quiet? Concrete? Rowdy? Do you like active verbs? Nouns? Reread "Jabberwocky" and "Counting-Out Rhyme" (pages 26 and 4); then try writing a poem for the pleasure of sound from your list.

You know the denotative meanings of *soup, snow, midnight, siren, candlelight, moon, terror, mist, escape, privacy.* List your connotations for each.

PIED[1] BEAUTY
(Gerard Manley Hopkins, 1844–1889)

Glory be to God for dappled things —
   For skies of couple-colour as a brinded cow;
     For rose-moles all in stipple upon trout that swim;
Fresh-firecoal chestnut-falls; finches' wings;
   Landscape plotted and pieced — fold, fallow, and plough;
     And all trades, their gear and tackle and trim.

All things counter, original, spare, strange;
   Whatever is fickle, freckled (who knows how?)
     With swift, slow; sweet, sour; adazzle, dim;
He fathers-forth whose beauty is past change:
            Praise him.

---

[1] *Pied:* patchy in color.

Reading this old favorite one day, I realized that in praising God for diversity, Hopkins, by his word choice, means also to praise God for the variety in language. The poem itself is "dappled," "stippled" with unusual words. Obviously, Hopkins delights in the sounds of *firecoal, rose-moles,* and *couple-colour.* In each line, the word choice reflects his admiration for the dappled things of the world *and* his joy in matching them to language.

Sound Patterns

In "Pied Beauty," Hopkins arranges certain sounds. If you look at each line, you'll see how often he repeats the initial consonants of words, as in line 4:

Fresh-firecoal chestnut-falls; finches' wings

Repeating an initial consonant sound is called **alliteration.** Like rhyme, alliteration ties sounds together, reinforcing, by repetition, a unity in the poem. By placing like sounds close together, the words are subtly linked, as in this line from the Preface to Walt Whitman's *Leaves of Grass:*

All beauty comes from beautiful blood and a beautiful brain.

Alliteration is one of the oldest formal devices of English poetry, older than rhyme. *Beowulf,* the Anglo-Saxon epic composed between 650 and 750 A.D., was written in short, strongly alliterative lines, a tradition still lively in English poetry.

According to this clattering poem of the fifteenth century, noise pollution is nothing new. Blacksmiths (smoked black smithys) working at night drove the anonymous poet to use the loudest words he could find for his complaint. He generally keeps to the traditional four alliterations per line.

THE BLACKSMITHS
(Anonymous)

Swarte smeked° smithes smatered with smoke	*black smoked*
Drive me to deth with din of here dintes.°	*their blows*
Swich° nois on nightes ne herd men never:	*such*
What knavene cry° and clatering of knockes!	*workmen shouting*
The cammede kongons° cryen after 'coal, coal'	*snub-nosed brutes*
And blowen here bellowes, that al here brain brestes:°	*bursts*
'Huf, puf!' said that one; 'haf, paf!' that other.	
They spitten and sprawlen and spellen many spelles;°	*curses*
They gnawen° and gnachen°, they grones togedere,	*grind, gnash*
And holden hem hote° with here hard hamers.	*keep themselves hot*
Of a bulle-hide been here barm-felles;°	*leather aprons*
Here shankes been shakled for the fire-flunderes;[1]	
Hevy hameres they han°, that hard been handled°,	*have, wielded*

---

[1] *shankes ... flunderes:* shanks have been protected against fire sparks.

Stark strokes they striken on a steled stokke:°   *steel anvil*
Lus, bus! las, das! rowten by rowe.°   *crash in turn*
Swich dolful a dreme° the devil it to-drive!   *noise*
The maister longeth a litel, and lasheth a lesse,

Twineth hem twain, and toucheth a treble;[2]
Tik, tak! hic, hac! tiket, taket! tik, tak!
Lus, bus! lus, das! swich lif they leden,
Alle clothemeres°: Crist hem give sorwe!   *horse-clothers*
May no man for bren-wateres[3] on night han his rest.

---

[2] *The maister . . . treble:* master smith lengthens a little piece and beats out a smaller one, twists the two together, and strikes a treble note.
[3] *bren-wateres:* water-sizzlers; refers to hot iron cooling in water.

Gerard Manley Hopkins was drawn to these early uses of sound patterning. He was interested also in forgotten language. He never hesitated to use words that had rested quietly in dictionaries for years. Observe the "new" words in the following poem. Note the addition of accents to words he wanted to stress:

INVERSNAID
(Gerard Manley Hopkins, 1844–1889)

This darksome burn, horseback brown,
His rollrock highroad roaring down,
In coop and in comb the fleece of his foam
Flutes and low to the lake falls home.

A winfpuff-bonnet of fáwn-fróth
Turns and twindles over the broth
Of a pool so pitchblack, féll-frówning,
It rounds and rounds Despair to drowning.

Degged with dew, dappled with dew
Are the groins of the braes that the brook treads through,

Wiry heathpacks, flitches of fern.
And the beadbonny ash that sits over the burn.

What would the world be, once bereft
Of wet and of wildness? Let them be left,
O let them be left, wildness and wet;
Long live the weeds and the wilderness yet.

"Degged with dew, dappled with dew" packs alliteration into the line. (Fortunately Hopkins did not go on to say, "Are the dips of the ditch that the drips drop through.") *Degged* means "sprinkled," "damped," "drizzled"—a perfectly good word rescued from oblivion. The key word is *burn*, the Scottish word for "brook." The words in the first three stanzas attempt to capture the fast-flowing motion of the burn. In stanza 4 the words slow down; the poem turns out to be a plea for the wilderness. A few minutes spent looking up unfamiliar words (such as *twindle, braes, flitches*) can make this poem come alive.

Consonance and **assonance** are, respectively, repetitions of consonant and vowel sounds. Consonance differs from alliteration only in that alliteration repeats the first letter, while consonance repeats sounds within a word. The line

His rollrock highroad roaring down

uses alliteration of the *r* in *roll* and *roar* and consonance in the *r* sounds within *rollrock, highroad*, and *roaring*. The line has five *o* sounds: assonance. Assonance is more pronounced in: "In coop and in comb the fleece of his foam."

Passages that arrange and repeat vowels (and smooth consonants: l, m, n, y, w) have **euphony**—that is, flowing and pleasing sound without disruption. These lines by Alfred, Lord Tennyson, are a famous example of euphony:

The moan of doves in immemorial elms,
And murmuring of innumerable bees.

Read "He Remembers Forgotten Beauty" aloud, thinking about how euphony works *with* the subject. Then compare the texture with "Inversnaid."

HE REMEMBERS FORGOTTEN BEAUTY
(William Butler Yeats, 1865–1939)

When my arms wrap you round I press
My heart upon the loveliness
That has long faded from the world;
The jewelled crowns that kings have hurled
In shadowy pools, when armies fled;
The love-tales wrought with silken thread
By dreaming ladies upon cloth
That has made fat the murderous moth;
The roses that of old time were
Woven by ladies in their hair,
The dew-cold lilies ladies bore
Through many a sacred corridor
Where such grey clouds of incense rose
That only God's eyes did not close:
For that pale breast and lingering hand
Come from a more dream-heavy land,
A more dream-heavy hour than this;
And when you sigh from kiss to kiss
I hear white Beauty sighing, too,
For hours when all must fade like dew,
But flame on flame, and deep on deep,
Throne over throne where in half sleep,
Their swords upon their iron knees,
Brood her high lonely mysteries.

Cacophony is the opposite quality, a group of harsh sounds:

double-tongued mud brain, hypocrite
hiss, the heft of blood's blind demand

As in "Inversnaid," the muscles of the tongue work hard in this example. The effect on meaning is also tensile. Since language is taut and hard, that quality infuses the meaning.

Nineteenth-century poets like Algernon Swinburne were especially fond of alliteration, consonance, and assonance. Swinburne had a weakness for **sibilance,** patterning *s* and hissing sounds. Note his use of *s*-sound patterns in this section from a longer poem:

from IN THE BAY
(Algernon C. Swinburne, 1837–1909)

XIX

The shadow stayed not, but the splendor stays,
Our brother, till the last of English days.
No day nor night on English earth shall be
Forever, spring nor summer, Junes nor Mays,
But somewhat as a sound or gleam of thee
Shall come on us like morning from the sea.

The Surprise of Language

Often a poem includes one or two little-known words, or an unusual use of a familiar word that ruffles the surface of the poem or shifts your attention just when you thought you knew where you were going. One poem by Theodore Roethke begins:

Once upon a tree
I came upon a time

A poem titled "Boustrophedon" sends you to the dictionary before you begin reading. In one of his "non-lectures," e.e. cummings says, "…although [my mother's] health eventually failed her, she kept her sense of humor to the beginning." The surprise word pulls the rug out from under our expectations. In the following poem, James Wright uses an ordinary word with a powerful effect.

AUTUMN BEGINS IN MARTINS FERRY, OHIO
(James Wright, 1927–1980)

In the Shreve High football stadium,
I think of Polacks nursing long beers in Tiltonsville,
And gray faces of Negroes in the blast furnace at Benwood,
And the ruptured night watchman of Wheeling Steel,
Dreaming of heroes

All the proud fathers are ashamed to go home.
Their women cluck like starved pullets,
Dying for love.

Therefore,
Their sons grow suicidally beautiful
At the beginning of October,
And gallop terribly against each other's bodies.

The language is exact. The names of the stadium, the town, the factory, the place where workers drink beer, all orient the reader clearly. The men Wright thinks of are *nursing* beers. Their faces turn gray in the furnace light; the watchman is *ruptured.* He compares the women to starved chickens. The words are concrete; we can see these people. Wright never generalizes or moralizes by resorting to abstractions about the tragic state of the steelworkers' lives; instead, with just a few words, he makes us see several precise views of these lives. Then, in the last stanza, the reflections take a turn. "Therefore," he says. The single word on a line by itself turns the poem inside out. Why? *Therefore* is not at all the kind of word he has used so far. If you read aloud, you'll also change your tone of voice at that point. *Therefore* catapults us toward a conclusion that suddenly seems to be the proof for an equation we did not realize was being set up. After *therefore*, he continues the change in language. The two words *suicidally beautiful* shock each other powerfully. The words, it turns out, allow us a new and more complex vision of an ordinary game of football. The unusual, disturbing juxtaposition of *suicidally beautiful* is reinforced by the additional pairing of other surprising words in the last line. *Gallop terribly* pairs words that jolt our attention. Wright's conclusions about the fall ritual at Shreve High provoke the reader to agree or argue with his explanation of football.

The Kinship of Words

A poem's language usually has a coherence we may be unaware of until it's interrupted. In Wright's poem, the word *Therefore* signals a switching of gears; from then on, the vivid, descriptive words intensify. **Diction** is a poem's entire word choice, the selection taken from the poet's whole knowledge of language. Diction is somewhat analogous to a recipe a chef devises from his whole familiarity with cuisines. A fiery pepper on a clam has consequences, as does a hot word in a cold poem. The chef wants his dish to balance and contrast tastes for the entire experience. The quality of every ingredient contributes to this.

"Words, words, words," Shakespeare wrote. Poems are mysteriously made of words, just as a great dish is, as one cook explained, "only a combination of ingredients." Words for a poem are generated from a particular area of language. In "The Foot," a finely articulated knowledge brings unlikely words into a poem.

THE FOOT
(Alice Jones)

Our improbable support, erected
on the osseous architecture
of the calcaneus, talus, cuboid,

navicular, cuneiforms, metatarsals,
phalanges, a plethora of hinges,

all strung together by gliding
tendons, covered by the pearly
plantar fascia, then fat-padded
to form the sole, humble surface
of our contact with earth.

Here the body's broadest tendon
anchors the heel's fleshy base,
the finely wrinkled skin stretches
forward across the capillaried arch,
to the ball, a balance point.

A wide web of flexor tendons
and branched veins maps the dorsum,
fades into the stub-laden bone
splay, the stuffed sausage sacks
of toes, each with a tuft

of proximal hairs to introduce
the distal nail, whose useless
curve remembers an ancestor,
the vanished creature's wild
and necessary claw.

We talk about rowing with a special vocabulary, as we do with ballet, gambling, law, and computer programming. Glassblowers and rabbit raisers, short-order cooks and moving van drivers — all have characteristic phrases and terms appropriate to their activities. Groups of words are particular to places also. Many words you'd say in Oregon you would not use in Maine or Australia. Poems often partake of special limitations of word choice. For a rabbit poem or a death poem, the writer dips into different dictions.

The **tone,** or mood, the poet wants the poem to have also influences word choice. In two poems about mountain climbing, the same poet may use similar technical terms and place names, but the diction will be guided differently by each poem's mood. Tension or exuberance lead the poet to make different word choices. In speech, you tell a lot about people's moods by their tones of voice. Even if you can't hear the words, you pick up quickly whether commotion in the street at night is someone getting mugged or someone going home from a party, whether the low voice on the telephone is a friend or an obscene caller, whether you don't mind that your teenager came in at four in the morning or you're barely hiding your fury. In poems, too, emotions and attitudes show in the *tone.* Anger, sarcasm, boisterousness, teasing, boredom, exultation, sadness, querulousness — these emotions are currents we sense running through word selection.

"Cherrylog Road" tells about a meeting that could take place in any rural area. But, at the outset, "kudzu" and "corn whiskey" begin to focus sharply on the specific location of the poem. What other words are *of* that place? Unlike Wright's "Autumn Begins in Martins Ferry, Ohio," this poem contains no shift in diction. It stays right in the hot Southern junkyard. Both the boy and Doris Holbrook climb through a series of cars. Doris has "escaped" from her father's farm; the boy imagines the Pierce-Arrow's former owner being driven to an orphanage. Even the sun is active "eating the paint in blisters / From a hundred car tops and hoods." Dickey chooses words of exhilarating motion and of location to lead to the wild parting at the end.

CHERRYLOG ROAD
(James Dickey, 1923–1997)

Off Highway 106
At Cherrylog Road I entered
The '34 Ford without wheels,
Smothered in kudzu,
With a seat pulled out to run
Corn whiskey down from the hills,

And then from the other side
Crept into an Essex
With a rumble seat of red leather
And then out again, aboard
A blue Chevrolet, releasing
The rust from its other color,

Reared up on three building blocks.
None had the same body heat;
I changed with them inward, toward
The weedy heart of the junkyard,
For I knew that Doris Holbrook
Would escape from her father at noon

And would come from the farm
To seek parts owned by the sun
Among the abandoned chassis,
Sitting in each in turn
As I did, leaning forward
As in a wild stock-car race

In the parking lot of the dead.
Time after time, I climbed in
And out the other side, like
An envoy or movie star
Met at the station by crickets.
A radiator cap raised its head,

Become a real toad or a kingsnake
As I neared the hub of the yard,
Passing through many states,
Many lives, to reach
Some grandmother's long Pierce-Arrow
Sending platters of blindness forth

From its nickel hubcaps
And spilling its tender upholstery
On sleepy roaches.
The glass panel in between
Lady and colored driver
Not all the way broken out,

The back-seat phone
Still on its hook.
I got in as though to exclaim,
"Let us go to the orphan asylum,
John: I have some old toys
For children who say their prayers."

I popped with sweat as I thought
I heard Doris Holbrook scrape
Like a mouse in the southern-state sun
That was eating the paint in blisters
From a hundred car tops and hoods.
She was tapping like code,

Loosening the screws,
Carrying off headlights,
Sparkplugs, bumpers,
Cracked mirrors and gear-knobs,
Getting ready, already,
To go back with something to show

Other than her lips' new trembling
I would hold to me soon, soon,
Where I sat in the ripped back seat
Talking over the interphone,
Praying for Doris Holbrook
To come from her father's farm

And to get back there
With no trace of me on her face
To be seen by her red-haired father
Who would change, in the squalling barn,
Her back's pale skin with a strop,
Then lay for me

In a bootlegger's roasting car
With a string-triggered 12-gauge shotgun
To blast the breath from the air.
Not cut by the jagged windshields,
Through the acres of wrecks she came
With a wrench in her hand,

Through dust where the blacksnake dies
Of boredom, and the beetle knows
The compost has no more life.
Someone outside would have seen
The oldest car's door inexplicably
Close from within:

I held her and held her and held her,
Convoyed at terrific speed
By the stalled, dreaming traffic around us,
So the blacksnake, stiff
With inaction, curved back
Into life, and hunted the mouse

With deadly overexcitement,
The beetles reclaimed their field
As we clung, glued together,
With the hooks of the seat springs
Working through to catch us red-handed
Amidst the gray breathless batting

That burst from the seat at our backs,
We left by separate doors
Into the changed, other bodies
Of cars, she down Cherrylog Road
And I to my motorcycle
Parked like the soul of the junkyard

Restored, a bicycle fleshed
With power, and tore off
Up Highway 106, continually
Drunk on the wind in my mouth,
Wringing the handlebar for speed,
Wild to be wreckage forever.

Both "Oh, Lovely Rock" and "Crystals Like Blood" use language that
focuses on geographical and geological terminology.

Oh, Lovely Rock
(Robinson Jeffers, 1887–1962)

We stayed the night in the pathless gorge of Ventana Creek, up
  the east fork.
The rock walls and the mountain ridges hung forest on forest
  above our heads, maple and redwood,
Laurel, oak, madrone, up to the high and slender Santa Lucian
  firs that stare up the cataracts
Of slide-rock to the star-color precipices.
  We lay on gravel and
Kept a little camp-fire for warmth
Past midnight only two or three coals glowed red in the cooling
  darkness; I laid a clutch of dead bay-leaves
On the ember ends and felted dry sticks across them and lay
  down again. The revived flame
Lighted my sleeping son's face and his companion's, and the
  vertical face of the great gorge-wall

Across the stream. Light leaves overhead danced in the fire's
    breath, tree-trunks were seen: it was the rock wall
That fascinated my eyes and mind. Nothing strange: light-gray
    diorite with two or three slanting seams in it,
Smooth-polished by the endless attrition of slides and floods; no
    fern nor lichen, pure naked rock . . . as if I were
Seeing rock for the first time. As if I were seeing through the
    flame-lit surface into the real and bodily
And living rock. Nothing strange . . . I cannot
Tell you how strange: the silent passion, the deep nobility and
    childlike loveliness: this fate going on
Outside our fates. It is here in the mountain like a grave smiling
    child. I shall die, and my boys
Will live and die, our world will go on through its rapid agonies
    of change and discovery; this age will die,
And wolves have howled in the snow around a new Bethlehem:
    this rock will be here, grave, earnest, not passive: the energies
That are its atoms will be bearing the whole mountain above: and
    I, many packed centuries ago,
Felt its intense reality with love and wonder, this lonely rock.

CRYSTALS LIKE BLOOD
(Hugh MacDiarmid, 1892–1978)

I remember how, long ago, I found
Crystals like blood in a broken stone.

I picked up a broken chunk of bed-rock
And turned it this way and that,
It was heavier than one would have expected
From its size. One face was caked
With brown limestone. But the rest
Was a hard greenish-gray quartz-like stone

Faintly dappled with darker shadows,
And in this quartz ran veins and beads
Of bright magenta.

And I remember how later on I saw
How mercury is extracted from cinnabar
—The double ring of iron piledrivers
Like the multiple legs of a fantastically symmetrical spider
Rising and falling with monotonous precision,
Marching round in an endless circle
And pounding up and down with a tireless, thunderous force,
While, beyond, another conveyor drew the crumbled ore
From the bottom and raised it to an opening high
In the side of a gigantic gray-white kiln.

So I remember how mercury is got
When I contrast my living memory of you
And your dear body rotting here in the clay
—And feel once again released in me
The bright torrents of felicity, naturalness, and faith
My treadmill memory draws from you yet.

Poems

FERN HILL
(Dylan Thomas, 1914–1953)

Now as I was young and easy under the apple boughs
About the lilting house and happy as the grass was green,
    The night above the dingle starry,
      Time let me hail and climb
    Golden in the heydays of his eyes,
And honoured among wagons I was prince of the apple towns

And once below a time I lordly had the trees and leaves
Trail with daisies and barley
Down the rivers of the windfall light.

And as I was green and carefree, famous among the barns
About the happy yard and singing as the farm was home,
In the sun that is young once only,
Time let me play and be
Golden in the mercy of his means,
And green and golden I was huntsman and herdsman, the calves
Sang to my horn, the foxes on the hills barked clear and cold,
And the sabbath rang slowly
In the pebbles of the holy streams.

All the sun long it was running, it was lovely, the hay
Fields high as the house, the tunes from the chimneys, it was air
And playing, lovely and watery
And fire green as grass.
And nightly under the simple stars
As I rode to sleep the owls were bearing the farm away,
All the moon long I heard, blessed among stables, the night-jars
Flying with the ricks, and the horses
Flashing into the dark.

And then to awake, and the farm, like a wanderer white
With the dew, come back, the cock on his shoulder: it was all
Shining, it was Adam and maiden,
The sky gathered again
And the sun grew round that very day.
So it must have been after the birth of the simple light
In the first, spinning place, the spellbound horses walking warm
Out of the whinnying green stable
On to the fields of praise.

And honoured among foxes and pheasants by the gay house
Under the new made clouds and happy as the heart was long,
    In the sun born over and over,
        I ran my heedless ways,
    My wishes raced through the house high hay
And nothing I cared, at my sky blue trades, that time allows
In all his tuneful turning so few and such morning songs
    Before the children green and golden
        Follow him out of grace,

Nothing I cared, in the lamb white days, that time would take me
Up to the swallow thronged loft by the shadow of my hand,
    In the moon that is always rising,
        Nor that riding to sleep
    I should hear him fly with the high fields
And wake to the farm forever fled from the childless land.
Oh as I was young and easy in the mercy of his means,
        Time held me green and dying
    Though I sang in my chains like the sea.

WHEN THAT I WAS AND A LITTLE TINY BOY[1]
(William Shakespeare, 1564–1616)

When that I was and a little tiny boy,
    With hey, ho, the wind and the rain,
A foolish thing was but a toy,
    For the rain it raineth every day.

But when I came to man's estate,
    With hey, ho, the wind and the rain,

---

[1] *When That I Was and a Little Tiny Boy:* the clown's song at the close of *Twelfth Night*.

'Gainst knaves and thieves men shut their gate,
 For the rain it raineth every day.

But when I came, alas! to wive,
 With hey, ho, the wind and the rain,
By swaggering could I never thrive,
 For the rain it raineth every day.

But when I came unto my beds,
 With hey, ho, the wind and the rain,
With toss-pots still had drunken heads,
 For the rain it raineth every day.

A great while ago the world begun,
 With hey, ho, the wind and the rain,
But that's all one, our play is done,
 And we'll strive to please you every day.

The Snowstorm
(Ralph Waldo Emerson, 1803–1882)

Announced by all the trumpets of the sky,
Arrives the snow, and, driving o'er the fields,
Seems nowhere to alight: the whited air
Hides hills and woods, the river, and the heaven,
And veils the farmhouse at the garden's end.
The sled and traveler stopped, the courier's feet
Delayed, all friends shut out, the housemates sit
Around the radiant fireplace, enclosed
In a tumultuous privacy of storm.
Come see the north wind's masonry.
Out of an unseen quarry evermore
Furnished with tile, the fierce artificer

Curves his white bastions with projected roof
Round every windward stake, or tree, or door.
Speeding, the myriad-handed, his wild work
So fanciful, so savage, nought cares he
For number or proportion. Mockingly,
On coop or kennel he hangs Parian[1] wreaths;
A swan-like form invests the hidden thorn;
Fills up the farmer's lane from wall to wall,
Maugre[2] the farmer's sighs; and, at the gate,
A tapering turret overtops the work.
And when his hours are numbered, and the world
Is all his own, retiring, as he were not,
Leaves, when the sun appears, astonished Art
To mimic in slow structures, stone by stone,
Built in an age, the mad wind's night-work,
The frolic architecture of the snow.

---

[1] *Parian:* marble.
[2] *maugre:* in spite of.

THE NIGHT IS FREEZING FAST
(A. E. Housman, 1859–1936)

The night is freezing fast,
To-morrow comes December;
And winterfalls of old
Are with me from the past;
And chiefly I remember
How Dick would hate the cold.

Fall, winter, fall; for he,
Prompt hand and headpiece clever,
Has woven a winter robe,

And made of earth and sea
His overcoat for ever,
And wears the turning globe.

SONNET LXXIII
(William Shakespeare, 1564–1616)

That time of year thou mayst in me behold
When yellow leaves, or none, or few, do hang
Upon those boughs which shake against the cold,
Bare ruined choirs, where late the sweet birds sang.
In me thou see'st the twilight of such day
As after sunset fadeth in the west;
Which by and by black night doth take away,
Death's second self, that seals up all in rest.
In me thou see'st the glowing of such fire,
That on the ashes of his youth doth lie,
As the deathbed whereon it must expire
Consumed with that which it was nourished by.
   This thou perceiv'st, which makes thy love more strong,
   To love that well which thou must leave ere long.

THE FISH
(Elizabeth Bishop, 1911–1979)

I caught a tremendous fish
and held him beside the boat
half out of water, with my hook
fast in a corner of his mouth.
He didn't fight.
He hadn't fought at all.
He hung a grunting weight,
battered and venerable

and homely. Here and there
his brown skin hung in strips
like ancient wallpaper,
and its pattern of darker brown
was like wallpaper:
shapes like full-blown roses
stained and lost through age.
He was speckled with barnacles,
fine rosettes of lime,
and infested
with tiny white sea-lice,
and underneath two or three
rags of green weed hung down.
While his gills were breathing in
the terrible oxygen
—the frightening gills,
fresh and crisp with blood,
that can cut so badly—
I thought of the coarse white flesh
packed in like feathers,
the big bones and the little bones,
the dramatic reds and blacks
of his shiny entrails,
and the pink swim-bladder
like a big peony.
I looked into his eyes
which were far larger than mine
but shallower, and yellowed,
the irises backed and packed
with tarnished tinfoil
seen through the lenses
of old scratched isinglass.
They shifted a little, but not
to return my stare.
—It was more like the tipping

of an object toward the light.
I admired his sullen face,
the mechanism of his jaw,
and then I saw
that from his lower lip
—if you could call it a lip—
grim, wet, and weaponlike,
hung five old pieces of fish-line,
or four and a wire leader
with the swivel still attached,
with all their five big hooks
grown firmly in his mouth.
A green line, frayed at the end
where he broke it, two heavier lines,
and a fine black thread
still crimped from the strain and snap
when it broke and he got away.
Like medals with their ribbons
frayed and wavering,
a five-haired beard of wisdom
trailing from his aching jaw.
I stared and stared
and victory filled up
the little rented boat,
from the pool of bilge
where oil had spread a rainbow
around the rusted engine
to the bailer rusted orange,
the sun-cracked thwarts,
the oarlocks on their strings,
the gunnells—until everything
was rainbow, rainbow, rainbow!
And I let the fish go.

BEAUTY
(Abraham Cowley, 1618–1667)

Beauty, thou wild fantastic ape,
Who dost in ev'ry country change thy shape!
Here black, there brown, here tawny, and there white;
Thou flatt'rer which compli'st with every sight!
    Thou babel which confound'st the eye
With unintelligible variety!
    Who hast no certain what, nor where,
But vary'st still, and dost thy self declare
    Inconstant, as thy she-professors are.

Beauty, love's scene and masquerade,
So gay by well-plac'd lights, and distance made;
False coin, with which th' impostor cheats us still;
The stamp and colour good, but metal ill!
    Which light, or base we find, when we
Weigh by enjoyment, and examine thee!
    For though thy being be but show,
'Tis chiefly night which men to thee allow:
And choose t'enjoy thee, when thou least art thou.

Beauty, thou active, passive ill!
Which diest thy self as fast as thou dost kill!
Thou tulip, who thy stock in paint dost waste,
Neither for physic good, nor smell, nor taste.
    Beauty, whose flames but meteors are,
Short-liv'd and low, though thou wouldst seem a star,
    Who dar'st not thine own home descry,
Pretending to dwell richly in the eye,
When thou, alas, dost in the fancy lie.

Beauty, whose conquests still are made
O'er hearts by cowards kept, or else betray'd!
Weak victor! who thy self destroy'd must be

When sickness storms, or time besieges thee!
   Thou unwholesome thaw to frozen age!
Thou strong wine, which youth's fever dost enrage,
   Thou tyrant which leav'st no man free!
Thou subtle thief, from whom nought safe can be!
Thou murth'rer which hast kill'd, and devil which wouldst
   damn me.

✿

UPSTATE
(Derek Walcott, 1930–)

A knife blade of cold air keeps prying
the bus window open. The spring country
won't be shut out. The door to the john
keeps banging. There're a few of us:
a stale drunk or stoned woman in torn jeans,
a Spanish-American salesman, and, ahead,
a black woman folded in an overcoat.
Emptiness makes a companionable aura
through the upstate village — repetitive,
but crucial in their little differences
of fields, wide yards with washing, old machinery — where people
   live
with the highway's patience and flat certainty.
Sometimes I feel sometimes
the Muse is leaving, the Muse is leaving America.
Her tired face is tired of iron fields,
its hollows sing the mines of Appalachia,
she is a chalk-thin miner's wife with knobbled elbows,
her neck tendons taut as banjo strings,
she who was once a freckled palomino with a girl's mane
galloping blue pastures plinkety-plunkety,
staring down at a tree-stunned summer lake,
when all the corny calendars were true.

The departure comes over me in smoke
from the far factories.

But were the willows lyres, the fanned-out pollard willows
with clear translation of water into song,
were the starlings as heartbroken as nightingales,
whose sorrow piles the looming thunderhead
over the Catskills, what would be their theme?
The spring hills are sun-freckled, the chaste white barns flash
through screening trees the vigour of her dream,
like a white plank bridge over a quarreling brook.
Clear images! Direct as your daughters
in the way their clear look returns your stare,
unarguable and fatal —
no, it is more sensual.
I am falling in love with America.

I must put the cold small pebbles from the spring
upon my tongue to learn her language,
to talk like birch or aspen confidently.
I will knock at the widowed door
of one of these villages
where she will admit me like a broad meadow,
like a blue space between mountains,
and holding her arms at the broken elbows
brush the dank hair from a forehead
as warm as bread or as a homecoming.

THAT SONG
(Pattiann Rogers, 1940–)

I will use the cormorant on his rope at night diving
Into the sea, and the fire on the prow, and the fish
Like ribbons sliding toward the green light in the dark.

I will remember the baneberry and the bladderwort
And keep the white crone under the bosackle tree
And the translucent figs and the candelabra burning alone
In the middle of the plains, and the twig girdler,
And the lizard of Christ running over the waves.

I will take the egg bubble on the flute
Of the elm and the ministries of the predacious
Caul beetle, the spit of the iris, the red juice shot
From the eye of the horny toad, and I will use
The irreducible knot wound by the hazel scrub
And the bog myrtle still tangling, and the sea horse
With his delicate horn, the flywheel of his maneuvering.

I will remember exactly each tab folded down
In the sin book of Sister Alleece and each prayer
Hanging in its painted cylinder above the door
And the desert goat at noon facing
The sun to survive.

I will include the brindled bandicoot and the barnacle
Goose and the new birds hatching from mussels
Under the sea and the migrating wildebeests humming
Like organs, moaning like men.

The sand swimmers alive under the Gobi plateau,
The cactus wren in her nest of thorns and the herald
Of the tarantula wasp and each yellow needle
In the spring field rising, everything will be there,
And nothing will be wasted.

MADRID

(Jay Wright, 1935–)

So the villa, having learned its many skills
through riding the bluish ochre waves of sand and clay,
has fooled us again. The moon is only a moon,
without the olive sheen and horse hoof of Granada.
No ruffled lace guitars clutch at the darkened windows.
The bilious green watermarks on old houses
only make you think of the candle wind,
gathering its hammer force season after season,
a tempered master with a gray design.
Even the wall has been undone by sierra loneliness.

Perhaps on some theatrical night,
Lope fell in love with Elena,
and acted out her virtues,
until the father bored him.
That could only end in scandalous verses,
cuffs and a ticket out of Madrid,
a cloaked night at a village gate,
a loping horse and lovers shedding
                    the acacia trees.
Better this picking at the poor brick and earth
than the bed where the mournful knight lies,
                    dreaming of dowry
          —some household furniture,
               an orchard, five vines, four beehives,
               forty-five hens, one cock and a crucible—
or the Italian guile and papal star of a duke's daughter.

It is late, and the voices of Tollán swing
on the porch of the Puerta de Alcalá.
Criollos dawdle in the Plaza Mayor,
brushing the white ruff of their provincial injuries.

The Panadería has gone, with its bull blood,
autos-da-fé and saints,
and the mimetic houses sink into shadow.
And yet that dead sun has awakened
the mountain mother in the oval plaza,
and these old women in black manta scudder
over the Manzares bed,
following the lights of Taxco silver, silk,
                     Luke's virgin and a good name.

It is late,
Palm Sunday,
on a day when the mask will drop
and a slouch hat and voluminous cloak
will uncover the exiled heart.
It is late,
the May day when the sun's red heart
                returns from its exile,
and the Emperor's horsemen fall and begin
the unraveling of a Morning Star.
It is late,
when the Queen has gone,
in gentleman's attire,
to exhibit her hunger for boar meat
and a Bourbon husband with a taste for peace.
It is late,
when the red flag of the most violent summer
calls an end to the nation's yearning.

It is time
for the jeweled humiliation of the chosen
              to be revealed.
Now when the snow falls on this crucible
of sullen winds and interrupted passions,
there will be the dark bell sound of a mother,

crying the name she can never have,
or having it, fulfill.

Mushroom Hunting in the Jemez Mountains
(Arthur Sze, 1950–)

Walking in a mountain meadow toward the north slope,
I see redcap amanitas with white warts and know
they signal cèpes. I see a few colonies of puffballs,
red russulas with chalk-white stipes, brown-gilled
Poison Pie. In the shade under spruce are two
red-pored boletes: slice them in half and the flesh
turns blue in seconds. Under fir is a single amanita
with basal cup, flaring annulus, white cap: is it
the Rocky Mountain form of *Amanita pantherina*?
I am aware of danger in naming, in misidentification,
in imposing the distinctions of a taxonomic language
onto the things themselves. I know I have only
a few hours to hunt mushrooms before early afternoon rain.
I know it is a mistake to think I am moving and
that agarics are still: they are more transient
than we acknowledge, more susceptible to full moon,
to a single rain, to night air, to a moment of sunshine.
I know in this meadow my passions are mycorrhizal
with nature. I may shout out ecstasies, aches, griefs,
and hear them vanish in the white-pored silence.

Words
(Sylvia Plath, 1932–1963)

Axes
After whose stroke the wood rings,
And the echoes!

Echoes traveling
Off from the center like horses.

The sap
Wells like tears, like the
Water striving
To re-establish its mirror
Over the rock

That drops and turns,
A white skull,
Eaten by weedy greens.
Years later I
Encounter them on the road —

Words dry and riderless,
The indefatigable hoof-taps.
While
From the bottom of the pool, fixed stars
Govern a life.

TODAY
(Frank O'Hara, 1926–1966)

Oh! kangaroos, sequins, chocolate sodas!
You really are beautiful! Pearls,
harmonicas, jujubes, aspirins! all
the stuff they've always talked about

still makes a poem a surprise!
These things are with us every day
even on beachheads and biers. They
do have meaning. They're strong as rocks.

3

Images:
The Perceptual Field

It is better to present one Image in a lifetime
than to produce voluminous works.

—EZRA POUND

When a runner describes the last quarter-mile of the marathon, he might say that his left calf felt tied in a granny knot and his lungs were on fire. He might say instead that he sailed along smoothly and finished like a boat slipping into the berth or that, when he saw the red ribbon ahead at the finish line, he felt a tidal wave of energy pulling him across.

These specific details give you an active sense of the runner's experience. The tight muscle, the pressure in his chest, the feeling of ease, the sight of the red ribbon—all these are images. We usually think of an image as a picture of something, like a photograph is an image of its subject, but an image is *any* physical sensation. In poetry, an **image** is a word "picture" of any sense impression, not necessarily the visual. We see the red ribbon; we can't see lungs on fire but we "picture" in our mind's eye the sensation of heat in the chest. The imaginative recreation of a sensation (touch, smell, auditory, visual, taste, motion) through words is an image. If the runner says, "I ran the marathon and the last quarter-mile was really hard," he conveys information; he doesn't recreate the experience. To use images is to show details that appeal directly to the senses as well as to the mind.

If you read, "He walks like a giraffe belly-deep in cold water," the words call up a humorous picture of a man moving along awkwardly, slowly, and laboriously. The image also recalls your own experience of the difficulty of moving in cold water. You recognize the sensation through your own body. This *showing* of the man is livelier than the writer's simply telling us, "The awkward man is walking with some difficulty." Physical detail makes the man's motion specific. The language is concrete, as opposed to abstract. **Concrete** derives from root words meaning "to grow together." **Abstract** comes from root words meaning "to remove" and "to pull away." Abstract words (*progress, jealousy, pleasure, experience*) seem distant, while concrete words (*sunlight, smile, fork, sandwich*) are solid and right next to direct experience. Abstract words and statements are sometimes important and necessary, but a string of them is tedious. Too much abstract language quickly begins to sound like white noise. Because we respond more to the particular than to the general, imagery is a most important element in the craft of poetry. The following examples clarify differences between "showing" and "telling."

To Tell	**To Show (with concrete details)**
She dresses sloppily.	She wears her clothes as if they were thrown on with a pitchfork. —*Jonathan Swift*
The sea is rough.	A sea Harsher than granite. —*Ezra Pound*
I saw the harvest moon come up.	And saw the ruddy moon lean over a hedge Like a red-faced farmer. —*T. E. Hulme*

The old woman got ready for bed.	You stood at the dresser, put your teeth away, washed your face, smoothed on Oil of Olay.
	—Mona Van Duyn
He'd do anything for her.	He'd cut off his thumbs for her.
	—C. D. Wright
She was absurdly pleased.	...pleased as a dog with two tails.
	—Ozark folk expression
He has an unpleasant hand.	A hand like a fat maggot.
	—Jean-Paul Sartre
The dog's eyes are unusually large.	The dog in the next room has eyes big as ferris wheels.
	—Forrest Gander

The sentences on the left suffer from what Henry James called "weak specification"; that is, the statements are too generalized. We understand "an unpleasant hand," but Sartre's "a hand like a fat maggot" stimulates the senses of touch and sight. "The sea is rough" is a clear enough sentence. But if the sea is "harsher than granite," then it has a *more* resistant quality: the waves appear to be as hard as rocks.

Three Image Poems

The next three poems make extensive use of sensory details. In "Gloire de Dijon," D. H. Lawrence almost paints a picture of a woman bathing by a window. He is not the first poet to compare a woman to a rose. Notice how unobtrusively the "I" participates, just enough to give the reader a grounded vantage point.

GLOIRE DE DIJON[1]
(D. H. Lawrence, 1885–1930)

When she rises in the morning
I linger to watch her;
She spreads the bath-cloth underneath the window
Glistening white on the shoulders,
While down her sides the mellow
Golden shadow glows as
She stoops to the sponge, and her swung breasts
Sway like full-blown yellow
Gloire de Dijon roses.

She drips herself with water, and her shoulders
Glisten as silver, they crumple up
Like wet and falling roses, and I listen
For the sluicing of their rain-disheveled petals,
In the window full of sunlight
Concentrates her golden shadow
Fold on fold, until it glows as
Mellow as the glory roses.

---

[1] *Gloire de Dijon* ("Glory of Dijon"): a kind of rose.

The sense most active here is the kinetic, the motions of spreading, swaying, swinging, stooping, dripping. These actions belong not only to the woman but to the roses the poet is comparing her with. Visually we see many colors and lights: white shoulders, gold shadow on her sides, the full-blown roses, her shoulder silvered when wet, a window full of sunlight, and her shadow glowing and golden. The watcher of the woman bathing recreates his experience through the careful selection and fusion of sensory details common to both the woman and the roses.

"What the Dog Perhaps Hears" concentrates on auditory images:

WHAT THE DOG PERHAPS HEARS
(Lisel Mueller, 1924–)

If an inaudible whistle
blown between our lips
can send him home to us,
then silence is perhaps
the sound of spiders breathing
and roots mining the earth;
it may be asparagus heaving,
headfirst, into the light
and the long brown sound
of cracked cups, when it happens.
We would like to ask the dog
if there is a continuous whirr
because the child in the house
keeps growing, if the snake
really stretches full length
without a click and the sun
breaks through clouds without
a decibel of effort;
whether in autumn, when the trees
dry up their wells, there isn't a shudder
too high for us to hear.

What is it like up there
above the shut-off level
of our simple ears?
For us there was no birth-cry,
the newborn bird is suddenly here,
the egg broken, the nest alive,
and we heard nothing when the world changed.

We can't actually hear "the long brown sound / of cracked cups" or
the snake's clicking sound as it stretches out. By speculating on what

the dog possibly hears, Mueller lets these sounds resonate playfully in the reader's imagination. By implication, too, she raises the question of other unperceived events around us. The poem works with primarily auditory images, but Mueller ties them to images involving other senses. The asparagus is "heaving, / headfirst, into the light," the sun "breaks through clouds," roots are "mining" and trees are drying up—all images of sight, motion, or touch.

Because it is grounded in the senses, Shakespeare's "Winter" still seems immediate to contemporary readers.

WINTER
(William Shakespeare, 1564–1616)

When icicles hang by the wall,
    And Dick the shepherd blows his nail,
And Tom bears logs into the hall,
    And milk comes frozen home in pail,
When blood is nipped, and ways be foul,
Then nightly sings the staring owl:
         "To-who!
Tu-whit, tu-who!" a merry note,
While greasy Joan doth keel[1] the pot.

When all aloud the wind doth blow,
    And coughing drowns the parson's saw,
And birds sit brooding in the snow,
    And Marian's nose looks red and raw,
When roasted crabs hiss in the bowl,
Then nightly sings the staring owl:
         "To-who!
Tu-whit, tu-who!" a merry note,
While greasy Joan doth keel the pot.

---

[1] *keel*: to cool by stirring.

Shakespeare appeals to many senses in this brief poem. We see frozen milk and Marian's red nose. We hear the wind blowing, crab apples hissing as they roast, and coughs drowning out the parson. The sense of touch is affected by "nipped," "greasy," "blows his nail," and Joan's stirring the pot. The icicles hang, the logs are brought in, the winds blow, and the birds sit brooding—all arresting images of motion or the lack of it. Smell and taste, the only senses not directly evoked, are hinted at as Joan stirs and the crab apples hiss.

Images and Perception

It is too extreme to maintain, as Theodore Roethke did in "The Waking" (page 337), that "We think by feeling. What is there to know?," but it is true that a large proportion of what we know, think, and remember is held in mind by images. Thought involves textures, smells, colors. Your own memories of winter, if you were writing a list of them, might include smoke rising from a factory chimney, a leak in the ceiling of a closet, the steamy smell of wool mittens drying on the radiator, charred marshmallows toasted over leaf smoke, your aunt's curried tomato soup simmering on the back burner. Such sensory experience is the basic material of imagery.

Each sense can divide and combine with others. Sight, the strongest sensory perception, also includes qualities of focus, shape, color, perspective, shadow, speed of movement, brightness, clarity, and composition. The auditory sense involves sounds of all pitches, ranges, and rhythms—along with silences (as in "What the Dog Perhaps Hears"). The kinetic sense Lawrence works with in "Gloire de Dijon" includes tension, the pull of weight, muscular balance, and gravity. Temperature, texture, and density are three qualities of the tactile sense, which is active in "Winter." The whole complex of tastes and smells, and the combinations of these, is crucial to perception. In addition to the five external senses, we also have an inner organic sense of pulse, heartbeat, cycles, and digestion.

No one knows exactly how images work. True, people have basically the same primary senses. True, language related closely to the senses is processed by the brain almost immediately, with no pause for complex connections to take place. We recognize "the hot aroma of dark roasted coffee" more quickly than "the complex acrid smell of a heating beverage." But why? Is one more pleasurable than the other? We respond immediately to language that seems to *be* experience, rather than language that seems to *describe* experience from a distance.

A whiff of a musty coat as you pass someone on the sidewalk can release a flood of memories of your grandfather's old age. Almost all of these will be images: his white mustache, his way of slurping his tea or jingling the change in his pocket, his habit of dabbing a white handkerchief at the corners of his eyes. Imagery is a constant sound-and-light show taking place in our heads. But the language of philosophical ideas and abstractions can be pleasurable, too. As you walk along the sidewalk with your grandfather's image in mind, you may begin to speculate and to draw conclusions about his life (he was a sweet man with a good sense of humor or he was a crotchety old grump) that are far removed from the intense first impression you got from the dank, mildewed smell. These ideas can be just as important and powerful as the images that provoke them. How imagery works is at the root of how we perceive and remember. As a reader told the ancient Chinese poet TuFu, "It is like being alive twice." The sharp focus of imagery on the senses guarantees a reader's emotional, connotative, and physical involvement. Generalizations or abstractions have a wider angle. A *particular* experience, such as one foot in the cold ocean, can evoke an experience of a place much more powerfully than a *general* statement about the coastal terrain. The painter Degas said he had many ideas for poems but couldn't manage to say what he wanted. His friend, the poet Mallarmé, replied, "My dear Degas, one does not make poetry with ideas but with words."

Describe to yourself the exact senses evoked in the following images and how each image focuses the experience described:

A tap at the pane, the quick sharp scratch
And blue spurt of a lighted match.   —*Robert Browning*

The old star eaten blanket of the sky.   —*T. E. Hulme*

Her knee feels like the face
Of a surprised lioness.   —*James Wright*

Purple is black blooming.   —*Christopher Smart*

With my whole body I taste these peaches.   —*Wallace Stevens*

I should have been a pair of ragged claws
Scuttling across the floors of silent seas.   —*T. S. Eliot*

The blindman placed
a tulip on his tongue for purple's taste.   —*May Swenson*

A woman so skinny I could smell her bones.   —*Miller Williams*

. . . a collarpoint of light.   —*Mei-Mei Berssenbrugge*

When you are old and gray and full of sleep,
And nodding by the fire, take down this book.   —*W. B. Yeats*

 In Your Notebook:

First memories are largely sensory. Write a list of your earliest memories, including all the colors, shapes, movements, tastes you can recall. Continue with other early memories.

Literal Images

The two kinds of images, literal and figurative, are different. "Her wet pink lips" is a literal image; "her ripe plum lips" is a figurative image. A **literal image** aims to replicate in words the object or experience. The poet tries to reproduce the subject realistically, without comparing it to anything else. A **figurative image** likens an object or experience to something else, usually something surprising, as in "his eye is like a burnt hole in a blanket"; a literal image would be "his black eye is almost swollen shut."

The Spanish writer Juan Ramón Jiménez said, "I want my word to be the thing itself, created by my soul a second time." William Carlos Williams's "Nantucket" is a clear word picture of the "thing itself." Nothing in the room is likened to anything else.

NANTUCKET
(William Carlos Williams, 1883–1963)

Flowers through the window
lavender and yellow

changed by white curtains —
Smell of cleanliness —

Sunshine of late afternoon —
On the glass tray

a glass pitcher, the tumbler
turned down, by which

a key is lying — And the
immaculate white bed.

The room in Nantucket is easy to enter, although we are not sure if it is a hotel, a summer house, a hospital, or what. Williams presents the room: its view of flowers, its clean smell, and its feeling of austerity. Everything in the room is "just so." The poem is like the room, spare and simple. The literal imagery seems appropriate to this room one might walk in and see.

"A Description of the Morning" takes place on a Dublin street in the early eighteenth century. Like "Nantucket," it sticks to literal imagery. Note how Swift presents the commotion of the city scene.

A Description of the Morning
(Jonathan Swift, 1667–1745)

Now hardly here and there an hackney-coach
Appearing, showed the ruddy morn's approach.
Now Betty from her master's bed had flown,
And softly stole to discompose her own.
The slipshod 'prentice from his master's door,
Had pared the dirt, and sprinkled round the floor.
Now Moll had whirled her mop with dex'rous airs,
Prepared to scrub the entry and the stairs.
The youth with broomy stumps began to trace
The kennel[1] edge, where wheels had worn the place.
The small-coal man was heard with cadence deep,
'Till drowned in shriller notes of chimney sweep,
Duns[2] at his lordship's gate began to meet,
And brickdust Moll had screamed through half a street.
The turnkey[3] now his flock returning sees,
Duly let out a-nights to steal for fees.
The watchful bailiffs take their silent stands;
And schoolboys lag with satchels in their hands.

---

[1] *kennel:* gutter.
[2] *duns:* bill collectors.
[3] *turnkey:* jailkeeper.

In Your Notebook:

After reading Swift's "A Description of Morning," reread Billy Collins's "Tuesday, June 4, 1991" (page xv). Try a similar approach, using only images.

For further practice in recognizing literal images, write three specific images of each of the following: speed, orange, fear, boredom, greed, yellow. (For example: *yellow*—petals of daffodils in a glass beaker, the last tooth in an old man's mouth, the bill of a duck.) Choose original images that *show* the subject.

The active sequence of people doing what needs to be done vivifies the description. Betty musses her bed so it will appear that she slept there, the apprentice tidies his master's workshop, schoolboys dawdle on the way to class. Each line is dense with imagery—shrill voices, screaming, the whirling mop—and with active verbs: *flown, stole, pared, sprinkled, scrubbed.* A description of a street in Baltimore or Atlanta today, packed with freeways, busses, digital clocks, and fast-food breakfasts, would not be remote in effect from Swift's Dublin street waking up.

Poems

TRAVELING THROUGH THE DARK
(William Stafford, 1914–1993)

Traveling through the dark I found a deer
dead on the edge of the Wilson River road.
It is usually best to roll them into the canyon:
that road is narrow; to swerve might make more dead.

By glow of the tail-light I stumbled back of the car
and stood by the heap, a doe, a recent killing;
she had stiffened already, almost cold.
I dragged her off; she was large in the belly.

My fingers touching her side brought me the reason —
her side was warm; her fawn lay there waiting,
alive, still, never to be born.
Beside that mountain road I hesitated.

The car aimed ahead its lowered parking lights;
under the hood purred the steady engine.
I stood in the glare of the warm exhauste turning red;
around our group I could hear the wilderness listen.

I thought hard for us all — my only swerving —,
then pushed her over the edge into the river.

PRELUDES
(T. S. Eliot, 1888–1965)

1

The winter evening settles down
With smell of steaks in passageways.
Six o'clock.
The burnt-out ends of smoky days.
And now a gusty shower wraps
The grimy scraps
Of withered leaves about your feet
And newspapers from vacant lots;
The showers beat

On broken blinds and chimney-pots,
And at the corner of the street
A lonely cab-horse steams and stamps.
And then the lighting of the lamps.

2

The morning comes to consciousness
Of faint stale smells of beer
From the sawdust-trampled street
With all its muddy feet that press
To early coffee-stands.
With the other masquerades
That time resumes,
One thinks of all the hands
That are raising dingy shades
In a thousand furnished rooms.

3

You tossed a blanket from the bed,
You lay upon your back, and waited;
You dozed, and watched the night revealing
The thousand sordid images
Of which your soul was constituted;
They flickered against the ceiling.

And when all the world came back
And the light crept up between the shutters
And you heard the sparrows in the gutters,
You had such a vision of the street
As the street hardly understands,
Sitting along the bed's edge, where
You curled the papers from your hair,

Or clasped the yellow soles of feet
In the palms of both soiled hands.

4

His soul stretched tight across the skies
That fade behind a city block,
Or trampled by insistent feet
At four and five and six o'clock;
And short square fingers stuffing pipes,
And evening newspapers, and eyes
Assured of certain certainties,
The conscience of a blackened street
Impatient to assume the world.

I am moved by fancies that are curled
Around these images and cling:
The notion of some infinitely gentle
Infinitely suffering thing.

Wipe your hand across your mouth, and laugh;
The worlds revolve like ancient women
Gathering fuel in vacant lots.

STUDY OF TWO PEARS
(Wallace Stevens, 1879–1955)

I

Opusculum paedagogum.[1]
The pears are not viols,

---

[1] *opusculum paedagogum:* a little
lesson that teaches.

Nudes or bottles.
They resemble nothing else.

II

They are yellow forms
Composed of curves
Bulging toward the base.
They are touched red.

III

They are not flat surfaces
Having curved outlines.
They are round
Tapering toward the top.

IV

In the way they are modelled
There are bits of blue.
A hard dry leaf hangs
From the stem.

V

The yellow glistens.
It glistens with various yellows,
Citrons, oranges and greens
Flowering over the skin.

VI

The shadows of the pears
Are blobs on the green cloth.
The pears are not seen
As the observer wills.

EPITAPH ON A HARE
(William Cowper, 1731–1800)

Here lies, whom hound did ne'er pursue,
    Nor swifter greyhound follow,
Whose foot ne'er tainted morning dew,
    Nor ear heard huntsman's halloo;

Old Tiney, surliest of his kind,
    Who, nursed with tender care,
And to domestic bounds confined,
    Was still a wild jack hare.

Though duly from my hand he took
    His pittance every night;
He did it with a jealous look,
    And, when he could, would bite.

His diet was of wheaten bread
    And mild, and oats, and straw;
Thistles, or lettuces instead,
    With sand to scour his maw.
On twigs of hawthorn he regaled,
    On pippins' russet peel;
And, when his juicy salads failed,
    Sliced carrot pleased him well.

A Turkey carpet was his lawn,
    Whereon he loved to bound,
To skip and gambol like a fawn,
    And swing his rump around.

His frisking was at evening hours,
    For then he lost his fear;

But most before approaching showers,
    Or when a storm drew near.

Eight years and five round-rolling moons
    He thus saw steal away,
Dozing out all his idle noons,
    And every night at play.

I kept him for his humor's sake,
    For he would oft beguile
My heart of thoughts that made it ache,
    And force me to a smile.

But now beneath this walnut shade
    He finds his long last home,
And waits, in snug concealment laid,
    Till gentler Puss shall come.

He, still more aged, feels the shocks,
    From which no care can save,
And, partner once of Tiney's box,
    Must soon partake his grave.

BADGER
(John Clare, 1793–1864)

When midnight comes a host of dogs and men
Go out and track the badger to his den,
And put a sack within the hole, and lie
Till the old grunting badger passes by.
He comes and hears — they let the strongest loose.
The old fox hears the noise and drops the goose.
The poacher shoots and hurries from the cry,
And the old hare half wounded buzzes by.

They get a forked stick to bear him down
And bait him all the day with many dogs,
And laugh and shout and fright the scampering hogs.
He runs along and bites at all he meets:
They shout and hollo down the noisy streets.

He turns about to face the loud uproar
And drives the rebels to their very door.
The frequent stone is hurled where'er they go;
When badgers fight, then everyone's a foe.
The dogs are clapped and urged to join the fray;
The badger turns and drives them all away.
Though scarcely half as big, demure and small.
He fights with dogs for hours and beats them all.
The heavy mastiff, savage in the fray,
Lies down and licks his feet and turns away.
The bulldog knows his match and waxes cold,
The badger grins and never leaves his hold.
He drives the crowd and follows at their heels
And bites them through — the drunkard swears and reels.

The frighted women take the boys away,
The blackguard laughs and hurries on the fray.
He tries to reach the woods, an awkward race,
But sticks and cudgels quickly stop the chase.
He turns again and drives the noisy crowd
And beats the many dogs in noises loud.
He drives away and beats them every one,
And then they loose them all and set them on.
He falls as dead and kicked by boys and men,
Then starts and grins and drives the crowd again;
Till kicked and torn and beaten out he lies
And leaves his hold and cackles, groans, and dies.

THE RUNNER
(Walt Whitman, 1819–1892)

On a flat road runs the well-train'd runner,
He is lean and sinewy with muscular legs,
He is thinly clothed, he leans forward as he runs,
With lightly closed fists and arms partially rais'd.

Figurative Images

Our use of language is naturally figurative. We say "slick as glass," "ugly as sin," "hard as rock," "soft as silk," "mad as a wet hen," "slow as molasses," "pale as a ghost," "dog-tired," "blood red," "weak as a kitten." We take for granted expressing one thing in terms of another. Some of the expressions above have become clichés that have lost their original surprise. Good figurative images seem new to the reader, not just decorative.

Figurative imagery functions quite differently from literal imagery. A literal image *remakes* something in words in order to describe a reality as vividly as possible. A figurative image establishes connections between things we normally would *not* associate. By using a figurative image, the poet intends to do one or all of these:

- *Expand sensory perception beyond the literal meaning.* "His death came slowly like a Mexican bus," adds other qualities to the fact of the slow death by connecting it to the characteristics of the old, over-laden Mexican buses that stop at every crossroad.
- *Give pleasure or surprise to the imagination.* We have never connected a slow death and a Mexican bus before. We experience finding the connection, which gives a sense of discovery and participation. We reach imaginatively beyond our usual grasp, yet

credulity is not destroyed. Yes, his death *could* come slowly like a Mexican bus.

- *Impart vigor by the inclusion of another active sensory detail.* The sudden appearance of the Mexican bus is a vivid image. It startles our normal expectations of where "His death came slowly..." was headed.
- *Intensify the deeper intention in the poem by adding the new dimension of the figurative image.* Any of us making an image for a slow death might have chosen a number of comparisons. *Only* this poet (Ann Gleeson) chose the Mexican bus, thereby putting *her* intuitive sense of death on the line. Like word choice, the choice of figurative images contributes to the overall mood, or tone, of the poem. "His death came slowly like an island emerging from the sea" would have to belong in a different poem than the more humorous bus image. Any image works within the whole poem as well as on its own.

In reading poems, ask *why* the poet uses a figurative image. What does the image add to the whole? As you read, consider the four intentions described above.

Figurative images fall into several distinct categories:

SIMILES

A *simile* is an explicit equation: A is like B. (The word *simile* comes from the Latin *similis*, meaning "similar" or "like.") *Like, as, as if,* and sometimes *seems* or *appears* are used in making the comparison.

> ... the bulb hangs in the hot dark
> like a white blood drop.   —*Michael Dennis Browne*

> The Roman Road runs straight and bare
> As the pale parting-line in hair.   —*Thomas Hardy*

> Jane, Jane
> Tall as a Crane.   —*Edith Sitwell*

I spied a very small brown duck
Riding the swells of the sea
Like a rocking-chair.   —*Galway Kinnell*

The blood of the children ran in the street
like the blood of children.   —*Pablo Neruda*

Saying Jane is as tall as a crane adds something to Jane's height: A crane seems to have little in common with a girl, but by linking the two, Sitwell gives Jane a particular angularity and a funny posture. The lightbulb, as seen by Browne, hangs like a drop of blood. We know white blood doesn't exist, but a drop of blood, about to fall, is in the *shape* of a lightbulb. We see the bulb in a different way than we could if he had not made the comparison. The simile by Neruda affects us because of the surprise. We expect a dissimilar comparison after *like*. By employing the simile construction, the poet tells us that there *can be* no figurative image which *adds* to the impact of the first statement.

A simile is usually weak if it is abstract, vague, or stale. The reader experiences not a glimmer of interest in

lazy as a day in June

clean as soap

the sun shone like hope

the rain fell like tears

If the comparison on the other side of *like* is not different *enough*, the simile will not work for the poem. For instance, if the small brown duck rides the waves like a seagull, we have simply a comparison between like things. The reader will discover something new only if the writer finds an image with enough electricity to travel back through the word *like* and recharge the original image. Similes that don't work sometimes use vague words with inappropriate comparatives, as in "...a lilac bush bloomed, pulsating / here and there like a delicate blue vein in the violet light." "Here and there" do not help the reader see anything, and clusters of lilac blossoms look nothing like pulsating veins. I could have made an interesting simile comparing the *color* of veins to lilacs. As it is, the simile is ineffective.

An **epic simile** makes an extended comparison. In Frost's poem below, "she" is compared to a tent in a field.

THE SILKEN TENT
(Robert Frost, 1874–1963)

She is as in a field a silken tent
At midday when a sunny summer breeze
Has dried the dew and all its ropes relent,
So that in guys it gently sways at ease,
And its supporting central cedar pole,
That is its pinnacle to heavenward
And signifies the sureness of the soul,
Seems to owe naught to any single cord,
But strictly held by none, is loosely bound
By countless silken ties of love and thought
To everything on earth the compass round,
And only by one's going slightly taut
In the capriciousness of summer air
Is of the slightest bondage made aware.

The simile spins out from "She is as...," the poem's first three words. The whole poem compares a woman to an exotic tent in a field at noon. Most tents are synthetic fabrics or rough canvas. This one is silk. The choice imparts a fine, luxurious quality to the woman. Even the ropes are silk. The tent flexes easily when the wind changes. At the same time, the center pole, signifying "the sureness of the soul," stands firmly in place and points toward heaven. The poem is one long sentence that seems free to billow and shift like the tent in the wind. In truth, the poem is tightly constructed in a traditional sonnet form, which determines length, rhyme, and a regular rhythmic beat. The countless ropes suggest that the woman is tied "To everything on earth the compass round," yet her life is so in harmony that she is free. Frost, both in meaning and in the poem's form, suggests that freedom is achieved through attachment to important "ties." Whether the woman would agree we don't know.

METAPHORS

Metaphors, like similes, connect unlike things having common qualities. How metaphor differs from simile is subtle but crucial.

Simile: My joy is like a river.

Metaphor: My joy is a river.
or: My joy, a river.

Poets use metaphor when they want a close, more direct comparison between the two things. But metaphor is not simply the removal of *like, as,* or other connectives. The word *metaphor* comes from Greek roots that mean "to transfer." When Shakespeare says, "Juliet is the sun," he *transfers* the sun's qualities to Juliet. More is at stake than if he'd said, "Juliet is like the sun." Juliet's life-giving powers, brightness, and all-importance are intensified by the direct link. There is only one sun in our solar system. Perhaps other woman could be "like the sun," but only one can *be* the sun.

Look at the difference:

No man is an island.   —*John Donne*

No man is like an island.

Like dilutes the assertive power of this image. Part of the reason for this is in the eye's response. Without the comparative word, the images have closer physical proximity on the page. *Like* and *as* call attention to themselves; we realize a comparison is taking place. Without them, a "transfer" occurs easily, almost automatically. Notice what happens when the biblical quote "God is love" is changed to "God is like love."

The following poem uses metaphor to express the bodily changes a woman experiences during pregnancy. The nine-line structure, with nine syllables in each line, wittily reinforces Plath's pregnant subject.

METAPHORS
(Sylvia Plath, 1932–1963)

I'm a riddle in nine syllables,
An elephant, a ponderous house,
A melon strolling on two tendrils.
O red fruit; ivory, fine timbers!
This loaf's big with its yeasty rising.
Money's new-minted in this fat purse.
I'm a means, a stage, a cow in calf.
I've eaten a bag of green apples,
Boarded the train there's no getting off.

Suppose Plath had named the poem "Similes" and proceeded through her list using *like* or *as* or *resembles*. If you read the poem again with that in mind you'll notice how different it feels.

In his *Poetics*, Aristotle said that metaphor is the "one thing that cannot be learned from others; and it is also a sign of genius, since a good metaphor implies an intuitive perception of the similarity in dissimilars." Metaphor is not simply a device writers use to ornament poems. William Butler Yeats wrote in "A Prayer for Old Age":

God guard me from those thoughts men think
In the mind alone;
He that sings a lasting song
Thinks in a marrow bone.

Metaphoric thinking constantly links the mind to the "marrow bone." Older civilizations than ours looked for signs all around them: fortunes in the leaves of tea, weather forecasts in the thickness of the goose's breastbone. Auspicious times for events were decided from the alignment of stars, flight patterns of birds, or droppings of animals. Augurs, the diviners of events, read these signs and made decisions or predictions from them. Although the use of metaphor is not as practically oriented as Roman augury, the this-is-that of metaphor touches the same core of thinking, the root that says unlike things have mysterious, informing links that we can discover.

Though metaphor works first on an intuitive level, it also works on a logical level. We can know exactly *how* "Juliet is the sun." Figurative language jumps off into imaginative territory but usually does not cut free from connections to reality. When the poet pushes an image too far, as in this example by Robert Browning, this can happen:

> The wild tulip, at the end of its tube, blows out its great red bell
> Like a thin clear bubble of blood for the children to pick and sell.

Children selling a bubble of blood? No. We don't *believe* that. Lovely as the first glass-blowing image is, the poor logic in the second line spoils the image.

When metaphors are poorly conceived, this kind of confusion results:

THE VINE
(James Thomson, 1700–1748)

The wine of love is music,
    And the feast of love is song:
When love sits down to banquet,
    Love sits long:
Sits long and rises drunken,
    But not with the feast and the wine;
He reeleth with his own heart,
    That great rich Vine.

If we remember Shakespeare's "If music be the food of love, play on" and similar treatments of the subject of love, we're ready to read this as a poem of that type. But these doubled-up metaphors get confusing. Vine, wine, feast, music, love — just which is the metaphor for what? None of the functions for figurative imagery are fulfilled; the tangle of imagery only obscures whatever significance that capital-letter "Vine" was supposed to have.

One step beyond vague metaphors are **mixed metaphors.** In these, the writer combines incompatible metaphors. If Shakespeare had written "If music be the fruit of love, play on, give me the whole nine yards," he would have run amuck with his metaphor. Mixed metaphors really do not occur much in poetry, except for comic effect.

This is a wonderful poem to memorize:

QUESTION
(May Swenson, 1919–1989)

Body my house
my horse my hound
what will I do
when you are fallen

Where will I sleep
How will I ride
What will I hunt

Where can I go
without my mount
all eager and quick
How will I know
in thicket ahead
is danger or treasure
when Body my good
bright dog is dead

How will it be
to lie in the sky
without roof or door
and wind for an eye

With cloud for shift
how will I hide?

Three metaphors for *body* work at once in "Question." The speaker's body is her "house," "hound," and "horse." As the title indicates, she is questioning the body's fate in terms of the three metaphors: What will I do when my body fails me? What becomes of "I" when the body fails? How does the "I" then sleep, ride, hunt? Questions are raised, not answered.

What are the qualities of the body she evokes by the three metaphors? "House" connotes a sense of security, the place to be at ease; "horse" links to quick mobility and liveliness; "hound" senses what's ahead in the hunt—that is, in the process of living. These are some of the first connections the metaphors make.

Swenson's metaphors also produce some more complex effects. Psychiatrist Carl Jung interpreted dreams of houses as a projection of the sense of self. A dream of wandering in a strange house, for instance, would be a metaphor for a quest within the self. In mythology, horses often represent the spiritual nature. In Greek legend, Pegasus, the winged horse who brought Zeus his thunderbolts, is associated with poetry. Hunting has many associations with quests and an intense, unpredictable pursuit of fate. Any discussion of a hunter brings up the old question, "Who is the hunter, who the hunted?"

May Swenson *may* have had some of these ideas in mind when she wrote "Question." For the reader, the metaphors are wide open to these and other interpretations. In the last stanza, *shift* means a dress. With only a cloud for a dress, how will "I" hide? With this final question, we see that all through the poem the speaker valued the body partly because some part of her is hidden within it. Without the protection of the body (with its attributes of security, liveliness, force) she questions the fate of the spirit, which will "lie in the sky / without roof or door."

Hungarian poet Attila József developed schizophrenia and committed suicide. I'm awed by his ability to write at all, but astonished by the playfulness he managed.

A JUST MAN
(Attila József, 1905–1937)

My eyes, you girls who milk the light,
turn over your pails.
Tongue, you tall handsome whooping young man,
leave your day-labour.
Breast, escape from me to Asia,
to the roots of sweating forests.
Backbone, collapse under the Eiffel Tower.
Nose, you sailing Greenland whaler,
keep your harpoon away from smells.
Hands, make a pilgrimage to Rome.
Legs, kick each other into a ditch.
Ears, surrender
your tympani, your tympani!
Leap over to Australia, my thigh,
you rose-pink marsupial.
Belly, you light balloon, soar
to Saturn, fly away!
Then I shall step out onto my lips,
with a curving shout jump into your ears,
and stopped clocks will start again,
and villages will shine like floodlights,
and the cities will be whitewashed,
and my vertebrae can scatter
in all directions of the globe,
because I'll be standing straight
among the crooked bodies of the dead.

—Translated by John Bátki

József lists wild, impossible metaphors for parts of the body: eyes are "girls who milk the light"; thigh, a "rose-pink marsupial"; belly, a "light balloon." He instructs these parts to head for distant places: Asia, Australia, the Eiffel Tower. As soon as he can get *out* of his body (which is flying apart anyway) he'll be "standing straight" among the dead.

What do you think József means by the last nine lines? Perhaps he means that after his death we will hear his poems. When that happens, the world will seem clean and new. He'll be both everywhere on the globe *and* able to feel justified.

Both "Question" and "A Just Man" travel far into the territory of the imagination. Why? Why not choose literal descriptions of the body? Refer to the four functions of figurative images described earlier in the chapter. How do they interconnect in these poems?

OTHER TROPES

As we've seen, metaphors and similes use words not literally, but figuratively. The generic term for any figurative image is a **trope**. English has many other special function tropes including synesthesia, metonymy, synecdoche, personification, oxymoron, and conceits.

SYNESTHESIA   I especially like to find one sensory perception expressed in terms of a different sense, doubling and interweaving the physical connections.

I know the seven fragrances of the rainbow   —*May Swenson*

... green wind ...   —*Federico García Lorca*

Light, chill and yellow
Bathes the serene
Foreheads of houses   —*Philip Larkin*

A crinkled paper makes a brilliant sound.   —*Wallace Stevens*

And the sabbath rang slowly
In the pebbles of the holy streams   —*Dylan Thomas*

...blind mouths....   —*John Milton*

METONYMY   An identifying emblem is substituted for the whole name. An "old salt" for a sailor, a "brown shirt" for a fascist, "red coats" for British soldiers. An *associated* quality speaks for the whole.

The pen is mightier than the sword.   —*Edward Bulwer-Lytton*

Her voice is full of money.   —*F. Scott Fitzgerald*

... doublet and hose
ought to show itself courageous to petticoat. —*William Shakespeare*

SYNECDOCHE   A piece or part of the whole represents the whole, as in "the long arm of the law," "Elvis the pelvis," "roof over one's head," "she's a brain." An active part, isolated, represents the whole more intensely. Someone who doesn't like "that look in your eye" probably finds your whole expression and demeanor disturbing; she emphasizes her objection by isolating the eye.

Was this the face that launched a thousand ships?
                                             —*Christopher Marlowe*

Send home my long strayed eyes to me
Which O! too long have dwelt on thee.   —*John Donne*

Worcester, get thee gone for I do see
Danger and disobedience in thine eye.   —*William Shakespeare*

The difference between synecdoche and metonymy is that synecdoche keeps *to itself* (face, eyes) for its representing image, while metonymy uses an emblem that is *outside itself* but associated, as salt is associated with the sea and therefore with sailors. When you disparagingly call someone a "redneck" (part of the person), you are using synecdoche; when you say "hayseed" (associated with farming), you're using metonymy. Although these distinctions among tropes seem like fine shadings, it's a pleasure to be able to identify the precise use of language a writer has chosen. Simile, metaphor, and synesthesia each use *comparisons* in different ways; synecdoche and metonymy both use closely identified *associations*.

PERSONIFICATION   An emotion or something inhuman, such as a mountain or love or a tree, is given human qualities. Sometimes the personification is named directly, as in "Death be not proud...." Other personifications:

Some flakes have lost their way, and grope back upwards.

—*Thomas Hardy*

the speechless cities of the night   —*Randall Jarrell*

whispers of wind in the listening sky   —*Stephen Spender*

the sleeping sea   —*William Sharp*

And in the soft ear of Spring, light voices sing. —*Marcel du Bon*

the last fingers of leaf
Clutch and sink into the wet bank.   —*T. S. Eliot*

The primary purpose of personification is to make nature seem to extend the emotions of the speaker by reflecting them. Many nature personifications are clichés: weeping skies, smiling sun, dying sunset, angry seas, hopeful sunrises. When the waves are "happy" or the rain "weeps," the natural world is credited with human feelings. In old movies, the camera pans to the beautiful sunset as the lovers kiss; storms break out when danger approaches. The skies act out the emotions of the actors. This kind of nature personification is called a **pathetic fallacy.**

Personification is also used to give a quality or action or idea a "presence" by addressing it like a person: "Good morning Midnight," or "Truth settled an old score."

OXYMORON   Contrasting words are juxtaposed in order to encompass contrary impressions or ideas. (The image of contradiction is reflected in the word itself: *oxymoron* comes from two Greek roots meaning "sharp" and "stupid.")

> Mis-shapen chaos of well-seeming forms!
> Feather of lead, bright smoke, cold fire, sick health!
> —*William Shakespeare*

>   as cold
> And passionate as the dawn.   —*William Butler Yeats*

CONCEIT   Conceit is a bold and/or extended simile or metaphor, such as

> Let us go then you and I
> When the evening is spread out against the sky
> Like a patient etherized upon a table   —*T. S. Eliot*

The two images compared amuse, surprise, or disturb you by their extreme contrast. "The Song of Solomon" in the Bible compares a woman's lips to scarlet thread, her cheeks to the halves of a pomegranate, then daringly compares her neck to the tower of David and her nose to the Tower of Lebanon, overlooking Damascus. Conceits involve risk: either captivating or repelling the reader. The conceit

In Your Notebook:

For practice in recognizing effective similes, complete each phrase with a concrete image of your own. Try to think of a connection that performs one of the four functions listed on pages 85–86. Look for a fresh image you've never seen in print before.

- The moon, broken off like . . .
- A red flower, brilliant as . . .
- Her fingers, delicate as . . .
- The island stretches out from the coast like . . .
- Your backbone ridged like . . .
- Soft as . . .
- That bicyclist, careening downhill like . . .
- Crazy bird! Its song like . . .
- His monotonous voice like . . .
- She spun off like . . .
- Days pass like . . .

Identify the following tropes by type:

honey-voiced
the dark blue notes of the cello
The flowers of the town are rotting away.   *—C. Day Lewis*

Death, O Death! Can't you spare me over
    for another year?   *—Kentucky Song*

When Poverty comes in the door,
Love goes out the window.   *—Georgia saying*

And winds went begging at each door.   *—Geoffrey Hill*

The sun, a demon's eye.   *—Edith Sitwell*

I ran my heedless ways,
My wishes raced through the house high hay.   *—Dylan Thomas*

In his devouring mind's eye. . . .   *—Washington Irving*

> Her jet appeared from nowhere,
> A needle punched through blue linen.   —*Neal Bowers*

Next, select a painting or a photograph and describe it so that you *show* the images. Use smell, touch, sound, taste, and motion as well as visual images.

Many metaphors are hidden in everyday speech. Once upon a time someone made the connection between the clock and the human face, between supports for the table and legs. These have long since become the face of the clock, the leg of the table. In the same way, it is natural to say the heart of the matter, the heel of Italy, the lip of the pitcher. Make a list of other metaphors embedded in everyday speech.

---

usually develops, making further connections between the two disparate images. John Donne's likening of two lovers' souls to drawing compasses is a famous conceit:

> If they be two, they are two so
>   As stiffe twin compasses are two,
> Thy soule the fixt foot, makes no show
>   To move, but doth, if the 'other doe.
>
> And though it in the center sit,
>   Yet when the other far doth rome,
> It leanes, and hearkens after it,
>   and growes erect, as that comes home.
>
> Such wilt thou be to mee, who must
>   Like th'other foot, obliquely runne;

Thy firmnes drawes my circle just,
And makes me end, where I begunne.

— from "A *Valediction: Forbidding Mourning*"

Symbols

A **symbol** is an image or action that stands for more than itself. A black and white mottled notebook reminds me of first grade, the teacher named Miss Gray, the reading circle, my polished shoes, and the line of alphabet letters around the blackboard. The black and white notebook is actually only itself, but to me it is symbolic. The image brings forth memories and ideas. Symbol comes from a Greek word meaning "to put together." Whereas metaphor and simile *name* connections between seemingly dissimilar images, a symbol *suggests* a range of connections.

A bare oak silhouetted against dark hills looks ominous, reminding you of lonely nights, loss, winter. A photograph of a highway leading away over rolling hills invites your imagination to go. The open road symbolizes escape, adventure, perhaps reminding you of the time you drove west alone. The notebook is a private symbol; the winter tree and open road images are common to many, though nuances may be particular to your experience. Some symbolic images cross cultures and time; harvest, sunrise, the full moon, and many more symbols are **archetypes,** images that have universal meaning. The connection between spring and rebirth belongs to everyone.

Poetry involves both kinds of symbolism, personal and universal. A nightingale may mean nothing to you, but after you read "Ode To a Nightingale" (page 378), Keats's own symbolic associations with the "immortal" bird's song may become alive and full of meaning. The meanings of a symbol gather as the poem develops. To awaken memories and associations, a symbol must join other qualities and perceptions. If I write about the notebook, no one will respond unless I cause the reader to experience some of the reasons this object has significance.

A knot in a piece of wood is the symbol working here:

THE KNOT
(Stanley Kunitz, 1905–)

I've tried to seal it in,
that cross-grained knot
on the opposite wall,
scored in the lintel of my door,
but it keeps bleeding through
into the world we share.
Mornings when I wake,
curled in my web,
I hear it come
with a rush of resin
out of the trauma
of its lopping-off.
Obstinate bud,
sticky with life,
mad for the rain again,
it racks itself with shoots
that crackle overhead,
dividing as they grow.
Let be! Let be!
I shake my wings
and fly into its boughs.

Kunitz's knot is a **private symbol;** readers do not come to it with symbolic associations of their own, as they would if the subject were, say, a wedding ring or the evening star. He develops this context: He has painted over the knot trying to seal it in, but it persistently pushes its own life through these cover-ups. Kunitz never says so, but we begin to see that this knot is like something in the speaker's life, which he has tried to obliterate but can't. A knot in wood results from the loss of a branch. We don't know the *exact* nature of the speaker's loss — which leaves the symbol open to our own associations — but we do know that something was lopped off. The symbol, in other words, isn't pinned down to *a* meaning, but the context establishes clear directions for meaning. Isn't there something you also try to push away that will not go away?

"The Knot" is straightforward. At times, symbolism gets extremely complex. Some poets have entire systems, secret cosmologies of symbols, which require extensive study. William Blake is one of these poets. The more familiar you are with his work, the richer Blake's symbols are, because the symbols interact among the poems. Two of his best-known lyrics show how each one amplifies the other.

THE LAMB
(William Blake, 1757–1827)

Little Lamb, who made thee?
　Dost thou know who made thee?
Gave thee life, and bid thee feed,
By the stream and o'er the mead;
Gave thee clothing of delight,
Softest clothing, woolly, bright;
Gave thee such a tender voice,
Making all the vales rejoice?
　Little Lamb, who made thee?
　Dost thou know who made thee?

Little Lamb, I'll tell thee,
Little Lamb, I'll tell thee:
He is callèd by thy name,

For he calls himself a Lamb.
He is meek, and he is mild;
He became a little child.
I a child, and thou a lamb,
We are callèd by his name.
　　Little Lamb, God bless thee!
　　Little Lamb, God bless thee!

THE TYGER
(William Blake, 1757–1827)

Tyger! Tyger! burning bright
In the forests of the night,
What immortal hand or eye
Could frame thy fearful symmetry?

In what distant deeps or skies
Burnt the fire of thine eyes?
On what wings dare he aspire?
What the hand dare seize the fire?

And what shoulder, and what art,
Could twist the sinews of thy heart?
And when thy heart began to beat,
What dread hand? and what dread feet?

What the hammer? what the chain?
In what furnace was thy brain?
What the anvil? what dread grasp
Dare its deadly terrors clasp?

When the stars threw down their spears,
And watered heaven with their tears,

Did he smile his work to see?
Did he who made the Lamb make thee?

Tyger! Tyger! burning bright
In the forests of the night,
What immortal hand or eye,
Dare frame thy fearful symmetry?

The lamb and the tiger symbolize opposites: innocence/experience, delight/terror, mildness/ferociousness. The lamb symbolizes *all* that is good, simple, gentle; the tiger, *all* that is predatory, mysterious, fearful. The first stanzas of both poems frame the question: Who is responsible for making you? Right away, we're shown that a large question is at stake; the poems are not just descriptions of animals. The speaker in "The Lamb" is childlike. The speaker in "The Tyger" is much more complex; the more sophisticated level of language reflects this difference. Considered alone, each poem loses some power because the poet is working with the idea that the creator who made the innocent lamb might have smiled also at his creation of the tiger. The pair of poems acknowledges the dual nature of creation and therefore of experience.

The following poem begins with a metaphor: "My Life had stood—a Loaded Gun." The third line introduces the "Owner" of the

---

 In Your Notebook:

Select an image from memory that is symbolic to you and write down all the images and ideas it brings to mind. It may be a red bike, a pencil box stenciled with your name, a sapphire pin your aunt wore at her throat, a pistol in a bedside drawer, the shape of a hill you could see from your window, a brown coat your mother wore to work every day.

---

gun. Both the gun and the owner, we quickly realize, are symbolic. (When a metaphor is extended, as it is in this poem, the distinction between metaphor and symbol blurs. The extended metaphor also becomes a symbol.) What does the "Owner" symbolize? Is he God? Could he be one part of the same person—body or soul? What other possibilities: Death? Sexuality? An internal conflict? This is a tough poem. The speaker seems perfectly secure in her logic, but no one can totally "explain" it. What are your ideas about the relationship of the gun and owner? About the last two lines?

754
(Emily Dickinson, 1830–1886)

My Life had stood—a Loaded Gun—
In Corners—till a Day
The Owner passed—identified—
And carried Me away—

And now We roam in Sovreign Woods—
And now We hunt the Doe—
And every time I speak for Him—
The Mountains straight reply—

And do I smile, such cordial light
Upon the Valley glow—
It is as a Vesuvian face
Had let its pleasure through—

And when at Night—Our good Day done—
I guard My Master's Head—
'Tis better than the Eider-Duck's
Deep Pillow—to have shared—

To foe of His—I'm deadly foe—
None stir the second time—

On whom I lay a Yellow Eye —
Or an emphatic Thumb —

Though I than He — may longer live
He longer must — than I —
For I have but the power to kill.
Without — the power to die —

A memorial is overtly symbolic. In "Facing It," the poet makes rich use of the reader's awareness of the Vietnam Veterans Memorial in Washington, D.C. He assumes our common associations to a war memorial but uses in the poem only a personal experience of the memorial itself. The black marble surface both reflects and absorbs. It becomes powerfully symbolic of his consciousness and conveys to the reader a nonverbal, intense reaction to the memorial. The author is black, and the first two lines immediately call up both the statistics of black dead in the Vietnam War and the power of the memorial itself to pull this viewer inside. Where does he establish the first link between himself and the memorial? Notice the images of light and black and white. What is the connection between "I'm stone" in the beginning and "I'm a window" near the end? Think about the contrasts in the poem, such as the carved names of the dead, and the liveliness of the reflections in the stone. What is the effect of the flashing brush strokes, the birds, the woman brushing the boy's hair?

FACING IT
(Yusef Komunyakaa, 1947–)

My black face fades,
hiding inside the black granite.
I said I wouldn't,
dammit: No tears.
I'm stone, I'm flesh.
My clouded reflection eyes me
like a bird of prey, the profile of night

slanted against morning. I turn
this way — the stone lets me go.
I turn that way — I'm inside
the Vietnam Veterans Memorial
again, depending on the light
to make a difference.
I go down the 58,022 names,
half-expecting to find
my own in letters like smoke.
I touch the name Andrew Johnson;
I see the booby trap's white flash.
Names shimmer on a woman's blouse
but when she walks away
the names stay on the wall.
Brushstrokes flash, a red bird's wings
cutting across my stare.
The sky. A plane in the sky.
A white vet's image floats
closer to me, then his pale eyes
look through mine. I'm a window.
He's lost his right arm
inside the stone. In the black mirror
a woman's trying to erase names:
No, she's brushing a boy's hair.

Poems

ALLEGRO
(Tomas Tranströmer, 1931–)

After a black day, I play Haydn,
and feel a little warmth in my hands.

The keys are ready. Kind hammers fall.
The sound is spirited, green, and full of silence.

The sound says that freedom exists
and someone pays no tax to Caesar.

I shove my hands in my haydnpockets
and act like a man who is calm about it all.

I raise my haydnflag. The signal is:
"We do not surrender. But want peace."

The music is a house of glass standing on a slope;
rocks are flying, rocks are rolling.

The rocks roll straight through the house
but every pane of glass is still whole.
                                        —Translated by Robert Bly

THE FORCE THAT THROUGH THE
GREEN FUSE DRIVES THE FLOWER
(Dylan Thomas, 1914–1953)

The force that through the green fuse drives the flower
Drives my green age; that blasts the roots of trees
Is my destroyer.
And I am dumb to tell the crooked rose
My youth is bent by the same wintry fever.

The force that drives the water through the rocks
Drives my red blood; that dries the mouthing streams
Turns mine to wax.

And I am dumb to mouth unto my veins
How at the mountain spring the same mouth sucks.

The hand that whirls the water in the pool
Stirs the quicksand; that ropes the blowing wind
Hauls my shroud sail.
And I am dumb to tell the hanging man
How of my clay is made the hangman's lime.

The lips of time leech to the fountain head;
Love drips and gathers, but the fallen blood
Shall calm her sores.
And I am dumb to tell a weather's wind
How time has ticked a heaven round the stars.

And I am dumb to tell the lover's tomb
How at my sheet goes the same crooked worm.

from BODY POEMS
(Coleman Barks, 1937–)

Big Toe

running running
running but clean
as a referee's whistle

& absolutely still
within my shoe
inside my sock:

he listens for mud.

Stomach

lunch paper sinking
into

the lake surface
the lake bottom

sleeping frogs
snapping turtles

Brain

a flashlight
looking through the empty
limbs

Appendix

one boxing glove
laced up
and ready

Bags Under the Eyes

the turnaround place
at the end of a lover's lane

why is that car coming back

Skeleton

on this jungle gym

Bruises

paint samples

Liver

a dripping locker room
full of older men

Yawn

(   )

Blood

the winery is on fire:

listen to the music

MY MOTHER WOULD BE A FALCONRESS
(Robert Duncan, 1919–1988)

My mother would be a falconress,
And I, her gay falcon treading her wrist,
would fly to bring back
from the blue of the sky to her, bleeding, a prize,
where I dream in my little hood with many bells
jangling when I'd turn my head.

My mother would be a falconress,
and she sends me as far as her will goes.
She lets me ride to the end of her curb
where I fall back in anguish.
I dread that she will cast me away,
for I fall, I mis-take, I fail in her mission.

She would bring down the little birds.
And I would bring down the little birds.

When will she let me bring down the little birds,
pierced from their flight with their necks broken,
their heads like flowers limp from the stem?

I tread my mother's wrist and would draw blood.
Behind the little hood my eyes are hooded.
I have gone back into my hooded silence,
talking to myself and dropping off to sleep.

For she has muffled my dreams in the hood she has made me,
sewn round with bells, jangling when I move.
She rides with her little falcon upon her wrist.
She uses a barb that brings me to cower.

She sends me abroad to try my wings
and I come back to her. I would bring down
the little birds to her
I may not tear into, I must bring back perfectly.

I tear at her wrist with my beak to draw blood,
and her eye holds me, anguisht, terrifying.
She draws a limit to my flight.
Never beyond my sight, she says.

She trains me to fetch and to limit myself in fetching.
She rewards me with meat for my dinner.
But I must never eat what she sends me to bring her.

Yet it would have been beautiful, if she would have carried me,
always, in a little hood with the bells ringing,
at her wrist, and her riding
to the great falcon hunt, and me
flying up to the curb of my heart from her heart
to bring down the skylark from the blue to her feet,
straining, and then released for the flight.

My mother would be a falconress,
and I her gerfalcon,[1] raised at her will,
from her wrist sent flying, as if I were her own
pride, as if her pride
knew no limits, as if her mind
sought in me flight beyond the horizon.

Ah, but high, high in the air I flew.
And far, far beyond the curb of her will,
were the blue hills where the falcons nest.
And then I saw west to the dying sun —
it seemd my human soul went down in flames.

I tore at her wrist, at the hold she had for me,
until the blood ran hot and I heard her cry out,
far, far beyond the curb of her will

to horizons of stars beyond the ringing hills of the world where
    the falcons nest
I saw, and I tore at her wrist with my savage beak.
I flew, as if sight flew from the anguish in her eye beyond her
    sight,

sent from my striking loose, from the cruel strike at her wrist,
striking out from the blood to be free of her.
My mother would be a falconress,
and even now, years after this,
when the wounds I left her had surely heald,
and the woman is dead,
her fierce eyes closed, and if her heart
were broken, it is stilld

---

[1] *gerfalcon*: large falcon.

I would be a falcon and go free.
I tread her wrist and wear the hood,
talking to myself, and would draw blood.

THE EVE OF ST. AGNES [1]
(John Keats, 1795–1821)

I

St. Agnes' Eve—Ah, bitter chill it was!
The owl, for all his feathers, was a-cold;
The hare limp'd trembling through the frozen grass,
And silent was the flock in woolly fold:
Numb were the Beadsman's fingers, while he told
His rosary, and while his frosted breath,
Like pious incense from a censer old,
Seem'd taking flight for heaven, without a death,
Past the sweet Virgin's picture, while his prayer he saith.

II

His prayer he saith, this patient, holy man;
Then takes his lamp, and riseth from his knees,
And back returneth, meagre, barefoot, wan,
Along the chapel aisle by slow degrees:
The sculptur'd dead, on each side, seem to freeze,
Emprison'd in black, purgatorial rails:
Knights, ladies, praying in dumb orat'ries,
He passeth by; and his weak spirit fails
To think how they may ache in icy hoods and mails.

---

[1] *Eve of St. Agnes:* January 20, when a maiden who performed certain
rituals (see stanza vi) would have a vision of her future lover or husband.

III

Northward he turneth through a little door,
And scarce three steps, ere Music's golden tongue
Flatter'd to tears this aged man and poor;
But no — already had his deathbell rung:
The joys of all his life were said and sung:
His was harsh penance on St. Agnes' Eve:
Another way he went, and soon among
Rough ashes sat he for his soul's reprieve,
And all night kept awake, for sinners' sake to grieve.

IV

That ancient Beadsman heard the prelude soft;
And so it chanc'd, for many a door was wide,
From hurry to and fro. Soon, up aloft,
The silver, snarling trumpets 'gan to chide:
The level chambers, ready with their pride,
Were glowing to receive a thousand guests:
The carved angels, ever eager-eyed,
Star'd, where upon their heads the cornice rests,
With hair blown back, and wings put cross-wise on their breasts.

V

At length burst in the argent revelry,
With plume, tiara, and all rich array,
Numerous as shadows haunting faerily
The brain, new stuff'd, in youth, with triumphs gay
Of old romance. These let us wish away,
And turn, sole-thoughted, to one Lady there,
Whose heart had brooded, all that wintry day,
On love, and wing'd St. Agnes' saintly care,
As she had heard old dames full many times declare.

VI

They told her how, upon St. Agnes' Eve,
Young virgins might have visions of delight,
And soft adorings from their loves receive
Upon the honey'd middle of the night,
If ceremonies due they did aright;
  As, supperless to bed they must retire,
  And couch supine their beauties, lilly white:
  Nor look behind, nor sideways, but require
Of Heaven with upward eyes for all that they desire.

VII

Full of this whim was thoughtful Madeline:
The music, yearning like a God in pain,
She scarcely heard: her maiden eyes divine,
Fix'd on the floor, saw many a sweeping train
Pass by — she heeded not at all: in vain
  Came many a tiptoe, amorous cavalier,
  And back retir'd: not cool'd by high disdain,
  But she saw not: her heart was otherwhere:
She sigh'd for Agnes' dreams, the sweetest of the year.

VIII

She danc'd along with vague, regardless eyes,
Anxious her lips, her breathing quick and short:
The hallow'd hour was near at hand: she sighs
Amid the timbrels,[2] and the throng'd resort
Of whisperers in anger, or in sport;
  'Mid looks of love, defiance, hate, and scorn,
  Hoodwink'd with faery fancy; all amort,

---

[2] *timbrels:* small drums.

Save to St. Agnes and her lambs unshorn,[3]
And all the bliss to be before to-morrow morn.

IX

So, purposing each moment to retire,
She linger'd still. Meantime, across the moors,
Had come young Porphyro, with heart on fire
For Madeline. Beside the portal doors,
Buttress'd from moonlight, stands he, and implores
All saints to give him sight of Madeline,
But for one moment in the tedious hours,
That he might gaze and worship all unseen;
Perchance speak, kneel, touch, kiss — in sooth such things have
been.

X

He ventures in: let no buzz'd whisper tell:
All eyes be muffled, or a hundred swords
Will storm his heart, Love's fev'rous citadel:
For him, those chambers held barbarian hordes,
Hyena foemen, and hot-blooded lords,
Whose very dogs would execrations howl
Against his lineage: not one breast affords
Him any mercy, in that mansion foul,
Save one old beldame, weak in body and in soul.

XI

Ah, happy chance! the aged creature came,
Shuffling along with ivory-headed wand,

---

[3] *lambs:* On St. Agnes's day two lambs were sacrificed and their wool was spun and
woven into cloth by the nuns.

To where he stood, hid from the torch's flame,
Behind a broad hall-pillar, far beyond
The sound of merriment and chorus bland:
He startled her; but soon she knew his face,
And grasp'd his fingers in her palsied hand,
Saying, "Mercy, Porphyro! hie thee from this place:
They are all here to-night, the whole blood-thirsty race!

XII

"Get hence! get hence! there's dwarfish Hildebrand;
He had a fever late, and in the fit
He cursed thee and thine, both house and land:
Then there's that old Lord Maurice, not a whit
More tame for his gray hairs—Alas me! flit!
Flit like a ghost away."—"Ah, Gossip dear,
We're safe enough; here in this arm-chair sit,
And tell me how"—"Good Saints! not here, not here;
Follow me, child, or else these stones will be thy bier."

XIII

He follow'd through a lowly arched way,
Brushing the cobwebs with his lofty plume,
And as she mutter'd "Well-a—well-a-day!"
He found him in a little moonlight room,
Pale, lattic'd, chill, and silent as a tomb.
"Now tell me where is Madeline," said he,
"O tell me, Angela, by the holy loom
Which none but secret sisterhood may see,
When they St. Agnes' wool are weaving piously."

XIV

"St. Agnes! Ah! it is St. Agnes' Eve—
Yet men will murder upon holy days:

Thou must hold water in a witch's sieve,[4]
And be liege-lord of all the Elves and Fays,
To venture so: it fills me with amaze
To see thee, Porphyro!—St. Agnes' Eve!
God's help! my lady fair the conjuror plays
This very night: good angels her deceive!
But let me laugh awhile, I've mickle[5] time to grieve."

XV

Feebly she laugheth in the languid moon,
While Porphyro upon her face doth look,
Like puzzled urchin on an aged crone
Who keepeth clos'd a wond'rous riddle-book,
As spectacled she sits in chimney nook.
But soon his eyes grew brilliant, when she told
His lady's purpose; and he scarce could brook
Tears, at the thought of those enchantments cold,
And Madeline asleep in lap of legends old.

XVI

Sudden a thought came like a full-blown rose,
Flushing his brow, and in his pained heart
Made purple riot: then doth he propose
A stratagem, that makes the beldame start:
"A cruel man and impious thou art:
Sweet lady, let her pray, and sleep, and dream
Alone with her good angels, far apart
From wicked men like thee. Go, go!—I deem
Thou canst not surely be the same thou didst seem."

---

[4] *witch's sieve:* a sieve bewitched so that no water can run through it.
[5] *mickle:* much.

XVII

"I will not harm her, by all saints I swear,"
Quoth Porphyro: "O may I ne'er find grace
When my weak voice shall whisper its last prayer,
If one of her soft ringlets I displace,
Or look with ruffian passion in her face:
Good Angela, believe me by these tears;
Or I will, even in a moment's space,
Awake, with horrid shout, my foemen's ears,
And beard them, though they be more fang'd than wolves and
  bears."

XVIII

"Ah! why wilt thou affright a feeble soul?
A poor, weak, palsy-stricken, churchyard thing,
Whose passing-bell may ere the midnight toll;
Whose prayers for thee, each morn and evening,
Were never miss'd" — Thus plaining, doth she bring
A gentler speech from burning Porphyro;
So woful, and of such deep sorrowing,
That Angela gives promise she will do
Whatever he shall wish, betide her weal or woe.

XIX

Which was, to lead him, in close secrecy,
Even to Madeline's chamber, and there hide
Him in a closet, of such privacy
That he might see her beauty unespied,
And win perhaps that night a peerless bride,
While legion'd faeries pac'd the coverlet,
And pale enchantment held her sleepy-eyed.

Never on such a night have lovers met,
Since Merlin paid his Demon all the monstrous debt.[6]

XX

"It shall be as thou wishest," said the Dame:
"All cates and dainties shall be stored there
Quickly on this feast-night: by the tambour frame[7]
Her own lute thou wilt see: no time to spare,
For I am slow and feeble, and scarce dare
On such a catering trust my dizzy head.
Wait here, my child, with patience; kneel in prayer
The while: Ah! thou must needs the lady wed,
Or may I never leave my grave among the dead."

XXI

So saying, she hobbled off with busy fear.
The lover's endless minutes slowly pass'd;
The dame return'd, and whisper'd in his ear
To follow her; with aged eyes aghast
From fright of dim espial. Safe at last,
Through many a dusky gallery, they gain
The maiden's chamber, silken, hush'd, and chaste;
Where Porphyro took covert, pleas'd amain.
His poor guide hurries back with agues in her brain.

XXII

Her falt'ring hand upon the balustrade,
Old Angela was feeling for the stair,

---

[6] *monstrous debt*: Merlin, son of a demon, paid the debt for his life by
performing evil deeds.
[7] *tambour frame*: embroidery frame.

When Madeline, St. Agnes' charmed maid,
Rose, like a mission'd spirit, unaware:
With silver taper's light, and pious care,
She turn'd, and down the aged gossip led
To a safe level matting. Now prepare,
Young Porphyro, for gazing on that bed;
She comes, she comes again, like ring-dove fray'd[8] and fled.

XXIII

Out went the taper as she hurried in;
Its little smoke, in pallid moonshine, died:
She clos'd the door, she panted, all akin
To spirits of the air, and visions wide:
No uttered syllable, or, woe betide!
But to her heart, her heart was voluble,
Paining with eloquence her balmy side;
As though a tongueless nightingale should swell
Her throat in vain, and die, heart-stifled, in her dell.

XXIV

A casement high and triple-arch'd there was,
All garlanded with carven imag'ries
Of fruits, and flowers, and bunches of knot-grass,
And diamonded with panes of quaint device,
Innumerable of stains and splendid dyes,
As are the tiger-moth's deep-damask'd wings;
And in the midst, 'mong thousand heraldries,
And twilight saints, and dim emblazonings,
A shielded scutcheon blush'd with blood of queens and kings.

---

[8] *fray'd*: alarmed

XXV

Full on this casement shone the wintry moon,
And threw warm gules[9] on Madeline's fair breast,
As down she knelt for heaven's grace and boon;
Rose-bloom fell on her hands, together prest,
And on her silver cross soft amethyst,
And on her hair a glory, like a saint:
She seem'd a splendid angel, newly drest
Save wings, for heaven: — Porphyro grew faint:
She knelt, so pure a thing, so free from mortal taint.

XXVI

Anon his heart revives: her vespers done,
Of all its wreathed pearls her hair she frees;
Unclasps her warmed jewels one by one;
Loosens her fragrant boddice; by degrees
Her rich attire creeps rustling to her knees:
Half-hidden, like a mermaid in sea-weed,
Pensive awhile she dreams awake, and sees,
In fancy, fair St. Agnes in her bed,
But dares not look behind, or all the charm is fled.

XXVII

Soon, trembling in her soft and chilly nest,
In sort of wakeful swoon, perplex'd she lay,
Until the poppied warmth of sleep oppress'd
Her soothed limbs, and soul fatigued away;
Flown, like a thought, until the morrow-day;
Blissfully haven'd both from joy and pain;

---

[9] *gules*: red.

Clasp'd like a missal where swart Paynims[10] pray;
Blinded alike from sunshine and from rain,
As though a rose should shut, and be a bud again.

XXVIII

Stol'n to this paradise, and so entranced,
Porphyro gazed upon her empty dress,
And listen'd to her breathing, if it chanced
To wake into a slumberous tenderness;
Which when he heard, that minute did he bless,
And breath'd himself: then from the closet crept,
Noiseless as fear in a wide wilderness,
And over the hush'd carpet, silent, stept,
And 'tween the curtains peep'd, where, lo!—how fast she slept.

XXIX

Then by the bed-side, where the faded moon
Made a dim, silver twilight, soft he set
A table, and, half anguish'd, threw thereon
A cloth of woven crimson, gold, and jet:—
O for some drowsy Morphean[11] amulet!
The boisterous, midnight, festive clarion,
The kettle-drum, and far-heard clarinet,
Affray his ears, though but in dying tone:—
The hall door shuts again, and all the noise is gone.

XXX

And still she slept an azure-lidded sleep,
In blanced linen, smooth, and lavender'd,

---

[10] *Paynims:* pagans.
[11] *Morphean:* refers to Morpheus, Greek god of sleep and dreams

While he from forth the closet brought a heap
Of candied apple, quince, and plum, and gourd;
With jellies soother than the creamy curd,
And lucent syrops, tinct with cinnamon;
Manna and dates, in argosy transferr'd
From Fez; and spiced dainties, every one,
From silken Samarcand to cedar'd Lebanon.

XXXI

These delicates he heap'd with glowing hand
On golden dishes and in baskets bright
Of wreathed silver: sumptuous they stand
In the retired quiet of the night,
Filling the chilly room with perfume light.—
"And now, my love, my seraph fair, awake!
Thou art my heaven, and I thine eremite:[12]
Open thine eyes, for meek St. Agnes' sake,
Or I shall drowse beside thee, so my soul doth ache."

XXXII

Thus whispering, his warm, unnerved arm
Sank in her pillow. Shaded was her dream
By the dusk curtains:—'twas a midnight charm
Impossible to melt as iced stream:
The lustrous salvers in the moonlight gleam;
Broad golden fringe upon the carpet lies:
It seem'd he never, never could redeem
From such a stedfast spell his lady's eyes;
So mus'd awhile, entoil'd in woofed phantasies.

---

[12] *eremite:* hermit.

XXXIII

Awakening up, he took her hollow lute,—
Tumultuous,—and, in chords that tenderest be,
He play'd an ancient ditty, long since mute,
In Provence call'd, "La belle dame sans mercy:"
Close to her ear touching the melody;—
Wherewith disturb'd, she utter'd a soft moan:
He ceased—she panted quick—and suddenly
Her blue affrayed eyes wide open shone:
Upon his knees he sank, pale as smooth-sculptured stone.

XXXIV

Her eyes were open, but she still beheld,
Now wide awake; the vision of her sleep:
There was a painful change, that nigh expell'd
The blisses of her dreams so pure and deep
At which fair Madeline began to weep;
And moan forth witless words with many a sigh;
While still her gaze on Porphyro would keep;
Who knelt, with joined hands and piteous eye,
Fearing to move or speak, she look'd so dreamingly.

XXXV

"Ah, Porphyro!" said she, "but even now
Thy voice was at sweet tremble in mine ear,
Made tuneable with every sweetest vow;
And those sad eyes were spiritual and clear:
How chang'd thou art! how pallid, chill, and drear!
Give me that voice again, my Porphyro,
Those looks immortal, those complainings dear!
Oh leave me not in this eternal woe,
For if thou diest, my Love, I know not where to go."

XXXVI

Beyond a mortal man impassion'd far
At these voluptuous accents, he arose,
Ethereal, flush'd, and like a throbbing star
Seen mid the sapphire heaven's deep repose;
Into her dream he melted, as the rose
Blendeth its odour with the violet, —
Solution sweet: meantime the frost-wind blows
Like Love's alarum pattering the sharp sleet
Against the window-panes; St. Agnes' moon hath set.

XXXVII

'Tis dark: quick pattereth the flaw-blown sleet:[13]
"This is no dream, my bride, my Madeline!"
'Tis dark: the iced gusts still rave and beat:
"No dream, alas! alas! and woe is mine!
Porphyro will leave me here to fade and pine. —
Cruel! what traitor could thee hither bring?
I curse not, for my heart is lost in thine,
Though thou forsakest a deceived thing; —
A dove forlorn and lost with sick unpruned wing."

XXXVIII

"My Madeline! sweet dreamer! lovely bride!
Say, may I be for aye thy vassal blest?
Thy beauty's shield, heart-shap'd and vermeil[14] dyed?
Ah, silver shrine, here will I take my rest
After so many hours of toil and quest,
A famish'd pilgrim, — sav'd by miracle.

---

[13] *flaw-blown sleet:* gust-blown sleet.
[14] *vermeil:* vermillion.

Thou I have found, I will not rob thy nest
    Saving of thy sweet self; if thou think'st well
To trust, fair Madeline, to no rude infidel.

XXXIX

"Hark! 'tis an elfin-storm from faery land,
    Of haggard seeming, but a boon indeed:
Arise—arise! the morning is at hand;—
    The bloated wassaillers will never heed:—
Let us away, my love, with happy speed;
    There are no ears to hear, or eyes to see,—
Drown'd all in Rhenish[15] and the sleepy mead:
    Awake! arise! my love, and fearless be,
For o'er the southern moors I have a home for thee."

XL

She hurried at his words, beset with fears,
    For there were sleeping dragons all around,
At glaring watch, perhaps, with ready spears—
    Down the wide stairs a darkling way they found.—
In all the house was heard no human sound.
    A chain-dropp'd lamp was flickering by each door;
The arras,[16] rich with horseman, hawk, and hound,
    Flutter'd in the besieging wind's uproar;
And the long carpets rose along the gusty floor.

XLI

They glide, like phantoms, into the wide hall;
    Like phantoms, to the iron porch, they glide;

---

[15] *Rhenish:* Rhine wine.
[16] *arras:* tapestry.

Where lay the Porter, in uneasy sprawl,
With a huge empty flaggon by his side:
The wakeful bloodhound rose, and shook his hide,
But his sagacious eye an inmate owns:
By one, and one, the bolts full easy slide: —
The chains lie silent on the footworn stones; —
The key turns, and the door upon its hinges groans.

XLII

And they are gone: aye, ages long ago
   These lovers fled away into the storm.
   That night the Baron dreamt of many a woe,
   And all his warrior-guests, with shade and form
   Of witch, and demon, and large coffin-worm,
   Were long be-nightmar'd. Angela the old
   Died palsy-twitch'd, with meagre face deform;
   The Beadsman, after thousand aves told,
For aye unsought for slept among his ashes cold.

FOG-HORN
(W. S. Merwin, 1927–)

Surely that moan is not the thing
That men thought they were making, when they
Put it there, for their own necessities.
That throat does not call to anything human
But to something men had forgotten,
That stirs under fog. Who wounded that beast
Incurably, or from whose pasture
Was it lost, full grown, and time closed round it
With no way back? Who tethered its tongue

So that its voice could never come
To speak out in the light of clear day,
But only when the shifting blindness
Descends and is acknowledged among us,
As though from under a floor it is heard,
Or as though from behind a wall, always
Nearer than we had remembered? If it
Was we that gave tongue to this cry
What does it bespeak in us, repeating
And repeating, insisting on something
That we never meant? We only put it there
To give warning of something we dare not
Ignore, lest we should come upon it
Too suddenly, recognize it too late,
As our cries were swallowed up and all hands lost.

UNIVERSITY OF IOWA HOSPITAL, 1976
(Edward Mayes, 1951–)

The last time I walked into
Ward C-22 I was stoned,
it was evening, I was picking
up my final paycheck—

where to begin in this never
ending blasted field of corpses.
Men looking like they had been
attacked repeatedly by a succession

of wild animals, throats half gone,
eyes bleeding, raw meat heaped
in piles. One walks around
sniffing through his long tubes.

A woman in a private room lies
curled like a Cro-Magnon mummy
in the museum. Where are
doctors of love, love apples,

the supervisors of love, love
administrators? Pain is a steady
fall from a high place, one with
no view, no vision outside

itself. Pain is a weed more
beautiful to look at than
rooms of flowers next to it.
It lasts through no rain.

resists scissors, takes over.
Last Christmas in the back room
an intern sat putting a black
jigsaw puzzle together, one thousand

pieces, one very long night. I
took a boy who had shot his face
off six months earlier on a walk
around the hospital grounds. He

was still uninterested after all
that damage. Another showed me 200
miles of scars, sixty years of making
that road. I know fifty people who are

now dead. One I watched die, his blood
pressure dove to nothing, and I had
to stuff him with cotton, tie
string around his penis, glue a label

on his forehead. I became extremely
careful driving home each day, I ate
good foods, slept the right amount,
lived the short life of convalescence.

FORK
(Charles Simic, 1937–)

This strange thing must have crept
Right out of hell.
It resembles a bird's foot
Worn around the cannibal's neck.
As you hold it in your hand,
As you stab with it into a piece of meat,
It is possible to imagine the rest of the bird:
Its head which like your fist
Is large, bald, beakless and blind.

THE BEST DAYS
(Quinton Duval, 1948–)

The sun was an old ball
in those days. The moon
was a dish of milk
in a blue night on sheets.
We were always thirsty
then. Wine flowed red
in our hearts. Love
was the way we felt
all over, every minute.
I'm not complaining

about now. I'm just lost
and not getting any help.
No one can break
the time we spent
together. We remember
the pink mud house,
startled cypresses
flickering in rain.
The morning we awoke
to the sound of summer
beating across the desert
driving clouds before it.
There is one half a red kiss
on your cup there
where you left it. It's still
warm because you just left.
This is a good day, maybe
one of the best. I don't know
for now. Those good days
are inside us, in heaven,
whatever you want to say.
They are more or less
gone, like you driving
to work, like me sitting here
with nothing to say
that isn't too ordinary or sad.

ON TIME
(John Milton, 1608–1674)

Fly envious Time, till thou run out thy race,
Call on the lazy leaden-stepping hours,

Whose speed is but the heavy Plummet's[1] pace;
And glut thy self with what thy womb devours,
Which is no more than what is false and vain,
And merely mortal dross;
So little is our loss,
So little is thy gain.
For when as each thing bad thou hast entomb'd,
And last of all, thy greedy self consum'd,
Then long Eternity shall greet our bliss
With an individual kiss;
And Joy shall overtake us as a flood,
When every thing that is sincerely good
And perfectly divine,
With Truth, and Peace, and Love shall ever shine
About the supreme Throne
Of him, t'whose happy-making sight alone,
When once our heav'nly-guided soul shall climb,
Then all this Earthy grossness quit,
Attir'd with Stars, we shall for ever sit,
Triumphing over Death, and Chance, and thee O Time.

---

[1] *Plummet*: The weight that moves the works of a clock. A manuscript note
indicates that Milton intended the poem "to be set on a clock case."

WHAT RUSHES BY US
(Patricia Goedicke, 1931–)

On the falling elevator trapped as the sixty-one floors blink
Like eyes in sequence, each possible resting place whipping by

Faster and faster, one after the other, Hello
Goodbye, my friends, yesterday we were talking, today we die

In our sleep, with the stars falling, surely it is the stars
In waterfalls of sparks, ribbons of light descending

With tennis racquets, Bibles, cars, violets, young men wearing
    hats
Ski lifts in winter, *The New York Times*, the Funnies.

All the intense conversations that will never end,
Your photograph on my wall, mine tucked in your billfold,

Do you know what you look like? Not now you don't,
Maybe one second ago you did, but the bit and pieces of
    yesterday

Are piling up, pushing (some even going on ahead),
There's Mother, there's Father, there's Edward from the first grade

And Beethoven's Ninth, and the Bach B Minor, each chord
Turns into a glissando, clusters of fireworks flying

With curses, cats wailing, the whine of the big guns
And desperate bombs going off, the little pot bellies

Of starved children, presidents, old beggars, vice-presidents,
Every newspaper headline, every last quarrel

We ever had, each hangover, each miraculous glass
Of the deep bourbon of love, even the pure silence of prayer

Is pouring past us like rain, like a blizzard of hard rice
Sliding by, sliding by, polished smooth as the ground

Each of us thinks he is standing on, certainly I do
Content, watching the world go by but suddenly

The bottom drops out, the stomach crazily catapults
Past the toes, the feet, the head follows, mountains

Exchange places with the back yard, even your face
Revolves in the sky, it's the Big Dipper, upside down

The wind roars in our ears, in the dizzy whirl of the blood
There's no turning back, on parallel tracks shooting

From the cliff of our birth we keep falling,
First you, then me, then me rushing by you.

4

The Speaker:
The Eye of the Poem

I hear bravuras of birds, bustle of growing wheat, gossip of flames,
  clack of sticks cooking my meals,
I hear the sound I love, the sound of the human voice. . . .
—WALT WHITMAN

A young writer wanted to write a poem about her friend's father's death. Visiting the friend's house around Christmas, she imagined what the family was feeling, tried to imagine death. How to approach such a poem? She thought of describing the family, tried describing the event of his death and her own feelings. Finally she decided to address the father directly.

UNTITLED
(*Ashley King, 1964–*)

You are dead now
your bones burning in the fire
cancer cells popping like oak
fine white oak your collar bone
and the branch from your leg

I think I see you
in the Christmas tree
smiling again like an ornament does
a red cardinal only for an instant

Your voice is the same voice but from back
far back in a line of ancestors
standing only briefly on the porch
faces outstretched into blanks
never moved since
They're all dead under the grass
and they're all still on the porch
with their reaching not grabbing faces

There was another picture of you happy
and not alone in the mountains
It's in somebody's wallet now
somebody who looks at it and wonders
how could you be a father
how could you smile like that with your hunting rifle

King chose not to say that the father was her friend's. Why? She speaks so that he seems almost present in the flash of the ornament twirling, the crackle of the fire. The memory of the sound of his voice seems as far removed as other long-dead ancestors who once gathered on a porch, perhaps to pose for a photograph. The other picture of him is in "somebody's" wallet. Probably she means her friend's wallet, but in the poem she chose to leave this somebody anonymous. By addressing the father as "you" and by leaving the photo in the possession of "somebody," King accomplishes two important things for the poem. She lets the reader "overhear" the speaker, "I," talking to a "you." Their connection is direct. What if at the end she'd said "in my friend's wallet" instead of "somebody's wallet"? "Somebody" is the more open choice; the reader feels included more than if the picture were only the friend's. The discovery lines for the reader, and probably for the writer, are "and they're all dead under the grass / and they're all still on the porch." She realizes that the dead are both dead in the earth *and* alive in memory, "reaching not grabbing." The choice of "somebody" reflects this broad realization about the dead: anyone can look at a photograph of the father and wonder at how present and yet how irretrievable he is.

Of course the writer doesn't know all this in advance. The poet *finds* the right speaker and the right listener, usually by trying out several approaches.

The Invented "I"

Authority, that quality in a poem that makes it believable and real, has the word *author* in it. The speaker the author selects establishes the presence and authority we respond to as we read. Who is speaking? And who is listening? Who is spoken about? The poet decides these for definite reasons. These choices determine the poem's fundamental orientation. The speaker's voice can have any number of tones, shades of expression, pitches, and changes. All these choices reveal the speaker's attitude toward the subject and the audience.

The next title lets us know right away that this will be an emotional poem spoken by a shepherd to his love. He speaks directly to her and no one else.

THE PASSIONATE SHEPHERD TO HIS LOVE
(*Christopher Marlowe, 1564–1593*)

Come live with me and be my love,
And we will all the pleasures prove
That valleys, groves, hills, and fields,
Woods, or steepy mountain yields.

And we will sit upon the rocks,
Seeing the shepherds feed their flocks,
By shallow rivers, to whose falls
Melodious birds sing madrigals.

And I will make thee beds of roses
And a thousand fragrant posies,
A cap of flowers, and a kirtle
Embroidered all with leaves of myrtle;

A gown made of the finest wool,
Which from our pretty lambs we pull;
Fair lined slippers for the cold,
With buckles of the purest gold;

A belt of straw and ivy buds
With coral clasps and amber studs:
And if these pleasures may thee move,
Come live with me and be my love.

The shepherd swains shall dance and sing
For thy delight each May morning:
If these delights thy mind may move,
Then live with me and be my love.

The speaker's gentle and persuasive tone remains insistent: three times he entreats his love (but in the imperative voice) to live with him. We can imagine that she is not displeased to hear him; she seems to stay put while he promises quite a few beds of roses and coral clasps. We overhear. We're invisible to them. Marlowe chose the voice of the shepherd for his love poem instead of writing from his own personal voice. Why? The imaginary shepherd can freely propose an idyllic world where "swains shall dance and sing / for thy delight each May morning." Four hundred years later, the shepherd's world still evokes response; we still propose enduring passion to those we love, still wish

for ideal circumstances. The shepherd is a **persona** (the Greek word
for "mask") for Marlowe. Speaking through the voices of others gives
poets wider possibilities than speaking always as a personal "I."

In addition to increased freedom of expression, a character voice
can heighten dramatic action. The character in "The Negress" is a
runaway slave who managed to get to Massachusetts and now writes
to her former mistress in the South:

THE NEGRESS:
HER MONOLOGUE OF DARK CRÊPE WITH EDGES OF LIGHT:
(Norman Dubie, 1945–)

Mistress Adrienne, I have been given a bed with a pink dresser
In the hot-house
Joining the Concord Public Library: the walls and roof are
Glass and my privacy comes from the apple-geraniums,
Violets, ferns, marigolds and white mayflags.
I get my meals
With the janitor and his wife and all of the books are mine
To use. I scour, sweep and dust.
I hope you don't think of me
As a runaway? I remember your kindness,
Your lessons in reading and writing on the piazza.
My journey was unusual. I saw some of the war
And it was terrible even far up into the North.
My first fright was at a train depot outside Memphis
Where some soldiers found me eating not yet ripened
Quinces and grapes, they took me prisoner: first
I helped some children carry tree limbs to the woodbox
Of the locomotive, then, I was shown to a gentleman
In the passenger car who was searching for his runaway
Negress in a purple dress; he wouldn't identify me,
And I was thrown in with about forty stray blacks into
An open boxcar and soon we were moving, next to me

A man was sucking on the small breasts of a girl
Maybe twelve years of age, across from them
A sad old woman smiled as she puffed on an old cigar end,
By afternoon she was dead, her two friends
Just kicked her out so that she rolled down into pasture
Frightening some hogs that ran off into a thicket.
The girl next to me whimpered and shook. Those quinces
Just ran straight through me and all I could do was
Squat in one corner that was supplied with ammonia-waters
And hay. We were given that night Confederate uniforms
To mend and when the others slept I dressed in three
Shirts and trousers and leapt from the moving train,
The padding helped some but I couldn't walk the next day.
I hid in a shack that seemed lonely but for a flock
Of turkeys, some young hens and a corn crib with tall
Split palings. The next morning from a hill
I watched field workers on a tobacco plantation, it took
Two men to carry a single leaf like a corpse from
A battle scene. That night I found a horse with a bit
In its mouth made of telegraph wire. He carried me up all

The way to Youngstown. *Chloe, you must*
Learn to swim in the pond and to ride the old sorrel.
I am grateful. I had to swim two rivers. I fished some
For perch, bream and trout and ate dried berries.
I stole a bushel of oysters from the porch of a farmhouse.
I treated my sores with blackgum from poplars. I witnessed
The hanging of three Confederate soldiers at a trestle:
Once they were done dancing, they settled in their greatcoats
Like dead folded birds. I have a hatred
Of men and I walked away from the trestle singing.
I spoke to The Concord Literary Club last Tuesday
About my experiences. I told them you never did
Abuse me. How we would sit out in the gazebo

And listen to the boys with their violins, tambourines,
Bones, drums and sticks. How we wept as girls
When the fox bit the head off our peahen and that
From that day how the peacock, missing his mate, would
See her in his reflection in a downstairs window
And fly at it increasing his iridescence with lacerations.
When I left you the windows were all missing and daubers
Were making their mud houses in the high corners
Of the hallway. With sugar-water and crêpe I have put a new
Hem on my purple dress.

At night I walk down the aisles
Of the library, the books climb twenty feet above me,
I just walk there naked with my tiny lamp.
I have the need to fling the lamp sometimes: but I resist it.
Mistress Adrienne, I saw three big cities burning!
Did you know ladies from Philadelphia rode for two days
In wagons to climb a hill where with spyglasses they watched
The war like a horse-pulling contest at a fair.
The man beside me on the train who was sucking the little
Girl's breasts, he was your stable boy, Napoleon. He said
He never had a bad word for you. His little mistress was
Still bare to the waist and before I leapt from the train,
And while he slept, I ran a rod into his eye. I stabbed him
In his brain. She stopped weeping.
Remember that French lullaby where two fleas in a gentleman's
Moustache die like a kiss between the lips of the gentleman
And his mistress. How we laughed at it!
I hope you were not long unconscious there beside the pond.
I just ran away from you, listening the whole night
For your father's hounds. I am
Afraid I split your parasol on your skull. If I
Don't hear from you I will try to understand. *Chloe.*

In her own voice, Chloe tells Mistress Adrienne the story of her escape. This is a **dramatic monologue,** a poem spoken by a persona who tells someone else a story or an event of significance. The poem is also an **epistle,** a poem written as a letter. Chloe is a good letter writer. She recreates her experience with vivid language and exact imagery. We even know exactly what blooms outside her window in her new home. Her intimate tone partly comes from Dubie's decision to make the poem a letter. Letters are directed to *a* reader, almost guaranteeing a one-to-one tone. As Chloe tells the horrifying details of the train ride, we experience them as we expect Mistress Adrienne did when she read. However, the poem surprises us in the end. Chloe's apology for the way she escaped—a whack on dear Mistress Adrienne's head—makes us revise what we thought Mistress Adrienne was hearing all along. The poem is more complex than we thought. Chloe is both violent and heroic and perhaps a little crazed: she thinks of setting the library on fire. The image of the peacock flying at his reflection is an important one. The two women seemed to be close; but to get her freedom, Chloe had to throw herself against her owner.

What did Dubie gain by allowing Chloe to speak? He could have written:

> She has been given a bed with a pink dresser
> In the hot-house....
> She gets her meals....

By choosing Chloe's voice, Dubie lets us hear a live speaker instead of a third-person description of her experience. A character gives a first-hand account. Does "listening" to the voice of an escaped slave give you new insight into the Civil War era? This account has more vivacity than the history books' paragraphs on the underground railroad routes and methods of escape.

The Personal "I" Speaker

Frequently the poem's "I" seems to be the actual voice of the author. When the first person is used this way, we respond to the immediacy of direct personal expression. Ideally the "I" voice, in developing the experience of the poem, also connects to the reader's experience, either internal or external. The poem's effect is not limited to the speaker.

The use of a character voice (Chloe's, for instance) has a very different dramatic impact from one's own voice telling an experience. Whereas with a character voice we keep some awareness of the fictional aspect of the poem, the personal "I" is more subjective. We feel near the voice of the poem. Poets adopt "I" because it conveys an often desired effect of immediacy, "as if" an experience were real. Although the "I" speaker in the poem and the author seem to be the same person, never assume the experience in the poem is an actual fact of the poet's life. "I" can be an invention as easily as any other voice. A poet can write about a morning in Barcelona in first person even if she has never been to Spain.

The choice of speaker is one of the big decisions the poet makes in determining the best stance for the poem. This choice focuses the poem in a particular way. Once the speaker is chosen, the poet still has infinite leeway in the tone of voice. Look at these two extremes in the use of "I":

I THINK CONTINUALLY OF THOSE
WHO WERE TRULY GREAT
(Stephen Spender, 1909–1995)

I think continually of those who were truly great.
Who, from the womb, remembered the soul's history
Through corridors of light where the hours are suns,
Endless and singing. Whose lovely ambition
Was that their lips, still touched with fire,

Should tell of the spirit clothed from head to foot in song.
And who hoarded from the spring branches
The desires falling across their bodies like blossoms.

What is precious is never to forget
The delight of the blood drawn from ageless aprings
Breaking through rocks in worlds before our earth;
Never to deny its pleasure in the simple morning light,
Nor its grave evening demand for love;
Never to allow gradually the traffic to smother
With noise and fog the flowering of the spirit.

Near the snow, near the sun, in the highest fields
See how those names are fêted by the waving grass,
And by the streamers of white cloud,
And whispers of wind in the listening sky;
The names of those who in their lives fought for life,
Who wore at their hearts the fire's centre.
Both of the sun they traveled a short while towards the sun,
And left the vivid air signed with their honour.

AUTOBIOGRAPHIA LITERARIA
(Frank O'Hara, 1926–1966)

When I was a child
I played by myself in a
corner of the schoolyard
all alone.

I hated dolls and I
hated games, animals were
not friendly and birds
flew away.

If anyone was looking
for me I hid behind a
tree and cried out "I am
an orphan."

And here I am, the
center of all beauty!
writing these poems!
Imagine!

O'Hara's "I" is campy, playful. His offbeat, gee-whiz tone makes fun of taking experience so seriously and, by implication, mocks those who would presume to write a "literary autobiography." Spender's "I," in contrast, venerates with deep seriousness the memory of those who lived valuable lives. His poem has a great ambition: to define a valuable life. His tone is somber. We can imagine the speaker addressing a large audience. He speaks to us in a tone of high purpose and importance. The structured appearance of the poem and the repetition of words add to the formality of the tone. Remembering the "author" in "authority," notice the absolutely unequivocal tone of the opening line and of "What is precious is never to forget...," "Never to deny...," and "Never to allow...." The author is certain of his values and presents them unfalteringly.

Do you think to yourself in the same way you speak to others? Some "I" poems record the interior voice. We overhear the speaker's private perceptions as they occur.

THE PARTIAL EXPLANATION
(Charles Simic, 1937–)

Seems like a long time
Since the waiter took my order.
Grimy little luncheonette,
The snow falling outside.

Seems like it has grown darker
Since I last heard the kitchen door
Behind my back
Since I last noticed
Anyone pass on the street.

A glass of ice water
Keeps me company
At this table I chose myself
Upon entering.

And a longing,
Incredible longing
To eavesdrop
On the conversation
Of cooks.

The speaker's interior tone shows in the sentence fragments; he wouldn't speak like this to anyone but himself. He thinks in random observations, which seem to float through his head. The glass of ice water keeping him company emphasizes his aloneness. This illogical thought is typical of the meanderings of someone musing to himself. No listener is implied. The speaker could be jotting notes on the napkin while we look over his shoulder.

Most "I" speakers do not assume a specific listener. The dramatic monologue is an exception. We experience the dramatic monologue as if we were standing with the intended listener. The **soliloquy**, also a solo voice, is another special use of "I." As in the dramatic monologue, a character is speaking. The speaker of a soliloquy usually is debating an action, not telling about an event. He or she is not aware of an audience; again, we overhear. Soliloquies are private, frequently used in plays to let the audience in on the inner thoughts of an actor, as in Hamlet's famous debate with himself.

FROM *HAMLET*

(William Shakespeare, 1564–1616)

(ACT III, SCENE I)

To be, or not to be, that is the question:
Whether 'tis nobler in the mind to suffer
The slings and arrows of outrageous fortune,
Or to take arms against a sea of troubles,
And by opposing end them. To die, to sleep—
No more; and by a sleep to say we end
The heartache, and the thousand natural shocks
That flesh is heir to. 'Tis a consummation
Devoutly to be wished—to die, to sleep—
To sleep, perchance to dream, ay there's the rub;
For in that sleep of death what dreams may come
When we have shuffled off this mortal coil[1]
Must give us pause—there's the respect[2]
That makes calamity of so long life.[3]
For who would bear the whips and scorns of time,
Th' oppressor's wrong, the proud man's contumely,
The pangs of despised love, the law's delay,
The insolence of office, and the spurns
That patient merit of th' unworthy takes,
When he himself might his quietus[4] make
With a bare bodkin?[5] Who would fardels[6] bear,
To grunt and sweat under a weary life,
But that the dread of something after death,
The undiscovered country, from whose bourn[7]

---

[1] *coil:* turmoil *or* rope ring, meaning flesh.
[2] *respect:* consideration.
[3] *so long life:* so long-lived.
[4] *quietus:* legal term meaning full discharge.
[5] *bodkin:* dagger.
[6] *fardels:* burdens.
[7] *bourn:* region.

No traveller returns, puzzles the will,
And makes us rather bear those ills we have
Than fly to others that we know not of?
Thus conscience does make cowards of us all;
And thus the native hue of resolution
Is sicklied o'er with the pale cast of thought,
And enterprises of great pitch[8] and moment
With this regard their currents turn awry
And lose the name of action. —

---

[8] *pitch:* height.

The Public Voice

When the speaker is "we," the poet presumes to speak for himself and others. "We" can be intimate, but usually "we" indicates that the poet will be concerned with a cultural or historical subject with broad scope and conclusions. The U.S. Constitution begins, "We, the people...." and "we" intends to represent all citizens. A poem that uses this kind of "we" is a **public voice poem.** The public voice speaks for a group of believers or participants in a common situation. The poet therefore wants a larger platform than a personal voice would offer. The choice of "we" stakes out a different territory than "I." Twentieth-century poets are less willing to venture to speak from the broad, homogeneous religious and political viewpoints that poets of earlier times took for granted. The plurality of our culture makes "we" a difficult choice.

Wilfred Owen's "we" is a troop of World War I soldiers. Owen, who died in that war, questions an ancient, accepted sentiment. The purpose of his poem is **didactic**—a moral lesson is intended. The irony here is that the poem disproves the lofty sentiment of the title. *Dulce et decorum est pro patria mori* ("It is sweet and dignified to die for one's country") is a common epitaph on the tombstones of European soldiers.

DULCE ET DECORUM EST
(Wilfred Owen, 1893–1918)

Bent double, like old beggars under sacks,
Knock-kneed, coughing like hags, we cursed through sludge,
Till on the haunting flares we turned our backs,
And towards our distant rest began to trudge.
Men marched asleep. Many had lost their boots,
But limped on, blood-shod. All went lame, all blind;
Drunk with fatigue; deaf even to the hoots
Of gas-shells dropping softly behind.

Gas! Gas! Quick, boys!—An ecstasy of fumbling,
Fitting the clumsy helmets just in time,
But someone still was yelling out and stumbling
And flound'ring like a man in fire or lime.
Dim through the misty panes and thick green light,
As under a green sea, I saw him drowning.

In all my dreams before my helpless sight
He plunges at me, guttering, choking, drowning.
If in some smothering dreams, you too could pace
Behind the wagon that we flung him in,
And watch the white eyes wilting in his face,
His hanging face, like a devil's sick of sin,

If you could hear, at every jolt, the blood
Come gargling from the froth-corrupted lungs
Bitten as the cud
Of vile, incurable sores on innocent tongues,—
My friend, you would not tell with such high zest
To children ardent for some desperate glory,
The old lie: *Dulce et decorum est*
Pro patria mori.

The Invisible Speaker

In a poem in the third person voice, the author acts as narrator, often not identifying himself at all except as a tone of voice. When a poem is about a "she" or "a woman" or "he" or "the people in apartment 4-C" or "a sparrow," the author-speaker intrudes on the subjects as little as possible. His voice sets the tone. This choice gives the poet a more objective stance than he has with "I," "we," or "you." The invisible speaker is close to the recording and accumulating camera eye.

AN ARUNDEL TOMB
(Philip Larkin, 1922–1985)

Side by side, their faces blurred,
The earl and countess lie in stone,
Their proper habits vaguely shown
As jointed armor, stiffened pleat,
And that faint hint of the absurd —
The little dogs under their feet.

Such plainness of the pre-baroque
Hardly involves the eye, until
It meets his left-hand gauntlet, still
Clasped empty in the other: and
One sees, with a sharp tender shock,
His hand withdrawn, holding her hand.

They would not think to lie so long.
Such faithfulness in effigy
Was just a detail friends would see:
A sculptor's sweet commissioned grace
Thrown off in helping to prolong
The Latin names around the base.

They would not guess how early in
Their supine stationary voyage
The air would change to soundless damage,
Turn the old tenantry away;
How soon succeeding eyes begin
To look, not read. Rigidly they

Persisted, linked, through lengths and breadths
Of time. Snow fell, undated. Light
Each summer thronged the glass. A bright
Litter of birdcalls strewed the same
Bone-riddled ground. And up the paths
The endless altered people came.

Washing at their identity.
Now, helpless in the hollow of
An unarmorial age, a trough
Of smoke in slow suspended skeins
Above their scrap of history,
Only an attitude remains:

Time has transfigured them into
Untruth. The stone fidelity
They hardly meant has come to be
Their final blazon, and to prove
Our almost-instinct almost true:
What will survive of us is love.

"An Arundel Tomb" describes the stone tomb carvings of the earl and countess of Arundel at their twelfth-century castle in Sussex, England. The invisible speaker presents the sculptures to the reader. He directs our looking rather formally—"One sees, with a sharp tender shock"—but with an observant eye. The speaker notices that the figures are holding hands. Through centuries of change, "undated" snow, and generations of birdsong, with thousands of people filing by to see them, they've lain there, hands joined, unchanging. The last two lines make a jump. From describing the characters in third person, the speaker shifts to a public voice. The shift suddenly includes *us*. Larkin moves from the particular earl and countess to a general idea about the survival of love. The medieval figures confirm *our* "almost-instinct." What if he'd said "and to prove / Our instinct true / What will survive of us is love"? But Larkin's conclusion is qualified; he carefully does not claim that our instinct *is* true.

Larkin's formal tone suits his description of the stone sculptures and the contemplative mood they arouse. The poem is addressed to any reader. Larkin maintains formality by the use of "one." If his speaker addressed "you," he'd hit a folksy, less dignified note. But this author does not break the objectivity built into "one" and his cool third-person descriptions of the earl and countess. Each choice he makes fits his philosophical conclusion.

Poems

CORINNA'S GOING A-MAYING
(Robert Herrick, 1591–1674)

Get up! get up for shame! the blooming morn
Upon her wings presents the god unshorn.
    See how Aurora[1] throws her fair
    Fresh-quilted colors through the air:
    Get up, sweet slug-a-bed, and see
    The dew bespangling herb and tree.
Each flower has wept and bowed toward the east
Above an hour since, yet you not dressed;
    Nay, not so much as out of bed?
    When all the birds have matins said,
    And sung their thankful hymns, 'tis sin,
    Nay, profanation to keep in,

----
[1] *Aurora*: goddess of dawn.

Whenas a thousand virgins on this day
Spring, sooner than the lark, to fetch in May.

Rise, and put on your foliage, and be seen
To come forth, like the springtime, fresh and green,
   And sweet as Flora.[2] Take no care
   For jewels for your gown or hair;
   Fear not; the leaves will strew
   Gems in abundance upon you;
Besides, the childhood of the day has kept,
Against you come, some orient[3] pearls unwept;
   Come and receive them while the light
   Hangs on the dew-locks of the night,
   And Titan[4] on the eastern hill
   Retires himself, or else stands still
Till you come forth. Wash, dress, be brief in praying:
Few beads are best when once we go a-Maying.

Come, my Corinna, come; and, coming mark
How each field turns a street, each street a park
   Made green and trimmed with trees; see how
   Devotion gives each house a bough
   Or branch: each porch, each door ere this,
   An ark, a tabernacle is.
Made up of whitethorn neatly interwove,
As if here were those cooler shades of love.
   Can such delights be in the street
   And open fields, and we not see 't?
   Come, we'll abroad; and let's obey
   The proclamation made for May,

---

[2] *Flora:* goddess of flowers.
[3] *orient:* eastern.
[4] *Titan:* the sun.

And sin no more, as we have done, by staying:
But, my Corinna, come, let's go a-Maying.

There's not a budding boy or girl this day
But is got up and gone to bring in May;
    A deal of youth, ere this, is come
    Back, and with whitethorn laden home.
    Some have dispatched their cakes and cream
    Before that we have left to dream;
And some have wept, and wooed, and plighted troth,
And chose their priest, ere we can cast off sloth.
    Many a green-gown has been given,
    Many a kiss, both odd and even,
    Many a glance, too, has been sent
    From out the eye, love's firmament;
Many a jest told of the keys betraying
This night, and locks picked; yet we're not a-Maying.

Come, let us go while we are in our prime,
And take the harmless folly of the time.
    We shall grow old apace, and die
    Before we know our liberty.
    Our life is short, and our days run
    As fast away as does the sun;
And, as a vapor or a drop of rain
Once lost, can ne'er be found again;
    So when or you or I are made
    A fable, song, or fleeting shade,
    All love, all liking, all delight
    Lies drowned with us in endless night.
Then while time serves, and we are but decaying,
Come, my Corinna, come, let's go a-Maying.

RESEMBLANCE
(Rena Williams, 1940–)

You passed me today in your ugly form.
It was almost you, with eyes fifteen years older
and a drunkard's nose
shining out of your face.

He plodded from the Greyhound station
down the sidewalk swinging a small dirty bag.
He probably came to meet a death;
he would be the brother who drifts in
for funerals and no one
knows quite what to say.

He headed for the telephone booth
in front of Grandmother's old white house.
Her ten children skated down
that deep chicken-run hall, dodging bats.
Four interchangable cubicles, enough for everyone,
opened into that hall which bristled,
bled with our scabby knees. We shouted
that space to life.

So you walk by in your ugly form
and I end missing my grandmother and the bats.
Students live there now, they've painted
LOVE on every sagging window, LOVE
in every purple shade and shape, and they
will not repeal a contrast so complete.

I watched you, mister, I know you well
and I'm the only person in this town
glad to see you.

YOU
(Frank Stanford, 1948–1978)

Sometimes in our sleep we touch
The body of another woman
And we wake up
And we know the first nights
With summer visitors
In the three storied house of our childhood.
Whatever we remember,
The darkest hair being brushed
In front of the darkest mirror
In the darkest room.

FOR A NEW CITIZEN
OF THESE UNITED STATES
(Li-Young Lee, 1957–)

Forgive me for thinking I saw
the irregular postage stamp of death;
a black moth the size of my left
thumbnail is all I've trapped in the damask.
There is no need for alarm. And

there is no need for sadness, if
the rain at the window now reminds you
of nothing; not even of that
parlor, long like a nave, where cloud-shadow,
wing-shadow, where father-shadow
continually confused the light. In flight,
leaf-throng and, later, soldiers and
flags deepened those windows to submarine.

But you don't remember, I know,
so I won't mention that house where Chung hid,
Lin wizened, you languished, and Ming—
Ming hush-hushed us with small song. And since you
don't recall the missionary
bells chiming the hour, or those words whose sounds
alone exhaust the heart—*garden,*
heaven, amen—I'll mention none of it.

After all, it was just our life,
merely years in a book of years. It was
1960, and we stood with
the other families on a crowded
railroad platform. The trains came, then
the rains, and then we got separated.
And in the interval between
familiar faces, events occurred, which
one of us faithfully pencilled
in a day-book bound by a rubber band.

But birds, as you say, fly forward.
So I won't show you letters and the shawl
I've so meaninglessly preserved.
And I won't hum along, if you don't, when
our mothers sing *Nights in Shanghai.*
I won't, each Spring, each time I smell lilac,
recall my mother, patiently
stitching money inside my coat lining,
if you don't remember your mother
preparing for your own escape.

After all, it was only our
life, our life and its forgetting.

MUSÉE DES BEAUX ARTS
(W. H. Auden, 1907–1973)

About suffering they were never wrong,
The Old Masters: how well they understood
Its human position; how it takes place
While someone else is eating or opening a window or just
    walking dully along;
How, when the aged are reverently, passionately waiting
For the miraculous birth, there always must be
Children who did not specially want it to happen, skating
On a pond at the edge of the wood:
They never forgot
That even the dreadful martyrdom must run its course
Anyhow in a corner, some untidy spot
Where the dogs go on with their doggy life and the torturer's
    horse
Scratches its innocent behind on a tree.
In Brueghel's *Icarus*,[1] for instance: how everything turns away
Quite leisurely from the disaster; the ploughman may
Have heard the splash, the forsaken cry,
But for him it was not an important failure; the sun shone
As it had to on the white legs disappearing into the green
Water; and the expensive delicate ship that must have seen
Something amazing, a boy falling out of the sky,
Had somewhere to get to and sailed calmly on.

---

[1] Brueghel's *Icarus:* In "Landscape with the Fall of Icarus," Brueghel shows everyday life
continuing without anyone noticing Icarus falling into the sea.

NANI

(Alberto Ríos, 1953–)

Sitting at her table, she serves
the sopa de arroz[1] to me
instinctively, and I watch her,
the absolute *mamá*, and eat words
I might have had to say more
out of embarrassment. To speak,
now-foreign words I used to speak,
too, dribble down her mouth as she serves
me albondigas.[2] No more
than a third are easy to me.
By the stove she does something with words
and looks at me only with her
back. I am full. I tell her
I taste the mint, and watch her speak
smiles at the stove. All my words
make her smile. Nani never serves
herself, she only watches me
with her skin, her hair. I ask for more.

I watch the *mamá* warming more
tortillas for me. I watch her
fingers in the flame for me.
Near her mouth, I see a wrinkle speak
of a man whose body serves
the ants like she serves me, then more words
from more wrinkles about children, words
about this and that, flowing more
easily from these other mouths. Each serves
as a tremendous string around her,

---

[1] *sopa de arroz:* rice soup.
[2] *albondigas:* meatballs.

holding her together. They speak
Nani was this and that to me
and I wonder just how much of me
will die with her, what were the words
I could have been, was. Her insides speak
through a hundred wrinkles, now, more
than she can bear, steel around her,
shouting, then. What is this thing she serves?
She asks me if I want more.
I own no words to stop her.
Even before I speak, she serves.

※

INVITING A FRIEND TO SUPPER
(Ben Jonson, 1573–1637)

Tonight, grave sir, both my poor house and I
   Do equally desire your company;
Not that we think us worthy such a guest,
   But that your worth will dignify our feast
With those that come, whose grace may make that seem
   Something, which else could hope for no esteem.
It is the fair acceptance, sir, creates
   The entertainment perfect, not the cates.[1]
Yet shall you have, to rectify your palate,
   An olive, capers, or some better salad
Ushering the mutton; with a short-legged hen,
   If we can get her, full of eggs, and then
Lemons, and wine for sauce; to these, a coney[2]
   Is not to be despaired of, for our money;
And, though fowl now be scarce, yet there are clerks,
   The sky not falling, think we may have larks.

---

[1] *cates:* food.
[2] *coney:* rabbit.

I'll tell you of more, and lie, so you will come:
    Of partridge, pheasant, woodcock, of which some
May yet be there, and godwit, if we can:
    Knat, rail, and ruff[3] too. Howsoe'r, my man
Shall read a piece of Virgil, Tacitus,
    Livy, or of some better book to us,
Of which we'll speak our minds, amidst our meat;
    And I'll profess no verses to repeat.
To this, if aught appear which I not know of,
    That will the pastry, not my paper, show of.
Digestive cheese and fruit there sure will be;
    But that which most doth take my Muse and me,
Is a pure cup of rich Canary wine,
    Which is the Mermaid's[4] now, but shall be mine;
Of which had Horace,[5] or Anacreon[6] tasted,
    Their lives, as do their lines, till now had lasted.
Tobacco, nectar, or the Thespian spring,
    Are all but Luther's beer to this I sing.
Of this we will sup free, but moderately,
    And we will have no Pooley, or Parrot[7] by,
Nor shall our cups make any guilty men;
    But, at our parting we will be as when
We innocently met. No simple word
    That shall be uttered at our mirthful board,
Shall make us sad next morning or affright
    The liberty that we'll enjoy tonight.

---

[3] *godwit ... knat ... rail ... ruff:* game birds considered delicacies in Jonson's time.
[4] *Mermaid:* a famous London pub and literary meeting place.
[5] *Horace* (65–8 B.C.): Roman poet and satirist.
[6] *Anacreon* (572–488 B.C.): Greek poet.
[7] *Pooley ... Parrot:* spies.

5

Rhyme
and Repetition

*All deep things are Song. It seems somehow the very
central essence of us, Song; as if all the rest were
but wrappages and hulls! . . . See deep enough,
and you see musically; the heart of Nature being
everywhere music, if you can only reach it.*
—THOMAS CARLYLE

We take rhyme and repetition so much for granted in poetry that it seems odd even to question why they're used. The common property of both is recurrence of sound. Both give pleasure. We like sounds that strike and chime and slide by each other. We respond to the here-it-comes-again refrain.

In the Cockney section of London, people were so fond of rhyme that they incorporated it into their daily speech. A friend remembers being carried up to bed by her father, who said, "Up those apples," a phrase that makes perfect sense to Cockneys, who know that their rhyme for stairs is "apples and pears," gradually shortened to "apples." "I've got to go home to my trouble and strife," "Call the hot potato," "Pass the Aristotle," "Answer the dog and bone," and "I'm out of bees and honey" are all clear to those in the know: *wife, waiter, bottle, phone,* and *money* are the less colorful translations. Besides being fun, rhyming slang (as it's called) worked as a disguise. Those who didn't know couldn't understand. Guards from the Hampstead neighbor-hood, for instance, couldn't always understand Cockney prisoners in London jails.

In America we have the Black tradition of "rapping" (or "toasting," as it used to be called), the roots of which go back to African creation myths, initiation rites, and songs. As in rhyming slang, the rhyming adds get-up-and-go. It provokes improvisation. Certain words or phrases repeat, with humor or irony gathering force as the rap goes on. Re-peating and rhyming also help stamp something in memory. In cul-tures that do not have written language, songs and chants pass on history and values. Repetition connects with the cycles of weather and crops in this Navajo song:

SONGS IN THE GARDEN OF THE HOUSE GOD

Now in the east
the white bean
& the great corn-plant
are tied with white lightning.
Listen! rain's drawing near!
The voice of the bluebird is heard.

Now in the east
the white bean
& the great squash
are tied with the rainbow.
Listen! the rain's drawing near!
The voice of the bluebird is heard.

From the top of the great corn-plant the water foams, I hear it.
Around the roots the water foams, I hear it.
Around the roots of the plant it foams, I hear it.
From their tops the water foams, I hear it.

The corn grows up. The waters of the dark clouds drop, drop.
The rain comes down. The waters from the corn leaves drop,
    drop.
The rain comes down. The waters from the plants drop, drop.
The corn grows up. The waters of the dark mists drop, drop.

Shall I cull this fruit of the great corn-plant?
Shall you break it?
    Shall I break it?
Shall I break it?
    Shall you break it?
Shall I?
    Shall you?
Shall I cull this fruit of the great squash vine?
    Shall you pick it up?
Shall I pick it up?
    Shall I pick it up?
Shall you pick it up?
    Shall I?
Shall you?

Speech and song uses of rhyme and repetition have everything to do with literary uses. All make rhymes and repeat words for surprise, for movement, for memory, for emphasis. Hopkins said, "Read with your ears," and we do. Along with word choice and sound patterns, the sound effects of rhyme and repetition help create the rhythm of the poem. Recurrence of a sound is itself a music. Like the chorus in a song, a refrain or rhyming pattern, once set up, rewards our anticipation.

Square-dance callers improvise their calls, sending the dancers into various patterns but always returning them to the circle. Elza White used this call at dances in Texas in the 1880s:

Salute your partner! Let her go!
Balance all and do-si-do!

Swing your gal, and all run away!
Right and left, and gents sashay!
Gents to the right and swing or cheat!
On to the next gal and repeat!
Balance to the next and don't be shy!
Swing your partner and swing her high!
Bunch the gals and circle around!
Whack your feet until they sound!
Form a basket! Break away!
Swing and kiss and all git gay!
All gents to the left and balance all!
Lift your hoofs and let 'em fall!
Swing your opp'sites! Swing again!
Kiss the sage-hens if you can!
Back to your partners, do-si-do!
Gents salute your little sweets!
Hitch up and promenade to your seats!

In "The Wheel," Wendell Berry draws us close to a deep unity of movement in dance. The title evokes the circular movement of the dance and also suggests the turning of the world, the clock, the wheel of fortune.

THE WHEEL
(Wendell Berry, 1934–)

At the first strokes of the fiddle bow
the dancers rise from their seats.
The dance begins to shape itself
in the crowd, as couples join,
and couples join couples, their movement
together lightening their feet.
They move in the ancient circle
of the dance. The dance and the song

call each other into being. Soon
they are one — rapt in a single
rapture, so that even the night
has its clarity, and time
is the wheel that brings it round.
In this rapture the dead return.
Sorrow is gone from them.
They are light. They step
into the steps of the living
and turn with them in the dance
in the sweet enclosure
of the song, and timeless
is the wheel that brings it round.

Berry's repetition of single words keeps them in motion. The rhythm also comes from alliteration and consonance, especially the high incidence of s sounds. Only five lines end with a period; the others run over to the next line. This sound flow adds to the endless circular motions of the dance. By implication, do you think Berry means that other formal patterns, perhaps the patterns in poetry, are also timeless? How do the dead "step / into the steps of the living"?

As in a square dance, the poem uses recurrence as an organizing principle. The dancers end in a circle; they end where they began — but meanwhile they have danced. Many poems begin and end with the same line. The ending line has accumulated meanings in the process; the reader comes full circle also. The patterns of rhymes resolve; nothing is left hanging over without its partnering rhyme. Rhyme and repetition unify the structure of the poem. Rhyming words resemble each other; repeating words and phrases, lines, or images are identical, though in succeeding contexts they often pick up different meanings and tones.

Reiteration gives balance and harmony. Along with the pleasure of hearing sounds echo, other subtle and distinct effects accrue through use of rhyme and repetition.

Rhyme

"Doesn't a poem have to rhyme?" people often wonder. The question reveals the strong inheritance of traditional poetry. Most, though not all, English poetry between the twelfth and twentieth centuries rhymed. The earliest poetry was alliterative. As English poets began to hear the rhymed lyrics of the Provençal troubadors drift across the channel, rhyme slowly began to prevail over alliteration as a formal device. By now, rhyme is an *option*. Poets use it on occasion but not as a regular practice. Why? Why not always use this tool that has pleased poets and readers for so many generations? The answer is part of the history of poetry, of course. There always was a parallel nonrhyming tradition in English poetry. In *Observations in the Art of English Poesie*, written in 1692, Thomas Campion said rhyme was "vulgar, unartificial, easy, rude, barbarous, shifting, sliding, and fat." Later, John Milton maintained that rhyme "is the invention of a barbarous Age, to set off wretched matter and lame meter." Rhyme, however, remained the strongest poetic convention until the twentieth century, when, with the breakup of other traditions, it became less common.

That World War I brought on a fragmentation of values and the breakdown of the coherent society in Western Europe is a concept familiar to most of us. Certainly all the arts reflect this. But if the disharmony of the age is responsible for changes in poetry, that is no negative judgment. Change in art is healthy. Poets began to focus on imagery instead of rhyme or other poetic conventions. As emphasis shifted away from formal devices, it shifted *to* the sound of the natural speaking voice or to the rhythm of breath; it shifted *to* new uses and arrangements of the line. These changes too are not permanent; the only thing permanent in art is change. T. S. Eliot thought "excessive devotion to rhyme has thickened the modern ear" and hoped the "shift away from rhyme might be a liberation *of* rhyme." "Freed from its exacting task…," he wrote, "it could be applied with greater effect where most needed."

KINDS OF RHYME

Rhyme is one of the strongest elements in the craft of poetry. It is simple — everyone knows what a rhyme is — but its effects are quite mysterious. At times it may seem merely ornamental, but a quick substitution of unrhyming synonyms shows how much intricate power the rhymes add to the meaning. Different kinds of rhymes cause different effects.

The most common rhymes are **pure rhymes.** In these, the initial sounds of the words differ and the rest of the sound is identical: hill/still, pit/lit, form/storm, wrong/song. If you want a pure rhyme for *bell*, you can run through the alphabet: cell, dell, fell, hell, and so on. Pure rhymes are bold. They call attention to themselves by their clear likeness.

Words that almost rhyme are **slant rhymes,** also called **off rhymes** or **half rhymes.** Here, the sounds are closely related but not identical: fear/care, face/dress, gone/moan, dizzy/easy. In a poem with pure rhymes, we catch on to the sound quickly, wait for the rhyming sounds to recur. With slant rhymes, we hear the corresponding sounds, but they're less obviously matched than pure rhymes. Pure rhymes have the satisfying sound of a lock clicking shut; the effect of slant rhyming is more subtle.

Emily Dickinson was a great inventor of slant rhymes. Her poems are often written with a metronome regularity. Because of this, the reader expects to hear rhyming that is just as obvious. Obvious, Dickinson is not. Her poetry is totally unpredictable. You never know where her next line will take you. In almost every poem there's at least one strange word that makes you stare and question. Her poems are often cryptic, as was the poet herself. In a letter about her rhymes, she said, "I need the little bells to cool me." Her use of slant rhyme repeatedly emphasizes the surprise and complexity of her subject. Her favored punctuation mark is the dash, which often replaces a comma or period. Read the dash as she intended it — as a charged pause in timing.

1052
(Emily Dickinson, 1830–1886)

I never saw a Moor—
I never saw the Sea—
Yet know I how the Heather looks
And what a Billow be.

I never spoke with God
Nor visited in Heaven—
Yet certain am I of the spot
As if the Checks were given—

Rhymes at the ends of lines are called **end rhymes.** They link the line ends together by echoing sounds. If a word within the line rhymes with the end rhyme, or with another word within the line, this is called **internal rhyme.** In the example below, internal rhyme tightens the sounds' unity. Also the end rhymes hit each other with force not only because they are pure but because their meanings collide.

> In autumn, the *mild* hunter brings down the *wild*
> *Boar,* the slow death *roar* sounds to the *child*

End rhymes with an accented last syllable (rĕ préss/uň dréss) or a single syllable (gó/nó) are called **rising rhymes.** Those ending with an unaccented last syllable (párt lў/smárt lў) are **falling rhymes.** Formerly, these were dubbed "masculine" (strong, stressed ending) and "feminine" (soft, unstressed ending) but I simply forbid that terminology. A rising rhyme or falling rhyme indicates whether the line ends emphatically or softly.

Poets go to great lengths to devise rhyming patterns. Consequently, you will encounter several kinds of rhyme. The list below introduces the most pleasing and efficacious:

apocopated rhyme: a cut-off rhyme. The last syllable of one of the rhymes is missing: gain/painless, hot/potted, lean/cleaner.

linked rhyme: the first syllable of a line echoes the last syllable of the previous line. This has the same effect as internal rhyme:

> Night weighs down the roof*top*
> *stops* the flashlight of a scared *cop*.

triple rhyme: words of three rhyming syllables with the first syllable of each as the accented one. "Snow in the Suburbs" by Thomas Hardy opens with a triple rhyme: "Every branch big with it/Bent every twig with it." Triples are often used for comic effect: higgledy/piggledy, Beelzebub/syllabub. In *"Death Came to Me,"* Stevie Smith, however, uses triple rhyme (plus internal rhyme) somberly:

> For underneath the superscription lurked I knew
> With pulse quickening and the blood thickening
> For fear in every vein the deadly strychnine.

head rhyme: not really a rhyme but another name for **alliteration** (repetition of consonant sounds at the beginning of a word):

> Western *w*ind, *w*hen *w*ill thou blow?

eye rhyme: words that look similar though they are pronounced differently: ties/eternities, cough/rough, care/caress, wind/find.

unpatterned rhyme: randomly placed rhyming words. Unpatterned rhyme gives *some* unity and a sense of linguistic spontaneity. In "To a Chameleon," Marianne Moore matches her rhyming craft to her changeable subject:

Hid by the august foliage and fruit
  of the grape-vine
  twine
    your anatomy
    round the pruned and polished stem,
      Chameleon
      Fire laid upon
    an emerald as long as
    the Dark King's massy
  one,
could not snap the spectrum up for food
  as you have done.

identical rhyme: not rhyme at all but a repetition of the *same* word where you would expect the next rhyming word. The word is restated, therefore reemphasized.

ENVOY
(Ernest Dowson, 1867–1900)

(Vitae summa brevis spem nos vetat incohare longam)[1]

They are not long, the weeping and the laughter,
  Love and desire and hate;
I think they have no portion is us after
    We pass the gate.

They are not long, the days of wine and roses:
  Out of a misty dream
Our path emerges for a while, then closes
    Within a dream.

---

[1]*Vitae ... longam:* Life's brevity prevents us from lengthy aspiration.

homonyms: not strictly rhymes but another unifying element like eye rhymes. Though the spelling differs, the same sound is repeated: time/thyme, sail/sale, praise/preys, pear/pair, reign/rain.

RHYME SCHEME

The **rhyme scheme** is the pattern of rhyme in an entire poem. To "read" the rhyme scheme give each new rhyme, as it appears, a letter. As a sound repeats, label it with the same letter as the word it rhymes with.

INFANT SORROW
(William Blake, 1757–1828)

My mother groaned, my father wept,	*a*
Into the dangerous world I leapt;	*a*
Helpless, naked, piping loud,	*b*
Like a fiend hid in a cloud.	*b*
Struggling in my father's hands,	*c*
Striving against my swaddling-bands,	*c*
Bound and weary, I thought best	*d*
To sulk upon my mother's breast.	*d*

Blake's rhyme scheme is aabb ccdd. If he had continued the poem, the pattern he set up would continue. "Infant Sorrow" is in two *stanzas*. In chapter 8 we will look in detail at different kinds of stanzas. For the moment, keep in mind that a stanza is a basic unit of thought and rhythm within a poem. The first stanza in a traditional poem establishes the rhythm, including the number of lines and the rhyme scheme that will be repeated in successive stanzas.

Occasionally you'll find a dangling rhyme or a disrupted rhyme scheme. Like a sudden shift in diction, this should alert you to something the poet wants you to notice. A broken-off, disjunctive, or incomplete rhyme will parallel a glitch or reversal in the poem's development.

MOON/JUNE RHYMES

If rhyme casts a spell by binding sounds together, the spell should be a good one. No device can destroy a poem more quickly than rhymes that clunk lifelessly down the right-hand edge of the poem. As an immediate test for hackneyed rhymes, see if you can predict the word coming up. If love/dove, sorrow/tomorrow, breath/death, moon/soon/June, true/blue, or pain/rain crop up, you know the poet got lazy and reached into the "poetry grab-bag" instead of working harder to sharpen the word choice. If the writer was satisfied with lazy rhymes, chances are the poem will be trite and imprecise. In such a poem, the rhyming word could be any number of choices:

> Seashell, seashell, what do you know?
> Tell your tale while the tide is [   ].
> Were you washed on a beach of pink.
> Where white caps sparkle and [   ].
> Did you witness a pirate's death
> Or swirl fast in a whale's deep [   ]
> *and so on*

The other hazard of rhyme is that a steady adherence to a rhyme scheme often forces extra, inappropriate words into the poem in order to fit the plan. Or it causes oddly twisted syntax, as in these lines about Lake Lemen by George Gordon, Lord Byron:

> Lemen's is fair; but think not I forsake
> the sweet remembrance of a dearer shore:
> Sad havoc time must with my memory make,
> Ere *that* or *thou* can fade these eyes before;

Three of the four lines turn normal phrasing around. The last line has been so wrenched to find a rhyme for "shore" that it hardly makes sense.

Rhyme and Meaning

Good rhyme works with meaning. In this little stanza from "Upon Julia's Clothes," Robert Herrick's sounds are part of what he's saying:

> Whenas in silks my Julia goes,
> Then, then, methinks, how sweetly flows
> that liquefaction of her clothes.

Goes, flows, and *clothes* cohere closely. Further, they all end in *s*. Herrick uses four other *s* sounds in the stanza, all mimicking the swishing of Julia's silks. The sounds are mutually supportive, each enhancing the other. In contrast, the following poem makes rhyme work with meaning in an opposite way:

Two in August
(John Crowe Ransom, 1888–1974)

> Two that could not have lived their single lives
> As can some husbands and wives
> Did something strange: they tensed their vocal cords
> And attacked each other with silences and words
> Like catapulted stones and arrowed knives.
>
> Dawn was not yet; night is for loving or sleeping,
> Sweet dreams or safekeeping;
> Yet he of the wide brows that were used to laurel
> And she, the famed for gentleness, must quarrel.
> Furious both of them, and scared, and weeping.
>
> How sleepers groan, twitch, wake to such a mood
> Is not well understood,
> Nor why two entities grown almost one
> Should rend and murder trying to get undone,
> With individual tigers in their blood.

She in terror fled from the marriage chamber
Circuiting the dark rooms like a string of amber
Round and round and back,
And would not light one lamp against the black,
And heard the clock that clanged: Remember, Remember.

And he must tread barefooted the dim lawn,
Soon he was up and gone;
High in the trees and night-mastered birds were crying
With fear upon their tongues, no singing nor flying
Which are their lovely attitudes by dawn.

Whether those bird-cries were of heaven or hell
There is no way to tell;
In the long ditch of darkness the man walked
Under the hackberry trees where the birds talked
With words too sad and strange to syllable.

"Two in August" concerns two warring people who are married. Ransom chooses rhymes that also rub uncomfortably against their mates. The rhyme scheme in each stanza is aabba. Like the two married people, the rhymes are linked in a formal arrangement. Notice the rhyming groups: lives/wives/knives; one/undone/mood/understood/blood; sleeping/safekeeping/weeping. One rhyme is abrasive in meaning to its partner, as in *sleeping* and *weeping*, *wives* and *knives*. The rhymes' simultaneous opposition in meaning and likeness in sound add drama and tension. This is unlike the Herrick stanza, where the rhyme is a force for harmony.

As you read rhymed poems, evaluate *how* the rhyme works. Is it a force for harmony, a reiteration of meaning? Or is it destabilizing, creating uncertainty, taking back with one hand what it gives with the other?

NOW WINTER NIGHTS ENLARGE
(Thomas Campion, 1567–1620)

Now winter nights enlarge
The number of their hours;

And clouds their storms discharge
    Upon the airy towers.
Let now the chimneys blaze
    And cups o'erflow with wine,
Let well-tuned words amaze
    With harmony divine.
Now yellow waxen lights
    Shall wait on honey love
While youthful revels, masques, and courtly sights
    Sleep's leaden spells remove.

This time doth well dispense
    With lover's long discourse;
Much speech hath some defense,
    Though beauty no remorse.
All do not all things well;
    Some measures comely tread,
Some knotted riddles tell,
    Some poems smoothly read.
The summer hath his joys,
    And winter his delights;
Though love and all his pleasures are but toys,
    They shorten tedious nights.

Poems

SONG
(John Donne, 1572–1631)

Go and catch a falling star,
    Get with child a mandrake root,[1]

---

[1] *Mandrake root:* The forked root of the
mandragora plant was associated with fertility.
It was said to shriek when pulled out of the
ground. Its shape resembled a human form.

Tell me where all past years are,
    Or who cleft the Devil's foot,
Teach me to hear mermaids singing,
Or to keep off envy's stinging,
            And find
            What wind
Serves to advance an honest mind.

If thou beest born to strange sights,
    Things invisible to see,
Ride ten thousand days and nights,
    Till age snow white hairs on thee.
Thou, when thou return'st, wilt tell me
All strange wonders that befell thee,
            And swear
            Nowhere
Lives a woman true, and fair.

If thou find'st one, let me know,
    Such a pilgrimage were sweet;
Yet do not, I would not go,
    Though at next door we might meet;
Though she were true when you met her,
And last till you write your letter,
            Yet she
            Will be
False, ere I come, to two, or three.

MAN AND WIFE
(Robert Lowell, 1917–1977)

Tamed by *Miltown*,[1] we lie on Mother's bed;
the rising sun in war paint dyes us red;

---

[1] *Miltown:* tranquilizers.

in broad daylight her gilded bed-posts shine,
abandoned, almost Dionysian.
At last the trees are green on Marlborough Street,
blossoms on our magnolia ignite
the morning with their murderous five days' white.
All night I've held your hand,
as if you had
a fourth time faced the kingdom of the mad —
its hackneyed speech, its homicidal eye —
and dragged me home alive.... Oh my *Petite*,
clearest of all God's creatures, still all air and nerve:
you were in your twenties, and I,
once hand on glass
and heart in mouth,
outdrank the Rahvs in the heat
of Greenwich Village, fainting at your feet —
too boiled and shy
and poker-faced to make a pass,
while the shrill verve
of your invective scorched the traditional South.

Now twelve years later, you turn your back.
Sleepless, you hold
your pillow to your hollows like a child;
your old-fashioned tirade —
loving, rapid, merciless —
breaks like the Atlantic Ocean on my head.

TO HER AGAINE, SHE BURNING IN A FEAVER
(Thomas Carew, 1595–1640)

> Now she burnes as well as I,
> Yet my heat can never dye;
> She burnes that never knew desire,

She that was yce, she now is fire,
Shee whose cold heart, chaste thoughts did arme
So, as Love flames could never warme
The frozen bosome where it dwelt,
She burnes, and all her beauties melt;
She burnes, and cryes, Loves fires are milde;
Feavers are Gods, and He's a childe.
Love; let her know the difference
Twixt the heat of soule, and sence.
Touch her with thy flames divine,
So shalt thou quench her fire, and mine.

AUBADE
(Edith Sitwell, 1887–1964)

Jane, Jane,
Tall as a crane,
The morning light creaks down again;

Comb your cockscomb-ragged hair,
Jane, Jane, come down the stair.

Each dull blunt wooden stalactite
Of rain creaks, hardened by the light,

Sounding like an overtone
From some lonely world unknown.

But the creaking empty light
Will never harden into sight,

Will never penetrate your brain
With overtones like the blunt rain.

The light would show (if it could harden)
Eternities of kitchen garden,

Cockscomb flowers that none will pluck,
And wooden flowers that 'gin to cluck.

In the kitchen you must light
Flames as staring, red and white,

As carrots or as turnips, shining
Where the cold dawn light lies whining.

Cockscomb hair on the cold wind
Hangs limp, turns the milk's weak mind. . . .

Jane, Jane,
Tall as a crane,
The morning light creaks down again!

THE CHANCES OF RHYME
(Charles Tomlinson, 1927–)

The chances of rhyme are like the chances of meeting —
    In the finding fortuitous, but once found, binding:
They say, they signify and they succeed, where to succeed
    Means not success, but a way forward
If unmapped, a literal, not a royal succession;
    Though royal (it may be) is the adjective or region
That we, nature's royalty, are led into.
    Yes. We are led, though we seem to lead
Through a fair forest, an Arden (a rhyme
    For Eden) — breeding ground for beasts
Not bestial, but loyal and legendary, which is more
    Than nature's are. Yet why should we speak

Of art, of life, as if the one were all form
    And the other all Sturm-und-Drang?[1] And I think
Too, we should confine to Crewe or to Mow
    Cop, all those who confuse the fortuitousness
Of art with something to be met with only
    At extremity's brink, reducing thus
Rhyme to a kind of rope's end, a glimpsed grass
    To be snatched at as we plunge past it—
Nostalgic, after all, for a hope deferred.
    To take chances, as to make rhymes
Is human, but between chance and impenitence
    (A half-rhyme) come dance, vigilance
And circumstance (meaning all that is there)
    Besides you, when you are there). And between
Rest-in-peace and precipice,
    Inertia and perversion, comes the varieties
Increase, lease, re-lease (in both
    Senses); and immersion, conversion—of inert
Mass, that is, into energies to combat confusion.
    Let rhyme be my conclusion.

———

[1] *Sturm-und-Drang:* storm and stress (German).

Repetition

Repetition allows the speaker or writer to emphasize what is important. Repetition is dramatic and rhythmic. Repetition can have a hypnotic effect. In *The Act of Creation*, Arthur Koestler describes riding on a train at a time of confusion and self-blame in his life. In the sound of the wheels speeding along the rails Koestler heard, compulsively, *I told you so, I told you so, I told you so*, until he felt almost mad. In *Anna Karenina*, Leo Tolstoy uses repetition both for its emphatic and its hypnotic effects. Kitty sees Anna at a ball and realizes that the man she wants, Vronsky, is attracted to Anna instead of to her:

Some supernatural force drew Kitty's eyes to Anna's face. She was fascinating in her simple black dress, fascinating were her round arms with their bracelets, fascinating was her firm neck with its thread of pearls, fascinating the straying curls of her loose hair, fascinating the graceful, light movements of her little feet and hands, fascinating was that lovely face in its eagerness, but there was something terrible and cruel in her fascination.

The recurring word marks each new aspect of Anna, and keeps our attention as rapt as Kitty's as she stares at her rival. The repetition becomes more emphatic at the end when Tolstoy reverses the sentence order, thereby giving the most emphasis to the words "terrible and cruel," which are Kitty's conclusions about Anna's beauty.

In chants and spells, prayers and songs, speeches and novels, as well as in poetry, repetition underscores, making what is said emphatic and memorable. Repetition is naturally rhythmic; words are set in motion by their recurrence. Waves breaking, a clock pendulum swinging, the pumping of bicycle pedals — regular patterns of sound create an expectation that the sound and pace will continue. And repetition is dramatic. That a line or word — or sometimes an image or idea — recurs signals that the writer thinks it bears repeating. Unless the sound is repeated too often or goes on too long, our attention is held. Each nuance of repetition has a slightly different effect.

SINGLE WORD REPETITION   When dethroned King Lear fantasizes taking revenge on those who usurped him, he said, "Then Kill, Kill, Kill, Kill, Kill, Kill." With each repetition, the word becomes more intense, a little wilder and more sinister. When Macbeth says:

> Tomorrow, and tomorrow, and tomorrow
> Creeps in this petty pace from day to day,
> To the last syllable of recorded time
> And all our yesterdays have lighted fools
> The way to dusty death. Out, out, brief candle!

the repetition of "tomorrow" sounds wearier each time the word occurs. The two commas and two conjunctions stretch out the sound even more. The short monosyllables "out, out" contrast with "tomorrow." Shakespeare made frequent use of the technique of repeating a single word, often with subtly different inflections depending on the context. "O Cressid! O false Cressid! false, false, false," from *Troilus and Cressida*, sounds childlike and petulant. In *Richard II*, the triple use of "little" sounds smaller with each use:

> And my large kingdom for a little grave,
> A little, little grave, an obscure grave

That "large" also begins with *l* heightens the contrast between the "large kingdom" and the "little grave."

ANAPHORA   The beginning word or words of a line repeat.

NIGHT SONG
(Lisel Mueller, 1924–)

Among rocks, I am the loose one,
among arrows, I am the heart,
among daughters, I am the recluse,
among sons, the one who dies young.

Among answers, I am the question,
between lovers, I am the sword,
among scars, I am the fresh wound,
among confetti, the black flag.

Among shoes, I am the one with the pebble,
among days, the one that never comes,
among the bones you find on the beach
the one that sings was mine.

Anaphora gives a songlike quality to "Night Song." Mueller interrupts the repetition twice, once in the middle and again at the conclusion; these lines break the pattern and keep the poem from becoming too lulling.

The next poem not only uses anaphora but playfully piles on internal rhymes and end rhymes. Gertrude Stein is the queen of repetition; for years she experimented in novels and poems with the myriad effects of insistent repetition. This is a section from her longer work, "A Valentine for Sherwood Anderson":

A VERY VALENTINE
(Gertrude Stein, 1874–1946)

Very fine is my valentine.
Very fine and very mine.
Very mine is my valentine very mine and very fine.
Very fine is my valentine and mine, very fine very mine and
mine is my valentine.

COMBINED REPETITION   Lines, phrases, and single words repeat extensively, tightly unifying the poem.

A RED, RED ROSE
(Robert Burns, 1759–1796)

O, my luve is like a red, red rose,
    That's newly sprung in June;
O, my luve is like the melodie
    That's sweetly play'd in tune.

As fair art thou, my bonnie lass,
    So deep in luve am I;
And I will luve thee still, my dear,
    Till a' the seas gang dry.

Till a' the seas gang dry, my dear,
   And the rocks melt wi' the sun:
And I will love thee still, my dear,
   While the sands o' life shall run.

And fare thee well, my only luve,
   And fare thee well a while!
And I will come again, my luve,
   Tho' it were ten thousand mile!

REFRAINS   Whole stanzas, concluding lines of stanzas, or multiple lines recur. Folk poetry and songs, ballads, carols, and hymns often use this kind of repetition, which reiterates the primary emotion, lesson, or situation. Critic Justus Lawler, writing about a poem by Yeats, speculates that in "the repetition . . . there may be a clue to the fascination of all poetic refrains. Over and over, almost spirally, they proclaim the unity that awaits the faithful wayfarer at the end of each stanza of his journey and ultimately at journey's end itself."

LORD RANDAL
(Anonymous, fifteenth century[?])

"O where hae ye been, Lord Randal, my son?
O where hae ye been, my handsome young man?"
"I hae been to the wild wood; mother, make my bed soon,
For I'm weary wi' hunting, and fain wald lie down."

"Where gat ye your dinner, Lord Randal, my son?
Where gat ye your dinner, my handsome young man?"
"I dined wi' my true-love; mother, make my bed soon,
For I'm weary wi' hunting, and fain wald lie down."

"What gat ye to your dinner, Lord Randal, my son?
What gat ye to your dinner, my handsome young man?"

"I gat eels boiled in broo; mother, make my bed soon,
For I'm weary wi' hunting, and fain wald lie down."

"What became of your bloodhounds, Lord Randal, my son?
What became of your bloodhounds, my handsome young man?"
"O they swelled and they died; mother, make my bed soon,
For I'm weary wi' hunting, and fain wald lie down."

"O I fear ye are poisoned, Lord Randal, my son!
O I fear ye are poisoned, my handsome young man!"
"O yes! I am poisoned; mother, make my bed soon,
For I'm sick at the heart, and I fain wald lie down."

OPENING AND CLOSING REPETITION When a poem ends with a line identical or similar to the opening line, the reader feels a sense of closure, as though the poem completes a full circle. If the poem is effective, the repeated line has gathered momentum and significance at the end. The ends of the short poems which follow repeat their openings with very different results.

BREAKFAST
(Wilfrid Gibson, 1878–1962)

We ate our breakfast lying on our backs
Because the shells were screeching overhead.
I bet a rasher to a loaf of bread
That Hull United would beat Halifax
When Jimmy Stainthorpe played full-back instead
Of Billy Bradford. Ginger raised his head
And cursed, and took the bet, and dropt back dead.
We ate our breakfast lying on our backs
Because the shells were screeching overhead.

SNAIL
(Federico García Lorca, 1898–1936)

They have brought me a snail.

Inside it sings
a map-green ocean.
My heart
swells with water,
with small fish
of brown and silver.

They have brought me a snail.
                                        —Translated by William Jay Smith

IMAGE REPETITION   The poet works with the repetition of an image or repeats a certain kind of imagery, such as smell or textures. For example, if you follow the sensuous color imagery in Keats's "The Eve of St. Agnes" (page 115), you can plot the lovers' emotions. Cool, silvery-white imagery heats to rich purple and red. If in a poem you find repeated images of wings, fire, roses, knives, any object or sensation, the repetition is integral to the meaning of the poem.

In the novel *Moby Dick*, Herman Melville made use of the color white in the same way image repetition works in poetry. Melville's narrator, Ishmael, says, "It was the whiteness of the whale that above all things appalled me," then launches into a nine-page catalogue of beautiful, then dreadful, images of whiteness: Japonicas, pearls, white-forked flame, brides, sacred snow-white bulls, ermine, milk-white steeds, then white sharks, bears, the pallor of the dead, an albatross, murderers in white hoods, a white squall, Antarctic seas, frost, and more. As we discover at the end of this meditation, Ishmael finds all colors a mask for white, the annihilation of color:

> ...the sweet tinge of sunset skies and woods...gilded velvets of
> butterflies, and the butterfly cheeks of young girls; all these are

but subtile deceits, not actually inherent in substances, but only laid on from without; so that all deified Nature absolutely paints like the harlot, whose allurements cover nothing but the charnel-house within; and when we proceed further, and consider that the mystical cosmetic which produces every one of her hues, the great principle of light, for ever remains white or colorless in itself, and it operating without medium upon matter, would touch all objects, even tulips and hoses, with its own blank tinge — pondering all this, the palsied universe lies before us a leper; and like wilful travellers in Lapland, who refuse to wear colored and coloring glasses upon their eyes, so the wretched infidel gazes himself blind at the monumental white shroud that wraps all the prospect around him. And all of these things the Albino whale was the symbol. Wonder ye then at the fiery hunt?

Anyone who reads *Moby Dick* remembers this central and powerful poetic section. The meditation on white reveals Ishmael's most basic relationship to nature and religion, in addition to his relationship to the great whale.

In poetry, this kind of repetition also causes the image to gather force and to achieve many of the effects of sound repetition: emphasis, memory, unity. It's beyond our scope here, but if you consider the repetition of images, even certain words, within a writer's whole body of work, you can identify that writer's major themes and concerns.

SYNTACTICAL REPETITION   In syntactical repetition, a sentence structure or a part of a sentence structure repeats. **Syntax** is the pattern of the word order in a sentence or phrase. In Macbeth's speech quoted earlier (page 185), notice that the repetition of "tomorrow" is followed by "in this petty pace," "from day," "to day," "to the last syllable," "of recorded time": five prepositional phrases. Unlike verbs, which keep the sentence moving, prepositional phrases are merely directional; they point our attention toward the action. The repetition of this pattern is, like the "tomorrows," slow and weary.

Note the use of "if" and "you would" below:

IF YOU SAW ME WALKING
(Gerald Stern, 1925–)

If you saw me walking one more time on the island
you would know how much the end of August meant to me;

and if you saw me singing as I slid over the wet stones
you would know I was carrying the secret of life in my hip pocket.

If my lips moved too much
you would follow one step behind to protect me;

if I fell asleep too soon
you would cover me in light catalpa or dry willow.

Oh if I wore a brace you would help me, if I stuttered
you would hold my arm, if my heart beat with fear

you would throw a board across the channel, you would put
out a hand to catch me, you would carry me on your back.

If you saw me swim back and forth through the algae
you would know how much I love the trees floating under me;

and if you saw me hold my leaf up to the sun
you would know I was still looking for my roots;

and if you saw me burning wood
you would know I was trying to remember the smell of maple.

If I rushed down the road buttoning my blue shirt—
if I left without coffee—if I forgot my chewed-up pen—

you would know there was one more day of happiness
before the water rose again for another year.

Depending on the context, repetition of a grammatical construction can be humorous, obsessive, insistent, or can portray other moods. For instance, the repetition of ten short declarative sentences makes a clipped, unequivocal sequence. Syntax has a psychological effect. Stern's poem plays off our expectation of *if* constructions. *If* is usually followed by a consequence — a *then*. We expect logic, but Stern steps around logic into playful and personal consequence of *if*. He repeats a pattern but surprises us each time.

When a syntactical pattern is repeated, in poetry or prose, there's a reason. The writer wants to evoke a certain response. Sentences strung together with *and* and *but* and *or* have different impacts than four-word sentences. How many phrases are used, where verbs occur, what type they are — many syntactical choices are important to how the reader experiences the sentence. In prose as well as poetry, writers make psychological use of sentence structure. As an extreme, look at the movement of this wayward and wild sentence from the life of William Davenant in *Aubrey's Brief Lives:*

> He was a next servant (as I remember, a Page also) to Sir Fulke Grevil, Lord Brookes, with whom he lived to his death, which was that a servant of his (that had long wayted on him, and his Lordship had often told him that he would doe something for him, but did not, but still putt him off with delayes) as he was trussing up his Lord's pointes comeing from Stoole (for then their breeches were fastned to the doubletts with points; then came in hookes and eies; which not to have fastened was in my boy-hood a great crime) stabbed him.

 In Your Notebook:

Choose a subject such as a hurricane, a robbery, a house, or a gift and write ten lines all in one continuous sentence. Then write ten sentences using (as Gerald Stern did) a repetitive sentence construction.

The parentheses and phrases of mundame detail delay and delay (just like the servant was "putt off" by his master) the final revelation of violent death. The syntax of the sentence is revealing and funny.

DANGERS OF REPETITION

Repetition has pitfalls. If the recurring words do not continue to help the work progress, a terrible monotony can result. If you sing

> 99 bottles of beer on the wall
> 99 bottles of beer
> If one of those bottles should happen to fall
> 98 bottles of beer on the wall. . . .

through to its compulsive end, you may be ordered out of the car. Without variation, overuse deadens, especially in a long poem. Turn-of-the-century schoolchildren memorized long sections of Robert Southey's "The Cataract of Lodore":

from THE CATARACT OF LODORE
(Robert Southey, 1774–1843)

> Collecting, projecting,
> Receding and speeding,
> And shocking and rocking,
> And darting and parting,
> And threading and spreading,
> And whizzing and hissing,
> And dripping and skipping,
> And hitting and splitting,
> And shining and twining,
> And rattling and battling,
> And shaking and quaking,
> And pouring and roaring,
> And waving and raving,
> And tossing and crossing,

And flowing and going,
And running and stunning,
And foaming and roaming,
And dinning and spinning,
And dropping and hopping,
And working and jerking,
And guggling and struggling,
And heaving and cleaving,
And moaning and groaning;
And glittering and frittering,
And gathering and feathering,
And whitening and brightening,
And quivering and shivering,
And hurrying and skurrying,
And thundering and floundering;
Dividing and gliding and sliding,
And falling and bawling and sprawling,
And driving and riving and striving,
And sprinkling and twinkling and wrinkling,
And sounding and bounding and rounding,
And bubbling and troubling and doubling,
And grumbling and rumbling and tumbling,
And clattering and battering and shattering;

How long can such crazy repeating go on? This is only a brief section.
   With liveliness, with progression, however, a long repetitive form will sustain interest. "Jubilate Agno" (Rejoice in the Lamb) is over twelve hundred lines long. Christopher Smart repeats the words *let* and *for* throughout. He adapted the exhaulted form of the responsive readings in the Anglican Church liturgy to write, in part, about an ordinary subject, his cat Jeoffry. However Smart intended us to take his choice of liturgical form, if we're accustomed to responsive readings in a church, the antics of the cat running through that form add to the poem's humor. His sharp observation of the cat's personality and movement keeps the poem lively. You almost can watch the cat.

from JUBILATE AGNO
(Christopher Smart, 1722–1771)

For I will consider my Cat Jeoffry.

For he is the servant of the Living God duly and daily serving him.

For at the first glance of the glory of God in the East he worships
in his way.

For is this done by wreathing his body seven times round with
elegant quickness.

For then he leaps up to catch the musk, which is the blessing of
God upon his prayer.

For he rolls upon prank to work it in.

For having done duty and received blessing he begins to consider
himself.

For this he performs in ten degrees.

For first he looks upon his fore-paws to see if they are clean.

For secondly he kicks up behind to clear away there.

For thirdly he works it upon stretch with the fore-paws extended.

For fourthly he sharpens his paws by wood.

For fifthly he washes himself.

For Sixthly he rolls upon wash.

For Seventhly he fleas himself, that he may not be interrupted
upon the beat.

For Eighthly he rubs himself against a post.

For Ninthly he looks up for his instructions.

For Tenthly he goes in quest of food.

For having consider'd God and himself he will consider his
neighbour.

For if he meets another cat he will kiss her in kindness.

For when he takes his prey he plays with it to give it chance.

For one mouse in seven escapes by his dallying.

For when his day's work is done his business more properly begins.

For he keeps the Lord's watch in the night against the adversary.

For he counteracts the powers of darkness by his electrical skin &
glaring eyes.

For he counteracts the Devil, who is death, by brisking about the life.

For in his morning orisons he loves the sun and the sun loves him.

For he is of the tribe of Tiger.

For the Cherub Cat is a term of the Angel Tiger.

For he has the subtlety and hissing of a serpent, which in goodness he suppresses.

For he will not do destruction, if he is well-fed, neither will he spit without provocation.

For he purrs in thankfulness, when God tells him he's a good Cat.

For he is an instrument for the children to learn benevolence upon.

For every house is incompleat without him & a blessing is lacking in the spirit.

For the Lord commanded Moses concerning the cats at the departure of the Children of Israel from Egypt.

For every family had one cat at least in the bag.

For the English Cats are the best in Europe.

For he is the cleanest in the use of his fore-paws of any quadrupede.

For the dexterity of his defence is an instance of the love of God to him exceedingly.

For he is the quickest to his mark of any creature.

For he is tenacious of his point.

For he is a mixture of gravity and waggery.

For he knows that God is his Saviour.

For there is nothing sweeter than his peace when at rest.

For there is nothing brisker than his life when in motion.

For he is of the Lord's poor and so indeed is he called by benevolence perpetually—Poor Jeoffry! poor Jeoffry! the rat has bit thy throat.

For he can catch the cork and toss it again.

For he is hated by the hypocrite and miser.

For the former is afraid of detection.

For the latter refuses the charge.

For he camels his back to bear the first notion of business.
For he is good to think on, if a man would express himself
   neatly.
For he made a great figure in Egypt for his signal services.
For he killed the Icneumon-rat very pernicious by land.
For his ears are so acute that they sting again.
For from this proceeds the passing quickness of his attention.
For by stroaking of him I have found out electricity.
For I perceived God's light about him both wax and fire.
For the Electrical fire is the spiritual substance, which God sends
   from heaven to sustain the bodies both of man and beast.
For God has blessed him in the variety of his movements.
For, tho he cannot fly, he is an excellent clamberer.
For his motions upon the face of the earth are more than any
   other quadrupede.
For he can tread to all the measures upon the musick.
For he can swim for life.
For he can creep.

Repetition in this Navajo chant, addressed to a god, seems to invite
us to dance or sing. You might test the power of repetition by reading
this aloud. Its power magnifies if read by several voices in unison.

from THE NIGHT CHANT

In Tsegihi
In the house made of the dawn
In the house made of evening twilight
In the house made of dark cloud
In the house made of rain & mist, of pollen, of grasshoppers
Where the dark mist curtains the doorway
The path to which is on the rainbow
Where the zigzag lightning stands high on top
Where the he-rain stands high on top

O male divinity
With your moccasins of dark cloud, come to us
With your mind enveloped in dark cloud, come to us
With the dark thunder above you, come to us soaring
With the shapen cloud at your feet, come to us soaring
With the far darkness made of the dark cloud over your head,
    come to us soaring
With the far darkness made of the rain & mist over your head,
    come to us soaring
With the zigzag lightning flung out high over your head
With the rainbow hanging high over your head, come to us soaring
With the far darkness made of the rain & the mist on the ends of
    your wings, come to us soaring
With the far darkness of the dark cloud on the ends of your wings,
    come to us soaring
With the zigzag lightning, with the rainbow high on the ends of
    your wings, come to us soaring

With the near darkness made of the dark cloud of the rain & the
    mist, come to us
With the darkness on the earth, come to us

With these I wish the foam floating on the flowing water over the
    roots of the great corn
I have made your sacrifice
I have prepared a smoke for you
My feet restore for me
My limbs restore, my body restore, my mind restore, my voice
    restore for me
Today, take out your spell for me

Today, take away your spell for me
Away from me you have taken it
Far off from me it is taken
Far off you have done it

Happily I recover
Happily I become cool

My eyes regain their power, my head cools, my limbs regain their
    strength, I hear again

Happily the spell is taken off for me
Happily I walk, impervious to pain I walk, light within I walk,
    joyous I walk

Abundant dark clouds I desire
An abundance of vegetation I desire
An abundance of pollen, abundant dew, I desire

Happily may fair white corn come with you to the ends of the
    earth
Happily may fair yellow corn, fair blue corn, fair corn of all kinds,
    plants of all kinds, goods of all kinds, jewels of all kinds, come
    with you to the ends of the earth

With these before you, happily may they come with you
With these behind, below, above, around you, happily may they
    come with you
Thus you accomplish your tasks

Happily the old men will regard you
Happily the old women will regard you
The young men & the young women will regard you
The children will regard you
The chiefs will regard you

Happily as they scatter in different directions they will regard you
Happily as they approach their homes they will regard you
May their roads home be on the trail of peace
Happily may they all return

In beauty I walk
With beauty before me I walk
With beauty behind me I walk
With beauty above me I walk
With beauty above & about me I walk
It is finished in beauty
It is finished in beauty

Poems

I Hear America Singing
(Walt Whitman, 1819–1892)

I hear America singing, the varied carols I hear,
Those of mechanics, each one singing his as it should be blithe
  and strong,
The carpenter singing his as he measures his plank or beam,
The mason singing his as he makes ready for work, or leaves off
  work,
The boatman singing what belongs to him in his boat, the
  deckhand singing on the steamboat deck,
The shoemaker singing as he sits on his bench, the hatter singing
  as he stands,
The wood-cutter's song, the plowboy's on his way in the morning,
  or at noon intermission or at sundown,
The delicious singing of the mother, or of the young wife at work,
  or of the girl sewing or washing,
Each singing what belongs to him or her and to none else,
The day what belongs to the day — at night the party of young
  fellows, robust, friendly,
Singing with open mouths their strong melodious songs.

ATOMIC BRIDE
(Thomas Sayers Ellis, 1963–)

FOR ANDRE FOXXE

A good show
Starts in the
Dressing room

And works its way
To the stage.
Close the door.

Andre's cross-
dressing, what
A drag. All

The world loves
A bride, something
About those gowns.

A good wedding
Starts in the
Department store

And works its way
Into the photo album.
Close the door.

Andre's tying
The knot, what
A drag. Isn't he

Lovely? All
The world loves
A bachelor, some-

thing about glamour
& glitz, white
Shirts, lawsuits.

A good dog
Starts in the yard
And works its way

Into da house.
Close your eyes,
Andre's wide open.

One freak of the week
Per night, what
A drag. Isn't

He lovely? All
The world loves
A nuclear family,

Something about
A suburban home,
Chaos in order.

A good bride starts
In the laboratory
And works his way

To the church.
Close the door,
Andre's thinking

Things over, what
A drag. Isn't
He lovely? All

The world loves
A divorce, something
About broken vows.

A good war starts
In the courtroom
And works its way

To the album cover.
Close the door,
Andre's swearing in,

What a drag.
Isn't he lovely? All
The world loves

A star witness,
Something about
Cross-examination.

A good drug starts
In Washington
And works its way

To the dancefloor.
Close the door,
Andre's strungout,

What a drag,
Isn't he lovely? All
The world loves

Rhythm guitar.
Something about
Those warm chords.

A good skeleton
Starts in the closet
And works its way

To the top of the charts.
Start the organ.
Andre's on his way

Down the aisle,
Alone, what an encore. All
The world loves

An explosive ending.
Go ahead Andre,
Toss the bouquet.

SOMNAMBULE[1] BALLAD
(Federico García Lorca, 1898–1936)

Green, how much I want you green.
Green wind. Green branches.
The ship upon the sea
and the horse in the mountain.
With the shadow on her waist
she dreams on her balcony,
green flesh, hair of green,
and eyes of cold silver.

---

[1] *Somnambule:* sleepwalker.

Green, how much I want you green.
Beneath the gypsy moon,
all things look at her
but she cannot see them.
Green, how much I want you green.
Great stars of white frost
come with the fish of darkness
that opens the road of dawn.
The fig tree rubs the wind
with the sandpaper of its branches,
and the mountain, a filching cat,
bristles its bitter aloes.
But who will come? And from where?
She lingers on her balcony,
green flesh, hair of green,
dreaming of the bitter sea.

—Friend, I want to change
my horse for your house,
my saddle for your mirror,
my knife for your blanket.
Friend, I come bleeding,
from the passes of Cabra.
—If I could, young man,
this pact would be sealed.
But I am no more I,
nor is my house now my house.
—Friend, I want to die
decently in my bed.
Of iron, if it be possible,
with sheets of fine holland.
Do you not see the wound I have
from my breast to my thoat?
—Your white shirt bears
three hundred dark roses.

Your pungent blood oozes
around your sash.
But I am no more I,
nor is my house now my house.
—Let me climb at least
up to the high balustrades:
let me come! Let me come!
up to the green balustrades.
Balustrades of the moon
where the water resounds.

Now the two friends go up
towards the high balustrades.
Leaving a trail of blood,
leaving a trail of tears.
Small lanterns of tin
were trembling on the roofs.
A thousand crystal tambourines
were piercing the dawn.

Green, how much I want you green,
green wind, green branches.
The two friends went up.
The long wind was leaving
in the mouth a strange taste
of gall, mint and sweet-basil.
Friend! Where is she, tell me,
where is your bitter girl?
How often she waited for you!
How often did she wait for you,
cool face, black hair,
on this green balcony!

Over the face of the cistern
the gypsy girl swayed.

Green flesh, hair of green,
with eyes of cold silver.
An icicle of the moon
suspends her above the water.
The night became as intimate
as a little square.
Drunken civil guards
were knocking at the door.
Green, how much I want you green.
Green wind. Green branches.
The ship upon the sea.
And the horse on the mountain.

— Translated by Stephen Spender and J. L. Gili

IN CHALK ROOMS
(Aina Kraujiete, 1923–)

let all the walls
about me be green
like a whole harvest
of summer's meadows
walls like light
sliding through green bottle-glass
walls like forest
moss-grown and damp
walls like mouldy
cheese on a knife
and walls like frogs
so cool and loud
walls with gentleness
like budding leaves
walls of juiciness
as of chopped turnip tops

walls in that tone
    in which rain soaks moss
and yellowed like cabbage
    butterflies abandoning cocoon
walls hard and green
    corrugated wet
encompassing me
    as have only woods and waters.

           but the world listens
           to me as to a gnat's song
           though I suffer terrible
           famine for greenness
           —Translated by Inara Cedrins

RESIDUE
(Carlos Drummond de Andrade, 1902–1987)

Of everything, a little stayed.
Of my fear. Of your temper.
Of stammered screams. Of the rose,
a little.

A little of the light stayed
pooled in the hat.
In the bully's eyes
a trace stayed, of gentleness
(only one).

A little of the dust
with which your white shoe
was covered. Random
clothes, some mass-veils, rotted,
a little, a little, a touch.

But of everything, a little stays.
Of the blasted bridge,
of two stalks of grass,
of the empty
box of cigarettes, a little stayed.

For of everything, a little stays.
The line of your chin stayed
in your daughter's.
Of your dry silence,
a little stayed, a little
in the angry walls,
in non-vocal leaves which spin.

A little of everything stayed
in the china saucer,
cracked dragon, pale flower;
the lines on your brow,
I mirror.

If a little stays of everything,
why shouldn't something mine stay,
too? in the train
running north, on a ship,
in newspaper ads;
a little of me in London,
some farther off?
in the consonant?
in the well?

A little buoy's in the drift
at the river's mouth
and fish don't mind it,
a little, it's not in books.

Of everything a little stays.
Not much: from the faucet drips
this ludicrous drop
half alcohol, half salt,
this frog-leg that leaps,
this wrist watch lens
split in a thousand hopes,
this swan neck,
this secret, infantile ...
Of everything, a little stays:
of me, of you; of Abelard.
Hair on my sleeve,
of everything a little stays,
wind in these ears,
buffoon burp, groan

from the abused entrails,
and tiny artifacts:
glass bell, honeycomb, shell
of revolver ... aspirin.
Of everything, a little stays.
Oh, open the lotion bottles
and smother
the intolerable stench of memory.

But of everything terrible, a little stays,
and under the beating waves
and under the clouds and the winds
and under the bridges and the tunnels
and under the flames and under the sarcasm
and under the drool and under the vomit
and under the sob within the cell, the forgotten prisoner
and under the performances and the scarlet death
and under the libraries, the asylums, the triumphant churches

and under you yourself and under your feet, half stiff already,
and under the gross canopy of family and class,
a little something always stays.
A button, sometimes. Sometimes a rat.

—Translated by Virginia de Araújo

TO GO TO LVOV
(Adam Zagajewski, 1945–)

To go to Lvov. Which station
for Lvov, if not in a dream, at dawn, when dew
gleams on a suitcase, when express
trains and bullet trains are being born. To leave
in haste for Lvov, night or day, in September
or in March. But only if Lvov exists,
if it is to be found within the frontiers and not just
in my new passport, if lances of trees
—of poplar and ash—still breathe aloud
like Indians, and if streams mumble
their dark Esperanto, and grass snakes like soft signs
in the Russian language disappear
into thickets. To pack and set off, to leave
without a trace, at noon, to vanish
like fainting maidens. And burdocks, green
armies of burdocks, and below, under the canvas
of a Venetian café, the snails converse
about eternity. But the cathedral rises,
you remember, so straight, as straight
as Sunday and white napkins and a bucket
full of raspberries standing on the floor, and
my desire which wasn't born yet,
only gardens and weeds and the amber
of Queen Anne cherries, and indecent Fredro.
There was always too much of Lvov, no one could

comprehend its boroughs, hear
the murmur of each stone scorched
by the sun, at night the Orthodox church's silence was unlike
that of the cathedral, the Jesuits
baptized plants, leaf by leaf, but they grew,
grew so mindlessly, and joy hovered
everywhere, in hallways and in coffee mills
revolving by themselves, in blue
teapots, in starch, which was the first
formalist, in drops of rain and in the thorns
of roses. Frozen forsythia yellowed by the window.
The bells pealed and the air vibrated, the cornets
of nuns sailed like schooners near
the theater, there was so much of the world that
it had to do encores over and over,
the audience was in frenzy and didn't want
to leave the house. My aunts couldn't have known
yet that I'd resurrect them,
and lived so trustfully, so singly;
servants, clean and ironed, ran for
fresh cream, inside the houses
a bit of anger and great expectation, Brzozowski
came as a visiting lecturer, one of my
uncles kept writing a poem entitled *Why*,
dedicated to the Almighty, and there was too much
of Lvov, it brimmed the container,
it burst glasses, overflowed
each pond, lake, smoked through every
chimney, turned into fire, storm,
laughed with lightning, grew meek,
returned home, read the New Testament,
slept on a sofa beside the Carpathian rug,
there was too much of Lvov, and now
there isn't any, it grew relentlessly
and the scissors cut it, chilly gardeners

as always in May, without mercy,
without love, ah, wait till warm June
comes with soft ferns, boundless
fields of summer, i.e., the reality.
But scissors cut it, along the line and through
the fiber, tailors, gardeners, censors
cut the body and the wreaths, pruning shears worked
diligently, as in a child's cutout
along the dotted line of a roe deer or a swan.
Scissors, penknives, and razor blades scratched,
cut, and shortened the voluptuous dresses
of prelates, of squares and houses, and trees
fell soundlessly, as in a jungle,
and the cathedral trembled, people bade goodbye
without handkerchiefs, no tears, such a dry
mouth, I won't see you anymore, so much death
awaits you, why must every city
become Jerusalem and every man a Jew,
and now in a hurry just
pack, always, each day,
and go breathless, go to Lvov, after all
it exists, quiet and pure as
a peach. It is everywhere.

—Translated by Renata Gorczynski

LUCKY LIFE
(Gerald Stern, 1925–)

Lucky life isn't one long string of horrors
and there are moments of peace, and pleasure, as I lie in between
    the blows.
Lucky I don't have to wake up in Phillipsburg, New Jersey,
on the hill overlooking Union Square or the hill overlooking

Kuebler Brewery or the hill overlooking SS. Philip and James
but have my own hills and my own vistas to come back to.

Each year I go down to the island I add
one more year to the darkness;
and though I sit up with my dear friends
trying to separate the one year from the other,
this one from the last, that one from the former,
another from another,
after a while they all get lumped together,
the year we walked to Holgate,
the year our shoes got washed away,
the year it rained,
the year my tooth brought misery to us all.

This year was a crisis. I knew it when we pulled
the car onto the sand and looked for the key.
I knew it when we walked up the outside steps
and opened the hot icebox and began the struggle
with swollen drawers and I knew it when we laid out
the sheets and separated the clothes into piles
and I knew it when we made our first rush onto
the beach and I knew it when we finally sat
on the porch with coffee cups shaking in our hands.

My dream is I'm walking through Phillipsburg, New Jersey,
and I'm lost on South Main Street. I am trying to tell,
by memory, which statue of Christopher Columbus
I have to look for, the one with him slumped over
and lost in weariness or the one with him
vaguely guiding the way with a cross and globe in
one hand and a compass in the other.
My dream is I'm in the Eagle Hotel on Chamber Street
sitting at the oak bar, listening to two

obese veterans discussing Hawaii in 1942,
and reading the funny signs over the bottles.
My dream is I sleep upstairs over the honey locust
and sit on the side porch overlooking the stone culvert
with a whole new set of friends, mostly old and humorless.

Dear waves, what will you do for me this year?
Will you drown out my scream?
Will you let me rise through the fog?
Will you fill me with that old salt feeling?
Will you let me take my long steps in the cold sand?
Will you let me lie on the white bedspread and study
the black clouds with the blue holes in them?
Will you let me see the rusty trees and the old monoplanes one
    more year?
Will you still let me draw my sacred figures
and move the kites and the birds around with my dark mind?

Lucky life is like this. Lucky there is an ocean to come to.
Lucky you can judge yourself in this water.
Lucky the waves are cold enough to wash out the meanness.
Lucky you can be purified over and over again.
Lucky there is the same cleanliness for everyone.
Lucky life is like that. Lucky life. Oh lucky life.
Oh lucky lucky life. Lucky life.

6

Meter: The Measured Flow

Poetry is nothing but time, rhythm perpetually creative.
—OCTAVIO PAZ

Put your finger on your pulse and feel the most basic rhythm we know: the tension/relaxation, tick/tock, yes/no, systole/diastole of our own circulation. All life on earth is rhythmic. Tides, breath, electro-magnetic fields, sound waves, sleep, the moon's phases, the mating dance of mockingbirds, even traffic on the freeway—each has its own pulse rate. From the rapid rhythm of our hearts pumping seventy barrels of blood a day, to the seventeen-year cycle of cicadas, to the slow orbit of a comet sweeping by every ninety years, there is intrinsic periodicity to life and nature.

The heartbeat is the rhythm of our earliest experience. The fetus curls close to the mother's heart. Once born, the baby is rocked back and forth. When the child can stand, he loves to bounce rhythmically in the crib and rattle the side slats. Long before the words make sense, the child holds up his hands to play Pat-a-Cake and moves his head to the beat of Mother Goose rhymes. The playground swing and seesaw:

back and forth, up and down. Rhythm is pleasurable. Later, he learns that rhythm is a key to most sports. The tennis or golf swing is a whole flow of acts in one motion. In football, synchronization with team-mates is crucial. To get a horse smoothly over a jump requires finding a rhythm that has to be set in motion long before the actual leap. Lovemaking, dancing, cooking, working on assembly lines — so much everyday living involves rhythm that we take its presence for granted.

From ancient times to the present, the song-stories of work, wars, and love have passed down the folk tradition in rhythmic forms. Chain gangs, field workers, railroaders, laborers of all kinds have joined the motions of their work to song and verse, both to facilitate the actual work motions and to lighten their labors.

LAMENT WHILE DESCENDING A SHAFT

> Down in the hole we go, boys,
> Down in the hole we go.
> The nine hundred level
> Is hot as the devil —
> I envy the man with the hoe.

Wisconsin river drivers at the turn of the twentieth century sang:

STIRLING'S HOTEL

There's old Molly Hogan who cooks from a book,
She's the chief chambermaid and the past-e-ry cook,
The pies that she bakes us, good God, how they smell!
A dog wouldn't eat them at Stirling's Hotel.

There's old Jack McKissick who cuts wood for his board:
But fishes instead, wouldn't work if he could.
The fish that he catches, good God, how they smell!
A dog wouldn't eat them at Stirling's Hotel.

And old Ed Starkes who works in the saloon,
The drinks that he gives, you could hold in a spoon.
For these little drinks he charges like hell,
And he gets all the money 'round Stirling's Hotel.

All our beds they are crummy with bugs and with lice,
And holes in the walls seem to vomit the mice;
And the breeze from the pantry has an old rotten smell,
It revives all the boarders at Stirling's Hotel.

"Clementine," "I've Been Working on the Railroad," "Blow the Man Down," and countless other sea chanteys, field songs, schoolyard tunes, and other handed-down songs preserve the distant rhythms of our ancestors' lives. Most of the poems and songs we know "by heart" are rhythmic — with rhymes, repetitive beats, alliteration, and other patterns of sound.

Meter is a strong element of rhythm. **Meter,** or *measure,* is the organization of words' accents into a pattern. Like rhyme and other patterns of sound, meter aids our recall and helps keep our attention on the unfolding of the poem or song. That the same sound comes around again rewards our expectations.

What Is Meter?

Language is rhythmical. Our voices naturally rise and fall, pause for breath, accent some syllables more than others, and intensify tone for emphasis. We speak of the Irish "lilt," the Southern "drawl," the Midwestern "twang," "rapid-fire" French, "musical" Italian. All these characteristics are part of inflection and pace. Each aspect of rhythm — rhyme, repetition, sound patterns, line, and meter — occurs in normal spoken and written English; as devices of poetry they are organized and heightened.

The unit of measurement in a metered poem is called a **foot**, reminding us that the original Greek rhythms were based on dance; some slow and steady, others ecstatic and wild. Much of the satisfaction of a regular beat stems from our breathing, turning, movement of muscles. If we no longer get up and dance around a stone altar or even sing the poem, subtle effects of meter still appeal to primary origins.

No *single* effect makes the rhythm of a poem. The call of an auctioneer in a tobacco barn, the words you put to the swish-swish of the windshield wipers, or the hypnotically repeated prayer of an old man on a park bench can remind us that rhythm is a part of a complex, overall perception. As the Spanish poet García Lorca warned, "Beneath all the statistics, there's a drop of duck's blood." Beyond all analysis, there is a mystery to rhythm, an essence or an energy as urgent and as unaccountable as our own heartbeat.

A poem is in meter if words are chosen and arranged so that accents (stresses) occur in a regular pattern. The meter of a poem works much like the beat of a song. It establishes a basic timing by organizing sounds. Of course absolute regularity of recurrence quickly gets monotonous. Poets usually vary meter or change it suddenly for emphasis. Musicians call this switch of timing **syncopation.** Some poets refer to it as *metrical tension* or *counterpoint.*

Listening carefully to the rise and fall of your own voice, say aloud these lines by Alfred, Lord Tennyson:

> The splendor falls on castle walls
> And snowy summits old in story:
> The long light shakes across the lakes,
> And the wild cataract leaps in glory.

and from A. E. Housman:

> And time shall put them both to bed
> But she shall lie with earth above,
> And he beside another love.

Your voice quickly "hears" a meter. You naturally emphasize, or **accent,** some words more than others. These stronger accents alternate with "weaker" sounds.

A thorough study of meter could be a life's work. Scholars have devised complex systems for evaluating the relative time and sound duration of accents on syllables as well as musical schemes for plotting meter. Such specialized theories are not our concern now. What concerns us is understanding basic metrical structure. We look at meter to see *how* it works concurrently with the poem's subject.

Scansion

Let's look at the easiest technique for discovering a poem's meter. In the Tennyson and Housman lines, if you mark the emphasized syllables with accents (´) and the unstressed syllables with the symbol ˘, you discover a pattern:

> The splen/dor falls/ on cas/tle walls
> And snow/y sum/mits old/ in story:
> The long/ light shakes/ across/ the lakes,
> And the wild/ cata/ract leaps /in glory.

and:

> And time/ shall put/ them both/ to bed
> But she/ shall lie/ with earth/ above.
> And he/ beside/ anoth/er love.

In the text, slashes (/) indicate where the metrical pattern starts to repeat; notice that the division can fall in the middle of a word. This process of noting accents and their intervals of recurrence is called **scansion.**

Scanning the lines above, we find the accents repeat in a two-syllable pattern: ˘´/˘´/˘´/˘´/. Each repeating set is called a foot. Both the Tennyson and Housman have four-foot patterns. Poems with four-foot lines are called *tetrameter*, meaning "four measures." But notice the variations. In the Tennyson lines a leftover *-y* hangs off *story* and *glory*. This kind of tag-end is metrically insignificant and is usually ignored. The fourth line departs radically from the pattern. Variations like these are important. In scanning a poem, first note the prevailing meter: that's the basic timing of the poem. Then see how the departures are working. "And the wild cataract leaps in glory" scrambles the lulling rhythm of the first three lines. "Wild cataract leaps" has four accents packed together. This intensifies the sudden motion of the cataract in contrast to the peace and quiet of the first lines.

Depending on the number of feet, lines are called: **monometer** (one foot), **dimeter** (two feet), **trimeter** (three feet), **tetrameter** (four feet), **pentameter** (five feet), **hexameter** or alexandrine (six feet), **heptameter** (seven feet), **octameter** (eight feet).

Identifying the number of feet is half the process of scansion. The other half is determining the order of the accents. The most common order in English poetry is an unaccented syllable (˘) followed by an accented syllable (´). This pair (˘´) is called an **iamb,** or an **iambic foot.** The overall accent pattern of the Tennyson and Housman lines above is iambic tetrameter.

Other important syllable patterns in English are:

´ ˘   **trochee:** óxfŏrd, áftĕr, stágnănt, bóxĕr
˘ ˘ ´   **anapest:** ănd thĕ móon, intĕrtwíne
´ ´   **spondee:** déadhéad, ríckráck, bíllbóard, póstcárd, "Nó, nó"

Of course the spondee cannot be sustained as a meter, since it consists of two strong stresses. It serves as a variation in a line for emphasis.

Other less common syllable patterns include:

´ ˘ ˘	dactyl
˘ ˘	pyrrhic
´ ˘ ´	cretic (also called amphimacer)
´ ´ ´	molossos
´ ˘ ˘ ´	choriamb
˘ ´ ˘	amphibrach
˘ ´ ´	bacchius
´ ´ ˘	antibacchius
˘ ˘ ˘	tribrach

Of these, the **dactyl** (as in métrĭcăl, déspĕrăte) turns up occasionally. Except to a specialist, most of the others are not of significant importance in reading a poem.

Scanning is not a precise technique. If you scan a line of a poem and compare it with someone else's version, you'll see differences. You may hear *billboard* as a spondee; someone else may hear it as a trochee. You may hear phrases differently according to your mood or emotions, which can change the way you accent words. What is important is discovering the overall metrical scheme and where and why there are variations. Don't look for rigid adherence to a meter—too much evenness makes dull poetry. Many poems begin strongly stressed, then shift into another pattern. Poets frequently want opening words to be dramatic so the reader is drawn right into the poem. Even if you scan just as the poet did, the meter will have reversals and gaps in it—spondees, extra syllables, or other feet.

To become comfortable with scansion, mark the accents in these words:

volume	difference	ornament
in a door	and the cat	interject
as they sang	blessing	under the
mystical	season	morning
endure	retire	lyrical

| lexicon | tietack | family |
| heartbreak | dog food | along |

If you want to practice scanning until it becomes familiar, reading aloud will help you determine how accents fall. Count a poem's syllables per line for a clue to meter: If there are eight or ten, the poem probably is in one of the most common meters, tetrameter or pentameter. Then mark the accents. Try scanning the following lines by Thomas Traherne or whole poems at the end of the chapter.

> How like an angel came I down!
>   How bright are all things here
> When first among his works I did appear,
>   O how their glory did me crown!
> The world resembled his eternity,
>   In which my soul did walk,
> And everything that I did see
>   Did with me talk.

Iambic Pentameter

Iambic pentameter is the most important meter in English. Five sets of two-syllable feet in the unaccented/accented pattern form the iambic pentameter line:

> Hŏw cán/ wĕ knów/ thĕ dánc/ĕr fróm/ thĕ dánce?

Besides a connection to the heartbeat, the iamb and trochee (the other two-syllable foot), correspond to the back-and-forth movement of walking, sowing, and rowing—some of the most basic human activities. Possibly some of our pleasure in meter comes from these organic connections. Greek legend says that the iamb rhythm originated not from such fundamentals but from a dance imitating the motions of a crippled quail! Whatever the origin of the meter, the pattern suits our muscular English language with its many consonants and alternating accents.

Iambic pentameter proves especially flexible as a meter. The five-foot line corresponds to a common sentence length: It's long enough to accommodate subject, verb, and object or prepositional phrase and short enough to say in one breath. In skillful hands, this makes iambic pentameter adaptable to a believable approximation of natural speech, even though the language is artificially arranged. This is not to say, as is often claimed, that English is naturally iambic. We do not walk around speaking in prevailing iambs. If you scan a newspaper article or a conversation, you will find no pattern of accents.

Read "Once by the Pacific" aloud, noticing how with each new line you breathe out or in. Even with a tight aabbccddeeffgg rhyme scheme and iambic pentameter, Robert Frost's poem keeps the cadence of a speaking voice.

ONCE BY THE PACIFIC
(Robert Frost, 1874–1963)

The shattered water made a misty din,
Great waves looked over others coming in,
And thought of doing something to the shore
That water never did to land before.
The clouds were low and hairy in the skies
Like locks blown forward in the gleam of eyes.
You could not tell, and yet it looked as if
The sand was lucky in being backed by cliff,
The cliff in being backed by continent.
It looked as if a night of dark intent
Was coming, and not only a night, an age.
Someone had better be prepared for rage.
There would be more than ocean water broken
Before God's last *Put out the light* was spoken.

When iambic pentameter is not rhymed, we call it **blank verse.** Because blank verse is even more adaptable to speech than rhymed iambic pentameter, Shakespeare chose to write his plays in it, often alternating blank verse sections with prose. You may read poems and plays in blank verse without being conscious of meter at all. So subtle are the effects that Samuel Johnson, the eighteenth-century writer, remarked that blank verse was verse for the eye alone. He meant that the iambic pentameter retains the same visual appearance of metered poetry, but the inconspicuous modulations of sound without rhyme make blank verse seem close to spoken English.

This discreet control gives blank verse power. The meter provides a light yoke of form without the appearance of artifice.

from AS YOU LIKE IT
(William Shakespeare, 1564–1616)

(ACT II, SCENE VII)

   All the world's a stage,
And all the men and women merely players:
They have their exits and their entrances;
And one man in his time plays many parts,
His acts being seven ages. At first the infant,
Mewling and puking in the nurse's arms.
And then the whining schoolboy, with his satchel,
And shining morning face, creeping like snail
Unwilling to school. And then the lover,
Sighing like furnace, with a woeful ballad
Made to his mistress' eyebrow. Then a soldier,
Full of strange oaths, and bearded like the pard,[1]
Jealous in honour, sudden and quick in quarrel,
Seeking the bubble reputation
Even in the cannon's mouth. And then the justice,

---

[1] *pard:* leopard.

In fair round belly with good capon lined,
With eyes severe and beard of formal cut,
Full of wise saws and modern instances;
And so he plays his part. The sixth age shifts
Into the lean and slippered pantaloon,
With spectacles on nose, and pouch on side;
His youthful hose, well saved, a world too wide
For his shrunk shank; and his big manly voice,
Turning again toward childish treble, pipes
And whistles in his sound. Last scene of all,
That ends this strange eventful history,
Is second childishness and mere oblivion,
Sans teeth, sans eyes, sans taste, sans everything.

An experienced actor can say these lines with naturalness. As you read aloud, you sense the alternating stresses in the sound of your voice—this alternation has a regularity prose lacks—but the meter hardly reveals itself otherwise. Rhyme makes a poem more noticeably a formal *object*. Blank verse, although capable of highly formal utterances, is closer to speech. Since meter is largely for the ear, not the eye, you catch it most readily when you read all poems aloud.

Blank verse provides poets with a distinctive, malleable tempo. In the seventeenth century, John Milton used blank verse for *Paradise Lost*, a long chronicle of Adam and Eve's fall from innocence. Blank verse accommodates itself to such extended works because it gives the poet a skeletal framework on which to build without making that framework invasive. John Dryden, a contemporary, was appalled by Milton's choice. Dryden wrote, "For imagination in a poet is a faculty so wild and lawless that, like an high-ranging spaniel, it must have clogs tied to it, less it outrun the judgment. The great easiness of blank verse renders the poet too luxuriant." Even so, most poets, then and now, frequently loosen or vary even the "luxuriant" blank verse. Syncopation saves any meter from falling into a sing-song silliness or hypnotic monotony. In the next poem, blank verse is the base line for Wallace Stevens. If you scan the whole poem, you'll find other types of feet used in almost every line, but the overall movement of the poem keeps to blank verse — unrhymed iambic pentameter.

SUNDAY MORNING
(Wallace Stevens, 1879–1955)

I

Complacencies of the peignoir, and late
Coffee and oranges in a sunny chair,
And the green freedom of a cockatoo
Upon a rug mingle to dissipate
The holy hush of ancient sacrifice.
She dreams a little, and she feels the dark
Encroachment of that old catastrophe,
As a calm darkens among water-lights.
The pungent oranges and bright, green wings
Seem things in some procession of the dead,
Winding across wide water, without sound.
The day is like wide water, without sound.
Stilled for the passing of her dreaming feet
Over the seas, to silent Palestine,
Dominion of the blood and sepulchre.

II

Why should she give her bounty to the dead?
What is divinity if it can come
Only in silent shadows and in dreams?
Shall she not find in comforts of the sun,
In pungent fruit and bright, green wings, or else
In any balm or beauty of the earth,
Things to be cherished like the thought of heaven?
Divinity must live within herself:
Passions of rain, or moods in a falling snow;

Grievings in loneliness, or unsubdued
Elations when the forest blooms; gusty
Emotions on wet roads on autumn nights;
All pleasures and all pains, remembering
The bough of summer and the winter branch.
These are the measures destined for her soul.

III

Jove in the clouds had his inhuman birth.
No mother suckled him, no sweet land gave
Large-mannered motions to his mythy mind.
He moved among us, as a muttering king,
Magnificent, would move along his hinds,
Until our blood, commingling, virginal,
With heaven, brought such requital to desire
The very hinds discerned it, in a star.
Shall our blood fail? Or shall it come to be
The blood of paradise? And shall the earth
Seem all of paradise that we shall know?
The sky will be much friendlier then than now,
A part of labor and a part of pain,
And next in glory to enduring love,
Not this dividing and indifferent blue.

IV

She says, "I am content when wakened birds,
Before they fly, test the reality
Of misty fields, by their sweet questionings;
But when the birds are gone, and their warm fields
Return no more, where, then, is paradise?"
There is not any haunt of prophecy,
Nor any old chimera of the grave,
Neither the golden underground, nor isle

Melodious, where spirits gat them home,
No visionary south, nor cloudy palm
Remote on heaven's hill, that has endured
As April's green endures; or will endure
Like her remembrance of awakened birds,
Or her desire for June and evening, tipped
By the consummation of the swallow's wings.

V

She says, "But in contentment I still feel
The need of some imperishable bliss."
Death is the mother of beauty; hence from her,
Alone, shall come fulfilment to our dreams
And our desires. Although she strews the leaves
Of sure obliteration on our paths,
The path sick sorrow took, the many paths
Where triumph rang its brassy phrase, or love
Whispered a little out of tenderness,
She makes the willow shiver in the sun
For maidens who were wont to sit and gaze
Upon the grass, relinquished to their feet.
She causes boys to pile new plums and pears
On disregarded plate. The maidens taste
And stray impassioned in the littering leaves.

VI

Is there no change of death in paradise?
Does ripe fruit never fall? Or do the boughs
Hang always heavy in that perfect sky,
Unchanging, yet so like our perishing earth,
With rivers like our own that seek for seas
They never find, the same receding shores
That never touch with inarticulate pang?

Why set the pear upon those river-banks
Or spice the shores with odors of the plum?
Alas, that they should wear our colors there,
The silken weavings of our afternoons,
And pick the strings of our insipid lutes!
Death is the mother of beauty, mystical,
Within whose burning bosom we devise
Our earthly mothers waiting, sleeplessly.

VII

Supple and turbulent, a ring of men
Shall chant in orgy on a summer morn
Their boisterous devotion to the sun,
Not as a god, but as a god might be,
Naked among them, like a savage source.
Their chant shall be a chant of paradise,
Out of their blood, returning to the sky;
And in their chant shall enter, voice by voice,
The windy lake wherein their lord delights,
The trees, like serafin, and echoing hills,
That choir among themselves long afterward,
They shall know well the heavenly fellowship
Of men that perish and of summer morn.
And whence they came and whither they shall go
The dew upon their feet shall manifest.

VIII

She hears, upon that water without sound,
A voice that cries, "The tomb in Palestine
Is not the porch of spirits lingering.
It is the grave of Jesus, where he lay."
We live in an old chaos of the sun.
Or old dependency of day and night.

Or island solitude, unsponsored, free,
Of that wide water, inescapable.
Deer walk upon our mountains, and the quail
Whistle about us their spontaneous cries;
Sweet berries ripen in the wilderness;
And, in the isolation of the sky,
At evening, casual flocks of pigeons make
Ambiguous undulations as they sink,
Downward to darkness, on extended wings.

More Key Meters

Iambic pentameter is the predominant choice of metrical poets writing in English. Though other meters are less flexible or harder to sustain, each has characteristics that are useful in different poetic situations.

The next poems illustrate different qualities of some standard meters. Meter, of course, determines line length. In each poem, notice how the metrical line length influences your reading pace: The line is a unit of time, and therefore has a major effect on the poem's rhythm.

IAMBIC TETRAMETER (˘ ´ ˘ ´ ˘ ´ ˘ ´)

With four feet, the iambic tetrameter line moves slightly faster than pentameter. The quickened tempo of a shorter line intensifies the rhythm and therefore the meaning. The shorter a line, the quicker the eye moves down the page. More vertical space is covered. The poem is falling, plunging, speeding rather than spreading across the page. Iambic tetrameter is shorter than pentameter, more compressed, with a slightly rushed breath rhythm. It is still long enough to seem close to speech. "The Passionate Shepherd to His Love" (page 140) is a fine example of the meter's virtues. We hear the shepherd's voice; the speed of tetrameter adds to his urgency and passion. The following poem is another of the meter's great moments:

TO HIS COY MISTRESS
(Andrew Marvell, 1621–1678)

Had we but World enough, and Time,
This coyness Lady were no crime.
We would sit down, and think which way
To walk, and pass our long Loves Day.
Thou by the Indian Ganges side
Should'st Rubies find: I by the Tide
Of Humber[1] would complain. I would
Love you ten years before the Flood:
And you should, if you please, refuse
Till the Conversion of the Jews.
My vegetable Love should grow
Vaster than Empires, and more slow.
An hundred years should go to praise
Thine Eyes, and on thy Forehead Gaze.
Two hundred to adore each Breast:
But thirty thousand to the rest.
An Age at least to every part,
And the last Age should show your Heart.
For Lady you deserve this State;
Nor would I love at lower rate.

But at my back I alwaies hear
Times winged Charriot hurrying near:
And yonder all before us lye
Deserts of vast Eternity.
Thy Beauty shall no more be found;
Nor, in thy marble Vault, shall sound
My ecchoing Song: then Worms shall try
That long preserv'd Virginity:
And your quaint Honour turn to dust;

---

[1] *Humber:* a river in Marvell's native area of Hull, England.

And into ashes all my Lust.
The Grave's a fine and private place,
But none I think do there embrace.
    Now therefore, while the youthful hew[2]
Sits on thy skin like morning glew,[3]
And while thy willing Soul transpires
At every pore with instant Fires,
Now let us sport us while we may;
And now, like am'rous birds of prey,
Rather at once our Time devour
Than languish in his slow-chapt[4] pow'r.
Let us roll all our Strength, and all
Our sweetness, up into one Ball:
And tear our Pleasures with rough strife,
Thorough the Iron gates of Life.
Thus, though we cannot make our Sun
Stand still, yet we will make him run.

---

[2] *hew*: hue.
[3] *glew*: glow.
[4] *slow-chapt*: slow jawed.

TROCHAIC TRIMETER (´˘ / ´˘ / ´˘)

A trochaic foot (´˘) reverses the iambic foot (˘´). Stress comes first.
The trochaic DA-da DA-da DA-da DA-da sound is called a **falling
rhythm,** whereas the iambic da-DA da-DA da-DA da-DA is a **rising
rhythm.** The sound falls off from the stress in the trochee and rises to
the stress in the iamb. In "To a Skylark," the short lines seem to "float
and run" like the bird. Each stanza ends with a stretched-out line.
The rhythm expands, contracts. This changes not only the rhythm
but the look of the poem on the page. Eye and ear respond to the sud-
den overflow into the longer meter, which is usually iambic hexame-
ter. Short meters are difficult to maintain for long because they easily
become monotonous. Shelley, by adding a longer line to each stanza
and varying the trochaic meter ensures against monotony.

TO A SKYLARK
(Percy Bysshe Shelley, 1792–1822)

Hail to thee, blithe spirit!
   Bird thou never wert,
That from heaven or near it
   Pourest thy full heart
In profuse strains of unpremeditated art.

Higher still and higher
   From the earth thou springest
Like a cloud of fire;
   The blue deep thou wingest,
And singing still dost soar, and soaring ever singest.

In the golden lightning
   Of the sunken sun,
O'er which clouds are brightening,
   Thou dost float and run;
Like an unbodied joy whose race is just begun.

The pale purple even
   Melts around thy flight;
Like a star of heaven,
   In the broad daylight
Thou art unseen, but yet I hear thy shrill delight,

Keen as are the arrows
   Of that silver sphere
Whose intense lamp narrows
   In the white dawn clear,
Until we hardly see, we feel that it is there.

All the earth and air
   With thy voice is loud,

As, when night is bare,
From one lonely cloud
The moon rains out her beams, and heaven is overflowed.

What thou art we know not;
What is most like thee?
From rainbow clouds there flow not
Drops so bright to see,
As from thy presence showers a rain of melody:

Like a poet hidden
In the light of thought,
Singing hymns unbidden,
Till the world is wrought
To sympathy with hopes and fears it heeded not;

Like a high-born maiden
In a palace tower,
Soothing her love-laden
Soul in secret hour
With music sweet as love, which overflows her bower;

Like a glow-worm golden
In a dell of dew,
Scattering unbeholden
Its aërial hue
Among the flowers and grass which screen it from the view;

Like a rose embowered
In its own green leaves,
By warm winds deflowered,
Till the scent it gives
Makes faint with too much sweet those heavy-wingèd thieves.

Sound of vernal showers
  On the twinkling grass,
Rain-awakened flowers,
  All that ever was
Joyous and clear and fresh, thy music doth surpass.

  Teach us, sprite or bird.
  What sweet thoughts are thine:
I have never heard
  Praise of love or wine
That panted forth a flood of rapture so divine.

Chorus hymeneal,
  Or triumphal chant,
Matched with thine would be all
  But an empty vaunt,
A thing wherein we feel there is some hidden want.

What objects are the fountains
  Of thy happy strain?
What fields, or waves, or mountains?
  What shapes of sky or plain?
What love of thine own kind? what ignorance of pain?

With thy clear keen joyance
  Languor cannot be;
Shadow of annoyance
  Never came near thee;
Thou lovest, but ne'er knew love's sad satiety.

Waking or asleep,
  Thou of death must deem
Things more true and deep
  Than we mortals dream,
Or how could thy notes flow in such a crystal stream?

We look before and after,
    And pine for what is not;
Our sincerest laughter
    With some pain is fraught;
Our sweetest songs are those that tell of saddest thought.

    Yet if we could scorn
        Hate and pride and fear,
    If we were things born
        Not to shed a tear,
I know not how thy joy we ever should come near.

    Better than all measures
        Of delightful sound,
    Better than all treasures
        That in books are found,
Thy skill to poet were, thou scorner of the ground!

    Teach me half the gladness
        That thy brain must know;
    Such harmonious madness
        From my lips would flow,
The world should listen then, as I am listening now.

IAMBIC TRIMETER (˘ ′ ˘ ′ ˘ ′)

The three-foot iambic is also a brief line length. The meter and short-
ness of the next poem correspond to meaning. Frost laments the
brevity of purity: The first tinge of green-gold in spring, the inno-
cence of Eve, dawn — all end quickly.

NOTHING GOLD CAN STAY
(Robert Frost, 1874–1963)

Nature's first green is gold,
Her hardest hue to hold.

Her early leaf's a flower;
But only so an hour.
Then leaf subsides to leaf.
So Eden sank to grief,
So dawn goes down to day.
Nothing gold can stay.

Quite different is this poem by Arthur Gorges — perhaps the most imaginative use of iambic trimeter ever made. Or *is* it iambic trimeter? The poem can be read straight across as three feet in iambic meter. Since the poet arranges each line in columns, we can also read each one separately as three *monometers*, or one-foot lines. The spacing of the phrases invites cross and vertical reading. The opening line, which repeats within each stanza, also closes the poem. Everything seems connected to and equal to everything else.

HER FACE	*HER TONGUE*	*HER WYTT*
	(Arthur Gorges, 1557–1625)	
Her face	Her tongue	Her wytt
So faier	So sweete	So sharpe
first bent	then drewe	then hitt
myne eye	myne eare	my harte
Myne eye	Myne eare	My harte
to lyke	to learne	to love
her face	her tongue	her wytt
doth leade	doth teache	doth move
Her face	Her tongue	Her wytt
with beames	with sounde	with arte
doth blynd	doth charm	doth knitt
myne eye	myne eare	my harte
Myne eye	Myne eare	My harte
with lyfe	with hope	with skill

| her face | her tongue | her witt |
| doth feede | doth feaste | doth fyll |

O face	O tongue	O wytt
with frownes	with cheeks	with smarte
wronge not	vex not	wounde not
myne eye	myne eare	my harte

This eye	This eare	This harte
shall Joye	shall yeald	shall swear
her face	her tongue	her witt

IAMBIC DIMETER (˘ ´/˘ ´)

Iambic dimeter consists of only two iambs. The line movement of "The Fly" suits a fly's motions and the poet's realization of his own life's brevity. Blake's poem is further unified by rhyme, which punctuates the quickness of the two-foot meter.

THE FLY
(William Blake, 1757–1827)

Little Fly,
Thy summer's play
My thoughtless hand
Has brush'd away.

Am not I
A fly like thee?
Or art not thou
A man like me?

For I dance,
And drink, & sing,
Till some blind hand
Shall brush my wing.

> If thought is life
> And strength & breath,
> And the want
> Of thought is death;
>
> Then am I
> A happy fly,
> If I live
> Or if I die.

ANAPESTIC TETRAMETER (˘˘′/˘˘′/˘˘′/˘˘′)

The anapest (˘˘′), a triple-syllable foot, is another rising rhythm. Note how the three-syllable foot extends the line length in tetrameter. After reading Browning's "Good News," you'll see why poems in this meter are rare:

HOW THEY BROUGHT THE GOOD NEWS FROM GHENT TO AIX
(Robert Browning, 1812–1889)

> I sprang to the stirrup, and Joris, and he;
> I galloped, Dirck galloped, we galloped all three;
> 'Good speed!' cried the watch, as the gate-bolts undrew;
> 'Speed!' echoed the wall to us galloping through;
> Behind shut the postern, the lights sank to rest,
> And into the midnight we galloped abreast.
>
> Not a word to each other: we kept the great pace
> Neck by neck, stride by stride, never changing our place;
> I turned in my saddle and made its girths tight,
> Then shortened each stirrup, and set the pique right,
> Rebuckled the cheek-strap, chained slacker the bit,
> Nor galloped less steadily Roland a whit.
>
> 'Twas moonset at starting; but while we drew near
> Lokeren, the cocks crew and twilight dawned clear;

At Boom, a great yellow star came out to see;
At Düffeld, 'twas morning as plain as could be;
And from Mecheln church-steeple we heard the half-chime,
So Joris broke silence with, 'Yet there is time!'

At Aerschot, up leaped of a sudden the sun,
And against him the cattle stood black every one,
To stare thro' the mist at us galloping past,
And I saw my stout galloper Roland at last,
With resolute shoulders, each butting away
The haze, as some bluff river headland its spray.

And his low head and crest, just one sharp ear bent back
For my voice, and the other pricked out on his track;
And one eye's black intelligence, — ever that glance
O'er its white edge at me, his own master, askance!
And the thick heavy spume-flakes which aye and anon
His fierce lips shook upwards in galloping on.

By Hasselt, Dirck groaned; and cried Joris, 'Stay spur!
Your Roos galloped bravely, the fault's not in her,
We'll remember at Aix' — for one heard the quick wheeze
Of her chest, saw the stretched neck and staggering knees,
And sunk tail, and horrible heave of the flank,
As down on her haunches she shuddered and sank.

So we were left galloping, Joris and I,
Past Looz and past Tongres, no cloud in the sky;
The broad sun above laughed a pitiless laugh,
'Neath our feet broke the brittle bright stubble like chaff;
Till over by Dalhem a dome-spire sprang white,
And 'Gallop,' gasped Joris, 'for Aix is in sight!'

'How they'll greet us!' — and all in a moment his roan
Rolled neck and croup over, lay dead as a stone;

And there was my Roland to bear the whole weight
Of the news which alone could save Aix from her fate,
With his nostrils like pits full of blood to the brim,
And with circles of red for his eye-sockets' rim.

Then I cast loose my buffcoat, each holster let fall,
Shook off both my jack-boots, let go belt and all,
Stood up in the stirrup, leaned, patted his ear,
Called my Roland his pet-name, my horse without peer;
Clapped my hands, laughed and sang, any noise, bad or good,
Till at length into Aix Roland galloped and stood.

And all I remember is, friends flocking round
As I sat with his head 'twixt my knees on the ground;
And no voice but was praising this Roland of mine,
As I poured down his throat our last measure of wine,
Which (the burgesses voted by common consent)
Was no more than his due who brought good news from Ghent.

If Browning's gait seems familiar, that's because both "The Star Spangled Banner" and "The Night Before Christmas" are written in the same meter. The outstanding characteristic of anapestic meter is a tharumping gallop. For this reason, it's difficult to maintain; few poems suit the pace.

DACTYLIC PENTAMETER (´˘˘/´˘˘/´˘˘/´˘˘/´˘˘)

The three-syllable dactyl becomes quite drawn out in a pentameter line. Impossible to maintain strictly, here the dactylic meter (´˘˘) prevails. With their falling rhythm and triple-syllable pattern, dactyls are even harder to sustain than anapests. They are used mainly as variation in iambic poems or (as here) in combination with other meters.

TO THE DRIVING CLOUD
(Henry Wadsworth Longfellow, 1807–1882)

Gloomy and dark art thou, O chief of the mighty Omahas;
Gloomy and dark as the driving cloud, whose name thou hast
    taken!
Wrapped in thy scarlet blanket, I see thee stalk through the city's
Narrow and populous streets, as once by the margin of rivers
Stalked those birds unknown, that have left us only their foot-
    prints.
What, in a few short years, will remain of thy race but the foot-
    prints?
How canst thou walk these streets, who has trod the green turf of
    the prairies?
How canst thou breathe this air, who has breathed the sweet air of
    the mountains?
Ah! 'tis in vain that with lordly looks of disdain thou dost challenge
Looks of disdain in return, and question these walls and these
    pavements,
Claiming the soil for thy hunting-grounds, while down-trodden
    millions
Starve in the garrets of Europe, and cry from its caverns that they,
    too,
Have been created heirs of the earth, and claim its division!
Back, then, back to thy woods in the regions west of the Wabash!
There as a monarch thou reignest. In autumn the leaves of the
    maple
Pave the floor of thy palace-halls with gold, and in summer
Pine-trees waft through its chambers the odorous breath of their
    branches.
There thou art strong and great, a hero, a tamer of horses!
There thou chasest the stately stag on the banks of the Elkhorn.
Or by the roar of the Running-Water, or where the Omaha
Calls thee, and leaps through the wild ravine like a brave of the
    Blackfeet!

Hark! what murmurs arise from the heart of those mountainous
    deserts?
Is it the cry of the Foxes and Crows, or the mighty Behemoth,
Who, unharmed, on his tusks once caught the bolts of the
    thunder,
And now lurks in his lair to destroy the race of the red man?
Far more fatal to thee and thy race than the Crows and the
    Foxes,
Far more fatal to thee and thy race than the tread of Behemoth,
Lo! the big thunder-canoe, that steadily breasts the Missouri's
Merciless current! and yonder, afar on the prairies, the campfires
Gleam through the night; and the cloud of dust in the gray of the
    daybreak
Marks not the buffalo's track, nor the Mandan's dexterous horse-
    race;
It is a caravan, whitening the desert where dwell the Camanches!
Ha! how the breath of these Saxons and Celts, like the blast of the
    east-wind,
Drifts evermore to the west the scanty smokes of thy wigwams!

Two Other Metrical Options

The preceding meters are all **accentual-syllabic:** both the number of
syllables and the number of accents count. The other two metrical
systems are simpler. **Accentual** meter counts only the number of
stresses per line. **Syllabic** meter counts only the number of syllables
per line, with no attention paid to the stresses at all.

ACCENTUAL METER

Accentual (or **strong-stress**) meter is the oldest formal metrical device
in English. Anglo-Saxon poetry was based on a four-stress line. The
stressed syllables were further linked by alliteration. The third ele-
ment was a pause (called **caesura,** the Latin word for "cut") in the

middle of the line. In the Middle Ages, Chaucer sometimes chose the old meter. He began his welcome to summer:

Nów welcom, sómer, with thy sonne softe

The strongly stressed, alliterated line with a caesura still survives, as in this example by e. e. cummings:

he sáng his dídn't he dancéd his díd

A twentieth-century example, cummings's line has all the elements of its ancient forebears. Although this caesura isn't punctuated, you hear a definite midline pause.

In 1797 Coleridge wrote "Christabel," an unfinished poem about the pure Christabel's mysterious meeting with a supernatural, powerful woman in the woods. He noted, ". . . the meter of Christabel is not properly speaking, irregular, though it may seem so from its being founded on a new principle: namely that of counting in each line the accents, not the syllables." His "new" meter wasn't new, only rediscovered.

from CHRISTABEL
(Samuel Taylor Coleridge, 1772–1834)

'Tis the middle of night by the castle clock,
And the owls have awakened the crowing cock;
Tu — whit! ——Tu — whoo!
And hark, again! the crowing cock,
How drowsily it crew.
Sir Leoline, the Baron rich,
Hath a toothless mastiff bitch;
From her kennel beneath the rock
She maketh answer to the clock,
Four for the quarters, and twelve for the hour;
Ever and aye, by shine and shower,

Sixteen short howls, not over loud;
Some say, she sees my lady's shroud.

Is the night chilly and dark?
The night is chilly, but not dark.
The thin gray cloud is spread on high,
It covers but not hides the sky.
The moon is behind, and at the full;
And yet she looks both small and dull.
The night is chill, the cloud is gray:
'Tis a month before the month of May,
And the Spring comes slowly up this way.

The lovely lady, Christabel,
Whom her father loves so well,
What makes her in the wood so late,
A furlong from the castle gate?
She had dreams all yesternight
Of her own betrothed knight;
And she in the midnight wood will pray
For the weal of her lover that's far away.

She stole along, she nothing spoke,
The sighs she heaved were soft and low,
And naught was green upon the oak
But moss and rarest mistletoe:
She kneels beneath the huge oak tree,
And in silence prayeth she.

The lady sprang up suddenly,
The lovely lady, Christabel!
It moaned as near, as near can be,
But what it is she cannot tell. —
On the other side it seems to be,
Of the huge, broad-breasted old oak tree.

The night is chill; the forest bare;
Is it the wind that moaneth bleak?
There is not wind enough in the air
To move away the ringlet curl
From the lovely lady's cheek—
There is not wind enough to twirl
The one red leaf, the last of its clan,
That dances as often as dance it can,
Hanging so light, and hanging so high,
On the topmost twig that looks up at the sky.

Poets are always rediscovering accentual meter. In the late nineteenth century, Gerard Manley Hopkins devised a system of rhythm derived from the early English roots. *Sprung rhythm*, as he named it, has as its strongest element the principle of accentual meter. Unaccented syllables are not taken into account. Hopkins's "Pied Beauty" (page 35), a litany of praise for all things "counter, original, spare, strange," hits four stresses in almost every line except for the suddenly shortened last line—where two words, equally stressed, bring the poem to an emphatic conclusion.

GOD'S GRANDEUR
(Gerard Manley Hopkins, 1844–1889)

The world is charged with the grandeur of God.
  It will flame out, like shining from shook foil;
  It gathers to a greatness, like the ooze of oil
Crushed. Why do men then now not reck[1] his rod?
Generations have trod, have trod, have trod;
  And all is seared with trade; bleared, smeared with toil;
  And wears man's smudge and shares man's smell: the soil
Is bare now, nor can foot feel, being shod.
And for all this, nature is never spent;

---

[1] *reck*: reckon with.

There lives the dearest freshness deep down things;
And though the last lights off the black West went
    Oh, morning, at the brown brink eastward, springs—
Because the Holy Ghost over the bent
    World broods with warm breast and with ah! bright wings.

SYLLABIC METER

Syllabic meter is simple. Only the number of syllables in a line matters. Accents are not considered. The poet either maintains a constant number of syllables in each line throughout the poem or constructs a pattern of lines arranged by syllable count, as in this example:

> 10 syllables
> 3 syllables
> 5 syllables
>
> 10 syllables
> 3 syllables
> 5 syllables

Syllabic meter, occasional in English poetry, is awkward to handle: Line endings are forced to fall where the syllable count ends. French and Japanese are friendlier languages for syllabics, since most syllables are equally weighted in those languages. Sometimes, however, the meter is used with felicity, even in English. Sylvia Plath manages to avoid pitfalls of dangling line endings in "Mushrooms." She allows herself five syllables per line and, with wit, gives mushrooms their first chance to "speak" their piece:

> *MUSHROOMS*
> *(Sylvia Plath, 1932–1963)*
>
> Overnight, very
> Whitely, discreetly,
> Very quietly

Our toes, our noses
Take hold on the loam.
Acquire the air.

Nobody sees us,
Stops us, betrays us;
The small grains make room.

Soft fists insist on
Heaving the needles,
The leafy bedding,

Even the paving.
Our hammers, our rams,
Earless and eyeless,

Perfectly voiceless,
Widen the crannies,
Shoulder through holes. We

Diet on water,
On crumbs of shadow,
Bland-mannered, asking

Little or nothing
So many of us!
So many of us!

We are shelves, we are
Tables, we are meek,
We are edible,

Nudgers and shovers
In spite of ourselves.
Our kind multiplies:

> We shall by morning
> Inherit the earth.
> Our foot's in the door.

One of my favorite syllabic poems is Dylan Thomas's lyric "Fern Hill" (page 50), a waterfall memoir about the ecstasy of childhood on a farm and about the inevitable fall into knowledge. On the first few readings, you might not recognize this as a syllabic poem. It is one of the most masterful uses of this form in the language because of the naturalness of the poem's movement and because of the way the meter works with the subject. Once you are aware of the syllabic control — each stanza repeats line for line the syllabic pattern of the previous stanza — you realize the triumph of the last line, "Though I sang in my chains like the sea" — that is exactly what the meter does. Though the poem appears to be free-wheeling and wild, it is, in fact, in check.

Rhythm and Meaning

"The Dance" is one of the best-known examples of rhythm working in lockstep with the subject of the poem. "The Dance" is based on a sixteenth-century Flemish painting of peasants dancing:

THE DANCE
(William Carlos Williams, 1883–1963)

> In Breughel's great picture, The Kermess,
> the dancers go round, they go round and
> around, the squeal and the blare and the
> tweedle of bagpipes, a bugle and fiddles
> tipping their bellies (round as the thick-
> sided glasses whose wash they impound)
> their hips and their bellies off balance
> to turn them. Kicking and rolling about

the Fair Grounds, swinging their butts, those
shanks must be sound to bear up under such
rollicking measures, prance as they dance
in Breughel's great picture, The Kermess.

Scanning "The Dance" for a regular pattern of accents is impossible.
Though the poem contains a large number of iambs and anapests,
the meter is irregular. The vigorous, tharumping anapests and the
quickly alternating iambs combine to make the poem itself kick and
swing. Notice that the rhythm spills over from line to line; Williams
uses only two sinuous sentences in all. The movement of the meter
works with alliteration and participles (by expressing continuous
action, -*ing* words seem to keep moving) to capture the rounded
shapes of the dancers, the overall circular motions of dance, and the
composition in the painting. Many of the words are short. This poem
reads as fast as a jig.

When meter is working well with the subject of the poem, as it is
above, there seem to be a seamless connection between both. How-
ever, rhythm is seldom as obvious as it is in "The Dance." And meter
in itself does not deliver meaning. A single meter can accommodate
racy, exuberant subjects as well as meditative and philosophical ones.
The whole effect of a metered poem depends on the interlocking re-
lationship of the subject with the poem's other components: rhyme,
repetition, word choice and order, imagery, vowel and consonant re-
lationships, *and* meter.

"Rhythm must have meaning," Ezra Pound insisted. Yes, and we
must discover the meaning through analysis of the whole poem. The
loose iambic pentameter of "Sunday Morning" (page 228), for in-
stance, gives the impression of a voice meditating and describing and
conjecturing. The low-key metrical pattern gives structure and for-
mality without drawing much attention to itself. The luxurious,
sprawling pentameter is the opposite of the don't-stop-for-a-moment
movement in "The Dance." Stevens's occasional use of rhyme is also
subtle: come/sun, sacrifice/water-light, else/herself. The quiet metri-
cal framework acts as ballast for the rich words and imagery. In con-

trast, "The Dance" hypes the rhythm, piles on the short, quick words, and works the language to a froth in twelve quick lines.

MY PAPA'S WALTZ
(Theodore Roethke, 1908–1963)

The whiskey on your breath
Could make a small boy dizzy;
But I hung on like death:
Such waltzing was not easy.

We romped until the pans
Slid from the kitchen shelf;
My mother's countenance
Could not unfrown itself.

The hand that held my wrist
Was battered on one knuckle;
At every step you missed
My right ear scraped a buckle.

You beat time on my head
With a palm caked hard by dirt,
Then waltzed me off to bed
Still clinging to your shirt.

In the poem above, the iambic trimeter is not the same as triple-time waltz rhythm but the three-beat line and the four-line stanza do connect with the waltz. All the rhythm belongs to Papa, drunk and exuberant. The child clings "like death," and the mother cannot "unfrown." The contrast between their fear and disdain and the father's romp drives the rhythm and the subject in opposing directions. The three are caught up in the rhythm, but each has a different emotion. In contrast, in Williams's "The Dance" everything in the poem conspires *with* the rhythm.

In Your Notebook:

The best way to understand meter thoroughly is to try writing in a particular meter. Write several lines each of iambic dimeter, iambic pentameter, trochaic trimeter, and anapestic tetrameter. Try a few lines of accentual meter and a short syllabic poem. Don't be concerned about writing the perfect poem. This is practice in experiencing the meters first hand.

Poems

MNEMONIC
(Samuel Taylor Coleridge, 1772–1834)

Trochee trips from long to short;
From long to long in solemn sort
Slow Spondee stalks; strong foot! yea ill able
Ever to come up with Dactyl's trisyllable.
Iambics march from short to long;
With a leap and a bound the swift Anapests throng.

HIS RUNNING MY RUNNING
(Robert Francis, 1901–1987)

Mid-autumn late autumn
At dayfall in leaf-fall
A runner comes running.

How easy his striding
How light his footfall
His bare legs gleaming.

Alone he emerges
Emerges and passes
Alone, sufficient.

When autumn was early
Two runners came running
Striding together

Shoulder to shoulder
Pacing each other
A perfect pairing.

Out of leaves falling
Over leaves fallen
A runner comes running

Aware of no watcher
His loneness my loneness
His running my running.

from ROMEO AND JULIET
(William Shakespeare, 1564–1616)

(ACT III, SCENE V)

JULIET
Wilt thou be gone? It is not yet near day.
It was the nightingale, and not the lark,
That pierced the fearful hollow of thine ear.
Nightly she sings on yond pomegranate tree.
Believe me, love, it was the nightingale.
ROMEO
It was the lark, the herald of the morn;
No nightingale. Look, love, what envious streaks
Do lace the severing clouds in yonder east.
Night's candles are burnt out, and jocund day

Stands tiptoe on the misty mountaintops.
I must be gone and live, or stay and die.
JULIET
Yond light is not daylight; I know it, I.
It is some meteor that the sun exhales
To be to thee this night a torchbearer
And light thee on thy way to Mantua.
Therefore stay yet; thou need'st not be gone.
ROMEO
Let me be ta'en, let me be put to death.
I am content, so thou wilt have it so.
I'll say yon gray is not the morning's eye,
'Tis but the pale reflex of Cynthia's brow[1]
Nor that is not the lark whose notes do beat
The vaulty heaven so high above our heads.
I have more care to stay than will to go.
Come death, and welcome! Juliet wills it so.
How is't, my soul? Let's talk; it is not day.
JULIET
It is, it is! Hie hence, be gone, away!
It is the lark that sings so out of tune,
Straining harsh discords and unpleasing sharps.
Some say the lark makes sweet division[2]
This doth not so, for she divideth us.
Some say the lark and loathèd toad change eyes;
O, now I would they had changed voices too,
Since arm from arm that voice doth us affray.[3]
Hunting thee hence with hunt's-up[4] to the day.
O, now be gone! More light and light it grows.
ROMEO
More light and light — more dark and dark our woes.

---

[1] *Cynthia's brow:* a reflection on the edge of the moon.
[2] *division:* melody.
[3] *affray:* frighten.
[4] *hunt's up:* a morning song for hunters.

RENDEZVOUS
(Alan Seeger, 1888–1916)

I have a rendezvous with Death
At some disputed barricade,
When Spring comes back with rustling shade
And apple-blossoms fill the air—
I have a rendezvous with Death
When Spring brings back blue days and fair.

It may be he shall take my hand
And lead me into his dark land
And close my eyes and quench my breath—
It may be I shall pass him still.
I have a rendezvous with Death
On some scarred slope of battered hill,
When Spring comes round again this year
And the first meadow-flowers appear.

God knows 'twere better to be deep
Pillowed in silk and scented down,
Where love throbs out in blissful sleep,
Pulse nigh to pulse, and breath to breath,
Where hushed awakenings are dear...
But I've a rendezvous with Death
At midnight in some flaming town,
When Spring trips north again this year,
And I to my pledged word am true,
I shall not fail that rendezvous.

IN MEMORY OF W. B. YEATS
(d. January, 1939)
(W. H. Auden, 1907–1973)

1

He disappeared in the dead of winter:
The brooks were frozen, the airports almost deserted,
And snow disfigured the public statues;
The mercury sank in the mouth of the dying day.
What instruments we have agree
The day of his death was a dark cold day.

Far from his illness
The wolves ran on through the evergreen forests,
The peasant river was untempted by the fashionable quays;
By mourning tongues
The death of the poet was kept from his poems.
But for him it was his last afternoon as himself,
An afternoon of nurses and rumors;
The provinces of his body revolted,
The squares of his mind were empty,
Silence invaded the suburbs,
The current of his feeling failed; he became his admirers.

Now he is scattered among a hundred cities
And wholly given over to unfamiliar affections,
To find his happiness in another kind of wood
And be punished under a foreign code of conscience.
The words of a dead man
Are modified in the guts of the living.

But in the importance and noise of tomorrow
When the brokers are roaring like beasts on the floor of the Bourse,[1]

---

[1] *Bourse*: stock exchange.

And the poor have the sufferings to which they are fairly
   accustomed,
And each in the cell of himself is almost convinced of his freedom,
A few thousand will think of this day
As one thinks of a day when one did something slightly unusual.
What instruments we have agree
The day of his death was a dark cold day.

2

You were silly like us; your gift survived it all:
The parish of rich women, physical decay,
Yourself. Mad Ireland hurt you into poetry.
Now Ireland has her madness and her weather still,
For poetry makes nothing happen: it survives
In the valley of its making where executives
Would never want to tamper, flows on south
From ranches of isolation and the busy griefs,
Raw towns that we believe and die in; it survives,
A way of happening, a mouth.

3

Earth, receive an honored guest;
William Yeats is laid to rest:
Let the Irish vessel lie
Emptied of its poetry.

Time that is intolerant
Of the brave and innocent,
And indifferent in a week
To a beautiful physique,

Worships language and forgives
Everyone by whom it lives;

Pardons cowardice, conceit,
Lays its honors at their feet.

Time that with this strange excuse
Pardoned Kipling and his views,
And will pardon Paul Claudel,
Pardons him for writing well.

In the nightmare of the dark
All the dogs of Europe bark,
And the living nations wait,
Each sequestered in its hate;

Intellectual disgrace
Stares from every human face,
And the seas of pity lie
Locked and frozen in each eye.

Follow, poet, follow right
To the bottom of the night,
With your unconstraining voice
Still persuade us to rejoice;

With the farming of a verse
Make a vineyard of the curse,
Sing of human unsuccess
In a rapture of distress:

In the deserts of the heart
Let the healing fountain start,
In the prison of his days
Teach the free man how to praise.

NATURE'S COOK
(Margaret, Duchess of Newcastle, 1625–1673)

Death is the cook of nature, and we find
Creatures drest several ways to please her mind;
Some Death doth roast with fevers burning hot,
And some he boils with dropsies in a pot;
Some are consumed for jelly by degrees,
And some with ulcers, gravy out to squeeze;
Some, as with herbs, he stuffs with gouts and pains,
Others for tender meat he hangs in chains;
Some in the sea he pickles up to keep,
Others he, as soused brawn,[1] in wine doth steep;
Some flesh and bones he with the Pox chops small,
And doth a French fricassee make withall;
Some on grid-irons of calentures[2] are broiled,
And some are trodden down, and so quite spoiled;
But some are baked, when smothered they do die,
Some meat he doth by hectick fevers fry;
In sweat sometimes he stews with savory smell,
An hodge-podge of diseases he likes well;
Some brains he dresseth with apoplexy,
Or fawce[3] of megrims,[4] swimming plenteously;
And tongues he dries with smoak from stomachs ill,
Which, as the second course he sends up still;
Throats he doth cut, blood puddings for to make,
And puts them in the guts, which cholicks rack;
Some hunted are by him for deer, that's red,
And some as stall-fed oxen knocked o'th' head;
Some singed and scald for bacon, seem most rare,
When with salt rheum and phlegm they powdered are.

---

[1] *soused brawn:* pickled hard.
[2] *calentures:* a tropical disease.
[3] *fawce:* sauce.
[4] *megrins:* migraines.

UPON HIS DEPARTURE HENCE
(Robert Herrick, 1591–1674)

Thus I
Passe by,
And die:
As One,
Unknown,
And gon:
I'm made
A shade,
And laid
I'th grave,
There have
My Cave.
Where tell
I dwell,
Farewell.

SAILING TO BYZANTIUM
(William Butler Yeats, 1865–1939)

That is no country for old men. The young
In one another's arms, birds in the trees
—Those dying generations—at their song,
The salmon-falls, the mackerel-crowded seas,
Fish, flesh, or fowl, commend all summer long
Whatever is begotten, born, and dies.
Caught in that sensual music all neglect
Monuments of unaging intellect.

An aged man is but a paltry thing,
A tattered coat upon a stick, unless
Soul clap its hands and sing, and louder sing
For every tatter in its mortal dress,
Nor is there singing school but studying
Monuments of its own magnificence;
And therefore I have sailed the seas and come
To the holy city of Byzantium.

O sages standing in God's holy fire
As in the gold mosaic of a wall,
Come from the holy fire, perne in a gyre,
And be the singing-masters of my soul.
Consume my heart away; sick with desire
And fastened to a dying animal
It knows not what it is; and gather me
Into the artifice of eternity.

Once out of nature I shall never take
My bodily form from any natural thing,
But such a form as Grecian goldsmiths make
Of hammered gold and gold enameling
To keep a drowsy Emperor awake;
Or set upon a golden bough to sing
To lords and ladies of Byzantium
Of what is past, or passing, or to come.

TO EARTHWARD
(Robert Frost, 1874–1963)

Love at the lips was touch
As sweet as I could bear;
And once that seemed too much;
I lived on air

That crossed me from sweet things,
The flow of—was it musk
From hidden grapevine springs
Down hill at dusk?

I had the swirl and ache
From sprays of honeysuckle
That when they're gathered shake
Dew on the knuckle,

I craved strong sweets, but those
Seemed strong when I was young;
The petal of the rose
It was that stung.

Now no joy but lacks salt
That is not dashed with pain
And weariness and fault;
I crave the stain

Of tears, the aftermark
Of almost too much love,
The sweet of bitter bark
And burning clove.

When stiff and sore and scarred
I take away my hand
From leaning on it hard
In grass and sand,

The hurt is not enough:
I long for weight and strength
To feel the earth as rough
To all my length.

RHYME

(Louise Bogan, 1897–1970)

What laid, I said.
My being waste?
'Twas your sweet flesh
With its sweet taste, —

Which, like a rose,
Fed with a breath,
And at its full
Belied all death.

It's at springs we drink;
It's bread we eat,
And no fine body,
Head to feet,

Should force all bread
And drink together,
Nor be both sun
And hidden weather.

Ah no, it should not;
Let it be.
But once heart's feast
You were to me.

STANZAS FOR MUSIC
(George Gordon, Lord Byron, 1788–1824)

There's not a joy the world can give like that it takes away,
When the glow of early thought declines in feelings' dull
    decay;
'Tis not on youth's smooth cheek the blush alone, which fades so
    fast,
But the tender bloom of heart is gone, ere youth itself be past.

Then the few whose spirits float above the wreck of happiness
Are driven o'er the shoals of guilt or ocean of excess:
The magnet of their course is gone, or only points in vain
The shore to which their shivered sail shall never stretch again.

Then the mortal coldness of the soul like death itself comes
    down;
It cannot feel for others' woes, it dare not dream its own;
That heavy chill has frozen o'er the fountain of our tears,
And though the eye may sparkle still, 'tis where the ice appears.

Though wit may flash from fluent lips, and mirth distract the
    breast,
Through midnight hours that yield no more their former hope of
    rest;
'Tis but as ivy-leaves around the ruined turret wreath,
All green and wildly fresh without, but worn and grey beneath.

Oh could I feel as I have felt,—or be what I have been,
Or weep as I could once have wept, o'er many a vanished scene:
As springs in deserts found seem sweet, all brackish though they
    be,
So, midst the withered waste of life, those tears would flow to me.

7

Free Verse

I have found the law of my own poems.
—WALT WHITMAN

Beginning in the twentieth century, ways of making poems multiplied. Poets felt dissatisfied with the restrictions of meter, set forms, and rhyme schemes that earlier poets took as the norm. They began to develop more diverse possibilities. Finding "the law of my own poems" means each poem is a "free verse," a new invention operating on its own terms instead of a marrying of subject, voice, and language to a pre-existing meter.

Meter, as we've seen, organizes accents into an overall pattern and more or less evenly times the lines. Meter provides an underlying orderly structure on which the poem can play out innumerable variations. But meter does more than that. It's not just a taut line on which you can hang your words and thoughts like wash flapping in the breeze. In a poem where the poet aspires for form to *be* content, content to *be* form, the choice of a certain meter means the poet hears the music in that key. Free verse poets hear differently. For both ways of writing, Thomas Carlyle's insight is apt: "See deep enough, and you see musically; the heart of Nature *being* everywhere music, if only you can reach it." Poets are always reaching for the music at the heart of the poem.

Free verse is improvisational. Poets compose with an irregular line, the speaking voice, language and imagery as their primary instruments. Lines do not necessarily follow the left margin; they may be placed in other arrangements. Blank space often is used for a pause within a line with or without punctuation. Some poems have no punctuation at all because the writer perceives it as an interruption. "I" is the most common speaker of the free verse poem; lines are broken to punctuate how the poet wants us to hear perceptions, individual speech, or breath rhythms.

No subject is taboo. In a contemporary poem, smog, rape, fallout, and cancer might meet waterfalls, birds of paradise, moonlight, and papaya on the same page. Keats might be amazed to read about crime and other "ugly" subjects, as well as about utterly mundane subjects:

BETWEEN WALLS
(William Carlos Williams, 1883–1963)

the back wings
of the

hospital where
nothing

will grow lie
cinders

in which shine
the broken

> pieces of a green
> bottle

These are some of the touchstone developments of free verse. This is not to say that all poets abandon the technical tools of traditional verse. A poem written tomorrow might well be at its best in trochaic tetrameter. Contemporary poems sometimes have the "ghost" of iambic pentameter or another meter working throughout the poem. And some poets still use the traditional meters entirely. Others use meter when particular poems benefit. Many, however, see meter as obsolete or as false to their purposes. American Charles Wright is not the only contemporary poet well versed in metrics who scans his poems to make sure that they do *not* accidentally fall into regular meter.

The Genesis of Free Verse

The roots of this change are old. Walt Whitman, carpenter, newspaper editor, and hospital volunteer in the Civil War, broke decisively with the verse of his time. He wrote long, rising and falling lines with hypnotic repetition and rolling movement. He insisted on "including" rather than paring down. He wanted an American poetry "proportionate to our continent, with its powerful races of men, its tremendous historical events, its great oceans, its mountains and its illimitable prairies."

Emily Dickinson, Whitman's contemporary, was his opposite. While Whitman hung out around docks and took large-stride steps over as much of the American landscape as possible, Dickinson closed herself off in her father's house and wrote privately, tying her poems into neat fascicles with string. She heard her own music. At times she used no meter; often her rhymes were based on Protestant hymns. If you grew up singing songs such as "Amazing Grace" or "The God of Abraham Praise," you can often "sing" Dickinson's poems to those tunes. What is striking is how she surprises the reader's expectations constantly by the subversive contrast of these common meters with her wild imagination and subjects. She counters the simplicity of the beat with startling word choices, juxtaposition of perceptions that have never been near each other before, and dissonant off-rhymes that sound distinctly at odds with other nineteenth-century verse.

In Ralph Waldo Emerson we find another precursor of free verse. Two of his distinctly modern percepts were "Ask the fact for the form" and "Any word, every word in language, every circumstance, becomes poetic in the hands of a higher thought." In nineteenth-century Concord, Massachusetts, Emerson envisioned a new poetry shaped from within and capable of including any subject.

Early American poets often had a quirky sense of rhythm; English traditions did not migrate unscathed. Writing in isolation, American poets devised their own poetic variations on the models at hand. In end-of-the-nineteenth-century England, some poets grew "sick to death of Swinburne," the poet so well known for his flowing style of rhymes and meters that he sometimes even made fun of himself. Thomas Hardy, Gerard Manley Hopkins, and (to a lesser extent) A. E. Housman, all born in the mid-1800s, broke out of the pervasive gentility with new subjects and more percussive sounds. French poets had established a *vers libre* ("free verse"), and their influences began to blow fast across the waters.

The poets most receptive to the influence from France were a group in England including the Americans H. D. (Hilda Doolittle) and Ezra Pound. By 1910, these poets were avidly reading Chinese poetry and discussing their own theories and values. The poetry they championed was based on clear, incisive images.

HEAT
(H. D. [Hilda Doolittle], 1896–1961)

> O wind, rend open the heat,
> cut apart the heat,
> rend it to tatters.

Fruit cannot drop
through this thick air—
fruit cannot fall into heat
that presses up and blunts
the points of pears
and rounds the grapes.

Cut the heat—
plough through it,
turning it on either side
of your path.

An image, Pound said, "is that which presents an intellectual and emotional complex in an instant of time." His famous one-image poem on the faces he saw as he emerged from the metro at La Concorde was distilled from a thirty-line poem:

IN A STATION OF THE METRO

The apparition of these faces in the crowd;
Petals on a wet, black bough.

"In a poem of this sort," Pound explained, "one is trying to record the precise instant when a thing outward and objective transforms itself, or darts into a thing inward and subjective."

As a unified group of writers, the Imagists blazed only briefly on the scene, but their initial contributions provided, as T. S. Eliot noted, "the starting point of modern poetry." Their principles of concentration, precise diction, and composition in the "sequence of the musical phrase not the sequence of a metronome" (Pound's advice) deeply influenced the poets who followed.

Developments in the arts always connect to the broader context of history. The changes in poetry early in the last century occurred as the

English-speaking world shifted values. Historians pinpoint World War I as the time of irreconcilable fragmentation of society. This break-up of values and coherence erupted in all the arts. Musical composers began to include dissonance and cacophony in their work; painters multiplied their perspectives; dancers broke out of the classical repertoire into spontaneous, sometimes contorted movements. The powerful camera eye of photography and movies had strong impact on writers. At the same time, belief in *a* poetics broke open. Comparing meter with free verse, poet Robert Hass says:

> The difference is, in some ways, huge; the metrical poem begins with an assumption of human life which takes place in a pattern of orderly recurrence with which the poet must come to terms, the free verse poem with an assumption of openness or chaos in which an order must be discovered.

This is the basic fact of free verse: each poem is shaped from within. In a way, poets always had this goal. Coleridge sought an "organic" form; Keats thought poetry should come into being "as naturally as leaves to a tree"; Milton wanted a "simple, sensuous, and impassioned" poetry. These approaches, however, only varied existing meters. Poets of the twentieth century made more decisive changes.

Without meter and rhyme scheme, what makes a poem a poem? When chloroform was invented, a famous doctor of the time remarked in dismay, "*Anyone* can be a surgeon now." When open forms began to strike a strong responsive chord in poets, many lamented like the good doctor. But the techniques of modern poetry, although different, are rigorous. A good poem remains difficult to achieve.

The Free Verse Craft of the Line

We know that the main difference between poetry and prose is that poetry is a line art and prose is a sentence art. Sentences run to the edge of the margin. Although lines of poems make sentences, the line lengths and breaks in poetry are crucial. (Prose poems are an exception to this. We'll read them later in the Open Forms chapter.) In both free verse and metered verse, lines are as important to the poem as rungs are to a ladder. Each line moves the poem along at a certain speed. A **line** is a unit of time; a line break is a punctuation, a slight halt in the flow. Where there is no comma or period, the line break indicates a slight pause, the equivalent of a half comma. The last work on a line always gets attention; that's where your eye stops before it returns to the beginning of the next line. You also attend to the first word in a line. Sometimes poets accentuate that first word more by capitalizing it. Whether short or long, free or metered, line length manages the flow of the poem and controls what words get the most attention. In free verse, therefore, lines often are irregular in length or are placed in arrangements on the page according to where the poet wants emphasis to fall. If the energy of one or a series of lines flags, the poem falls off in interest. What the line is *not*, necessarily, is a unit of sense. In all poetry, lines often **enjamb** (run on) to the next, as in these iambic tetrameter lines by W. D. Snodgrass:

> The green catalpa tree has turned
> All white; the cherry blooms once more.

The second line is **end-stopped:** the sense of the line terminates with a period. Pauses and emphases are expressive of the poem's content.

Typed as conventional prose, an e. e. cummings poem reads:

> Buffalo Bill's defunct, who used to ride a water-smooth, silver stallion and break one, two, three, four, five pigeons just like that. Jesus, he was a handsome man. And what I want to know is, how do you like your blue-eyed boy, Mister Death?

These are lively words. But look at the increase of effect when they're arranged in lines:

from PORTRAITS
(e. e. cummings, 1894–1962)

VIII

Buffalo Bill's
defunct
        who used to
        ride a watersmooth-silver
                    stallion
and break onetwothreefourfive piegonsjustlikethat
                                            Jesus

he was a handsome man
                    and what i want to know is
how do you like your blueeyed boy
Mister Death

The isolation of words on the short lines gives each word special importance. The long, jolting, run-together line speeds up the middle of the poem violently, then drops off suddenly to exclaim "Jesus." We can hear a speaking voice in the rhythm. When the voice concludes "how do you like your blueeyed boy / Mister Death," we're surprised at the shift from the exuberant descriptions of Buffalo Bill to a direct question asked of Death. It is a surprise that works mainly because the line break between "man" and "and what" downshifts from fast talk to a question but also continues the conversational voice.

Usually the use of the line is more subtly modulated than in "Buffalo Bill." In these cases, we have to look closely at how the line works to reveal emotions or movements of thought.

THE ELDER SISTER
(Sharon Olds, 1942–)

When I look at my elder sister now
I think how she had to go first, down through the

birth canal, to force her way
head-first through the tiny channel,
the pressure of Mother's muscles on her brain,
the tight walls scraping her skin.
Her face is still narrow from it, the long
hollow cheeks of a Crusader on a tomb,
and her inky eyes have the look of somone who has
been in prison a long time and
knows they can send her back. I look at her
body and think how her breasts were the first to
rise, slowly, like swans on a pond.
By the time mine came along, they were just
two more birds on the flock, and when the hair
rose on the white mound of her flesh, like
threads of water out of the ground, it was the
first time, but when mine came
they knew about it. I used to think
only in terms of her harshness, sitting and
pissing on me in bed, but now I
see I had her before me always
like a shield. I look at her wrinkles, her clenched
jaws, her frown-lines — I see they are
the dents on my shield, the blows that did not reach me.
She protected me, not as a mother
protects a child, with love, but as a
hostage protects the one who makes her
escape as I made my escape, with my sister's
body held in front of me.

The poem starts quickly with "When I look at my elder sister now," which places the reader exactly where the speaker is: considering the older sister. Each line of the poem is strong, a ladder rung taking us decisively through ways the speaker regards her sister. All but three lines are enjambed. These run-on lines, plus the use of several conjunctions, emphasize midsentence words and the forceful flow of the speaker's voice. A few lines end with *the* or in the middle of an infinitive ("to / rise"). These give a dangling or suspended quality to the line, as though we hear an odd pause in the speaker's voice. The third end-stopped line ("...the blows that did not reach me") marks the end of the story of the sister. The next five lines summarize what the younger sister now realizes. Throughout the poem, the lines seem close to the pace of breathing. They slightly expand and contract in length, slowing and speeding the pace as you read. Note the internal rhymes (now/how/down) and other intensifying, unifying sound patterns (pressure/muscles/scraping/skin) throughout the poem.

In e. e. cummings's poem, the line use establishes an individual speech rhythm: We hear a voice speaking and we listen to it. In Olds's poem, the fierce lines seem almost deployed, fired down onto the page. "The Elder Sister" is a **continuous form:** it proceeds without stanza breaks. This uninterrupted form intensifies the urgent all-at-onceness of the enjambed lines.

A break for a stanza is a break in timing, a big pause. William Carlos Williams chose continuous lines for the rhythm of "The Great Figure." He wanted lines to *go* at the speed of the truck:

THE GREAT FIGURE
(William Carlos Williams, 1883–1963)

> Among the rain
> and lights
> I saw the figure 5
> in gold
> on a red
> firetruck
> moving
> tense
> unheeded
> to gong clangs
> siren howls

and wheels rumbling
through the dark city.

Williams's line becomes the movement of the action in the poem.

Lines can rush like a fuse burning, drop down like a rock in water, drift about musically, or curve as though the writer were hemming a circular skirt. The line is *expressive* of the content. In free verse, rhythm is individualized. A subtle poem, laid out to reveal the motions of the mind in the process of perception, will not strike you with its movement. You must judge each poem's way of using the line.

Although we're looking at functions of lines separately, remember that usually several forces are working together. cummings's Buffalo Bill poem, for example, uses a speech rhythm, but also at work is the passionate rush of fear and wonder at death.

The next poem's short lines are restless like the wind; they also seem to reflect the quick movement of the poet's perception. *Scirocco* is a seasonal, harsh wind.

SCIROCCO
(Jorie Graham, 1951–)

In Rome, at 26
        Piazza di Spagna,
at the foot of a long
        flight of
stairs, are rooms
        let to Keats

in 1820,
        where he died. Now
you can visit them,
        the tiny terrace,
the bedroom. The scraps
        of paper

on which he wrote
    lines
are kept behind glass,
    some yellowing,
some xeroxed or
    mimeographed....

Outside his window
    you can hear the scirocco
working
    the invisible.
Every dry leaf of ivy
    is fingered,

refingered. Who is
    the nervous spirit
of this world
    that must go over and over
what it already knows,
    what is it

so hot and dry
    that's looking through us,
by us,
    for its answer?
In the arbor
    on the terrace

the stark hellenic
    forms
of grapes have appeared.
    They'll soften
till weak enough
    to enter

our world, translating
    helplessly
from the beautiful
    to the true....
Whatever the spirit,
  the thickening grapes

are part of its looking,
    and the slow hands
that made this mask
    of Keats
in his other life,
    and the old woman,

the memorial's
    custodian,
sitting on the porch
    beneath the arbor
sorting chick-peas
    from pebbles

into her cast-iron
    pot.
See what her hands
    know—
they are its breath,
    its mother

tongue, dividing,
    discarding.
There is light playing
    over the leaves,
over her face,
    making her

abstract, making
    her quick
and strange. But she
    has no care
for what speckles her,
    changing her,

she is at
    her work. Oh how we want
to be taken
    and changed,
want to be mended
    by what we enter.

Is it thus
    with the world?
Does it wish us
    to mend it,
light and dark,
    green

and flesh? Will it
    be free then?
I think the world
    is a desperate
element. It would have us
    calm it,

receive it. Therefore this
    is what I
must ask you
    to imagine: wind;
the moment
    when the wind

> drops; and grapes,
>   which are nothing,
> which break
>   in your hands.

The very short lines of "Scirocco" work *for* the complex subjects of the poem. Keats died at 25; his brief life ended in Rome, where he'd gone to escape the English climate. The brief lines — fleeting, delicate — break on important words. The additional attention the eye gives to the end words and to the single-word lines emphasizes more words than we would in longer lines.

Notice the old woman sorting peas. We see her on the porch under the arbor — a wide focus. Then she's sorting peas into her pot. Then the focus narrows further: We're shown her hands, the light on her face as the wind moves the leaves. The lines both present and time the image by zooming in closer and closer on the woman. We see her in stages, as the poet saw.

"Scirocco" is a speculative poem with no single meaning, certainly no easily paraphrasable meaning. In "Ode on a Grecian Urn," Keats wrote:

> "Beauty is truth, truth beauty," — that is all
> Ye know on earth, and all ye need to know.

Graham's speaker echoes this famous quote as she looks out Keats's window "from the beautiful / to the true. . . ." All that is past and present seems to be part of the restless impulse of the inquiring spirit personified by the wind. We're invited in to hear the speaker's meditation and, lastly, to imagine simultaneously the constant wind and the perfect "hellenic" forms of the grapes, which cannot endure.

Did Graham decide on the form in advance? Probably not. In writing, a poet may notice a shape starting to form in the rough draft; here, a contracting and expanding line might have determined the form. Once the shape emerges, the poet starts to work with it, just as

Michelangelo claimed to have *released* the shapes of his sculptures from giant blocks of marble.

A vastly different line rhythm is used by C. K. Williams. His books are sometimes printed in a wide format to accommodate his very long lines—longer than most prose. This book isn't wide enough to print his lines without breaking them. Imagine each indented line as part of the line above it. Although many poets occasionally work with a long line, no one else since Whitman has consistently used this stretched-to-the-limit length. Williams's poems have stories to tell. He uses lines in layers to build his story gradually. The eye must travel all the way across the page. Further, he uses many conjunctions. The rhythm may remind you of the Old Testament, with its rolling *and* and *thens* gathering cumulative power. Williams's poems expand. They do not pare down, compress. They are urban poems that combine fact, memory, and imagination with a landscape that is *inclusive* like Whitman's, but inclusive of squad cars, urban renewal, and winos.

BLADES
(C. K. Williams, 1936–)

When I was about eight, I once stabbed somebody, another kid, a
    little girl.
I'd been hanging around in front of the supermarket near our
    house
and when she walked by, I let her have it, right in the gap
    between her shirt and her shorts
with a piece of broken-off car antenna I used to carry around in
    my pocket.
It happened so fast I still don't know how I did it: I was as shocked
    as she was
except she squealed and started yelling as though I'd plunged a
    knife in her
and everybody in the neighborhood gathered around us, then
    they called the cops,

then the girl's mother came running out of the store saying
  "What happened? What happened?"
and the girl screamed, "He stabbed me!" and I screamed back, "I
  did not!" and she you did too
and me I didn't and we were both crying hysterically by that time.
Somebody pulled her shirt up and it was just a scratch but we
  went on and on
and the mother, standing between us, seemed to be absolutely
  terrified.
I still remember how she watched first one of us and then the
  other with a look of complete horror —
You did too! I did not! — as though we were both strangers, as
  though it was some natural disaster
she was beholding that was beyond any mode of comprehension
  so all she could do
was stare speechlessly at us, and then another expression came
  over her face,
one that I'd never seen before, that made me think she was going
  to cry herself
and sweep both of us, the girl and me, into her arms to hold us
  against her.
The police came just then, though, quieted everyone down, put
  the girl and the mother
into a squad-car to take to the hospital and me in another to take
  to jail
except they really only took me around the corner and let me go
  because the mother and daughter were black
and in those days you had to do something pretty terrible to get
  into trouble that way.
I don't understand how we twist these things or how we get them
  straight again
but I relived that day I don't know how many times before I
  realized I had it all wrong.
The boy wasn't me at all, he was another kid: I was just there.

284 / THE DISCOVERY OF POETRY

And it wasn't the girl who was black, but him. The mother was
   real, though.
I really had thought she was going to embrace them both and I
   had dreams about her for years afterwards: that I'd be being
   born again
and she'd be lifting me with that same wounded sorrow or she
   would suddenly appear out of nowhere,
blotting out everything but a single, blazing wing of holiness.
Who knows the rest? I can still remember how it felt the old
   way.
How I make my little thrust, how she crushes us against her, how
   I turn and snarl
at the cold circle of faces around us because something's torn in
   me,
some ancient cloak of terror we keep on ourselves because we'll
   do anything,
anything, not to know how silently we knell in the mouth of
   death
and not to obliterate the forgivenesses and the lies we offer one
   another and call innocence.
This is innocence. I touch her, we kiss.
And this. I'm here or not here. I can't tell. I stab her. I stab her
   again. I still can't.

A metrical line is easy to grasp. We hear the harmony of the repeating
pattern of syllables and line length. Without metrical standards, you
learn to pay attention to the poet's sense of how rhythm works in each
poem — whether it captures speech rhythms, underscores meaning,
mirrors the motion of the mind as it perceives, or captures an actual
physical motion.

In crafting a poem in free verse, the writer is not "free" just because
the conventions of meter and rhyme scheme are abandoned. Free
verse challenges the poet to make imaginative and expressive use of
the line. The free verse line is like the sensitive needle on the seis-
mograph, tracing the movement and tremors of the earth.

Remember that the way a line is crafted constantly interacts with other elements. Line use is inseparable in its effect from elements such as sound patterns, imagery, repetition. All of these elements merge with the voice of the poem.

Voice

> *We convince by our presence.*
> —*Walt Whitman*

Someone's voice is mysterious. You answer a call from someone you haven't talked to in years and recognize her just from the way she says your name. If you're familiar with a writer's work, you can recognize the author's voice in even a few unsigned lines. If you know Mozart well, you'll spot even unfamiliar works as his. These recognitions have to do with characteristic sounds and tones. When a parent says, "Don't speak to me in that tone of voice," you know what is meant. You also know the difference in the way you sound speaking to someone and the more fragmented way you think, muse, and imagine to yourself. A poem's tone of voice is similarly revealing. The forceful, direct tone in "The Elder Sister" tells you that the poem's message is unequivocal. The voice leaves nothing ambiguous. It is an outside, direct-address voice. In contrast, the voice in "Scirocco" moves back and forth from an outer voice addressing "you" to an inner, contemplative voice thinking to itself. This poem requires more participation from the reader. The voice in "Blades" is casual at first. The speaker says "about eight," "another kid," and "hanging around." He could be telling you this over coffee. His storyteller mode (this happened, then this, then this) continues until the break. The last section shifts: He realizes the story did not happen that way at all. Reality and fantasy change places in memory. In the last seven lines, Williams speeds up the rhythm, drops the casual words and writes about "holiness," "death," "forgiveness." The language shift indicates an opening of the speaker's perception into larger questions: What is the truth of memory,

In Your Notebook:

You can experience the power of line breaks by rewriting prose paragraphs as free verse. Try different line arrangements with this paragraph from Arlene Blum's book about mountain climbers in the Himalayas, *Annapurna: A Woman's Place.* After you find the line arrangement that best emphasizes the motion and drama of the paragraph, edit the words for further intensification.

> I was just beginning to cross the mounts of avalanche debris when I saw, but didn't hear, a great cloud of snow and ice coming down from the right side of the Sickle. It looked as though the three members ahead of me were directly in its path. I turned around and ran, occasionally looking back at its progress. I got so winded running full speed with my pack that I had to slow to a fast walk. When I felt I was out of the way, I looked around for the others. All I saw was a great cloud of snow engulfing the area where they'd been. I knelt down, breathing fast and hard. I didn't know what to do. Should I probe for them? What if another avalanche came down? Should I run back to Camp II for help? What if I forgot the place where I'd last seen them? . . . What should I do?

Then rewrite this passage from Wright Morris's novel *Ceremony at Lone Tree* as free verse. Try two versions, one with longer lines and one with shorter.

> Come to the window. The one at the rear of the Lone Tree Hotel. The view is to the west. There is no obstruction but the sky. Although there is no one outside to look in, the yellow blind is drawn low at the window, and between it and the pane a fly is trapped. He has stopped buzzing. Only the crawling shadow can be seen. Before the whistle of the train is heard the loose pane rattles like a simmering pot, then stops, as if pressed by a hand, as the train goes past. The blind sucks inward and the dangling cord drags in the dust on the sill.

how do we protect ourselves, what is innocence? The last line of the poem contains six clipped, contradictory sentences. In dramatic complement to their meaning, the truncated, blurted last sentences also contradict the leisurely syntax of the long lines.

Free Verse, the Tradition and Beyond

After free verse took hold, poetry changed irrevocably. Free verse evolved into a complex craft and tradition in itself, with criteria as rigorous as metrical verse. By now the art of poetry exists in such an open field that the term *free verse* seems to belong to a period long ago.

What makes a poem good applies to any poetry. What's good seems new; it is not predictable. The language is precise and fresh. The ideas or emotions develop. The craft holds our interest as the development takes place. There are compelling reasons for the poem to exist.

Open forms and metrics are not an either/or choice. Poets in any age use whatever tool is available to forge the poems they want to write. Someone right now, given the right subject, can use trochees or anapests to make a memorable contemporary poem. In someone else's hand, a metered poem will seem dated, dressed up in a bustle and high-buttoned shoes. The forms and techniques of traditional poetry are alive. They're here, along with later craft developments, available for the right use.

Poems

SNOW
(Louis MacNeice, 1907–1963)

The room was suddenly rich and the great bay-window was
Spawning snow and pink roses against it
Soundlessly collateral and incompatible:
World is suddener than we fancy it.

World is crazier and more of it than we think,
Incorrigibly plural. I peel and portion
A tangerine and spit the pips and feel
The drunkenness of things being various.

And the fire flames with a bubbling sound for world
Is more spiteful and gay than one supposes—
On the tongue on the eyes on the ears in the palm of one's
    hands—
There is more than glass between the snow and the huge roses.

STARLIGHT
(Philip Levine, 1928–)

My father stands in the warm evening
on the porch of my first house.
I am four years old and growing tired.
I see his head among the stars,
the glow of his cigarette, redder
than the summer moon riding
low over the old neighborhood. We
are alone, and he asks me if I am happy.
"Are you happy?" I cannot answer.
I do not really understand the word,
and the voice, my father's voice, is not
his voice, but somehow thick and choked,
a voice I have not heard before, but
heard often since. He bends and passes
a thumb beneath each of my eyes.
The cigarette is gone, but I can smell
the tiredness that hangs on his breath.
He has found nothing, and he smiles
and holds my head with both his hands.
Then he lifts me to his shoulder,

and now I too am there among the stars,
as tall as he. Are you happy? I say.
He nods in answer, Yes! oh yes! oh yes!
And in that new voice he says nothing,
holding my head tight against his head,
his eyes closed up against the starlight,
as though those tiny blinking eyes
of light might find a tall, gaunt child
holding his child against the promises
of autumn, until the boy slept
never to awaken in that world again.

CAT & THE WEATHER
(May Swenson, 1919–1989)

Cat takes a look at the weather:
snow;
puts a paw on the sill;
his perch is piled, is a pillow.

Shape of his pad appears:
will it dig? No,
not like sand,
like his fur almost.

But licked, not liked:
too cold.
Insects are flying, fainting down.
He'll try

to bat one against the pane.
They have no body and no buzz,
and now his feet are wet;
it's a puzzle.

Shakes each leg,
then shakes his skin
to get the white flies off;
looks for his tail,

tells it to come on in
by the radiator.
World's turned queer
somehow: all white,

no smell. Well, here
inside it's still familiar.
He'll go to sleep until
it puts itself right.

POEM
(William Carlos Williams, 1883–1963)

As the cat
climbed over
the top of

the jamcloset
first the right
forefoot

carefully
then the hind
stepped down

into the pit of
the empty
flowerpot

*

LONG RANGE PATROL
(D. F. Brown, 1949–)

Tense
again there as a
cat and sure   I
can see in the dark
this blanket bulletproof
the attack will come
on the other side
they won't
get me they don't   I am
home   it is
daylight
            then
our sentry blows
his claymore   we
all let go and I wish
I had dug deeper or it
wasn't me or
my friends hold me
I am home   it is
daylight

*

I KNOW A MAN
(Robert Creeley, 1926–)

As I sd to my
friend, because I am
always talking—John, I

sd, which was not his
name, the darkness sur-
rounds us, what

can we do against
it, or else, shall we &
why not, buy a goddamn big car,

drive, he sd, for
christ's sake, look
out where yr going.

MEDITATION AT LAGUNITAS
(Robert Hass, 1941–)

All the new thinking is about loss.
In this it resembles all the old thinking.
The idea, for example, that each particular erases
the luminous clarity of a general idea. That the clown-
faced woodpecker probing the dead sculpted trunk
of that black birch is, by his presence,
some tragic falling off from a first world
of undivided light. Or the other notion that,
because there is in this world no one thing
to which the bramble of *blackberry* corresponds,
a word is elegy to what it signifies.
We talked about it late last night and in the voice
of my friend, there was a thin wire of grief, a tone
almost querulous. After a while I understood that,
talking this way, everything dissolves: *justice,*
pine, hair, woman, you and *I*. There was a woman
I made love to and I remembered how, holding
her small shoulders in my hands sometimes,

I felt a violent wonder at her presence
like a thirst for salt, for my childhood river
with its island willows, silly music from the pleasure boat,
muddy places where we caught the little orange-silver fish
called *pumpkinseed.* It hardly had to do with her.
Longing, we say, because desire is full
of endless distances. I must have been the same to her.
But I remember so much, the way her hands dismantled bread,
the thing her father said that hurt her, what
she dreamed. There are moments when the body is as numinous
as words, days that are the good flesh continuing.
Such tenderness, those afternoons and evenings,
saying *blackberry, blackberry, blackberry.*

BLACKBERRYING
(Sylvia Plath, 1932–1963)

Nobody in the lane, and nothing, nothing but blackberries,
Blackberries on either side, though on the right mainly,
A blackberry alley, going down in hooks, and a sea
Somewhere at the end of it, heaving. Blackberries
Big as the ball of my thumb, and dumb as eyes
Ebon in the hedges, fat
With blue-red juices. These they squander on my fingers.
I had not asked for such a blood sisterhood; they must love me.
They accommodate themselves to my milkbottle, flattening their
    sides.

Overhead go the choughs in black, cacophonous flocks—
Bits of burnt paper wheeling in a blown sky.
Theirs is the only voice, protesting, protesting.
I do not think the sea will appear at all.
The high, green meadows are glowing, as if lit from within.

I come to one bush of berries so ripe it is a bush of flies,
Hanging their bluegreen bellies and their wing panes in a
   Chinese screen.

The honey-feast of the berries has stunned them; they believe in
   heaven.
One more hook, and the berries and bushes end.

The only thing to come now is the sea.
From between two hills a sudden wind funnels at me,
Slapping its phantom laundry in my face.
These hills are too green and sweet to have tasted salt.
I follow the sheep path between them. A last hook brings me
To the hills' northern face, and the face is orange rock
That looks out on nothing, nothing but a great space
Of white and pewter lights, and a din like silversmiths
Beating and beating at an intractable metal.

TO A POOR OLD WOMAN
(William Carlos Williams, 1883–1963)

munching a plum on
the street a paper bag
of them in her hand

They taste good to her
They taste good
to her. They taste
good to her

You can see it by
the way she gives herself

to the one half
sucked out in her hand

Comforted
a solace of ripe plums
seeming to fill the air
They taste good to her

THIRTEEN WAYS OF LOOKING AT A BLACKBIRD
(Wallace Stevens, 1879–1955)

I

Among twenty snowy mountains,
The only moving thing
Was the eye of the blackbird.

II

I was of three minds,
Like a tree
In which there are three blackbirds.

III

The blackbird whirled in the autumn winds.
It was a small part of the pantomime.

IV

A man and a woman
Are one.

A man and a woman and a blackbird
Are one.

V

I do not know which to prefer,
The beauty of inflections
Or the beauty of innuendoes,
The blackbird whistling
Or just after.

VI

Icicles filled the long window
With barbaric glass.
The shadow of the blackbird
Crossed it, to and fro.
The mood
Traced in the shadow
An indecipherable cause.

VII

O thin men of Haddam,
Why do you imagine golden birds?
Do you not see how the blackbird
Walks around the feet
Of the women about you?

VIII

I know noble accents
And lucid, inescapable rhythms;
But I know, too,

That the blackbird is involved
In what I know.

IX

When the blackbird flew out of sight,
It marked the edge
Of one of many circles.

X

At the sight of blackbirds
Flying in a green light,
Even the bawds of euphony
Would cry out sharply.

XI

He rode over Connecticut
In a glass coach.
Once, a fear pierced him,
In that he mistook
The shadow of his equipage
For blackbirds.

XII

The river is moving.
The blackbird must be flying.

XIII

It was evening all afternoon.
It was snowing

And it was going to snow.
The blackbird sat
In the cedar-limbs.

For the Anniversary of My Death
(W. S. Merwin, 1927–)

Every year without knowing it I have passed the day
When the last fires will wave to me
And the silence will set out
Tireless traveller
Like the beam of a lightless star
Then I will no longer
Find myself in life as in a strange garment
Surprised at the earth
And the love of one woman
And the shamelessness of men
As today writing after three days of rain
Hearing the wren sing and the falling cease
And bowing not knowing to what

GIORNI [1]
(Edward Mayes, 1951–)

Gather the pears of St. Peter before the first *vespa*[2] begins to suck
out the white juice, and gather the *nocciole*[3] on St. Philibert's day,

hence their other name, before something I can't see bores small
holes into the brown shells. The long cords of the families
   continue to

---

[1] *giorni:* days
[2] *vespa:* wasp
[3] *nocciole:* hazelnuts

unravel, on one end a weight down an old well, green snakes at
the bottom.
Gather cabbages when their outer leaves are large enough to
wrap

a child in, or when one leaf can be floated in a bucket of water
with a honey
jar on top. The recipes get longer when I want them shorter,
shorter when

I want them longer. The moon is waxing and now what should I
be gathering?
Gather the *pomodori, sempre.*[4] Snap them off their thick green
stems and eat,

the heat of them in your hands. Make a fist of your hand, make a
hand of your
fist. What's the first stop after death, or the next stop? I remember
the years

I spent, cumulatively, below zero, frozen families. Then thawed
families, gathering
for some reason, and then leaving, saying *tanti auguri,*[5] and may
there be one

hundred of these days. The sun gathers the darkness somehow
because each
day here I sense two minutes less of light. Exactly two, as if
someone holds

up two fingers and someone else in the control room nods.
Gather the *melone,*

---

[4] *pomodori, sempre:* tomatoes, always
[5] *tanti auguri:* best wishes

small and sweet, hundreds of seeds in the wet center. Think of
    the seeds

the families have sown, have scattered. It has been all of us here
    who have
gathered, even casually, such as, I gather that you're in a hurry, I
    gather that

this it the last time we'll see each other alive. It is I, talking,
    speaking correctly,
writing one last word followed by another last word. I somehow
    need to

gather darkness around me like the shield I want to be carried
    home on.
When we gather, we recognize what we've gathered. And all the
    days,

more than the one hundred, more than the thirty thousand we've
    been allotted,
all these days repeat *this is us, it is you, here, it is I, here, sono io.*[6]

---

[6] *sono io:* it is I

8

Traditional and Open Forms

*In poetry you have a form looking for a subject and a
subject looking for a form. When they come together
successfully you have a poem.*
—W. H. AUDEN

Form is the first thing I notice about a poem. At a glance, my eye picks
up many subtle clues that orient me. Is the poem dense, or is it sur-
rounded by a lot of white space? Do words appear scattered, or are
they justified along the left margin? Any irregular spacing attracts the
eye, alerts you to listen to the poem's particular music. Stanzas indi-
cate a formal coherence. If the stanzas are couplets (two lines) or qua-
trains (four lines), the unrolling of those equally formed verses down
the page contributes right away to a sense of harmony and order.

How does form relate to the poem's overall impact? And why?
Does form contribute meaning? What is it exactly?

Form doesn't hold a poem like a pitcher holds milk. Form is more
like a satin dress that fits tight as a second skin. That's the right fit,
but form can't come off like a dress. Although the accepted wisdom,
"Form follows function," works for architecture, it isn't quite accu-
rate for poetry. "Sound must seem an echo to the sense," the famous

dictum of Alexander Pope, also just misses. "Echo" and "follow" are misleading words. They imply that the inside and the outside of the poem are separable.

The poem's form and content are interactive systems. Form without balanced content is hollow; content without form is chaos. The poem *is* the form; the form *is* the poem.

The American Heritage Dictionary lists many meanings for form. First, "the contour and structure of something as distinguished from its substance." Second, "the body or outward appearance (of a person or animal) considered separately from the face or head." Those definitions won't do for our purposes. If all parts of a poem work together as a whole, form cannot be "separated" or "distinguished from" other elements. I read at definition eight: "fitness, as of an athlete or animal, with regard to health or training." This is getting close. Certainly the life of the poem depends on a strong form, but this definition too misses something. Form is not simply a well-trained body that gets the poem over the finish line. All these are helpful, but we're after the precise relationship of form and substance.

All the way down at definition number nineteen, I find "the resting place of a hare." The resting place and the hare give a good figurative image for the intertwining of form and substance in poetry: the live animal and the moment of its shaping the grass. The resting place of the rabbit, a swirl of grasses, occurs simultaneously with the wild animal settling into it. The form of a good poem occurs simultaneously with the meaning, not as a separate phenomenon. The better the poem, the more natural the form seems.

Yeats makes interesting use of the same image:

MEMORY
(William Butler Yeats, 1865–1939)

One had a lovely face,
And two or three had charm,
But charm and face were in vain
Because the mountain grass

Cannot but keep the form
Where the mountain hare has lain.

Yeats's metaphor of the hare and grass reveals that because of his iden-
tity with the woman, he cannot help but retain within himself a place
for her presence: He is formed *only* for her. The poem's form, ideally,
has the same inevitability.

Looking at Forms

What first impressions do you get from a shape?

EASTER WINGS
(George Herbert, 1593–1633)

Lord, who createdst man in wealth and store,
Though foolishly he lost the same,
Decaying more and more,
Till he became
Most poor:
With thee
O let me rise
As larks, harmoniously,
And sing this day thy victories:
Then shall the fall further the flight in me.

My tender age in sorrow did begin;
And still with sicknesses and shame
Thou didst so punish sin,
That I became
Most thin.
With thee
Let me combine,
And feel this day thy victory;
For, I imp my wing on thine,
Affliction shall advance the flight in me.

Written in the seventeenth century, "Easter Wings" represents an
extreme use of form. The shape of the poem actually makes a vi-
sual image of wings. Poets since the Greeks have experimented with

304 / THE DISCOVERY OF POETRY

portraying graphically the relationship of subject and form. **Con-crete poetry** (or *shaped* poetry) is the name for poetry with this in-tent. In "Easter Wings," notice how the expansion and contraction of the line lengths works. The line expands for God, contracts for mankind and "I." Herbert's subject is, broadly, the possibility of res-urrection inspired by Easter. The term *imp* in the next-to-last line means "to graft." Falconers imped extra feathers on wings so their birds could be more powerful. Herbert uses the term as a metaphor for attaching his spirit to God's. The poem's concrete image of wings underscores this metaphor.

Poems have been constructed, often with wit, in the shape of crosses, swans, lambs, hourglasses, and apples. Sometimes the concrete poem is *only* shape; the image or typographical arrangement *is* the poem, as in this example by Aram Saroyan:

eyeye

Concrete poems surprise us with novelty. After the first reaction to the typography wears off, however, the poem might not be very inter-esting. The shape can seem to call too much attention to itself, over-shadowing content. But some concrete poems, like "Easter Wings," offer more than a quick impression; even though the balance is some-what tipped, our interest in the content isn't overwhelmed by the vi-sual impact.

For most poets, shaped or concrete poems are merely occasional pieces. Not every poem about a tulip benefits from the tulip shape. But often the desire to make the poem into an image of content in-fluences the form. Just as line placement is expressive, a poem's over-all shape subtly expresses something too.

The form of "The Shape of Death" borrows some of the impact of a concrete poem. The appearance is disturbing. A white, jagged shape runs down the middle. With the title in mind, we begin reading the poem with a sense of intrigue: Is death this ghostly hole down the middle? Do we read straight across or down? Does the gap in each line work as a long caesura? As we read, the white space becomes an imaginative blank that counterpoises love (small as a cell that can't be split) and death (large as a nuclear blast). Central to the poem is a questioning, which the mysterious, shifting white space actively reinforces. The hole down the middle remains ambiguous. Unlike concrete poems, which make a visual image such as an apple or a flower, this internal shaping uses the line and the stanza to express important tension in the poem.

THE SHAPE OF DEATH
(May Swenson, 1919–1989)

What does love look like?   We know the shape of death.
Death is a cloud, immense   and awesome. At first a
lid is lifted from the   eye of light. There is a
clap of sound. A white   blossom belches from the
jaw of fright. A   pillared cloud churns from
white to gray, like a   monstrous brain that bursts
and burns—then turns   sickly black, spilling
away, filling the whole   sky with ashes of dread.
Thickly it wraps, between   the clean seas and the
moon, the earth's green   head. Trapped in its
cocoon, its choking   breath, we know the shape
of death. Death is a   cloud. What does love look

like? Is it a particle,   a star, invisible entirely,
beyond the microscope and   Palomar? A dimension past
the length of hope? Is   it a climate far and fair,
that we shall never dare   discover? What is its
color, and its alchemy?   Is it a jewel in the earth,
can it be dug? Or   dredged from the sea? Can
it be bought? Can it be   sown and harvested? Is it
a shy beast to be caught?   Death is a cloud—immense

a clap of sound. Love is
nests within each cell,
is a ray, a seed, a note,
our air and blood. It is
our very skin, a sheath

little and not loud. It
and it cannot be split. It
a word, a secret motion of
not alien — it is near —
to keep us pure of fear.

"The Shape of Death" is an **open form**: The shape is unique to this particular poem. Open forms sometimes are called **nonce forms,** nonce meaning "for an occasion."

A poem's form doesn't always make a visual statement. Most poems line up in blocks or move straight down the page. A practiced reader of poetry recognizes right away if a poem is one of the traditional forms of English poetry. The next poem is a **sonnet.** Unless you already know the form, its shape offers little immediate information. The sonnet has fourteen lines and is the great English poetic form. There is some choice about how these lines are divided into stanzas; but basically, when you spot a fourteen-line poem, most probably a sonnet is at hand.

BRIGHT STAR
(John Keats, 1795–1821)

Bright star, would I were stedfast as thou art —
　　Not in lone splendour hung aloft the night
And watching, with eternal lids apart,
　　Like nature's patient, sleepless Eremite,[1]
The moving waters at their priestlike task
　　Of pure ablution round earth's human shores,
Or gazing on the new soft-fallen mask
　　Of snow upon the mountains and the moors —
No — yet still stedfast, still unchangeable,
　　Pillow'd upon my fair love's ripening breast,
To feel for ever its soft fall and swell,

---

[1] *Eremite:* hermit.

Awake for ever in a sweet unrest,
Still, still to hear her tender-taken breath,
And so live ever — or else swoon to death.

A poet who chooses the sonnet form is committed to a meter and rhyme scheme, and to a small space and fast development. The usual rhyme scheme of the sonnet demands a strong closing rhyme, which tends toward a resolved ending. The end bangs shut. These "givens" offer some advantages to the writer, but also some dangers. Since so many great poems exist in the form, just choosing it reminds the reader of other sonnets and invites comparisons. Obviously, using the inherited form becomes a rich complement when the poem is good and a tremendous liability otherwise. When the writer tries the sonnet, or other traditional forms, often ideas come from the set form. The sonnet possesses a momentum of its own and may channel the poet's mind in new directions.

The poems above represent three approaches to structure: making a concrete visual image out of words, developing an expressive shape, and using an inherited form. In a good poem, no matter what its structure, *the form is the content.*

Traditional Forms

STANZAS

In Italian, *stanza* means "room"; a stanza is to the poem as a room is to the house. Each stanza does different work and each is necessary to the poem's whole structure. Like verses in a song, a stanza follows a set pattern, stops, then starts the pattern again. Usually there's a line space between stanzas.

Why is a poem written in stanzas? Think of the stanza as a *section of development.* A stanza works like a paragraph. New paragraph, new viewpoint or subject. The same holds for poetry, although the change is sometimes subtle.

Stanzas, like meters, have no inherent significance. They are plastic, accommodating themselves to massacres as well as love songs, to nonsense as well as high seriousness. As with each other element in poetry, we must always look to the whole for meaning, not to any one part.

These are examples of stanzas commonly used in English. Stanzas may, of course, be unrhymed, although in traditional poetry we expect a rhyme scheme.

Couplet: two lines. Sometimes the couplet is set off in stanzas but, rhymed, the couplet is often employed for long uninterrupted verse. An aa rhyme identifies the couples. The **heroic couplet** is rhymed iambic pentameter, as in these lines by Alexander Pope:

> The hungry judges soon the sentence sign,
> And wretches hang that jurymen may dine.

Tercet (also called **triplet**): three lines, as in this example by Percy Bysshe Shelley. Usual rhyme schemes are aaa (all end words rhyme) or aba.

> O wild West Wind, thou breath of Autumn's being,
> Thou, from whose unseen presence the leaves dead
> Are driven, like ghosts from an enchanter fleeing,

Tercets that are rhyme-linked (aba, bcb, cdc, and so on) are called **terza rima.** This is the stanza used in Dante's *Divine Comedy.*

Quatrain: four lines. Ballads and many hymns are written in quatrains. Many types of quatrains exist, with varied meters and rhyme schemes. A quatrain called **common measure** alternates a four-foot iambic line with a three-foot iambic line, rhyming abcb. Quatrains are the most frequently used of all the types of stanzas, as in this example by Walter Savage Landor.

> I strove with none, for none was worth my strife;
> Nature I loved; and next to Nature, Art.
> I warm'd both hands against the fire of life;
> It sinks, and I am ready to depart.

Quintet: five lines with no prescribed rhyme. This example by William Blake from "The School Boy" rhymes ababb:

> How can the bird that is born for joy
> Sit in a cage and sing?
> How can a child, when fears annoy,
> But droop his tender wing,
> And forget his youthful spring?

Sestet: six lines variously rhymed, or unrhymed. Here's an example from "I Wandered Lonely as a Cloud" by William Wordsworth:

> For oft, when on my couch I lie
> in vacant or in pensive mood,
> They flash upon that inward eye
> Which is the bliss of solitude;
> And then my heart with pleasure fills,
> And dances with the daffodils.

Septet (or **Chaucerian stanza** or **rhyme royal**): seven lines. Chaucer was the first to write septets (rhyming ababbcc) in English, but because King James I of Scotland once wrote the same stanza form, it is sometimes called rhyme royal, as in these lines from *The Canterbury Tales*. When used with other rhyme schemes, this stanza is simply called a septet.

With so glad cheere his gestes° she receyveth.   *guests*
And so konnyngly° everich° in his degree,   *adeptly, each one*
That no defaute° no man aperceyveth°   *fault, perceived*
But ay they wondren what she myghte be
That in so poure array was for to se
And koude° swich honour and reverence,   *was familiar with*
And worthily they preysen° hir prudence.   *praised*

Octave: eight lines. An octave may have any rhyme scheme, or none. **Ottava rima** is a special form of the octave rhyming ababcc, as in this example from "Don Juan" by George Gordon, Lord Byron.

But sweeter still than this, than these, than all,
    Is first and passionate love—it stands alone,
Like Adam's recollection of his fall;
    The tree of knowledge has been plucked—all's known—
And life yields nothing further to recall
    Worthy of this ambrosial sin, so shown,
No doubt in fable, as the unforgiven
Fire which Prometheus filched for us from heaven.

Spenserian Stanza: nine lines with an ababbcbcc rhyme. An unusual stanza because eight lines in iambic pentameter are followed by a longer hexameter (six-foot) line. As in these lines from "The Eve of St. Agnes" by John Keats, the Spenserian stanza makes an effective visual and rhythmic break in a long poem.

And they are gone: aye, ages long ago
These lovers fled away into the storm.
That night the Baron dreamt of many a woe,
And all his warrior-guests, with shade and form
Of witch, and demon, and large coffin-worm,

Were long be-nightmared. Angela the old
Died palsy-twitched, with meager face deform;
The Beadsman, after thousand aves told,
For aye unsought-for slept among his ashes cold.

These nine lengths are the major building blocks of stanzaic poetry. Poets often combine several types of stanzas in one poem. For instance, notice that the sonnets in the next section are made of quatrains and couplets or octaves and sestets. Shelley's "Ode to the West Wind" (page 329) combines the terza rima stanza with a couplet at the end of each section.

A thorough study of stanza combinations, variations, and the traditional forms used in poetry could fill several volumes. We will look at forms with distinctly different qualities.

SONNET

Sonneto means "little song" in Italian. The **sonnet** is a lyric with fourteen rhyming lines in iambic pentameter. Before the twentieth century, almost every major writer, along with thousands of minor ones, selected this form at some time. Early poets were partial to the **sonnet sequence** (a group of sonnets on a theme) and to **sonnet crowns** (seven linked sonnets in which the last line of one becomes the first line of the next, and the last line of the final poem repeats the first line of the first poem). Because the sonnet form is short, it lends itself to such groupings. But short also means difficult. Many poets write sonnets about the sonnet, revealing their love/hate feelings for the requirements of the form. The form is exacting, particularly at the end. Early sonnets are primarily love poems, but every subject finds a home in the form. Hundreds of experiments and adaptations have bent and continue to bend the form to various ends.

Why is the sonnet the great traditional English form? Partly because English poets fell in love with the sonnets of the Italian Renaissance and wanted to write their own versions. Fortunately, the imported form adapted to our language. Once on English soil, the form naturalized. Iambic pentameter conducts a seemingly effortless flow of English, and the short form seems conducive to English also, like the usual length of a prose paragraph.

The three major types of sonnet are Shakespearean, Petrarchan, and Spenserian. Each is a tight structure. Their challenging rhyme schemes all produce a coherent, packed, and therefore charged form.

The **Shakespearean sonnet** (also called the **English sonnet**) consists of three quatrains rhyming abab, cdcd, and efef, followed by a concluding couplet rhyming gg. The action of the poem proceeds, then, like three quick spins and a sudden leap. The final rhyme, coming so close to its partner, closes the poem with finality; there is no doubting the end. Therefore, this kind of sonnet suits subjects that need strong closure. If the subject does not, the form can sound forced toward a conclusion not demanded by the quatrains.

SONNET XCVIII
(William Shakespeare, 1564–1616)

From you have I been absent in the spring,
When proud-pied April, dress'd in all his trim,
Hath put a spirit of youth in every thing,
That heavy Saturn laugh'd and leap'd with him.
Yet nor the lays of birds, nor the sweet smell
Of different flowers in odour and in hue,
Could make me any summer's story tell,
Or from their proud lap pluck them where they grew:
Nor did I wonder at the lily's white,
Nor praise the deep vermilion in the rose;
They were but sweet, but figures of delight,
Drawn after you, you pattern of all those.
Yet seem'd it winter still, and, you away,
As with your shadow I with these did play.

The **Petrarchan sonnet** form, named after the fourteenth-century Italian poet Petrarch, is in two parts: an octave rhyming abbaabba and a sestet of varying rhyme schemes, often cdcdcd. Between the octave and sestet, where the rhyme break occurs, there is usually a psychological break called the *turn*. Here, after the rather leisurely eight-line opening where the subject is laid forth, the poem changes course. Words such as *but, thus, so,* or *because* often further pinpoint the change in thought or direction that this turn signals. After the turn, the sestet resolves or consolidates or reflects on the concerns of the octave. The subject of the poem must lend itself to this kind of resolution in order for the form to fit.

The Petrarchan is hard to sustain in English because the writer works with only four different rhymes instead of the six of the Shakespearean sonnet; thus four words must rhyme with each other instead of only two. Some poets object to this tighter rhyme scheme; Keats called it "pouncing rhyme."

ON FIRST LOOKING INTO CHAPMAN'S HOMER[1]
(John Keats, 1795–1821)

Much have I traveled in the realms of gold,
    And many goodly states and kingdoms seen;
    Round many western islands have I been
Which bards in fealty to Apollo hold.
Oft of one wide expanse had I been told
    That deep-browed Homer ruled as his demesne[2];
    Yet did I never breathe its pure serene
Till I heard Chapman speak out loud and bold:
Then felt I like some watcher of the skies

---

[1] *Chapman's Homer:* George Chapman, Elizabethan poet, translated Homer.
[2] *demesne:* realm.

When a new planet swims into his ken;
Or like stout Cortez[3] when with eagle eyes
    He stared at the Pacific—and all his men
Looked at each other with a wild surmise—
    Silent, upon a peak in Darien.

—————

[3] *Cortez:* Keats mistakes Cortez for Balboa, the explorer
who first reached the Pacific in 1513.

The **Spenserian sonnet** is the least favored of the three major types.
Like the Spenserian stanza, this sonnet is named for the innovative
sixteenth-century poet, Edmund Spenser. His abab, bcbc, cdcd, ee
rhyme scheme links even the quatrains together. These interwoven
rhymes give an intensely lyrical effect, blending the lines together.

SONNET LXXV
(Edmund Spenser, 1522–1599)

One day I wrote her name upon the strand,
    But came the waves and washed it away;
    Again I wrote it with a second hand.
    But came the tide and made my pains his prey.
"Vain man," said she, "that dost in vain assay
    A mortal thing so to immortalize,
    For I myself shall like to this decay,
    And eke my name be wiped out likewise."
"Not so," quod I, "let baser things devise
    To die in dust, but you shall live by fame;
    My verse your virtues rare shall eternize
    And in the heavens write your glorious name,
Where, whenas death shall all the world subdue,
    Our love shall live, and later life renew."

Not quite a traditional love sonnet, "Sonnet Reversed" begins with the couplet, which usually closes a sonnet. What point does this reversal of form make?

SONNET REVERSED
(Rupert Brooke, 1887–1915)

Hand trembling towards hand; the amazing lights
Of heart and eye. They stood on supreme heights.

Ah, the delirious weeks of honeymoon!
    Soon they returned, and, after strange adventures,
Settled at Balham by the end of June.
    Their money was in Can. Pacs. B. Debentures,
And in Antofagastas. Still he went
    Cityward daily; still she did abide
At home. And both were really quite content
    With work and social pleasures. Then they died.
They left three children (besides George, who drank):
    The eldest Jane, who married Mr Bell,
William, the head-clerk in the County Bank,
    And Henry, a stock-broker, doing well.

VILLANELLE
Although imported to England from France, the villanelle also originated in Italy, where it was a folk song form in the late fifteenth century. In English, as in Italian, it is primarily a lyric form.

IF I COULD TELL YOU
(W. H. Auden, 1907–1973)

Time will say nothing but I told you so,
Time only knows the price we have to pay;
If I could tell you I would let you know.

If we should weep when clowns put on their show,
If we should stumble when musicians play,
Time will say nothing but I told you so.

There are no fortunes to be told, although,
Because I love you more than I can say,
If I could tell you I would let you know.

The winds must come from somewhere when they blow,
There must be reasons why the leaves decay;
Time will say nothing but I told you so.

Perhaps the roses really want to grow,
The vision seriously intends to stay;
If I could tell you I would let you know.

Suppose the lions all get up and go,
And all the brooks and soldiers run away;
Will Time say nothing but I told you so?
If I could tell you I would let you know.

Understanding the structure of this appealing form becomes easier after reading and hearing the repeating lines. The **villanelle** consists of nineteen lines: five tercets and a concluding quatrain. Each tercet rhymes aba. The quatrain at the end rhymes abaa. The first line of the poem repeats as the end of stanzas 2 and 4; it also repeats in the penultimate line. The last line of stanza 1 repeats as the last line of stanzas 3 and 5, and also at the last line of the poem. No set metrical pattern is required, though lines usually are close to the same syllabic length.

The repetition cannot be static. Each time a repeating line reappears, it should have added significance. Rhythmically, the repetition seems to push the poem forward, like waves breaking behind waves. The repetition of both recurrent lines at the end seems to deliver all the rhythm of the poem to the closing.

SESTINA

The most mysterious form used in English is the **sestina** (see page 319). As the word suggests, the form is based on sixes. Six six-line stanzas end with a tercet. The last words on each line in the first stanza are repeated as the last words in the following stanzas, in a defined order. All six key words also appear in the tercet, three as end words and one in the middle of each line. Notice too that the last word of a stanza ends the first line in the next stanza. Finally, the last word of the poem repeats the last word of the first line. Trace the recurrences in this example, which I wrote to exorcise my bird phobia.

SESTINA FOR THE OWL

True, I am afraid of birds, but the <u>owl</u>	A
has yellow round eyes that open and <u>close</u>	B
like a human's. I'm fixed in that <u>stare</u>.	C
Every day at Mother's table, the owl is <u>over</u>	D
me, blinking. I do not hear her <u>fly</u>	E
in, flatten quietly against the wall. <u>Terror</u>	F
of her gleaming talons as I blow the soup. <u>Terror</u>	F
of her feathers ruffling. In the frame she's "The Snowy <u>Owl</u>,"	A
pretending. I sip the soup. She spots prey, <u>flies</u>.	E
Devours on the spot and I <u>close</u>	B
my fists, vomit fur tooth bone. Over and <u>over</u>	D
at dinner she calls, oooo . . . eee. I run <u>upstairs</u>.	C
I won't sleep. I won't sleep because she <u>stares</u>	C
down from the high rafters above my bed. <u>Terror</u>	F
of her cry, you . . . me. . . . In the dark, <u>over</u>	D
my body she is waiting. If I sleep, the <u>owl</u>	A
will fall, rake out my palms with her talons, <u>close</u>	B
my sharp eyes. If I slowly drift, she <u>flies</u>	E

at me, my mouth fills with feathers, <u>flies</u>   E
down, hard beak gouging. Wild, she <u>stares</u>   C
flapping until I scream for Mother, Hold me <u>close</u>!   B
There's no such thing! I can't trust her, my <u>terror</u>   F
chattering my teeth, her snowy gown white as <u>owl's</u>.   A
The night will never be <u>over</u>.   D

Now, in the dream the old woman in a coat hunches <u>over</u>   D
the hill, returns, turns fierce, turns owl, <u>flies</u>   E
for me. And at the museum I see the very <u>owl's</u>   A
soft plumage, the angel bird, immovable eyes. I <u>stare</u>   C
a long time deeply stirred. Could I feel the <u>terror</u>   F
of the field mouse lifted high in my hooks, <u>close</u>   B

to my breast, smothering, thrilled. The stuffed owl <u>closes</u>   B
her eyes. No it will never be <u>over</u>.   D
In the field she is always circling, her shadow a <u>terror</u>   F
over small creatures. My red coat draws her eye. She <u>flies</u> E
around and around me, narrowing my chances. I <u>stare</u>   C
up at the sky where she sails in wide rings. The <u>owl</u>   A

swoops <u>close</u> and flies, swoops close. <u>Flies</u>   (B) E
into the body of a woman and <u>over</u> the child running
    <u>downstairs</u>   (D) C
wings spreading <u>terror</u>. You, me, you, me, sings the <u>owl</u>.   (F) A

If the end words in stanza one are lettered ABCDEF, the pattern for repeating the words is:

1. ABCDEF
2. FAEBDC
3. CFDABE
4. ECBFAD
5. DEACFB
6. BDFECA
7. ECA (with BDF midline)

When the sestina was first used in the early twelfth century, the numerology of the sixes probably had a mystical meaning that is lost to us now. What is still fascinating, on inspection of the form, is that each end word is positioned next to every other end word twice in the poem. If we make a hexagon of end words (called ABCDEF) and connect each end word as it touches all the other end words in every stanza, we see that the poem is indeed graphically complete (see figure).

THE SESTINA

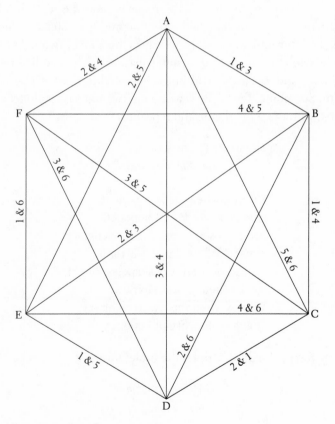

Letters = end words
Numbers = stanzas where words are next to each other; for example,
E is next to D in stanzas 1 and 5

This locked network, along with the incantatory effect of the return of the word in different contexts in each stanza, *creates* the sestina's closed, weblike structure. Subjects must call for intricacy in order for the form to fit. The sestina especially suits exploring compulsive subjects, problems without solution, obsessions, or dream states. Possibly these are the reasons the sestina remains a popular form in contemporary poetry.

THREE LYRIC FORMS

Three similar French forms that made their way into the repertoire of English poetry are the triolet, the rondeau, and the rondel. All are light lyrics. Their concentrated repetition and lyric qualities demonstrate both the difficulty and the felicity of these highly wrought forms.

The **triolet** is one octave rhyming abaaabab. The first line repeats at lines 4 and 7. The second line is repeated as the last line of the poem. Sometimes the triolet is written in two stanzas, a quintet and a triplet, with the same rhyme and repeat pattern.

FIRST PHOTOS OF FLU VIRUS
(Harold Witt, 1923–)

Viruses, when the lens is right,
change into a bright bouquet.
Are such soft forms of pure delight
viruses? When the lens is right,
instead of swarms of shapeless blight,
we see them in a Renoir way.
Viruses when the lens is right
change into a bright bouquet.

"Early Supper" skillfully triples the triolet form.

EARLY SUPPER
(Barbara Howes, 1914–)

Laughter of children brings
    The kitchen down with laughter.

While the old kettle sings
Laughter of children brings
To a boil all savory things.
    Higher than beam or rafter,
Laughter of children brings
    The kitchen down with laughter.

So ends an autumn day,
    Light ripples on the ceiling,
Dishes are stacked away;
So ends an autumn day,
The children jog and sway
    In comic dances wheeling.
So ends an autumn day,
    Light ripples on the ceiling.

They trail upstairs to bed,
    And night is a dark tower.
The kettle calls: instead
They trail upstairs to bed,
Leaving warmth, the coppery-red
    Mood of their carnival hour.
They trail upstairs to bed,
    And night is a dark tower.

The most common—**rondeau**—consists of fifteen lines arranged in a quintet, quatrain, and sestet. The first few words of the first line act as a refrain in lines 9 and 15. These refrain lines do not rhyme, but repeating the fragment seems to imply the rest of the line, including the rhyme. The rhyme, therefore, acts invisibly. The rondeau's usual rhyme scheme is aabba, aab*Refrain*, aabba*Refrain*. An eight-syllable line is traditional.

DEATH OF A VERMONT FARM WOMAN
(Barbara Howes, 1914–)

Is it time now to go away?
July is nearly over; hay

Fattens the barn, the herds are strong,
Our old fields prosper; these long
Green evenings will keep death at bay.

Last winter lingered; it was May
Before a flowering lilac spray
Barred cold for ever. I was wrong.
                    Is it time now?

Six decades vanished in a day!
I bore four sons: one lives; they
Were all good men; three dying young
Was hard on us. I have looked long
For these hills to show me where peace lay...
                    Is it time now?

Rondels are similar to rondeaux. Thirteen or fourteen lines use two refrains. Line 1 comes back at 7; line 2 repeats at 8. The first two lines close the poem. The chosen rhyme scheme determines which will be the last line. Two quatrains followed by a quintet or sestet is the usual structure. The rhyme scheme varies: Often it is abba, abab, abbaa.

TOO HARD IT IS TO SING
(Austin Dobson, 1840–1921)

(Too hard it is to sing
    In these untuneful times,
When only coin can ring,
    And no one cares for rhymes!

Alas! for him who climbs
    To Aganippe's spring:[1]

---

[1] *Aganippe's spring*: spring on Mount Helicon, sacred to the muses.

Too hard it is to sing
    In these untuneful times!

His kindred clip his wing;
    His feet the critic limes:
If Fame her laurel bring,
    Old age his forehead rimes:
Too hard it is to sing
    In these untuneful times!)

OTHER TRADITIONS: HAIKU AND PANTOUM

The forms we've considered so far all evolved in England and western Europe. Haiku and pantoum are two forms from more distant sources.

Japanese **haikus** appear to be simple. Many of us learned to write them in grade school. The form is only seventeen syllables, arranged in three lines of 5-7-5 syllables. The form may have originated as long ago as the thirteenth century in the linked verses of medieval Japan. The haiku is related to the **tanka,** a slightly longer poem of 31 syllables in five lines, arranged 5-7-5-7-7. The haiku construction corresponds to the first three lines of the tanka form. Traditional Japanese poetry is based on the alternation of 5-7-5 lines, the short length corresponding to the culture's appreciation for simplicity. In the twentieth century, the haiku form became extraordinarily popular in English. Technically it is next to impossible to write a true haiku in our language. Japanese is a language without stresses and with different grammatical constructions. English cannot condense, without wrenching the meaning, to the extent Japanese can.

We can sense the compression possible in Japanese by looking at the word-for-word translation of a haiku: "bell fading out flower's scent as for strike evening." A translator wanting to make this meaningful to an English reader has to keep the economy of the original while supplying more connectives. We might write:

As bell tones fade,
flower scents take up the ringing—
evening breeze.

With these difficulties in mind, the English approximations of haikus can be satisfying on their own terms. Often, because of the language differences, translators of haiku sacrifice the correct syllable count in an attempt to keep to the economical compression of the original. Haiku composed in English keeps closer to the 5-7-5 form.

Whether a haiku is a translation or an English original, the form must work as quickly as the brush stroke in a Japanese ink sketch. The immediacy of a single image—bell notes, cherry blossoms, birds— joined to a seasonal allusion suggests a time passing or a change in a human condition.

These translations are by R. H. Blyth:

The silence!
The voice of the cicada
Penetrates the rocks.   —*Basho*

The coolness:
The voice of the bell
As it leaves the bell!   —*Buson*

It is deep autumn
My neighbor—
How does he live?   —*Buson*

The wind-bells ringing,
While the leeks
Sway.   —*Shosei*

New Year's Day;
The hut just as it is,
Nothing to ask for.   —*Nanshi*

Ah, grief and sadness!
The fishing-line trembles
    In the autumn breeze.   —*Buson*

How long the day:
The boat is talking
    With the shore.   —*Shiki*

The snake slid away,
But the eyes that glared at me,
    Remained in the grass.   —*Kyoski*

For an imported form to take root, it must fill a need for a certain kind of expression. Before the haiku was adopted, English had nothing like it in size or intent. Closest in tone and length was the **epigram,** a rhyming couplet or quatrain such as this one by Alexander Pope:

> But when to mischief mortals bend their will,
> How soon they find fit instruments of ill!

But epigrams have very different qualities. An anonymous Latin epigram describes itself:

> Three things must epigrams, like bees, have all,
> A sting, and honey, and a body small.

Epigrams *comment.* Though often funny or ironic, their primary function is to impart wisdom.* The haiku may be wise also, but the chief purpose is to reveal a momentary, often quite complex perception. Writers in English adopted the haiku because they responded to the delicate sensibility inherent in the form.

---

* *Note:* Don't confuse *epigram* with *epitaph* (the inscription on a tombstone) or with *epigraph* (a quote at the beginning of a poem or story).

The **pantoum** also has qualities not found in English. The form is a Malayan one from the fifteenth century, with older roots in Chinese and Persian poetry. The sound effect is close to chanting, with extensive use of repetition. A pantoum consists of an indefinite number of quatrains of any line length. The second and fourth lines of each stanza become the first and third lines of the next stanza. Sometimes the pantoum is rhymed abab, bcbc, cdcd (and so on), but usually in English it is unrhymed. The pantoum circles back. Like some of the French lyric forms, it ends where it began: The last line of the poem repeats the first line. The second line of the last stanza repeats the third line of stanza 1. Often the pantoum develops two ideas. The first starts in the first two lines of the poem and the second starts in the last two lines of stanza 1. Because of the pattern of the repeating lines, the two subjects work their way down the poem in a back-and-forth, push-pull movement.

ATOMIC PANTOUM
(Peter Meinke, 1932–)

In a chain reaction
the neutrons released
split other nuclei
which release more neutrons

The neutrons released
blow open some others
which release more neutrons
and start this all over

Blow open some others
and choirs will crumble
and start this all over
with eyes burned to ashes

And choirs will crumble
the fish catch on fire
with eyes burned to ashes
in a chain reaction

The fish catch on fire
because the sun's force
in a chain reaction
has blazed in our minds

Because the sun's force
with plutonium trigger
has blazed in our minds
we are dying to use it

With plutonium trigger
curled and tightened
we are dying to use it
torching our enemies

Curled and tightened
blind to the end
torching our enemies
we sing to Jesus

Blind to the end
split up like nuclei
we sing to Jesus
in a chain reaction

In Your Notebook:

Keats and his friends often had fifteen-minute sonnet competitions. "Sonnet Right Off the Bat" inspires you to set the timer to fifteen minutes and go. Choose a rhyme scheme and try your own.

SONNET RIGHT OFF THE BAT
(Lope de Vega, 1562–1635)

"Write me a sonnet. On the spot," said she.
Now there's a bind I wasn't in before.
A sonnet's fourteen lines, I hear — no more
No less. But look, just jabbering I did three.
You'd think the rhymes would have me up a tree,
But here I'm halfway through the second four.
So, if I up by two my present score
The octave's a dead duck. No stopping me!

Well look at Lope entering line nine!
I must have knocked it off in nothing flat
And breezed half through the sestet. Doing fine
Nearing the finish. As to where I'm at,
I rather think it's — hmmm — the thirteenth line.
Here's fourteen. Care to count them? And that's that.
— Translated by John Frederick Nims

Poems

SONNET CXVI
(William Shakespeare, 1564–1616)

Let me not to the marriage of true minds
Admit impediments. Love is not love

Which alters when it alteration finds.
Or bends with the remover to remove:
O, no! it is an ever-fixed mark,
That looks on tempests and is never shaken;
It is the star to every wandering bark,
Whose worth's unknown, although his height be taken.
Love's not Time's fool, though rosy lips and cheeks
Within his bending sickle's compass come;
Love alters not with his brief hours and weeks,
But bears it out even to the edge of doom.
If this be error and upon me proved,
I never writ, nor no man ever loved.

ODE TO THE WEST WIND
(Percy Bysshe Shelley, 1792–1822)

I

O wild West Wind, thou breath of Autumn's being,
Thou, from whose unseen presence the leaves dead
Are driven, like ghosts from an enchanter fleeing,

Yellow, and black, and pale, and hectic red,
Pestilence-stricken multitudes! O thou
Who chariotest to their dark wintry bed

The winged seeds, where they lie cold and low,
Each like a corpse within its grave, until
Thine azure sister of the spring shall blow

Her clarion o'er the dreaming earth, and fill
(Driving sweet buds like flocks for feed in air)
With living hues and odours plain and hill:

Wild spirit, which art moving everywhere;
Destroyer and preserver; hear, Oh hear!

II

Thou on whose stream, 'mid the steep sky's commotion,
Loose clouds like earth's decaying leaves are shed,
Shook from the tangled boughs of heaven and ocean,

Angels of rain and lightning: there are spread
On the blue surface of thine airy surge,
Like the bright hair uplifted from the head

Of some fierce Maenad,[1] even from the dim verge
Of the horizon to the zenith's height,
The locks of the approaching storm. Thou dirge

Of the dying year, to which this closing night
Will be the dome of a vast sepulchre,
Vaulted with all thy congregated might

Of vapours, from whose solid atmosphere
Black rain, and fire, and hail will burst: O hear!

III

Thou who didst waken from his summer dreams
The blue Mediterranean, where he lay.
Lulled by the coil of his crystalline streams,

Beside a pumice isle in Baiae's bay,[2]
And saw in sleep old palaces and towers
Quivering within the wave's intenser day,

---

[1] *Maenad:* wild, frenzied woman; originally a member of the cult of
Dionysus, Greek god of wine and fertility.
[2] *Baiae's bay:* northwestern part of the Bay of Naples.

All overgrown with azure moss and flowers
So sweet, the sense faints picturing them! Thou
For whose path the Atlantic's level powers

Cleave themselves into chasms, while far below
The sea-blooms and the oozy woods which wear
The sapless foliage of the ocean, know

Thy voice, and suddenly grow gray with fear,
And tremble and despoil themselves: O hear!

IV

If I were a dead leaf thou mightest bear;
If I were a swift cloud to fly with thee;
A wave to pant beneath thy power, and share

The impulse of thy strength, only less free
Than thou, O uncontrollable! if even
I were as in my boyhood, and could be

The comrade of thy wanderings over heaven,
As then, when to outstrip thy skiey speed
Scarce seemed a vision; I would ne'er have striven

As thus with thee in prayer in my sore need.
O! lift me as a wave, a leaf, a cloud!
I fall upon the thorns of life! I bleed!

A heavy weight of hours has chained and bowed
One too like thee: tameless, and swift, and proud.

V

Make me thy lyre, even as the forest is:
What if my leaves are falling like its own?
The tumult of thy mighty harmonies

In Your Notebook:

Writing in forms is a good way to understand their power. Try writing a sestina. Select six words related to a subject you'd like to explore—a specific activity such as sailing or dancing or an emotion such as jealousy or joy. Following the pattern for the sestina, map your six end words along a right margin, then work with the lines. You may want to change words after you get started. Or try other forms, perhaps haiku, pantoum, or villanelle.

Will take from both a deep autumnal tone,
Sweet though in sadness. Be thou, spirit fierce,
My spirit! Be thou me, impetuous one!

Drive my dead thoughts over the universe,
Like withered leaves, to quicken a new birth;
And, by the incantation of this verse,

Scatter, as from an unextinguished hearth
Ashes and sparks, my words among mankind!
Be through my lips to unawakened earth

The trumpet of a prophecy! O wind,
If winter comes, can spring be far behind?

from HOLY SONNETS
(John Donne, 1572–1631)

SONNET 7

At the round earth's imagined corners, blow
Your trumpets, angels, and arise, arise
From death, you numberless infinities
Of souls, and to your scattered bodies go;

All whom the flood did, and fire shall o'erthrow;
All whom war, dearth, age, agues, tyrannies,
Despair, law, chance, hath slain, and you whose eyes
Shall behold God, and never taste death's woe.
But let them sleep, Lord, and me mourn a space,
For if above all these my sins abound,
'Tis late to ask abundance of thy grace
When we are there; here on this lowly ground
Teach me how to repent; for that's as good
As if thou hadst sealed my pardon with thy blood.

SESTINA: VANISHING POINT
(Marilyn Krysl, 1942–)

A city, alive with sleeping people. Awake, the man
feels in his pockets. A roll of film, loose change,
ticket stubs, a book of matches. All he owns
can be quickly summarized. The drift of moonlight
across the dark floor is more to the point
here. Some things don't pin down. The woman

he thought was his is now another woman
in another city. Luminous, she leaves the man
his own flesh, a roll of film. The vanishing point
is that moment when the phone's ringing changes
to silence, and we are vibrant and alone, and moonlight
seems like the only thing that's left worth owning

and we attend its shifting configuration, own it
by our attention. His fist is empty. The woman
is on the move. Like many lovers the moonlight
waxes, illumines her, and wanes, and the man's
heart will beat until it stops. We are a cellchange,
we vanish and reappear, and there's a point

at which you are not who you were. At some point—
but where? She knows no location, only her own
shifting configuration, the play of loose change
in Heisenberg's pocket, nude descending a staircase. A woman
dies but her fingernails grow after death. The man
caught her once, asleep beside a shaft of moonlight

but he moved: the photo's blurred, moonlight
and flesh in slow fog, through their point
of vanishing and gone. There's not a man
on earth or moon can claim to own
white clarity for long. Or was it the woman
dreaming an earthquake, buckling rock changing

the lay of the land? At some point she wakes, changes
cities, names, cuts her hair. Like moonlight
we occur and reoccur. He's not wrong, but the woman
in the photo is dead, the moon's set. What's the point
of trying to buy time? What this man owns
isn't what he needs in the dark. This is the man

who wanted to remember the point at which he fell
asleep. But he's awake, without moonlight or a plan,
on his own, on the move, changing like a woman leaving a man.

SESTINA
(Elizabeth Bishop, 1911–1979)

September rain falls on the house.
In the failing light, the old grandmother
sits in the kitchen with the child
beside the Little Marvel Stove,
reading the jokes from the almanac,
laughing and talking to hide her tears.

She thinks that her equinoctial tears
and the rain that beats on the roof of the house
were both foretold by the almanac,
but only known to a grandmother.
The iron kettle sings on the stove.
She cuts some bread and says to the child,

It's time for tea now; but the child
is watching the teakettle's small hard tears
dance like mad on the hot black stove,
the way the rain must dance on the house.
Tidying up, the old grandmother
hangs up the clever almanac

on its string. Bird-like, the almanac
hovers half open above the child,
hovers above the old grandmother
and her teacup full of dark brown tears.
She shivers and says she thinks the house
feels chilly, and puts more wood in the stove.

It was to be, says the Marvel Stove.
I know what I know, says the almanac.
With crayons the child draws a rigid house
and a winding pathway. Then the child
puts in a man with buttons like tears
and shows it proudly to the grandmother.

But secretly, while the grandmother
busies herself about the stove,
the little moons fall down like tears
from between the pages of the almanac
into the flower bed the child
has carefully placed in the front of the house.

Time to plant tears, says the almanac.
The grandmother sings to the marvellous stove
and the child draws another inscrutable house.

DO NOT GO GENTLE INTO THAT GOOD NIGHT
(Dylan Thomas, 1914–1953)

Do not go gentle into that good night,
Old age should burn and rave at close of day;
Rage, rage against the dying of the light.

Though wise men at their end know dark is right,
Because their words had forked no lightning they
Do not go gentle into that good night.

Good men, the last wave by, crying how bright
Their frail deeds might have danced in a green bay,
Rage, rage against the dying of the light.

Wild men who caught and sang the sun in flight,
And learn, too late, they grieved it on its way,
Do not go gentle into that good night.

Grave men, near death, who see with blinding sight
Blind eyes could blaze like meteors and be gay,
Rage, rage against the dying of the light.

And you, my father, there on the sad height,
Curse, bless, me now with your fierce tears, I pray.
Do not go gentle into that good night.
Rage, rage against the dying of the light.

THE WAKING
(Theodore Roethke, 1908–1963)

I wake to sleep, and take my waking slow.
I feel my fate in what I cannot fear.
I learn by going where I have to go.

We think by feeling. What is there to know?
I hear my being dance from ear to ear.
I wake to sleep, and take my waking slow.

Of those so close beside me, which are you?
God bless the Ground! I shall walk softly there,
And learn by going where I have to go.

Light takes the Tree; but who can tell us how?
The lowly worm climbs up a winding stair;
I wake to sleep, and take my waking slow.

Great Nature has another thing to do
To you and me; so take the lively air,
And, lovely, learn by going where to go.

This shaking keeps me steady. I should know.
What falls away is always. And is near.
I wake to sleep, and take my waking slow.
I learn by going where I have to go.

WHAT IS AN EPIGRAM?
(Samuel Taylor Coleridge, 1772–1834)

What is an epigram? a dwarfish whole,
Its body brevity, and wit its soul.

SOLDIERS BATHING
(F. T. Prince, 1912–)

The sea at evening moves across the sand.
Under a reddening sky I watch the freedom of a band
Of soldiers who belong to me. Stripped bare
For bathing in the sea, they shout and run in the warm air;
Their flesh worn by the trade of war, revives
And my mind towards the meaning of it strives.

All's pathos now. The body that was gross,
Rank, ravenous, disgusting in the act or in repose,
All fever, filth and sweat, its bestial strength
And bestial decay, by pain and labour grows at length
Fragile and luminous. 'Poor bare forked animal,'
Conscious of his desires and needs and flesh that rise and fall,
Stands in the soft air, tasting after toil
The sweetness of his nakedness: letting the sea-waves coil
Their frothy tongues about his feet, forgets
His hatred of the war, its terrible pressure that begets
A machinery of death and slavery,
Each being a slave and making slaves of others: finds that he
Remembers his old freedom in a game
Mocking himself, and comically mimics fear and shame.

He plays with death and animality;
And reading in the shadows of his pallid flesh, I see
The idea of Michelangelo's cartoon
Of soldiers bathing, breaking off before they were half done
At some sortie of the enemy, an episode
Of the Pisan wars with Florence. I remember how he showed
Their muscular limbs that clamber from the water,

And heads that turn across the shoulder, eager for the slaughter,
Forgetful of their bodies that are bare,
And hot to buckle on and use the weapons lying there.
—And I think too of the theme another found
When, shadowing men's bodies on a sinister red ground,
Another Florentine, Pollaiuolo,
Painted a naked battle: warriors, straddled, hacked the foe,
Dug their bare toes into the ground and slew
The brother-naked man who lay between their feet and drew
His lips back from his teeth in a grimace.

They were Italians who knew war's sorrow and disgrace
And showed the thing suspended, stripped: a theme
Born out of the experience of war's horrible extreme
Beneath a sky where even the air flows
With lacrimae Christi.[1] For that rage, that bitterness, those blows,
That hatred of the slain, what could they be
But indirectly or directly a commentary
On the Crucifixion? And the picture burns
With indignation and pity and despair by turns,
Because it is the obverse of the scene
Where Christ hangs murdered, stripped, upon the Cross. I mean,
That is the explanation of its rage.

And we too have our bitterness and pity that engage
Blood, spirit, in this war. But night begins,
Night of the mind: who nowadays in conscious of our sins?
Though every human deed concerns our blood,
And even we must know, what nobody has understood,
That some great love is over all we do,
And that is what has driven us to this fury, for so few
Can suffer all the terror of that love:

---

[1] *lacrimae Christi*: tears of Christ.

The terror of that love has set us spinning in this groove
Greased with our blood.
                              These dry themselves and dress,
Combing their hair, forget the fear and shame of nakedness.
Because to love is frightening we prefer
The freedom of our crimes. Yet, as I drink the dusky air,
I feel a strange delight that fills me full,
Strange gratitude, as if evil itself were beautiful,
And kiss the wound in thought, while in the west
I watch a streak of red that might have issued from Christ's breast.

DOVER BEACH
(Matthew Arnold, 1822–1888)

The sea is calm to-night,
The tide is full, the moon lies fair
Upon the Straits;—on the French coast, the light
Gleams, and is gone; the cliffs of England stand,
Glimmering and vast, out in the tranquil bay.
Come to the window, sweet is the night air!
Only, from the lone line of spray
Where the ebb meets the moon-blanch'd sand,
Listen! you hear the grating roar
Of pebbles which the waves suck back, and fling.
At their return, up the high strand,
Begin, and cease, and then again begin,
With tremulous cadence slow, and bring
The eternal note of sadness in.

Sophocles long ago
Heard it on the Aegean, and it brought
Into his mind the turbid ebb and flow
Of human misery; we

Find also in the sound a thought,
Hearing it by this distant northern sea.

The sea of faith
Was once, too, at the full, and round earth's shore
Lay like the folds of a bright girdle furl'd;
But now I only hear
Its melancholy, long, withdrawing roar,
Retreating to the breath
Of the night-wind down the vast edges drear
And naked shingles of the world.

Ah, love, let us be true
To one another! for the world, which seems
To lie before us like a land of dreams,
So various, so beautiful, so new,
Hath really neither joy, nor love, nor light,
Nor certitude, nor peace, nor help for pain;
And we are here as on a darkling plain
Swept with confused alarms of struggle and flight,
Where ignorant armies clash by night.

Open Forms

A poem is in open form when the shape is invented for the particular poem. No *set* pattern of stanzas or formal structure determine anything. But each poem does have a form. It may present a striking appearance, like May Swenson's poem at the beginning of this chapter. It may have verse paragraphs of two-, six-, four-, and seven-line sections. Or it could be a continuous long poem in free verse with no breaks at all. The shape is made anew for each poem.

Although the terms usually are used interchangeably, verse paragraphs and stanzas are different. The stanza is a unit of a *set* number of lines. The **verse paragraph** has no such regularity. The verse paragraphs of a poem could be of two, five, eight, and six lines whereas a poem in stanzas is a series or patterned mix of quatrains, octaves, or whatever the poet chooses. Both verse paragraphs and stanzas may rhyme or be metrical, though this is much more expected in stanzaic poems. Although verse paragraphs keep to no established repeating pattern or number of lines, stanzas and verse paragraphs function similarly. Like a stanza, a new verse paragraph indicates a change in perspective, action, or subject.

Verse paragraphs, continuous form (uninterrupted by breaks), and one-of-a-kind shapes such as concrete poems are all *open forms*. Although many contemporary poems are in open form, it would be a mistake to lump all free verse into this category because sometimes free verse is arranged in regular stanzas.

Many poems in Chapter 7 were in open forms, where we focused on voice and line. Now we'll concentrate on the overall shapes of some interesting examples of poems in open form.

EFFORT AT SPEECH BETWEEN TWO PEOPLE
(Muriel Rukeyser, 1913–1980)

: Speak to me.   Take my hand.   What are you now?
  I will tell you all.   I will conceal nothing.
  When I was three, a little child read a story about a rabbit
  who died, in the story, and I crawled under a chair   :
  a pink rabbit   :   it was my birthday, and a candle
  burnt a sore spot on my finger, and I was told to be happy.

: Oh, grow to know me.   I am not happy.   I will be open:
  Now I am thinking of white sails against a sky like music,
  like glad horns blowing, and birds tilting, and an arm about me.
  There was one I loved, who wanted to live, sailing.

: Speak to me.   Take my hand.   What are you now?
  When I was nine, I was fruitily sentimental,

fluid : and my widowed aunt played Chopin,
and I bent my head on the painted woodwork, and wept.
I want now to be close to you.   I would
link the minutes of my days close, somehow, to your days.

: I am not happy.   I will be open.
I have liked lamps in evening corners, and quiet poems.
There has been fear in my life.   Sometimes I speculate
On what a tragedy his life was, really.

: Take my hand.   Fist my mind in your hand.   What are you now?
When I was fourteen, I had dreams of suicide,
and I stood at a steep window, at sunset, hoping toward death :
if the light had not melted clouds and plains to beauty,
if light had not transformed that day, I would have leapt,
I am unhappy.   I am lonely.   Speak to me.

: I will be open.   I think he never loved me:
he loved the bright beaches, the little lips of foam
that ride small waves, he loved the veer of gulls:
he said with a gay mouth: I love you.   Grow to know me.

: What are you now?   If we could touch one another,
if these our separate entities could come to grips,
clenched like a Chinese puzzle . . . yesterday
I stood in a crowded street that was live with people,
and no one spoke a word, and the morning shone.
Everyone silent, moving. . . . Take my hand.   Speak to me.

The first thing to notice about "Effort at Speech Between Two People" is the odd line of colons along the left margin. Other colors appear within the poem, as does staggered white space within the lines. The grammatical function of a colon is to indicate an addition to what has just been written. Rukeyser's choice of this punctuation mark does not just separate the two "efforts at speech." The section breaks could do that. She indicates by the colon that there is a connection *between* the sections. The isolation of one speaker emphasizes the isolation of the other. Though the two lone voices speak back and forth, the two speakers seem not to hear each other. The halting progression of the speech and the short sentences and phrases with wide spacing remind us of the word *effort* in the title. The form incorporates the silent pauses, the irregular movement of thought changing into speech. The poem ends with the words that began it: "Speak to me." The last image is of a crowd (an expanded version of the two speakers) where "no one spoke a word."

THE HOWLING OF WOLVES
(Ted Hughes, 1930–1998)

Is without world.

What are they dragging up and out on their long leashes of sound

That dissolve in the mid-air silence?

Then crying of a baby, in this forest of starving silences,
Brings the wolves running.
Tuning of a violin, in this forest delicate as an owl's ear,
Brings the wolves running — brings the steel traps clashing and
    slavering,
The steel furred to keep it from cracking in the cold,
The eyes that never learn how it has come about
That they must live like this,

That they must live

Innocence crept into minerals.

The wind sweeps through and the hunched wolf shivers.
It howls you cannot say whether out of agony or joy.

The earth is under its tongue,
A dead weight of darkness, trying to see through its eyes.
The wolf is living for the earth.
But the wolf is small, it comprehends little.

It goes to and fro, trailing its haunches and whimpering horribly.

It must feed its fur.

The night snows stars and the earth creaks.

"The Howling of Wolves" has two powerful fragment lines. The beginning, "Is without world," actually completes the title; but set on its own line, it starts the poem with a sense of dangling. The eerie sounds of the wolves are outside our world. They call up dark forces, primitive instincts. In the middle of the poem the author isolates the line "That they must live," the completion being "Innocence crept into minerals." That is, the animals living for basic survival can have no innocence. Innocence belongs to what is inanimate. Other plaintive sounds — the baby's cry, the tuning up of a violin — bring back to mind the wolves' cry underneath everything. The language is dramatic and elemental, like the subject. The single-line verse paragraphs put white space above and below many lines. This adds to their importance by focusing our attention. White space functions as punctuation. The eye must pause for it. What did Hughes want when he used this form? Why not construct the poem in quatrains or couplets? As it is, the form seems to move as thoughts occur: slowly then quickly, long then short. We "hear" a person thinking. A formal stanza would have impressed us with its order, undercutting the awareness of the bestial undercurrents that this dark poem brings to us.

Prose Poems

In poetry there are exceptions to every rule. One useful rule we've learned is that poetry is written in lines and prose is written in sentences. But prose poems are not written in lines, and still they are poems.

Not everyone agrees. Diehards maintain that the writer of prose poems didn't take the trouble to find a form; it's some aberration, like the fish in Florida that crawls out of water and walks.

But the short block of prose *is* the form. Line breaks aside, the prose poem keeps the craft tools of free verse working as hard as in other forms. Density can give an implosive quality to a subject; the lack of white space intensifies the impression that everything is happening at once. Some prose poems have a relaxed appearance, skipping lines or including conversation. Because of the prose appearance, the writer, at times, seems freed from the serious idea of Poetry with a capital *P* and admits more humor, conversation, description, or irony into the poem.

Look at the unexpected effects of prose in this poem set in El Salvador during a civil war:

THE COLONEL
(Carolyn Forché, 1950–)

What you have heard is true. I was in his house. His wife carried a tray of coffee and sugar. His daughter filed her nails, his son went out for the night. There were daily papers, pet dogs, a pistol on the cushion beside him. The moon swung bare on its black cord over the house. On the television was a cop show. It was in English. Broken bottles were embedded in the walls around the house to scoop the kneecaps from a man's legs or cut his hands to lace. On the windows there were gratings like those in liquor stores. We had dinner, rack of lamb, good wine, a gold bell was on the table for calling the maid. The maid brought green mangoes, salt, a type of bread. I was asked how I enjoyed the country. There was a brief commercial in Spanish. His wife took everything away. There was some talk then of how difficult it had become to govern. The parrot said hello on the terrace. The colonel told it to shut up, and pushed himself from the table. My friend said to

me with his eyes: say nothing. The colonel returned with a sack
used to bring groceries home. He spilled many human ears on
the table. They were like dried peach halves. There is no other
way to say this. He took one of them in his hands, shook it in our
faces, dropped it into a water glass. It came alive there. I am tired
of fooling around he said. As for the rights of anyone, tell your
people they can go fuck themselves. He swept the ears to the
floor with his arm and held the last of his wine in the air. Some-
thing for your poetry, no? he said. Some of the ears on the floor
caught this scrap of his voice. Some of the ears on the floor were
pressed to the ground.

The narrative in this poem is highly charged. The poet makes a wise
choice for her form. The flat tone of statement, at war with the vio-
lence within the poem, maintains tension. Line breaks would increase
that tension, pushing the poem too far toward the melodramatic. It's
easy to see the poetic craft at work in "The Colonel": the intimate tone
of the voice speaking directly to you, the repetition of the same declar-
ative sentence structure, the compressed event. The deliberate plain-
ness of the statements is important. (As Forché says, "There is no other
way to say this.") The cumulative effect of the simple style emphasizes
the growing horror of what is revealed.

We widen our conception of poetry a bit to admit the prose poem.
When is a piece of prose a prose poem? No exact definition exists. A
prose poem may use any or all of the assets of poetry except the line.
Primarily, the form must be needed: the margin-to-margin line, the
density and concentration should be part of the effect necessary to
the subject.

We could lift whole prose poems out of novels by James Joyce,
Virginia Woolf, Herman Melville, Thomas Wolfe, or Colette. Prose
poems also have links to fairy tales and parables. Sections of the Bible
could be called prose poems. In mid-nineteenth-century France,
Charles Baudelaire codified the modern poets' version of the form. In
the preface to his *Little Poems in Prose*, Baudelaire asks, "Which of
us, in his ambitious moments, has not dreamed of the miracle of a

poetic prose...?" As with haiku and pantoum, the prose poem offers a mode of writing unavailable in other forms. As with all others, this form's special characteristics are part of what is being said.

Open Forms Poems

TULIPS
(Sylvia Plath, 1932–1963)

The tulips are too excitable, it is winter here.
Look how white everything is, how quiet, how snowed-in.
I am learning peacefulness, lying by myself quietly
As the light lies on these white walls, this bed, these hands.
I am nobody; I have nothing to do with explosions.
I have given my name and my day-clothes to the nurses
And my history to the anaesthetist and my body to surgeons.

They have propped my head between the pillow and the sheet-
   cuff
Like an eye between two white lids that will not shut.
Stupid pupil, it has to take everything in.
The nurses pass and pass, they are no trouble,
They pass the way gulls pass inland in their white caps,
Doing things with their hands, one just the same as another,
So it is impossible to tell how many there are.

My body is a pebble to them, they tend it as water
Tends to the pebbles it must run over, smoothing them gently.
They bring me numbness in their bright needles, they bring me
   sleep.
Now I have lost myself I am sick of baggage —
My patent leather overnight case like a black pillbox,
My husband and child smiling out of the family photo;
Their smiles catch onto my skin, little smiling hooks.

I have let things slip, a thirty-year-old cargo boat
Stubbornly hanging on to my name and address.
They have swabbed me clear of my loving associations.
Scared and bare on the green plastic-pillowed trolley
I watched my tea-set, my bureaus of linen, my books
Sink out of sight, and the water went over my head.
I am a nun now, I have never been so pure.

I didn't want any flowers, I only wanted
To lie with my hands turned up and be utterly empty.
How free it is, you have no idea how free —
The peacefulness is so big it dazes you,
And it asks nothing, a name tag, a few trinkets.
It is what the dead close on, finally; I imagine them
Shutting their mouths on it, like a Communion tablet.

The tulips are too red in the first place, they hurt me.
Even through the gift paper I could hear them breathe
Lightly, through their white swaddlings, like an awful baby.
Their redness talks to my wound, it corresponds.
They are subtle: they seem to float, though they weigh me down,
Upsetting me with their sudden tongues and their color,
A dozen red lead sinkers round my neck.

Nobody watched me before, now I am watched.
The tulips turn to me, and the window behind me
Where once a day the light slowly widens and slowly thins,
And I see myself, flat, ridiculous, a cut-paper shadow
Between the eye of the sun and the eyes of the tulips,
And I have no face, I have wanted to efface myself.
The vivid tulips eat my oxygen.

Before they came the air was calm enough,
Coming and going, breath by breath, without any fuss.

Then the tulips filled it up like a loud noise.
Now the air snags and eddies round them the way a river
Snags and eddies round a sunken rust-red engine.
They concentrate my attention, that was happy
Playing and resting without committing itself.

The walls, also, seem to be warming themselves.
The tulips should be behind bars like dangerous animals;
They are opening like the mouth of some great African cat,
And I am aware of my heart: it opens and closes
Its bowl of red blooms out of sheer love of me.
The water I taste is warm and salt, like the sea,
And comes from a country far away as health.

DEAF POEM
(Tess Gallagher, 1943–)

Don't read this one out loud. It isn't
to be heard, not even in the sonic zones
of the mind should it trip the word "explosion"
and detonate in the silent room. My love
needs a few words that stay out of
the mouth and vocal cords. No vibrations, please.
He needs to put his soul's freshly inhuman capacity
into scattering himself deeper into
the forest. It's part of the plan that birds
will eat the markings. It's okay. He's not coming
that way again. He likes it where he is. Or if he
doesn't, I can't know anything about it. Let
the birds sing. He always liked to hear them
any time of day. But let this poem meet
its deafness. It pays attention another way, like he
doesn't when I bow my head and press my forehead

in the swollen delusion of love's power to
manifest across distance the gladness that joined us.
Wherever he is he still knows I have two feet
and one of them is broken from dancing.
He'd come to me if he could. It's nice to be sure
of something when speaking of the dead. Sometimes
I forget what I'm doing and call out to him. It's me! How
could you go off like that? Just as things were
getting good. I'm petulant, reminding him of his promise
to take me in a sleigh pulled by horses
with bells. He looks back in the dream — the way
a violin might glance across a room at its bow
about to be used for kindling. He doesn't
try to stop anything. Not the dancing. Not the deafness
of my poems when they arrive like a sack of wet
stones. Yes, he can step back into life just long enough
for eternity to catch hold, until one of us
is able to watch and to write the deaf poem,
a poem missing even the language
it is unwritten in.

❉

LIVING
(C. D. Wright, 1949–)

If this is Wednesday, write Lazartigues, return library books,
pick up passport form, cancel the paper.

If this is Wednesday, mail B her flyers and K her shirts. Last
thing I asked as I walked K to her car, "You sure you have
everything?" "Oh yes," she smiled, as she squalled off. Whole
wardrobe in front closet.

Go to Morrison's for paint samples, that's where
housepainter has account (near Pier One), swing by Gano St.

for another bunch of hydroponic lettuce. Stop at cleaners if
there's parking.

Pap smear at 4. After last month with B's ear infections, can't
bear sitting in damn doctor's office. Never a magazine or
picture on the wall worth looking at. Pack a book.

Ever since B born, nothing comes clear. My mind like a
mirror that's been in a fire. Does this happen to the others.

If this is Wednesday, meet Moss at the house at noon. Pick B
up first, call sitter about Friday evening. If she prefers, can bring
B to her (hope she keeps the apartment warmer this year).

Need coat hooks and picture hangers for office. Should take
car in for air filter, oil change. F said one of back tires low.
Don't forget car payment, late last two months in a row.

If this is Wednesday, there's a demo on the green at 11. Took
B to his first down at Quoinset Point in August. Blue skies.
Boston collective provided good grub for all. Long column of
denims and flannel shirts. Smell of Patchouli made me so
wistful, wanted to buy a wood stove, prop my feet up, share a J
and a pot of Constant Comment with a friend. Maybe some
zucchini bread.

Meet with honors students from 1 to 4. At the community
college I tried to incite them to poetry. Convince them this line
of work beats the bejesus out of a gig as gizzard splitter at the
processing plant or cleaning up after a leak at the germ warfare
center. Be all you can be, wrap a rubber band around your
trigger finger until it drops off.

Don't forget to cancel the goddamned paper. At the very least
quit reading editorials and police reports—local boys caught

throwing sewer caps off the overpass again, not to mention
recreational violence in the park next to our cashew-colored
house every night of the year.

Swim at 10:00 before picking up B, before demo on the
green, and before meeting Moss, if it isn't too crowded. Only
three old women talking about their daughters-in-law last
Wednesday at 10:00.

Phone hardware to see if radon test arrived.

Keep an eye out for a new yellow blanket. Left B's on the
plane, though he seems over it already. Left most recent issue of
Z in the seat. That will make a few businessmen boil. I liked the
man who sat next to me, he was sweet to B. Hated flying, said
he never let all of his weight down.

Need to get books in the mail today. Make time pass in line at
the p.o. imagining man in front of me butt naked. Fellow in the
good-preacher-blue suit, probably has a cold, hard bottom.

Call N for green tomato recipe. Have to get used to the
yankee growing season. If this is Wednesday, N goes in hospital
today. Find out how long after marrow transplant before
can visit.

Mother said she read in paper that Pete was granted a divorce.
His third. My highschool boyfriend. Meanest thing I could have
done, I did to him, returning the long-saved-for engagement
ring in a band-aid box, while he was stationed in Danang.

Meant to tell F this morning about dream of eating
grasshoppers, fried but happy. Our love a difficult instrument
we are learning to play. Practice, practice.

No matter where I call home anymore, feel like a boat under
the trees. Living is strange.

This week only: bargain on laid paper at East Side
Copy Shop.

Woman picking her nose at the stoplight. Shouldn't look,
only privacy we have anymore in the car. Isn't that the woman
from the colloquium last fall, who told me she was a stand-up
environmentalist. What a wonderful trade, I said, because the
evidence of planetary wrongdoing is overwhelming. Because
because because of the horrible things we do.

If this is Wednesday, meet F at Health Department at 10:45
for AIDS test.

If this is Wednesday, it's trash night.

MARIN HEADLANDS
(Jane Miller, 1949–)

Grief as we know it
and pity as we know it,
the roaring foggy darkness as we know it,
love as we know it
and beauty and magnetism,
energy, as we know it,
as we have come to know it,
relationship and intimacy, as we know,
the great earthquake, life, as we know it,
tension, destiny, family,
movement at the subtlest level of function, as we know it,
human beings as we know them,

California, the blue dolphin,
the eucalyptus, the umbrella pine, the coastline,
as we have come to know them,
the mist, the lovers, the children,
the aging, the homebound, the irreversible,
these, as we have come to know them, the homosexual's parade,
the mayor's limousine, the homeless's cape of newspaper,
as we call them, our plate of food our rings our fresh haircuts
our meager donation our writers our poetry, as we have come to
    know it
our education our manner our estate our transportation our travel
our privacy our privilege as we have come to know it our sexuality
our vision as we know it

lightning as it is known, plants, peaches, wine,
failure, esteem, faith,
the future, as it is known, the noun,
as we have come to know it,
a "thought" as we know it, a "commitment" a "vote" a "religion"
as we know them,
ghosts, tempests, gods — the days, the instances,

the dream, as we know it, the poetic, the pacific, the allegorical,
the excuse, as we know it, the error,
the meaning, as we have come to know it, far away,
as we have come to know it, death, as we know,
heaven as it is known, and timelessness and grace, as is
expected to know, and as we have come to,

loathing, avarice,
a drink, a safety net, a parent, a dog, a weapon, a
response, a paddle, a marine, a debutante, a quarter,
a parasite, without knowing it, a minor actor, a case in point,
a husband, a weekend, without knowing, an admission,
a clue, without knowing, a country, a pope,

land rights, tenants, garages, inventory,
without knowing them, a twenty-seven year old, without knowing
    it,
it, itself, them, themselves,
as we know without knowing

private parties with ribs barbequed, embroidery of dead names,
the state of Russian music, the modern sensibility, as it is known,
the telecommunications network, the criminal element, as they
    are
known, the "wall," the "bomb," the "communist," the "TV," the
    "free,"
as they are variously known
and now me, without knowing, as is generally known,
me, as the sea and sky appear to know without knowing,
and you, knowing full well, without knowing,

"plump girls pinched with butter," "babies with roses and baby
    roses,"
January, February, June and July,
lipstick and blood, as they are associated and known,
as we have come to know our home, our place, our time, our
hour, our
favorite,
dark beach as we have come to,

in agreement, with little else to say, as a matter of course,
silenced, not a moment too soon, without further ado, without
a word in edgewise

the mere mention of three in the afternoon, a Tuesday in
    summer,
memories, as they are variously known
and were to have been understood and, commonly, forgiven,

this choice and those images and that situation
and this conclusion,
these approximations and those generalizations, as we know
and fear them,
as is our nature, toothy, hairy, spiny,

a faultline of carmine poppies, raspberries,
spring green gullies, grasses
and ravens,
a place never seen, the imagination as we know it,
bugless and treeless and airless and waterless and sunless.

❧

POPPIES
(Mary Oliver, 1935–)

The poppies send up their
orange flares; swaying
in the wind, their congregations
are a levitation

of bright dust, of thin
and lacy leaves.
There isn't a place
in this world that doesn't

sooner or later drown
in the indigos of darkness,
but now, for a while,
the roughage

shines like a miracle
as it floats above everything

with its yellow hair.
Of course nothing stops the cold,

black, curved blade
from hooking forward —
of course
loss is the great lesson.

But also I say this: that light
is an invitation
to happiness,
and that happiness,

when it's done right,
is a kind of holiness,
palpable and redemptive.
Inside the bright fields,

touched by their rough and spongy gold,
I am washed and washed
in the river
of earthly delight —

and what are you going to do —
what can you do
about it —
deep, blue night?

SINISTER
(Forrest Gander, 1956–)

As if a distinction might be drawn at the edge of a continuum.
As if this might shake us by the teeth.

You know that vagrant at hogkilling time he goes
farm to farm collecting dried bladders.
This is the bone he stuck in your gate.

As if the salted beer foam and boiled egg were
repercussions of our own feeling,
as if the barn swallows told us nothing.

He burns a scent into his clothes
to cover the hogstink, he chews on cloves.

As if this sentence were a cliff
and a witness, that dry birdnote its postulate.

Shows up at The Triangle one Saturday a month,
sits across from the mirror.

As if transformation came
from the isomorphic pressure
of close attention. As if, tenting his fingers,
his beauty were purified by restraint.

Outside the package store, with that Polaroid
you gave me, I took his photograph.
I've had these sooty paw prints under my eyes,
he said, *since time out of mind.*

As if the sadness of pictures
had to do with our exclusion,
even from those in which we appear.

As though our theories unfit us for wholeness,
and the surfaces were crazed,
and there were not time
to recover the yolk of ourselves.

He admired his likeness. *My wife's blind,*
he told me. *Last night in the yard,*
fireflies come out. Fireflies, I said.
She nodded yes. Then I heard, far off,
what she heard, horseshoes clanging.

INK FISH
(Toni Mirosevich, 1951–)

We gather around his latest gift, turn our noses at the smell. Taking what is offered she moves to the cutting board, has learned early on to gut salmon, perch, halibut, cod. Here is the arrangement. She will cook what he brings in.

A gray mess spills out as the newspaper opens, squid the metal color of the sea when the day is overcast, a gray weather that depresses her. She takes the good knife, first slices the heads off, then down one side to open them up. Freed of form the squid slip through her fingers, evade her grasp, elusive as a husband drawn by the sea.

She slides out the dark sack of intestines, the squid marks her, her hands now black with ink. We dance around the kitchen, yell *inkfish inkfish*, the only name we've ever known. If we took fountain pens, placed them in the mouth of the squid, pulled the hammer back, we could fill up each cartridge with secrets of the sea.

Their bodies lie flat on the newsprint like dull sheets left hanging on the line to dry. Their wetness alters the print. Every story blurs.

This is what he tells us. There are nights when a grayness enters his bones, a grayness that depresses. It's then he bends over the bow, called, as he is always called, to look deep into the waves. Then he sees us: this image at the table, his wife inside a circle, his family gathered round. When he misses her he sees her dark form in the waves.

She skims off what is left of ocean, the slickness, then pounds them tender. We hear each squid slap the board, see the small dents the knife handle makes. She readies the pan, tosses them in. With the slightest heat they curl, turn opaque. Nothing is ever clear. At the sink she rinses off her hands. The ink goes down the drain. A story finds its way back to the sea.

GIRL
(Jamaica Kincaid, 1949–)

Wash the white clothes on Monday and put them on the stone heap; wash the color clothes on Tuesday and put them on the clothesline to dry; don't walk barehead in the hot sun; cook pumpkin fritters in very hot sweet oil; soak your little cloths right after you take them off; when buying cotton to make yourself a nice blouse, be sure that it doesn't have gum in it, because that way it won't hold up well after a wash; soak salt fish overnight before you cook it; is it true that you sing benna in Sunday School?; always eat your food in such a way that it won't turn someone else's stomach; on Sundays try to walk like a lady and not like the slut you are so bent on becoming; don't sing benna in Sunday school; you mustn't speak to wharf-rat boys, not even to give directions; don't eat fruits on the street — flies will follow you; *but I don't sing benna on Sundays at all and never in Sunday school*; this is how to sew on a button; this is how to make a buttonhole for the button you have just sewed on; this is how to hem a dress when you see the hem coming down and so to prevent yourself from looking like the slut I know you are so bent on becoming; this is how you iron your father's khaki shirt so that it doesn't have a crease; this is how you iron your father's khaki pants so that they don't have a crease; this is how you grow okra — far from the house, because okra tree harbors red ants; when you are growing dasheen, make sure it gets plenty of water or else it makes your throat itch when you are eating it; this is how you sweep a corner; this is how you sweep a whole house; this is how you sweep a yard; this is how you smile to someone you don't like too much; this is how you smile to someone you don't like at all; this is how you smile to someone you like completely; this is how you set a table for tea; this is how you set a table for dinner; this is how you set a table for dinner with an important guest; this is how you set a table for lunch; this is how you set a table for breakfast; this is how to behave in the presence of men who don't know you very well, and this way they won't recognize immediately the slut I have warned you against becoming; be sure to wash every day, even if it is with your own spit; don't squat down to play marbles—you are not a boy, you know; don't pick people's flowers—you might catch something; don't throw stones at blackbirds, because it might not be a blackbird at all; this is how to make a bread pudding; this is how to make doukona; this is how to make pepper pot; this is how to make a good medicine for a cold; this is how to make a good medicine to throw away a child before it even becomes a child; this is how to catch a fish; this is how to throw back a fish you don't like, and that way something bad won't fall on you; this is how to bully a man; this is how a man bullies you; this is how to love a man, and if this doesn't work there are other ways, and if they don't work don't feel too bad about giving up; this is how to spit up in the air if you feel like it, and this is how to move quick so that it doesn't fall on you; this is how to make ends meet; always squeeze bread to make sure it's fresh; *but what if the baker won't let me feel the bread?*; you mean to say that after all you are really going to be the kind of woman who the baker won't let near the bread?

9

Subject and Style

All the fun's in how you say a thing.
—ROBERT FROST

While one great poem begins with a philosophical speculation on the vicissitudes of history, another may start with someone sitting in the sun clipping her toenails. Fleas and angels, ecstasy and flowers, rain and potatoes, war and pinball—anything is a potential subject for a poem.

By now you've read dozens of poems on many subjects and in many forms and voices. It may surprise you to hear Chilean poet Pablo Neruda's opinion that there are only eleven subjects for poetry. Neruda didn't say exactly what the eleven are. His point was that all poetry revolves around a few basic human situations and universal concerns.

Various lists of eleven subjects—or nine or eighteen—might exist; surely some common denominators are love, death, conflict, identity, politics, memory, art, nature, spirituality. What else? Perhaps loss, joy, time, power, mortality, beginnings. Quickly the subjects begin to blur together—perhaps loss is an aspect of memory or death, joy an aspect of love. The categories don't matter. What matters is that poems have essential concerns that people of any time recognize as important to their own living. In contrast to the old saw "There's nothing new under the sun," each subject becomes new to new generations. The ancient Greek tragedy of Medea killing her own children still hits the modern reader with force. A contemporary poem on the fear of war or the pleasure of petting a horse in a meadow would have moved someone living centuries ago.

Types of Poems

Some subjects written about over and over have been codified into types of poems. A **pastoral,** for example, features a rural landscape. The pastoral often involves the lives or loves of nymphs and shepherds. Writers choose this setting because of a special effect: The idyllic landscape releases the subject from the real world of complex, mundane situations. No petty details, class differences, or world events can get to the lovers. For the space of the poem, they're together in an Edenlike landscape. In "Michael," the shepherd knows "the meaning of all winds." The last four lines of this excerpt make clear what the fields and hills of Michael's home meant to him. In pastorals, the setting takes on the same role as a person: It is an active force in the poem.

from MICHAEL, A PASTORAL
(William Wordsworth, 1770–1850)

Of shepherds, dwellers in the valleys, men
Whom I already loved; not verily
For their own sakes, but for the fields and hills
Where was their occupation and abode.
And hence this tale, while I was yet a boy
Careless of books, yet having felt the power

Of Nature, by the gentle agency
Of natural objects, led me on to feel
For passions that were not my own, and think
(At random and imperfectly indeed)
On man, the heart of man, and human life.
Therefore, although it be a history
Homely and rude, I will relate the same
For the delight of a few natural hearts;
And, with yet fonder feeling, for the sake
Of youthful poets, who among these hills
Will be my second self when I am gone.

Upon the forest side in Grasmere Vale
There dwelt a shepherd, Michael was his name;
An old man, stout of heart, and strong of limb.
His bodily frame had been from youth to age
Of an unusual strength; his mind was keen,
Intense, and frugal, apt for all affairs,
And in his shepherd's calling he was prompt
And watchful more than ordinary men.
Hence had he learned the meaning of all winds,
Of blasts of every tone; and, oftentimes,
When others heeded not, he heard the south
Make subterraneous music, like the noise
Of bagpipers on distant Highland hills.
The shepherd, at such warning, of his flock
Bethought him, and he to himself would say,
"The winds are now devising work for me!"
And, truly, at all times, the storm, that drives
The traveler to a shelter, summoned him
Up to the mountains; he had been alone
Amid the heart of many thousand mists,
That came to him, and left him, on the heights.
So lived he till his eightieth year was past.

And grossly that man errs, who should suppose
That the green valleys, and the streams and rocks,
Were things indifferent to the shepherd's thoughts.
Fields, where with cheerful spirits he had breathed
The common air; hills, which with vigorous step
He had so often climbed; which had impressed
So many incidents upon his mind
Of hardship, skill or courage, joy or fear;
Which, like a book, preserved the memory
Of the dumb animals, whom he had saved,
Had fed or sheltered, linking to such acts
The certainty of honorable gain;
Those fields, those hills — what could they less? had laid
Strong hold on his affections, were to him
A pleasurable feeling of blind love,
The pleasure which there is in life itself.

The pastoral tradition goes back to the third century B.C. poems of Theocritus, who described the Sicilian landscape of his childhood. Today, since nymphs and shepherds are in short supply, we use the term *pastoral* for any poem describing a rural scene.

Other common subject-types of poems are:

Ars poetica (the art of poetry): a poem written on the subject of the poetic art, usually to explain the poet's reasons for writing.

ARS POETICA?
(Czeslaw Milosz, 1911–)

I have always aspired to a more spacious form
that would be free from the claims of poetry or prose
and would let us understand each other without exposing
the author or reader to sublime agonies.

In the very essence of poetry there is something indecent:
a thing is brought forth which we didn't know we had in us,
so we blink our eyes, as if a tiger had sprung out
and stood in the light, lashing his tail.

That's why poetry is rightly said to be dictated by a daimonion,
though it's an exaggeration to maintain that he must be an angel.
It's hard to guess where that pride of poets comes from,
when so often they're put to shame by the disclosure of their
    frailty.

What reasonable man would like to be a city of demons,
who behave as if they were at home, speak in many tongues,
and who, not satisfied with stealing his lips or hand
work at changing his destiny for their convenience?

It's true that what is morbid is highly valued today,
and so you may think that I am only joking
or that I've devised just one more means
of praising Art with the help of irony.

There was a time when only wise books were read
helping us to bear our pain and misery.
This, after all, is not quite the same
as leafing through a thousand works fresh from psychiatric clinics.

And yet the world is different from what it seems to be
and we are other than how we see ourselves in our ravings.
People therefore preserve silent integrity
thus earning the respect of their relatives and neighbors.

The purpose of poetry is to remind us
how difficult it is to remain just one person,

for our house is open, there are no keys in the doors,
and invisible guests come in and out at will.

What I'm saying here is not, I agree, poetry,
as poems should be written rarely and reluctantly,
under unbearable duress and only with the hope
that good spirits, not evil ones, choose us for their instrument.
                    —Translated by the author and Lillian Vallee

Aubade (or **alba**): a poem composed at dawn, usually in the
voice of a departing lover.

ALBA
(Derek Walcott, 1930–)

Dawn breaking as I woke,
With the white sweat of the dew
On the green, new grass.
I walked in the cold, quiet as
If it were the world beginning;
Peeling and eating a chilled tangerine.
I may have many sorrows,
Dawn is not one of them.

Carpe diem: a poem urging one to live in the moment because
time passes quickly. Named from a poem by Horace, which be-
gins, *"Carpe diem, quam minimum credula postero"* ("Seize
today, and trust tomorrow little").

TO THE VIRGINS, TO MAKE MUCH OF TIME
(Robert Herrick, 1591–1674)

Gather ye rosebuds while you may,
  Old time is still a-flying;

And this same flower that smiles today
 Tomorrow will be dying.

The glorious lamp of heaven, the sun,
The higher he's a-getting,
The sooner will his race be run,
 And nearer he's to setting.

That age is best which is the first,
 When youth and blood are warmer;
But being spent, the worse, and worst
 Times still succeed the former.

Then be not coy, but use your time,
 And, while ye may, go marry;
For, having lost but once your prime,
 You may forever tarry.

Dithyramb: originally a poem about Dionysus, the Greek god of fertility and procreation. The subject gradually widened to include any poem about the adventures of the gods. In modern times *dithyramb* has come to mean a poem of revelry or praise, or any exaggerated, passionate composition.

A SMART* DITHYRAMB
(Susan MacDonald, 1937–)

*(CHRISTOPHER SMART, 1722–1771)

Let us consider the Great Gray Whale
For his skin is a mystery to our fingers and on those we can count
 his blessings
For first he has adopted a medium where all movement is
 graceful

For secondly, in that darkness, he opens his great harp mouth
and gives us sidelong smiles as small fish enter his belly to pray
For thirdly he is forty tons heavy
For fourthly he can stand on his tail
For fifthly he likes company and when the temperature drops
travels in cheap charters to southern lagoons
For sixthly he is blessed with very close friends, barnacles and lice
For seventhly when he rises to the surface and blows
God lifts himself from the deep and becomes noise
For eighthly are we moved to awe when he mates
seeing only fin and fluke, conjuring the rest
For ninthly he is playful, Heaven's great child
For tenthly his language is inaudible
For he is bored by encounters with our elite
No sparrow falls where he might notice it
The credentials of colour slide easily past his grey back
For he has an archbishop's dignity
One moment solid as land, the next only a slick
glossing the water's surface, our breath floundering in his wake

For praise is in his eye, which sights land and remembers

For his long journey is a meditation
The stippled hinds of his cow and calf glittering in the evening
  sun
Let us give thanks for there is no meanness in him
For our spirits soar with his breach which cracks the world's rim

He dives beyond reach, takes with him the remnants of our
  imagination

Elegy: a poem written for or about someone dead. The poet usually contemplates the meaning of death and often finds some consolation.

On My First Son
(Ben Jonson, 1573–1637)

Farewell, thou child of my right hand,[1] and joy;
My sin was too much hope of thee, loved boy;
Seven years thou wert lent to me, and I thee pay,
Exacted by thy fate, on the just day.[2]
O could I lose all father now! for why
Will man lament the state he should envy,
To have so soon 'scaped world's and flesh's rage,
And, if no other misery, yet age?
Rest in soft peace, and asked, say, "Here doth lie
Ben Jonson his best piece of poetry."
For whose sake henceforth all his vows be such
As what he loves may never like too much.

----

[1] *child of my right hand:* Jonson's son's name was Benjamin,
which means "child of my right hand" in Hebrew.
[2] *the just day:* the child died on his birthday.

Encomium: originally a celebration for a hero or heroine, now
a laudatory poem for a legendary or real person.

To Toussaint L'Ouverture[1]
(William Wordsworth, 1770–1850)

Toussaint, the most unhappy man of men!
Whether the whistling rustic tend his plough
Within thy hearing, or thy head be now
Pillowed in some deep dungeon's earless den —
O miserable chieftain! where and when

----

[1] *Toussaint L'Ouverture:* Black Haitian revolutionary who
declared independence from France. He was defeated and sent
to a French prison, where he died in 1803.

Wilt thou find patience! Yet die not; do thou
Wear rather in thy bonds a cheerful brow:
Though fallen thyself, never to rise again,
Live, and take comfort. Thou hast left behind
Powers that will work for thee; air, earth, and skies;
There's not a breathing of the common wind
That will forget thee: thou has great allies;
Thy friends are exultations, agonies,
And love, and man's unconquerable mind.

Epithalamium: a celebration for a wedding.

from EPITHALAMIUM
(Edmund Spenser, 1522–1599)

Wake, now my love, awake; for it is time,
The Rosy Morne long since left Tithones[1] bed,
All ready to her silver coche° to clyme.   *coach*
And Phoebus[2] gins° to shew his glorious hed.   *begins*
Hark how the cheerefull birds do chaunt theyr laies° *lays, songs*
And carroll of loves praise.
The merry Larke hir mattins sings aloft,
The thrust replyes, the Mavis° descant° playes, *thrush, accompaniment*
The Ouzell° shrills, the Ruddock° warbles soft, *blackbird, robin*
So goodly all agree with sweet consent,
To this dayes merriment.
Ah my deere love why doe ye sleepe thus long,
When meeter were that ye should now awake,
T' awayt the comming of your joyous make,°   *mate*
And hearken to the birds lovelearnèd song,
The deawy leaves among.

---

[1] *Tithones:* a mortal loved by the goddess of dawn.
[2] *Phoebus:* the sun god, also called Apollo.

For they of joy and pleasance to you sing,
That all the woods them answer and theyr eccho ring.

My love is now awake out of her dreame,
And her fayre eyes like stars that dimmèd were
With darksome cloud, now shew theyr goodly beams
More bright then Hesperus[3] his head doth rere.
Come now ye damzels, daughters of delight,
Helpe quickly her to dight,
But first come ye fayre houres which were begot
In Joves sweet paradice, of Day and Night,
Which doe the seasons of the yeare allot,
And al that ever in this world is fayre
Doe make and still repayre.
And ye three handmayds of the Cyprian Queene,[4]
The which doe still adorne her beauties pride,
Helpe to addorne my beautifullest bride:
And as ye her array, still throw betweene
Some graces to be seene,
And as ye use to Venus, to her sing,
The whiles the woods shal answer and your eccho ring.

Now is my love all ready forth to come,
Let all the virgins therefore well awayt,
And ye fresh boyes that tend upon her groome
Prepare your selves; for he is comming strayt.
Set all your things in seemely good aray
Fit for so joyfull day,
The joyfulst day that ever sunne did see.
Faire Sun, shew forth thy favourable ray,
And let thy lifull° heat not fervent be   *lifeful, vital*

---

[3] *Hesperus*: evening star, also called Venus.
[4] *Cyprian queen*: Venus, associated in myth with the island of Cyprus.

For feare of burning her sunshyny face,
Her beauty to disgrace.
O fayrest Phoebus, father of the Muse,
If ever I did honour thee aright,
Or sing the thing, that mote° thy mind delight,   *might*
Doe not thy servants simple boone° refuse,   *prayer*
But let this day let this one day be myne,
Let all the rest be thine.
Then I thy soverayne prayses loud wil sing,
That all the woods shal answer and theyr eccho ring. [etc. . . .]

Other types are the **madrigal,** a short poem (12 or 13 lines, usually with a rhyming couplet at the end) about nature and love; the **rune,** a magical chant or incantation; and the **palinode,** a poem retracting a regretted statement or previous poem.

These types of poems are not forms but simply the names of common subjects. An aubade, pastoral, or other type may be in any shape or meter. Thousands of poems, of course, do not fall neatly into any subject category.

"What are your poems about?" must be the question poets hate most.

A profound, brilliant writer may have to answer, "Blackbirds, childhood in Ohio, and weather." A terrible writer might answer, "Traveling through the Yucatan on foot and serving time in an Arab jail." So what? As poet William Matthews noted, "It is not, of course, the subject that is or isn't dull but the quality of attention we do or do not pay to it, and the strength of our will to transform."

How does the writer *transform* a subject? Besides craft, besides choice of speaker and subject, what connective tissue in the poem holds it together?

Style

Writers often feel that everything that could be said on any subject has been said before—and better—by other writers. A young poet

SUBJECT AND STYLE / 375

comparing her new poem to one by Yeats is bound to fear at some point that the new work, so engrossing while she was writing it, hardly bears considering. Yeats is great! But what keeps writers sharpening their pencils is a hope that one's own *way* with the subject, one's own poem on spring or love, will stand out. The art of poetry is largely the art of *revisioning*, in one's own time and style, the subjects that always have concerned writers.

The interplay of everything the poet brings to the art makes up **style**. *Style* is an elusive term; we can recognize style more easily than we can describe it. When you say that a friend "really has style," you mean not only her looks and dress but her whole way of talking, walking, expressing herself, and regarding life. When someone tells you, "That sounds like something only you would think of," *your* way of being is recognized, something of your essential style noticed.

A poet's style is made up of characteristic words and images, prevalent concerns, tone of voice, patterns of syntax, and form. When we read enough of an author, we begin to know the kind of power he has over language and the resources of language at his disposal. What makes us recognize the author, even if a poem is not identified, is style. In a long career, style changes. Early Yeats is different from late Yeats. We can trace his growth in power, the enlargement of his subjects. Still, Yeats is Yeats. Certain traits—a trace in the phrasing here, an identifying word there—mark the style, as, at times, in an old face you glimpse the younger person.

Sometimes a writer grows overly aware of style and begins to sound repetitive. The reader says, "Oh no, there he goes again, pressing the same set of buttons." He has gone lazy on himself, doing too easily what he knows how to do. The work becomes a parody of itself.

The poet who keeps evolving is the one who pays new attention to the subject of each poem, essentially starting over with each attempt to write. To find out what only *he* could say is to find—and keep—a singular, unmistakable style. "Make it new" was Ezra Pound's advice to poets. This requires delving into one's own unique imagination, intellect, and experience and forging from those a piece of art. "Finding your own voice" isn't like looking for the proverbial needle in the haystack; it is being able to hear yourself clearly. One test of style is to ask whether someone else could have written the poem. If not, why? That *why* is the key to the poem's style.

Keats's Style

Like fine paper held up to the light, a good poem is stamped with the poet's watermark, a distinctive complex of qualities that make up the writer's style. If we read several poems by John Keats, we see his watermarks—a richness and complexity of imagery and an honest, clear voice full of life. His constant subjects are ordinary ones: love, death, seasons, the transience of life. He was interested in myth and dramatic narratives. In frustration with the sonnet form, he developed the ten-line stanza to use in his odes. This stanza compresses the fourteen-line sonnet length and uses a metrically longer last line. Keats found a form that was adaptable to his exploring, speculative mode.

Because Keats died at 25, he did not have long to try his skills; but by experimenting constantly, he pushed into new areas to an astonishing degree. In his letters, Keats wrote: "We hate poetry that has a palpable design upon us.... Poetry should be great and unobtrusive, a thing which enters into one's soul, and does not startle it or amaze it with itself but with its subject." And: "I think Poetry should surprise by a fine excess and not by singularity—it should strike the Reader as a wording of his own highest thoughts, and appear almost a Remembrance." Keats's own work meets these standards. The poems seem to unfold naturally, with sincerity and without dogmatism. A Keats poem always has a sense of newness, as though the ink were still wet.

Keats also wrote that he valued *gusto*—there's the word most appropriate to his own vitality with language. The texture of a Keats poem is crowded with fully formed images and surprising juxtapositions of words, as in "nervy knees," "listening fear," "pleasant pain," "icy trance." He also gives an ongoing and present quality to the poems through frequent use of participle endings: *tasting, winding, opening, passing*. Assonance, consonance, and alliteration are hard at work to unify the images by sound. No writer except Shakespeare uses imagery as sensuously as Keats. Recall his description of Madeline kneeling under the stained glass window in "The Eve of St. Agnes" (page 115):

> A casement high and triple-arch'd there was,
> All garlanded with carven imag'ries
> Of fruits, and flowers, and bunches of knot-grass,
> And diamonded with panes of quaint device,
> Innumerable of stains and splendid dyes,
> As are the tiger-moth's deep damask'd wings;
> And in the midst, 'mong thousand heraldries,
> And twilight saints, and dim emblazonings,
> A shielded scutcheon blush'd with blood of queens and kings.
>
> Full on this casement shone the wintry moon,
> and threw warm gules[1] on Madeline's fair breast,
> As down she knelt for heaven's grace and boon;
> Rose-bloom fell on her hands, together presst,
> And on her silver cross soft amethyst,
> And on her hair a glory, like a saint:
> She seem'd a splendid angel, newly dresst,
> Save wings, for heaven: — Porphyro grew faint:
> She knelt, so pure a thing, so free from mortal taint.

---

[1] *gules:* reds.

Keats often doubles the impact of his imagery by using *synesthesia* (one sense experience in terms of another) or by using a second image to reinforce the first.

> Forlorn! the very word is like a bell
>
> convuls'd with scarlet pain
>
> moist scent of flowers

hushed, cool rooted flowers, fragrant eyed

But here is no light
Save what from heaven is with the breezes blown

...the small warm rain
Melts out the frozen incense from all flowers

Music's golden tongue

the silver snarling trumpets

Sudden a thought came like a full-blown rose
Flushing his brow, and in his pained heart
Made purple riot

thine own soft-conched ear

In this great ode, notice especially the sound imagery. What *does* the speaker know that the nightingale "hast never known" and how can the poet attain the "full-throated ease" of the bird?

ODE TO A NIGHTINGALE
(John Keats, 1795–1821)

My heart aches, and a drowsy numbness pains
   My sense, as though of hemlock I had drunk,
Or emptied some dull opiate to the drains
   One minute past, and Lethe-wards[1] had sunk:
'Tis not through envy of thy happy lot,
   But being too happy in thy happiness,—
     That thou, light wingèd Dryad[2] of the trees,

---

[1] *Lethe-wards:* towards Lethe, river in Hades whose water induces forgetfulness.
[2] *Dryad:* wood nymph.

In some melodious plot
Of beechen green, and shadows numberless,
    Singest of summer in full-throated ease.

O for a draught of vintage! that hath been
    Cooled a long age in the deep-delvèd earth,
Tasting of Flora[3] and the country green,
    Dance, and Provençal song, and sunburnt mirth!
O for a beaker full of the warm South,
    Full of the true, the blushful Hippocrene,[4]
        With beaded bubbles winking at the brim,
            And purple-stainèd mouth;
That I might drink, and leave the world unseen,
    And with thee fade away into the forest dim:

Fade far away, dissolve, and quite forget
    What thou among the leaves hast never known,
The weariness, the fever, and the fret
    Here, where men sit and hear each other groan;
Where palsy shakes a few, sad, last grey hairs,
    Where youth grows pale, and spectre-thin, and dies;
        Where but to think is to be full of sorrow
            And leaden-eyed despairs,
    Where Beauty cannot keep her lustrous eyes,
        Or new Love pine at them beyond to-morrow.

Away! away! for I will fly to thee,
    Not charioted by Bacchus[5] and his pards,
But on the viewless wings of Poesy,
    Though the full brain perplexes and retards:
Already with thee! tender is the night,
    And haply the Queen-Moon is on her throne,

---

[3] *Flora:* goddess of flowers.
[4] *Hippocrene:* fountain of the muses.
[5] *Bacchus:* god of wine and fertility. His chariot was pulled by leopards.

Clustered around by all her starry Fays,[6]
    But here there is no light,
Save what from heaven is with the breezes blown
    Through verdurous glooms and winding mossy ways.

I cannot see what flowers are at my feet,
    Nor what soft incense hangs upon the boughs,
But, in embalmèd darkness, guess each sweet
    Wherewith the seasonable month endows
The grass, the thicket, and the fruit tree wild;
    White hawthorn, and the pastoral eglantine;
        Fast fading violets covered up in leaves;
            And mid-May's eldest child,
The coming musk rose, full of dewy wine,
    The murmurous haunt of flies on summer eves.

Darkling I listen; and, for many a time
    I have been half in love with easeful Death,
Called him soft names in many a musèd rhyme,
    To take into the air my quiet breath;
Now more than ever seems it rich to die,
    To cease upon the midnight with no pain,
        While thou art pouring forth thy soul abroad
            In such an ecstasy!
    Still wouldst thou sing, and I have ears in vain —
    To thy high requiem become a sod.

Thou wast not born for death, immortal Bird!
    No hungry generations tread thee down;
The voice I hear this passing night was heard
    In ancient days by emperor and clown:
Perhaps the self-same song that found a path

---

[6] *Fays:* fairies.

In Your Notebook:

When you hear the first few bars of music by a group you like, you recognize their style immediately. Read all the poems by Emily Dickinson in this book. What enables you to recognize her style?

Other poets with high-profile styles are Gerard Manley Hopkins, William Butler Yeats, and Walt Whitman. Review poems by each and think about their distinctive aspects and differences.

Go back and read all the poems in this book by Dylan Thomas. You'll quickly identify the hallmarks of his style.

> Through the sad heart of Ruth,[7] when, sick for home,
>   She stood in tears amid the alien corn;
>   The same that oft-times hath
> Charmed magic casements, opening on the foam
>   Of perilous seas, in faery lands forlorn.
>
> Forlorn! the very word is like a bell
>   To toll me back from thee to my sole self!
> Adieu! the fancy cannot cheat so well
>   As she is famed to do, deceiving elf.
> Adieu! adieu! thy plaintive anthem fades
>   Past the near meadows, over the still stream,
>   Up the hillside; and now 'tis buried deep
>   In the next valley glades:
>   Was it a vision, or a waking dream?
>   Fled is that music:—Do I wake or sleep?

---

[7] *Ruth*: faithful Biblical wife who followed her husband's family to a foreign country.

THE WINDHOVER[1]
(Gerard Manley Hopkins, 1844–1889)

TO CHRIST OUR LORD

I caught this morning morning's minion, kingdom of daylight's
   dauphin, dapple-dawn-drawn Falcon, in his riding
     Of the rolling level underneath him steady air, and striding
High there, how he rung upon the rein of a wimpling wing
In his ecstasy! then off, off forth on swing,
     As a skate's heel sweeps smooth on a bow-bend: the hurl
       and gliding
     Rebuffed the big wind. My heart in hiding
Stirred for a bird, — the achieve of, the mastery of the thing!

Brute beauty and valor and act, oh, air, pride, plume, here
     Buckle! And the fire that breaks from thee then, a billion
Times told lovelier, more dangerous, O my chevalier!

   No wonder of it: shéer plód makes plough down sillion
Shine, and blue-bleak embers, ah my dear,
     Fall, gall themselves, and gash gold-vermilion.

----

[1] *Windhover:* a small hawk.

Poems on Four Subjects

With Pound's "Make it new" in mind, I've gathered the following
groups of poems on ordinary subjects. How do poets' approaches to
the same subject differ? Compare styles, keeping in mind that the
style includes voice, craft, and subject. A writer's style in a whole
body of work may differ from your impression in a particular poem,
but it is useful to look at single poems and to ask what is distinctive
about each. Look at imagery, diction, and style.

AUTUMN

Almost every poet at some time writes on the subject of autumn. The change of summer into fall stirs all of us to consider how the year is passing, how time is passing, how one's own life is changing and moving toward death, how each time in life and each season are unique.

GRAPPA[1] IN SEPTEMBER
(Cesare Pavese, 1908–1950)

The mornings run their course, clear and deserted
along the river's banks, which at dawn turn foggy,
darkening their green, while they wait for the sun.
In the last house, still damp, at the field's edge,
they sell tobacco, which is blackish in color
and tastes of sugar: it gives off a bluish haze.
They also have grappa there, the color of water.

There comes a moment when everything stands still
and ripens. The trees in the distance are quiet,
their darkness deepens, concealing fruit so ripe
it would drop at a touch. The occasional clouds
are swollen and ripe. Far away, in city streets,
every house is mellowing in the mild air.

This early, you see only women. The women don't smoke,
or drink. All they can do is stand in the sunlight,
letting it warm their bodies, as if they were fruit.
The air, raw with fog, has to be swallowed in sips,
like grappa. Everything here distills its own fragrance.
Even the water in the river has absorbed the banks,
steeping them to their depths in the soft air. The streets
are like the women. They ripen by standing still.

---

[1] *grappa*: a strong drink distilled from grape husks after the juice has been pressed for wine.

This is the time when every man should stand
still in the street and see how everything ripens.
There's even a breeze, which doesn't move the clouds
but somehow succeeds in maneuvering the bluish haze
without scattering it. The smell drifting by is a new smell,
the tobacco is tinged with grappa. So it seems
the women aren't the only ones who enjoy the morning.
                              —Translated by William Arrowsmith

TO AUTUMN
(John Keats, 1795–1821)

I

Season of mists and mellow fruitfulness,
    Close bosom friend of the maturing sun,
Conspiring with him how to load and bless
    With fruit the vines that round the thatch-eaves run:
To bend with apples the mossed cottage-trees,
And fill all fruit with ripeness to the core;
        To swell the gourd, and plump the hazel shells
    With a sweet kernel; to set budding more,
And still more, later flowers for the bees,
Until they think warm days will never cease,
        For summer has o'er-brimmed their clammy cells.

II

Who hath not seen thee oft amid thy store?
    Sometimes whoever seeks abroad may find
Thee sitting careless on a granary floor,
    Thy hair soft-lifted by the winnowing wind;
Or on a half-reaped furrow sound asleep,
    Drowsed with the fume of poppies, while thy hook
        Spares the next swath and all its twinèd flowers;
And sometimes like a gleaner thou dost keep

Steady thy laden head across a brook.
Or by a cider-press, with patient look,
  Thou watchest the last oozings hours by hours.

III

Where are the songs of spring? Aye, where are they?
  think not of them, thou hast thy music too —
While barrèd clouds bloom the soft-dying day,
  And touch the stubble-plains with rosy hue.
Then in a wailful choir the small gnats mourn
  Among the river sallows, borne aloft
    Or sinking as the light wind lives or dies;
And full-grown lambs loud bleat from hilly bourn;
  Hedge-crickets sing; and now with treble soft
  The red-breast whistles from a garden-croft;
    And gathering swallows twitter in the skies.

THE WILD SWANS OF COOLE
(William Butler Yeats, 1865–1939)

The trees are in their autumn beauty,
The woodland paths are dry,
Under the October twilight the water
Mirrors a still sky;
Upon the brimming water among the stones
Are nine-and-fifty swans.

The nineteenth autumn has come upon me
Since I first made my count;
I saw, before I had well finished,
All suddenly mount
And scatter wheeling in great broken rings
Upon their clamorous wings.

I have looked upon those brilliant creatures,
And now my heart is sore.
All's changed since I, hearing at twilight,
The first time on this shore,
The bell-beat of their wings above my head,
Trod with a lighter tread.

Unwearied still, lover by lover,
They paddle in the cold
Companionable streams or climb the air;
Their hearts have not grown old;
Passion or conquest, wander where they will,
Attend upon them still.

But now they drift on the still water,
Mysterious, beautiful;
Among what rushes will they build,
By what lake's edge or pool
Delight men's eyes when I awake some day
To find they have flown away?

THE END OF AUTUMN
(Francis Ponge, 1899–1988)

In the end, autumn is no more than a cold infusion. Dead leaves of all essences steep in the rain. No fermentation, no resulting alcohol; the effect of compresses applied to a wooden leg will not be felt till spring.

The stripping is messily done. All the doors of the reading room fly open and shut, slamming violently. Into the basket, into the basket! Nature tears up her manuscripts, demolishes her library, furiously thrashes her last fruits.

She suddenly gets up from her work table; her height at once immense. Unkempt, she keeps her head in the mist. Arms

In Your Notebook:

Write a poem exploring your personal connotations of October.

---

dangling, she rapturously inhales the icy wind that airs her thoughts. The days are short, night falls fast, there is no time for comedy.

The earth, amid the other planets in space, regains its seriousness. Its lighted side is narrower, infiltrated by valleys of shadow. Its shoes, like a tramp's, slosh and squeak.

In this frog pond, this salubrious amphibiguity, everything regains strength; hops from rock to rock, and moves on to another meadow. Rivulets multiply.

That is what is called a thorough cleaning, and with no respect for conventions! Garbed in nakedness, drenched to the marrow.

And it lasts, does not dry immediately. Three months of healthy reflection in this condition; no vascular reaction, no bathrobe, no scrubbing brush. But its hearty constitution can take it.

And so, when the little buds begin to sprout again, they know what they are up to and what is going on—

—Translated by Beth Brombert

FOUR LOVE POEMS

SOMEWHERE I HAVE NEVER TRAVELLED
(e.e. cummings, 1894–1962)

somewhere i have never travelled, gladly beyond
any experience, your eyes have their silence:
in your most frail gesture are things which enclose me,
or which i cannot touch because they are too near

your slightest look easily will unclose me
though i have closed myself as fingers,
you open always petal by petal myself as Spring opens
(touching skilfully, mysteriously) her first rose

or if your wish be to close me, i and
my life will shut very beautifully, suddenly,
as when the heart of this flower imagines
the snow carefully everywhere descending;

nothing which we are to perceive in this world equals
the power of your intense fragility whose texture
compels me with the colour of its countries,
rendering death and forever with each breathing

(i do not know what it is about you that closes
and opens; only something in me understands
the voice of your eyes is deeper than all roses)
nobody, not even the rain, has such small hands

I Will Enjoy Thee Now
(Thomas Carew, 1595–1640)

I will enjoy thee now, my Celia, come,
And fly with me to Love's Elysium.
The giant, Honour, that keeps cowards out
Is but a masquer, and the servile rout
Of baser subjects only bend in vain
To the vast idol; whilst the nobler train
Of valiant lovers daily sail between
The huge Colossus' legs, and pass unseen
Unto the blissful shore. Be bold and wise,
And we shall enter; the grim Swiss denies

Only to tame fools a passage, that not know
He is but form and only frights in show
The duller eyes that look from far; draw near
And thou shalt scorn what we were wont to fear.
We shall see how the stalking pageant goes
With borrow'd legs, a heavy load to those
That made and bear him; not, as we once thought,
The seed of gods, but a weak model wrought
By greedy men, that seek to enclose the common,
And within private arms empale free woman.
Come, then, and mounted on the wings of Love
We'll cut the flitting air and soar above
The monster's head, and in the noblest seats
Of those blest shades quench and renew our heats.
There shall the queens of love and innocence,
Beauty and Nature, banish all offence
From our close ivy-twines; there I'll behold
Thy baréd snow thy unbraided gold;
There my enfranchised hand on every side
Shall o'er thy naked polish'd ivory slide.
No curtain there, though of transparent lawn,
Then, as the empty bee that lately bore
Into the common treasure all her store,
Flies 'bout the painted field with nimble wing,
Deflow'ring the fresh virgins of the spring,
So will I rifle all the sweets that dwell
In my delicious paradise, and swell
My bag with honey, drawn forth by the power
Of fervent kisses from each spicy flower.
I'll seize the rose-buds in their perfumed bed,
The violet knots, like curious mazes spread
Shall be before thy virgin-treasure drawn;
But the rich mine, to the enquiring eye
Exposed, shall ready still for mintage lie,

And we will coin young Cupids. There a bed
Of roses and fresh myrtles shall be spread,
Under the cooler shades of cypress groves;
Our pillows of the down of Venus' doves,
Whereon our panting limbs we'll gently lay,
In the faint respites of our active play;
That so our slumbers may in dreams have leisure
To tell the nimble fancy our past pleasure,
And so our souls, that cannot be embraced,
Shall the embraces of our bodies taste.
Meanwhile the bubbling stream shall court the shore,
Th' enamour'd chirping wood-choir shall adore
In varied tunes the deity of love;
The gentle blasts of western winds shall move
The trembling leaves, and through their close boughs breathe
Still music, whilst we rest ourselves beneath
Their dancing shade; till a soft murmur, sent
From souls entranced in amorous languishment,
Rouse us, and shoot into our veins fresh fire,
Till we in their sweet ecstasy expire.
O'er all the garden, taste the ripen'd cherry,
The warm firm apple, tipp'd with coral berry;
Then will I visit with a wand'ring kiss
The vales of lilies and the bower of bliss;
And where the beauteous region doth divide
Into two milky ways, my lips shall slide
Down those smooth alleys, wearing as they go
A track for lovers on the printed snow;
Thence climbing o'er the swelling Apennine,
Retire into thy grove of eglantine,
Where I will all those ravish'd sweets distill
Through Love's alembic, and with chemic skill
From the mix'd mass one sovereign balm derive,
Then bring that great elixir to thy hive.

NEW BODY
(Jane Miller, 1949–)

There's a sort of eternity
when we're in bed together
whether silently you awaken
me with the flat of your hand
or sleep breathing with a small scratch
in your throat, or quietly attach
a bird to the sky I dream
as a way in to my body —

Now you have made me excited
to accept heaven as an idea
inside us, perpetual
waters, because you let yourself
fall from a sky you invented
to a sea I vaulted
when it was small rain
accumulating — My heart drained

there and fills now in time
to sketch in the entire
desert landscape we remember
as an ocean port,
that part of me accepting
your trust, a deep
voluptuous thrust into my hours,
that has no earthly power

but lives believing you were made for me
to give in to completely,

every entry into you the lip
of water that is in itself scant hope
broken into like sleep
by kisses — Policed in the desert
by a shooting star, we are the subversive
love scratched out of sky, o my visitor.

EVERY DAY YOU PLAY
(Pablo Neruda, 1904–1973)

Every day you play with the light of the universe.
Subtle visitor, you arrive in the flower and the water.
You are more than this white head that I hold tightly
as a cluster of fruit, every day, between my hands.

You are like nobody since I love you.
Let me spread you out among yellow garlands.
Who writes your name in letters of smoke among the stars of the
    south?
Oh let me remember you as you were before you existed.

Suddenly the wind howls and bangs at my shut window.
The sky is a net crammed with shadowy fish.
Here all the winds let go sooner or later, all of them.
The rain takes off her clothes.

The birds go by, fleeing.
The wing. The wind.

I can contend only against the power of men.
The storm whirls dark leaves
and turns loose all the boats that were moored last night to the sky.

You are here. Oh, you do not run away. You will answer me to the
    last cry.
Cling to me as though you were frightened.
Even so, at one time a strange shadow ran through your eyes.

Now, now too, little one, you bring me honeysuckle,
and even your breasts smell of it.
While the sad wind goes slaughtering butterflies
I love you, and my happiness bites the plum of your mouth.

How you must have suffered getting accustomed to me,
my savage, solitary soul, my name that sends them all running.
So many times we have seen the morning star burn, kissing our
    eyes,
and over our heads the grey light unwind in turning fans.

My words rained over you, stroking you.
A long time I have loved the sunned mother-of-pearl of your
    body.
I go so far as to think that you own the universe.
I will bring you happy flowers from the mountains, bluebells,
dark hazels, and rustic baskets of kisses.
I want
to do with you what spring does with the cherry trees.

—Translated by W. S. Merwin

All of these love poems have in common a tone of intimacy. They are
written to or about a person, not about love as a subject. How do they
differ in their approaches to the other person? Think of the role of the
person addressed in each poem.

    The next poem, "Proclamation," suffers in comparison with the
poems above. Why? With a common subject such as love, written
about in thousands of poems, how did the other poets avoid these
problems?

In Your Notebook:

Write a poem that expresses love. Try to find the precise language that touches the unmistakable source of feelings you have for someone. Your poem can be about any kind of love, not necessarily romantic love.

PROCLAMATION

I love you though 'tis wrong to say.
My thoughts are with you every day.

You are on my mind and in my heart.
It's hard to bear that we're apart.

For I will love you as long as day
turns from blue to black, I say.

And if it does not please you,
Even then I will still be true.

Though you lie in the arms of another,
with love over your soul always I hover.

PAINTING

Three poets look at the same painting by Pieter Brueghel, Flemish painter of the sixteenth century.

THE HUNTERS IN THE SNOW
(William Carlos Williams, 1883–1963)

The over-all picture is winter
icy mountains
in the background the return

from the hunt it is toward evening
from the left
sturdy hunters lead in

their pack the inn-sign
hanging from a
broken hinge is a stag a crucifix

between his antlers the cold
inn yard is
deserted but for a huge bonfire

that flares wind-driven tended by
women who cluster
about it to the right beyond

the hill is a pattern of skaters
Brueghel the painter
concerned with it all has chosen

a winter-struck bush for his
foreground to
complete the picture

WINTER LANDSCAPE
(John Berryman, 1914–1972)

The three men coming down the winter hill
In brown, with tall poles and a pack of hounds
At heel, through the arrangement of the trees,
Past the five figures at the burning straw,
Returning cold and silent to their town,

Returning to the drifted snow, the rink
Lively with children, to the older men,
The long companions they can never reach,

The blue light, men with ladders, by the church
The sledge and shadow in the twilit street,

Are not aware that in the sandy time
To come, the evil waste of history
Outstretched, they will be seen upon the brow
Of that same hill: when all their company
Will have been irrecoverably lost,

These men, this particular three in brown
Witnessed by birds will keep the scene and say
By their configuration with the trees,
The small bridge, the red houses and the fire,
What place, what time, what morning occasion

Sent them into the wood, a pack of hounds
At heel and the tall poles upon their shoulders,
Thence to return as now we see them and
Ankle-deep in snow down the winter hill
Descend, while three birds watch and the fourth flies.

HUNTERS IN THE SNOW: BRUEGHEL
(Joseph Langland, 1917–)

Quail and rabbit hunters with tawny hounds,
Shadowless, out of late afternoon
Trudge toward the neutral evening of indeterminate form.
Done with their blood-annunciated day
Public dogs and all the passionless mongrels
Through deep snow
Trail their deliberate masters
Descending from the upper village home in hovering light.
Sooty lamps
Glow in the stone-carved kitchens.
This is the fabulous hour of shape and form

When Flemish children are grey-black-olive
And green-dark-brown
Scattered and skating informal figures
On the mill ice pond.
Moving in stillness
A hunched dame struggles with her bundled sticks,
Letting her evening's comfort cudgel her
While she, like jug or wheel, like a wagon cart
Walked by lazy oxen along the old snowlanes,
Creeps and crunches down the dusky street.
High in the fire-red dooryard
Half unhitched the sign of the Inn
Hangs in wind
Tipped to the pitch of the roof.
Near it anonymous parents and peasant girl,
Living like proverbs carved in the alehouse walls,
Gather the country evening into their arms
And lean to the glowing flames.

Now in the dimming distance fades
The other village; across the valley
Imperturbable Flemish cliffs and crags
Vaguely advance, close in, loom,
Lost in nearness. Now
The night-black raven perched in branching boughs
Opens its early wing and slipping out
Above the grey-green valley
Weaves a net of slumber over the snow-capped homes.
And now the church, and then the walls and roofs
Of all the little houses are become
Close kin to shadow with small lantern eyes.
And now the bird of evening
With shadows streaming down from its gliding wings
Circles the neighboring hills
Of Hertogenbosch, Brabant.

Darkness stalks the hunters,
Slowly sliding down,
Falling in beating rings and soft diagonals.
Lodged in the vague vast valley the village sleeps.

The subject of each poem is "The Hunters in the Snow." How does each poem use Brueghel's painting? Are the poems able to stand alone? How does seeing the painting influence your reaction? Does the tone in each poem correspond in any way to the style of the painting?

LOOKING AT OBJECTS

"The Red Wheelbarrow," the first poem in this group, is one of the most famous twentieth century poems — a plain presentation of a simple image. On a farm much *does* depend on a wheelbarrow, of course, but by showing it to us carefully, line by line, timing the images by his line breaks, Williams makes a subtle case that an object itself is worth close attention. We see almost a watercolor image: the red wheelbarrow glazed with rain beside white chickens, with no comments attached, aside from "so much depends." The poem exemplifies Williams's belief, "No ideas but in things."

In contrast, Keats's and Neruda's objects prooke them to profound thoughts. The objects are present *and* are points of departure. Stein's piano may already be playing music. The poem is both verbal music and a way of seeing — Stein's way. Influenced by the Cubist painters, who fractured "normal" visual images to create new angular forms, Stein broke up the continuity of language in the interest of creating new patterns of seeing. Her poem doesn't "mean" in the conventional sense; instead, it breaks up and rearranges our straight-on view of an object.

THE RED WHEELBARROW
(William Carlos Williams, 1883–1963)

so much depends
upon

a red wheel
barrow

glazed with rain
water

beside the white
chickens.

ODE ON A GRECIAN URN
(John Keats, 1795–1821)

1

Thou still unravished bride of quietness,
   Thou foster-child of silence and slow time,
Sylvan historian, who canst thus express
   A flowery tale more sweetly than our rhyme:
What leaf-fringed legend haunts about thy shape
   Of deities or mortals, or of both,
      In Tempe or the dales of Arcady?
   What men or gods are these? What maidens loth?
What mad pursuit? What struggle to escape?
   What pipes and timbrels? What wild ecstasy?

2

Heard melodies are sweet, but those unheard
   Are sweeter; therefore, ye soft pipes, play on;
Not to the sensual ear, but, more endeared,
   Pipe to the spirit ditties of no tone:
Fair youth, beneath the trees, thou canst not leave
   Thy song, nor ever can those trees be bare;
      Bold Lover, never, never canst thou kiss,

Though winning near the goal—yet, do not grieve;
    She cannot fade, though thou hast not thy bliss,
  Forever wilt thou love, and she be fair!

3

Ah, happy, happy boughs! that cannot shed
  Your leaves, nor ever bid the Spring adieu;
And, happy melodist, unwearied,
  Forever piping songs forever new;
More happy love! more happy, happy love!
  Forever warm and still to be enjoyed,
    Forever panting, and forever young;
And breathing human passion far above,
    That leaves a heart high-sorrowful and cloyed,
      A burning forehead, and a parching tongue.

4

Who are these coming to the sacrifice?
  To what green altar, O mysterious priest,
Lead'st thou that heifer lowing at the skies,
  And all her silken flanks with garlands dressed?
What little town by river or sea shore,
  Or mountain-built with peaceful citadel,
    Is emptied of this folk, this pious morn?
And, little town, thy streets forevermore
  Will silent be; and not a soul to tell
    Why thou art desolate, can e'er return.

5

O Attic shape! Fair attitude! with brede
  Of marble men and maidens overwrought,
With forest branches and the trodden weed;
  Thou, silent form, dost tease us out of thought

As doth eternity: Cold Pastoral!
  When old age shall this generation waste,
    Thou shalt remain, in midst of other woe
    Than ours, a friend to man, to whom thou say'st,
  "Beauty is truth, truth beauty," — that is all
    Ye know on earth, and all ye need to know.

ODE TO A WATCH AT NIGHT
(Pablo Neruda, 1904–1973)

At night, in your hand
my watch shone
like a firefly.
I heard
its ticking:
like a dry rustling
coming
from your invisible hand.
Then your hand
went back to my dark breast
to gather my sleep and its beat.

The watch
went on cutting time
with its little saw.
As in a forest
fragments
of wood fell,
little drops, pieces
of branches or nests
without the silence changing,
without the cool darkness ending,
so
the watch went on cutting

from its invisible hand
time, time,
and minutes
fell like leaves,
fibres of broken time,
little black feathers.
As in the forest
we smelled roots,
the water somewhere released
a fat plopping
as of wet grapes.
A little mill
milled night,
the shadow whispered
falling from your hand
and filled the earth.
Dust,
earth, distance,
my watch in the night
ground and ground
from your hand.

I placed
my arm
under your invisible neck,
under its warm weight,
and in my hand
time fell,
the night,
little noises
of wood and of forest,
of divided night,
of fragments of shadow,
of water that falls and falls:
then

sleep fell
from the watch and from
both your sleeping hands,
it fell like a dark water
from the forests,
from the watch
to your body,
out of you it made the nations,
dark water,
time that falls
and runs
inside us.

And that was the way it was that night,
shadow and space, earth
and time,
something that runs and falls
and passes.

And that is the way all the nights
go over the earth,
leaving nothing but a vague
black odour, a leaf falls,
a drop
on the earth,
its sound stops,
the forest sleeps, the waters,
the meadows,
the fields,
the eyes.

I hear you and breathe,
my love,
we sleep.

          —Translated by W. S. Merwin

404 / Te Dscovery of Petry

 In Your Notebook:

Write a poem that simply presents an object in its context, such as a glass bottle on a windowsill or a motorcycle in the snow or a bowl of peaches on a table. Then try a Stein-like view of the same object.

A PIANO
(Gertrude Stein, 1874–1946)

If the speed is open, if the color is careless, if the selection of a strong scent is not awkward, if the button holder is held by all the waving color and there is no color, not any color. If there is no dirt in the pin and there can be none scarcely, if there is not then the place is the same as up standing.

This is no dark custom and it even is not acted in any such a way that a restraint is not spread. That is spread, it shuts and it lifts and awkwardly the centre is in standing.

The approach to objects in this group of poems varies enormously. Hopkins said, "If you look hard enough at an object, it begins to look back at you." Which object among the poems begins to "look back" — that is, starts to cause reflections and speculations in you? Why?

Poems

ALBA
(Ezra Pound, 1885–1972)

As cool as the pale wet leaves of lily-of-the-valley
She lay beside me in the dawn.

VERITÀ[1]
(Edward Mayes, 1951–)

Vincerò,[2] sings
Jussi Bjorling,
Puccini's *Turandot*
crackling on 78
turned into CD.
These are the late
'90s. That was
the late '30s.
He had better
lungs than God.
Verily I say unto
you that it is easier
to listen to *Turandot*
than to have composed
it. Truth is farther
than one can see,
more than one
can hear. If Keats
took truth to his
grave, he was
a beautiful corpse.
Gimme body
any day. I say it
as a hedge
against mortality.
All of those
gathering for
the *vendemmia,*[3]
cutting a few

---

[1] *verità:* truth
[2] *vincerò:* I will win
[3] *vendemmia:* harvest

pounds of truth
from the vines,
with one beautiful
stroke of the knife.
Whenever I'm feeling
overly spiritual, I fly
around this room
for a while, then
become self-conscious,
and crash into
the furniture. Earth
is truth, too.
What we walk upon,
what we go down
into. Stevens said that the world's
ugly, that everyone on it
is sad. If what we
touch touches us
back, if what we hear
hears us back, if
what we taste
tastes us back,
if what we smell
smells us back, if what
we see sees us back.
Isn't *Inferno* better
than *Paradiso*? Isn't it
that when we write
happiness we mean
beauty? Puccini writes
it, Jussi sings it,
we hear it, coming
out the double doors
into the front yard,

mixing with the jasmine
and geraniums,
the hyssop,
the stŭ-ōne
of the stone walls,
I will win, he sings,
whether it's beauty
or truth, who knows,
and has he won
already, past tense,
since that's all he
knows on earth,
this earth upon which
we will soon gather
for the olive harvest,
when not long ago white
oxen snorted in the cold
fields, for spring had
called, and said it would
soon return, to turn
the soil, the earth,
the truth, turn it with plow
and shovel, *aratro*[4] and *vanga*,[5]
find the beauty
that will come,
prepare for it,
use well the hoe,
the *zappa*,[6] get down
on your knees and dig.

---

[4] *aratro:* plow
[5] *vanga:* shovel
[6] *zappa:* hoe

MADRIGAL
(Anonymous, 1602)

My Love in her attire doth show her wit,
  It doth so well become her;
For every season she hath dressings fit,
  For Winter, Spring, and summer.
    No beauty she doth miss
      When all her robes are on:
    But Beauty's self she is
      When all her robes are gone.

VILLAGE FOR A WEDDING
(Jan Boleslaw Ożóg, 1913–1991)

Sky like pigeon's little belly.

Sky like goldfinch egg,
sky like starling's tune
greenishblue.

But fields like sundrenched sea
where roe-deer bound through oats
like fish through sea of rye.

And the village distant from a hummock
like a chain on a bicycle.

Iris in golden glimmer like pilot-flame.

But trees deeprooted like ponds
of green broth.
But grass like prayers
from lips of decaying willows.

And the village distant from a hummock
harrows gouged by nails
instead of stakes.

Lady bugs slide off lindens,
cockroaches to pick in a kerchief.

In barns peasant gears groan
cranking round the chaffcutter,
and frightened wasps play
like a heathen church at high mass.

Red beaks of carrots
circle higher than storks.

And the power station beyond the village
limping on crutches
like bent herdsman on crook.

Here the morning scented with hemp
saltily with bundle of clover.

Here my beloved hides for the night
safe from the boys in the kneading trough.
But up the ladder to the attic
carrying a measure of rye on his back
like a good husband

Here you are invited to the wedding.
                              —Translated by Leonard Kress

THE DAY LADY[1] DIED
(Frank O'Hara, 1926–1966)

It is 12:20 in New York a Friday
three days after Bastille day, yes
it is 1959 and I go get a shoeshine
because I will get off the 4:19 in Easthampton
at 7:15 and then go straight to dinner
and I don't know the people who will feed me

I walk up the muggy street beginning to sun
and have a hamburger and a malted and buy
an ugly NEW WORLD WRITING to see what the poets
in Ghana are doing these days
                                                        I go on to the bank
and Miss Stillwagon (first name Linda I once heard)
doesn't even look up my balance for once in her life
and in the GOLDEN GRIFFIN I get a little Verlaine
for Patsy with drawings by Bonnard although I do
think of Hesiod, trans. Richmond Lattimore or
Brendan Behan's new play or *Le Balcon* or *Les Nègres*
of Genet, but I don't, I stick with Verlaine
after practically going to sleep with quandariness

and for Mike I just stroll into the PARK LANE
Liquor Store and ask for a bottle of Strega and
then I go back where I came from to 6th Avenue
and the tobacconist in the Ziegfeld Theatre and
casually ask for a carton of Gauloises and a carton
of Picayunes, and a NEW YORK POST with her face on it

---

[1] *Lady*: Singer Billie Holiday, known as "Lady Day."

and I am sweating a lot by now and thinking of
leaning on the john door at the 5 SPOT
while she whispered a song along the keyboard
to Mal Waldron and everyone and I stopped breathing

I CARE NOT FOR THESE LADIES
(Thomas Campion, 1567–1620)

I care not for these ladies,
That must be wooed and prayed:
Give me kind Amaryllis,
The wanton country maid.
Nature art disdaineth,
Her beauty is her own.
    Her when we court and kiss,
    She cries, "Forsooth, let go!"
    But when we come where comfort is,
    She never will say no.

If I love Amaryllis,
She gives me fruit and flowers:
But if we love these ladies,
We must give golden showers.
Give them gold, that sell love,
Give me the nut-brown lass,
    Who, when we court and kiss,
    She cries, "Forsooth, let go!"
    But when we come where comfort is,
    She never will say no.

These ladies must have pillows,
And beds by strangers wrought;

Give me a bower of willows,
Of moss and leaves unbought,
And fresh Amaryllis,
With milk and honey fed;
   Who, when we court and kiss,
   She cries, "Forsooth, let go!"
   But when we come where comfort is,
   She never will say no.

My Sweetest Lesbia
(Thomas Campion, 1567–1620)

My sweetest Lesbia, let us live and love,
And though the sager sort our deeds reprove,
Let us not weigh them. Heaven's great lamps do dive
Into their west, and straight again revive,
But soon as once set is our little light,
Then must we sleep one ever-during night.

If all would lead their lives in love like me,
Then bloody swords and armor should not be;
No drum nor trumpet peaceful sleeps should move,
Unless alarm came from the camp of love.
But fools do live, and waste their little light,
And seek with pain their ever-during night.

When timely death my life and fortune ends,
Let not my hearse be vexed with mourning friends,
But let all lovers, rich in triumph, come
And with sweet pastimes grace my happy tomb;
And Lesbia, close up thou my little light,
And crown with love my ever-during night.

THE EXPIRATION
(John Donne, 1572–1631)

So, so, breake off this last lamenting kisse,
    which sucks two soules, and vapors Both away,
Turn thou ghost that way, and let me turn this,
    And let our selves benight our happiest day.
We ask'd none leave to Love, not will we owe
    Any, so cheap a death, as saying, Go;

Go; and if that word have not quite kill'd thee,
    Ease me with death, by bidding me go too.
Oh, if it have, let my word work on me,
    And a just office on a murderer do.
Except it be too late, to kill me so,
    Being double dead, going, and bidding, go.

A VALEDICTION: FORBIDDING MOURNING
(John Donne, 1572–1631)

As virtuous men passe mildly away,
    And whisper to their soules, to goe,
Whilst some of their sad friends doe say,
    The breath goes now, and some say, no:

So let us melt, and make no noise,
    No teare-floods, nor sigh-tempests move,
T'were prophanation of our joyes
    To tell the layetie our love.

Moving of th'earth brings harmes and feares,
    Men reckon what it did and meant,
But trepidation of the spheares,
    Though greater farre, is innocent.

Dull sublunary lovers love
   (Whose soule is sense) cannot admit
Absence, because it doth remove
   Those things which elemented it.

But we by a love, so much refin'd,
   That our selves know not what it is,
Inter-assured of the mind,
   Care lesse, eyes, lips, and hands to misse.

Our two soules therefore, which are one,
   Though I must goe, endure not yet
A breach, but an expansion,
   Like gold to ayery thinnesse beate.

If they be two, they are two so
   As stiffe twin compasses are two,
Thy soule the fixt foot, makes no show
   To move, but doth, if th'other doe.

And though it in the center sit,
   Yet when the other far doth rome,
It leanes, and hearkens after it,
   And growes erect, as that comes home.

Such wilt thou be to mee, who must
   Like th'other foot, obliquely runne;
Thy firmnes drawes my circle just,
   And makes me end, where I begunne.

THE RELIQUE
(John Donne, 1572–1631)

When my grave is broke up again
Some second guest to entertain,
(For graves have learn'd that woman-head
To be to more than one a Bed)
    And he that digs it, spies
A bracelet of bright hair about the bone,
    Will he not let us alone,
And think that there a happy couple lies,
Who thought that this device might be some way
To make their souls, at the last busy day,
Meet at this grave, and make a little stay?

    If this fall in a time, or land
    Where mis-devotion doth command,
    then, he that digs us up, will bring
    Us, to the Bishop, and the King,
        To make us Reliques; then
Thou shalt be a Mary Magdalen, and I
        A something else thereby:
All women shall adore us, and some men;
And since at such time, miracles are sought,
I would have that age by this paper taught
What miracles we harmless lovers wrought.

    First, we lov'd well and faithfully,
    Yet knew not what we loved, nor why;
    Difference of sex no more we knew,
    Than our Guardian Angels do;
        Coming and going, we
Perchance might kiss, but not between those meals;
    Our hands ne'er toucht the seals

Which nature, injur'd by late law, sets free:
The miracles we did; but now alas,
All measure, and all language, I should pass,
Should I tell what a miracle she was.

ON DONNE'S POETRY
(Samuel Taylor Coleridge, 1772–1834)

With Donne, whose muse on dromedary trots,
Wreathe iron pokers into true-love knots;
Rhyme's sturdy cripple, fancy's maze and clue,
Wit's forge and fire-blast, meaning's press and screw.

NIGHT FEEDING
(Muriel Rukeyser, 1913–1980)

Deeper than sleep but not so deep as death
I lay there dreaming and my magic head
remembered and forgot. On first cry I
remembered and forgot and did believe.

I knew love and I knew evil:
woke to the burning song and the tree burning blind,
despair of our days and the calm milk-giver who
knows sleep, knows growth, the sex of fire and grass,
renewal of all waters and the time of the stars
and the black snake with gold bones.

Black sleeps, gold burns; on second cry I woke
fully and gave to feed and fed on feeding.
Gold seed, green pain, my wizards in the earth
walked through the house, black in the morning dark.

Shadows grew in my veins, my bright belief,
my head of dreams deeper than night and sleep.
Voices of all black animals crying to drink,
cries of all birth arise, simple as we,
found in the leaves, in clouds and dark, in dream,
deep as this hour, ready again to sleep.

THE MOTHER
(Gwendolyn Brooks, 1917–2000)

Abortions will not let you forget.
You remember the children you got that you did not get,
The damp small pulps with a little or with no hair,
The singers and workers that never handled the air.
You will never neglect or beat
Them, or silence or buy with a sweet.
You will never wind up the sucking-thumb
Or scuttle off ghosts that come.
You will never leave them, controlling your luscious sigh,
Return for a snack of them, with gobbling mother-eye.

I have heard in the voices of the wind the voices of my dim
killed children.
I have contracted. I have eased
My dim dears at the breasts they could never suck.
I have said, Sweets, if I sinned, if I seized
Your luck
And your lives from your unfinished reach,
If I stole your births and your names,
Your straight baby tears and your games,
Your stilted or lovely loves, your tumults, your marriages,
     aches, and your deaths,
If I poisoned the beginnings of your breaths,

Believe that even in my deliberateness I was not deliberate.
Though why should I whine,
Whine that the crime was other than mine? —
Since anyhow you are dead.
Or rather, or instead,
You were never made.
But that too, I am afraid,
Is faulty: oh, what shall I say, how is the truth to be said?
You were born, you had body, you died.
It is just that you never giggled or planned or cried.

Believe me, I loved you all.
Believe me, I knew you, though faintly, and I loved, I loved you
All.

WHEN THE CEILING CRIES
(Russell Edson, 1935–)

A mother tosses her infant so that it hits the ceiling.
   Father says, why are you doing that to the ceiling?
   Do you want my baby to fly away to heaven? the ceiling is
      there so that the baby will come back to me, says
      mother.
   Father says, you are hurting the ceiling, can't you hear it crying?
   So mother and father climb a ladder and kiss the ceiling.

GIACOMETTI'S DOG
(Robin Becker, 1951–)

She moves so gracefully on her bronze legs
that they form the letter M beneath her.
There is nothing more beautiful than the effort
in her outstretched neck, the simplicity of the head;

but she will never curl again in the comfortable basket,
she will never be duped by the fireplace and the fire.

Though she has sniffed out cocaine in the Newark Airport,
we can never trust her good nose again.
She'll kill a chicken in her master's yard,
she'll corner a lamb in the back pasture.
She's resigning her post with the Seeing Eye.

Giacometti's *Dog* will not ask for water
though she's been tied to a rope in Naples
for three days under the hot sun.
Giacometti's *Dog* will not see a vet
though someone kicks her and her liver fills with blood.
Though she's fed meat laced with strychnine.
Though her mouth fills with porcupine quills.

Giacometti's *Dog* is coming back
as a jackal, snapping at the wheels
of your bicycle, following behind in her
you-can't-touch-me-now suit.
Giacometti's *Dog* has already forgotten
when she lost the use of her back legs
and cried at the top of the stairs
and you took pity on her.

She's taking a modern-day attitude.
She knows it's a shoot-or-get-shot situation.
She's not your doggie-in-the-window.
She's not racing into a burning house or taking your shirt
between her teeth and swimming to the beach.
She's looking out for Number One,
she's doing the dog paddle and making it
to shore in this dog-eat-dog world.

BLACK POET, WHITE CRITIC
(Dudley Randall, 1914–)

A critic advises
not to write on controversial subjects
like freedom or murder,
but to treat universal themes
and timeless symbols
like the white unicorn.

A white unicorn?

10

Interpretation: The Wide Response

Try to be one of the people on whom nothing is lost.
—HENRY JAMES

Folk wisdom has it that spiders hatch their eggs by staring at them. Reading poems requires the same concentration. An African tribe dries reeds for flutes. When the instruments are carved, a musician ceremoniously breathes into each one, imparting a soul. This kind of life giving is also needed each time you read a poem.

We may analyze a poem in terms of rhythm, language, metaphor, or any aspect, and it still may remain inert unless the elements fuse. Coleridge coined a word for the ability to fuse the parts of a poem into a whole: *esemplastic,* "to shape into one." The poem's total effect *is* the unity of perception. The best reader lets imagination work along with analysis and listens for the widest possibilities of the words. This requires both staring and giving.

Think about the craft and meaning(s) of this poem:

LYING IN A HAMMOCK AT WILLIAM DUFFY'S FARM
IN PINE ISLAND, MINNESOTA
(James Wright, 1927–1980)

Over my head, I see the bronze butterfly,
Asleep on the black trunk,
Blowing like a leaf in green shadow.
Down the ravine behind the empty house,
The cowbells follow one another
Into the distances of the afternoon.

To my right,
In a field of sunlight between two pines,
The droppings of last year's horses
Blaze up into golden stones.
I lean back, as the evening darkens and comes on.
A chicken hawk floats over, looking for home.
I have wasted my life.

First, you might be moved by the poem and surprised by the ending. The most important immediate response is how the poem affects you. What emotions does it arouse, what memories does it evoke, where does it take your imagination, what does it remind you of? Then, *why?* How do you respond to the images and line use? How does looking at the craft add to your first impression? What won't "hatch"?

Here are one young writer's notes on Wright's poem:

```
Wright was the first poet I felt a connection
with. And the first contemporary poet I under-
stood. When I read the poem "Lying in a Ham-
mock . . ." one afternoon, I must have been a bit
weary of things in general. Maybe that's why the
title so appealed to me. I had never seen a poem
that had a title so long or so particular. Oh! to
be on a farm at that moment, I thought. There
```

things are easier, one can rest, relax, breathe in clean country air. Nature! I thought, would cure the emptiness, loneliness I was feeling at the moment.

I read it again. Several days later I came back to it. I read it again and again, to the point where I had memorized it, I had taken it far within me. I still didn't "understand" everything, I felt.

One fall day I was taking a walk. All the trees were beautiful in their hardwood colors—this was Minnesota. Fall always brought a certain sadness that came out of the wonderful beauty of that season, the smells, the colors, the light, the air. If this isn't a glimpse of beauty, what is? What is beauty? While I was on this walk, Wright's poem came into my mind—perhaps it was there all along—and I started saying it to myself. Being outside, it was almost as if I were lying in a hammock, observing the world around me. I remember looking in the gutter of the street which was filling up with fallen leaves; mixed in were cigarette butts, plastic bottles, a can—the usual litter, but somehow it all looked transfigured, like Bishop's looking at the old worn-out fish she caught one day and proclaiming that everything was "rainbow, rainbow, rainbow." (See "The Fish," page 55.) I felt then that I understood the Wright poem—not just theoretically, but on the level of the senses.

After this, reading other poems became much easier. I had made a breakthrough in understanding: Poems are written by men and women. We all share common experiences. Poets are different from others in that they feel their experience is remarkable—that is, something to make remarks on. Poets don't simply ignore this kind of ordinary scene. They go one step further.

I still like the poem. Look at the senses Wright touches: Sight: "I see" butterfly, black trunk. He shifts to hearing: cowbells. Back to sight: field, year-old horse droppings. Sight: chicken hawk overhead. Not only these particular ones; he seems to be surrounded with those things that touch his senses. I like his yoking of words that call up a particular emotion: black trunk and empty house. The empty house hooks up with the second-to-last line, "looking for home." This kind of emptiness he feels is populated by some quite amazing sights, feelings. The butterfly is bronze, like a work of art: unreal, very unordinary. It's "asleep"—though how he knows this, who knows! It just shows that he has been looking at it for a long time, admiring it, the bronze against the black. And this bronze butterfly is in "green" shadow. How a shadow can be green!

The second sentence gives us only sound: he's true to his point of view. He can't see the cows; he only can hear the bells—that kind of melancholy sound. The o sounds in the line make the bell notes follow each other across the page. This pleased and surprised me. He thought of that! A poem tries for surprise, tries to get the reader to see something other than what he or she is accustomed to seeing. How pedestrian to have said "into the distances of the field" or "into the late afternoon."

The third sentence: He sees to the right of him piles of droppings. He thinks they're about a year old. They "blaze up into golden stones." Here we have to say, "Enough!" We allowed you to go on about the butterfly turning into a leaf, and there just being cowbells instead of cows, but manure into gold bricks! If we believe this, we'll believe anything!

The last image he gives is less an image than a straight statement. The hawk overhead doesn't seem quite as charged as the other images. What it's doing, though, and what the poet thinks it's doing might be two different things. Wright anthropomorphizes the hawk. The hawk is perhaps looking for its next meal, a rat or a gopher or a snake. But Wright says the hawk is "looking for home," meaning that it has a home to look for. However, it's Wright (or "the speaker") who is troubled by "home." This kind of projection seems a shade corny.

What's Wright doing through this poem? On the one hand, he's simply the observer; that's all he can do. In a hammock—resting, suspended between earth and sky. Also, the hammock is on someone else's place—Wright seems to make a point of that in the title—he denotes a very specific place. It's as if he's giving you clues—when, Evening: where, a Farm: and so on—and wants you to solve some problem he has.

It seems he's giving you clues because of that last line he throws out, almost like a cry. How to explain, or respond to, this last line? I take Wright seriously, but have to ask why he feels this way. Does the last line follow from the images before it? It's a very drastic statement to make: what happens after you say that to yourself? We don't know in the case of Wright—he doesn't tell us any more; he leaves us with that statement ringing in our ears. Interesting that he ends the poem with "my life." Key words, I think. He opens the poem up to some broader considerations. He's openly saying what many of us at one time or another will have to confront: What has been the worth of my life? Have I "wasted" it? How do you "waste" a life? This seems one of the fundamentals of poetry. Poetry raises questions.

This writer fully reacted to and explored the poem. Anything one does wholly requires a kind of rapt attention that lets the most happen. Understanding poems sometimes demands living with the poem for a while, as this writer did.

Wright was familiar with "Archaic Torso of Apollo," by the German poet Rainer Maria Rilke:

ARCHAIC TORSO OF APOLLO
(Rainer Maria Rilke, 1875–1926)

We have no idea what his fantastic head
was like, where the eyeballs were slowly swelling. But
his body now is glowing like a gas lamp,
whose inner eyes, only turned down a little,

hold their flame, shine. If there weren't light, the curve
of the breast wouldn't blind you, and in the swerve
of the thighs a smile wouldn't keep on going
toward the place where the seeds are.

If there weren't light, this stone would look cut off
where it drops clearly from the shoulders,
its skin wouldn't gleam like the fur of a wild animal,

and the body wouldn't send out light from every edge
as a star does . . . for there is no place at all
that isn't looking at you. You must change your life.
                                        —Translated by Robert Bly

Clearly, there's a relationship between the two poems. A further insight may strike if you read Wright's "A Blessing" and "Autumn Comes to Martins Ferry, Ohio" again. All four poems hinge on an illumination at the end. Each leads to a transforming revelation about ordinary experience. Other poems by an author often illuminate the poem at hand.

After all this, what about that startling last line in "Lying in a Hammock..."? Obviously, it's an electrical charge that arcs back to touch each line with significance. It resists a simple analysis. To some extent, each reader must be the African musician who gives soul to a dried reed by breathing into it. The line says what it says clearly: "I have wasted my life." But exactly *how* that means is richly open to interpretation.

What Is Meaning?

Often we hear "What does the poem mean?" That's an odd question, a reductive question that sounds as if the poem is sitting there on the page while "meaning" hovers above it like a little white cloud; as if we must read the cloud formations to find the real poem. Instead, think of **meaning** as *everything* you perceive about the poem. Many poems *suggest* multiple meanings. These are not always paraphrasable. Wright's poem begins with mundane experience (easy enough to talk about), but it ends with a startling perception that bears thinking about at length.

Rather than being *about* experience, think of a poem *as* an experience—sometimes with memorable insights, sometimes not. Every good poem establishes its own parameters. Sometimes sound takes precedence over meaning, sometimes verbal juxtapositions make *a* meaning irrelevant, except as each person interprets the poem. Gertrude Stein's work is an example of this. To read "A Piano" (page 404) and say that it "doesn't make sense" is to miss the point. (After one of Stein's perfectly logical lectures on poetry, a reporter asked her why she didn't write the way she spoke. She replied, "Why don't you read the way I write?") We have to learn to read on the poem's terms. We can't always know what the poet intended, but by a careful reading, we can by now see the writer's approach to the subject. Poems do not mean what they do not say or suggest. We must trust the text; then we understand by remaining open to the poem's widest possibilities. Karl

Shapiro paid his fellow poet Randall Jarrell this compliment: "He was a great, you might say a dangerous, listener."

The more you bring with you, the more you get back. Reading Rilke's poem and Wright's other work deepens your response to Wright's poem. In his essay "The Prerequisites," Robert Frost wrote:

> A poem is best read in the light of all other poems ever written. We read A the better to read B (we have to start somewhere; we may get very little out of A). We read B the better to read C, C the better to read D, D the better to go back and get something more out of A. Progress is not the aim, but circulation. The thing is to get among the poems where they hold each other apart in their places as the stars do.

Excellent advice: Get *among* the poems and circulate.

Gaps and Holes

Craft. Analysis of the text. Our own interpretations. And still there is something else at work in a poem. Dylan Thomas was aware of significant "holes and gaps" in this passage from "Poetic Manifesto":

> You can tear a poem apart to see what makes it technically tick, and say to yourself, when the works are laid out before you, the vowels, the consonants, the rhymes or rhythms, "Yes, this is *it*. This is why the poem moves me so. It is because of the craftsmanship." But you're back again where you began!
>
> You're back with the mystery of having been moved by words. The best craftsmanship always leaves holes and gaps in the works of the poem so that something that is *not* the poem can creep, crawl, flash, or thunder in.

In the fragments of Anakreon, a Greek poet of the sixth century B.C., the "gaps and holes" are obvious because parts of the poems are lost. We're drawn toward what is not said, or to what is understated — the poem between the lines. We must participate, supplying our own imaginative complement to what's there. In the fragments below, imagination goes to work on the enticing brackets, which mark lost portions of the ancient worm-eaten papyrus from which these translations were made. What's not said but suggested is definitely a part of our experience.

TRANSLATIONS OF ANAKREON[1]
(Anakreon, sixth century B.C.)

3.

```
[                                              ]
[              ] all[nig]ht long [             ]
[                                              ]
Both delight and [                            ]
[                                              ]
But loving [                                  ]
Offerings at hand [                           ]
Of the Pierides [                             ]
[                                              ]
And Graces [                                  ]
And then the [                                ]
[                                              ]
[                                              ]
[              ] beaut[iful] [                 ]
[                                              ]
Flitter we all the night [                    ]
Fishing with bait [                           ]
Golden-helmeted Pallas [                      ]
```

---

[1] *Anakreon:* Anakreon lived in Teos, now Sighalik in Turkey, and later in Athens in the sixth century B.C. His work is often confused with that of an Alexandrian imitation, or homage, to him, written by a group of poets and later misunderstood to be the real work of Anakreon. These fragments are by the real, historical Anakreon.

[   ] from afar [   ]
Flowering [   ]
[   ]

20.

Can myrrh rubbed on a chest
Sweeten the great round heart inside?

32.

[   ]
Whose heart is green and young again
And dances to a lissome tune on the flute.

39.

[   ] loved pitiful war.

40.

The servant girl poured
Honied wine from the jug
On her shoulder.0

85.

[   ] bedroom
In which he, unmarrying,
Was married [   ].

91.

You carry on over it
  Far too much.

92.

He sleeps soundly
With his bedroom door
Always unbolted.

105.

[   ]
Glowing with desire,
Gleaming with spiced oil
[   ].

112.

Walking along with a haughty neck.

113.

Chattering swallow.

114.

Wine-server.

123.

Pretty.

124.

Stalks of slim white celery
In a wicker basket.

158.

[   ]

161.

[   ]
Again [   ] island
[   ] we two in love,
We pray *O ears that hear prayers,*
Our very solemn [   ]
[   ] *Lady in the stars*
[   ] Eros stalking
On the balls of his feet [   ]
The happy [   ] who
Of those I love [   ]
Until my dream [   ]
Hail! Kyllanas [   ]
[   ] the sea [   ]
We kneel at Aphrodite's altar
[   ]
Sacred mother [   ]
Of Kypris [   ]
[   ]
Excite [   ]
[   ]
Glossy [   ]
[   ]
Sweet [   ]
Hail [   ]
Sight [   ]
I hug your knees [   ]
Young [   ]
You, boy [   ]

Come to me! [   ]
Look [   ]
[   ]

—Translated by Guy Davenport

The jolting phrases of Emily Dickinson invite our participation in a
way similar to the fragments of Anakreon:

425
(Emily Dickinson, 1830–1886)

Good Morning—Midnight—
I'm coming Home—
Day—got tired of Me—
How could I—of Him?

Sunshine was a sweet place—
I liked to stay—
But Morn—didn't want me—now—
So—Goodnight—Day!

I can look—can't I—
When the East is Red?
The Hills—have a way—then—
That puts the Heart—abroad—

You—are not so fair—Midnight—
I chose—Day—
But—please take a little Girl—
He turned away!

Rather than proceeding smoothly, the sense or meaning jerks and
jumps. Phrases abut each other like wires that get close enough to
spark. The halts (dashes) are, of course, part of the meaning. They

connect and separate at once. Here's where the reader's imagination must come into play. We follow the poet's thought process as it occurs, close to the act of perception.

When a poem is extraordinarily difficult to understand fully on first or tenth reading, as much of Dickinson is, we become fascinated, like a mother who prefers the difficult child. We respond strongly without knowing why. The mystery of such a poem is that someday — after we, not the poem, have changed — we may be able to read it. Thomas's "There Was a Saviour," a poem crowded with symbols and private religious associations, seems deliberately cryptic.

THERE WAS A SAVIOUR
(Dylan Thomas, 1914–1953)

There was a saviour
Rarer than radium,
Commoner than water, crueller than truth;
Children kept from the sun
Assembled at his tongue
To hear the golden note turn in a groove,
Prisoners of wishes locked their eyes
In the jails and studies of his keyless smiles.

The voice of children says
From a lost wilderness
There was calm to be done in his safe unrest,
When hindering man hurt
Man, animal, or bird
We hid our fears in that murdering breath,
Silence, silence to do, when earth grew loud,
In lairs and asylums of the tremendous shout.

There was glory to hear
In the churches of his tears,

Under his downy arm you sighed as he struck,
　　　O you who could not cry
　　　On to the ground when a man died
　　Put a tear for joy in the unearthly flood
And laid your cheek against a cloud-formed shell:
Now in the dark there is only yourself and myself.

　　　Two proud, blacked brothers cry,
　　　Winter-locked side by side,
　　To this inhospitable hollow year,
　　　O we who could not stir
　　　One lean sigh when we heard
　　Greed on man beating near and fire neighbour
　　But wailed and nested in the sky-blue wall
Now break a giant tear for the little known fall,

　　　For the drooping of homes
　　　That did not nurse our bones,
　　Brave deaths of only ones but never found,
　　　Now see, alone in us,
　　　Our own true strangers' dust
　　Ride through the doors of our unentered house.
Exiled in us we arouse the soft,
Unclenched, armless, silk and rough love that breaks all rocks.

Did Thomas know everything about his poem? Generally the poet knows his business; otherwise the poems falter or skid. Occasionally a poet writes a luminous, mysterious poem that puzzles him more than the reader. Reader or writer, you do not always understand everything.

The ancient fragments and the obscure Thomas poem require us to sharpen our oyster knives and to pry into them. The active reader always brings an *imaginative complement* to a poem, a readiness to participate fully in the experience. Nothing is as necessary to the poem as a flexible reader.

Power Sources

In his book *On Surgery*, Richard Seltzer says that between the dermis and the epidermis there exists a layer of "pure energy." Dylan Thomas wrote about "the force that through the green fuse drives the flower." Forces and energies also impel or organize the poem.

Most good poems are alive with strong emotion or experience. Thomas's "gaps and holes," though not as apparently as rhythm, meter, and imagery, also fuel the poem. And there are many other discernible forces. Each of the following poems brings to your attention something particular about a poem's infrastructure. A way of proceeding, an idea, a moment of sudden revelation: Each is that "layer of pure energy" operating with meaning and craft.

IDEA

The primary power comes from an idea that engages our minds. We tend to solve a poem like "The Tortoise" by sorting through our own reactions for agreement. What emotions are behind the idea in this poem?

THE TORTOISE
(Cid Corman, 1924–)

Always to want to
go back, to correct
an error, ease a

guilt, see how a friend
is doing. And yet
one doesn't, except

in memory, in
dreams. The land remains
desolate. Always

the feeling is of
terrible slowness
overtaking haste.

ASSOCIATION

A string of associations propels the poem — and the reader's imagination. The mind is naturally associative: One thing reminds you of another, without logical connection. The smell of rain on hot streets may catapult you to a feeling you had for someone, which in turn reminds you of a red motorcycle and pots of hyacinths on a windowsill. No logic, just sensory links buried in the psyche. Poems using this approach depend on the reader's willingness to make imaginative leaps with the author. I especially like poems that allow one image to spark another. The motion seems close to the way thought actually occurs.

In André Breton's "Free Union," each association has to do with a subject, the speaker's wife. The poem is **surreal** (meaning "beyond realism"), a free way of associating by allowing subconscious or dreamlike imagery to surface and guide the poem.

Surreal poems often have a dream logic. The poet dips into the psyche, leaps from image to image. The surreal poet values the spontaneity of subconscious associations. **Surrealism** was originally a French movement in poetry spearheaded by Breton, who wrote in 1924:

Everything leads one to believe that there exists a certain point in the mind from which life and death, the real and the imaginary, the past and the future, what is communicable and what is incommunicable, the high and the low, cease to be perceived as contradictory.

This mysterious "point" was the pole star that inspired and guided the surrealists' fantastic experiments in painting and poetry.

438 / THE DISCOVERY OF POETRY

from FREE UNION
(André Breton, 1896–1966)

My wife with the woodfire hair
With the heat lightning thoughts
And the hourglass waist
My wife with the waist of an otter in the tiger's jaws
My wife with the mouth of cockade and clustering maximal stars
With teeth like the spoor of white mice on white earth
With a tongue of rubbed amber and glass
With a tongue like a daggered host
The tongue of a doll whose eyes open and close
A tongue of unbelievable stone
My wife with eyelashes like the strokes of childish writing
With eyebrows like the rim of a swallow's nest
My wife with the temples of slate on a glasshouse roof
And steam on windows
My wife with the champagne shoulders
Like a dolphin-headed fountain under ice
My wife with the matchstick wrists
My wife with the fingers of chance and the ace of hearts
With the fingers of new-mown hay
My wife with the armpits of marten and beechnut
And Midsummer Night
Of privet and wentletrap nests
With the arms of sea-surf and mill-dam foam
And of wheat and mill mixed
My wife with the spindle legs
Moving like clockwork and despair
My wife with the calves of elder pith
My wife with the feet of initials
With the feet of key-bunches with the feet of drinking caulkers
My wife whose neck is pearl barley
Whose throat is a golden dale
With rendez-vous in the very bed of the torrent

With the breasts of night
My wife with the breasts of marine molehills
My wife with the ruby crucible breasts
With breasts like the ghost of a rose under dew
My wife with a belly like the unfolding fan of the days
A belly like a giant claw
My wife with back like a bird in vertical flight
With back of quicksilver
Back of light
With a nape of rolled stone and moist chalk
And the fall of a glass just drained
My wife with the skiff hips
Hips of chandelier and arrow feathers
Hips of the ribs of white peacock plumes
And imperceptibly swinging scales
My wife with the buttocks of sandstone and mountain flax
My wife with the swan's back buttocks
My wife with the springtime buttocks
And gladiolus sex
My wife with the placer and water-mole sex
My wife with sex of seaweed and stale sweets
My wife with mirror sex
My wife with eyes full of tears
With eyes of violet panoply and magnetic needle
My wife with savannah eyes
My wife with eyes of water to drink in prison
My wife with eyes of wood always under the axe
With eyes of water level air level the level of earth and fire
                              —Translated by Kenneth White

TENSION

A major force of the poem is sometimes tension. The use of opposites, words or concepts, gives a push-pull tautness. The poem proceeds by juxtaposition of opposites or by the use of **paradox,** a statement that seems to contradict itself. For example, Shakespeare wrote, "When my love swears that she is made of truth / I do believe her, though I know she lies."

BITTER-SWEET
(George Herbert, 1593–1633)

Ah, my dear angry Lord,
Since thou dost love, yet strike;
Cast down, yet help afford;
Sure I will do the like.

I will complain, yet praise;
I will bewail, approve;
And all my sour-sweet days
I will lament and love.

ALOGICAL STRUCTURE

An alogical structure proceeds other than by sequential logic. Like surreal poems, these poems refuse to be pinned down to *meaning*. They remain wide open to interpretation, or sometimes just to listening. The example below is a **sound poem,** written for the ear. When an alogical poem seems composed by chance, it is called an **aleatory** poem.

The example that follows is highly structured and conscious, but not organized along a one-two-three logical track.

A CHORALE* OF CHEROKEE NIGHT MUSIC AS HEARD THROUGH AN OPEN WINDOW IN SUMMER LONG AGO
(Jonathan Williams, 1929–)

uhu wahuhu wahuhu wahuhu wahuhu wahuhu wahuhu wahuhu wahuhu w
guku uguku uguku uguku uguku uguku uguku uguku uguku uguku uguku
huhu huhu huhu huhu huhu huhu huhu huhu huhu huhu huhu huhu huh

---

*screech owl, hoot owl, yellow-breasted chat, jar-fly, carolina chickadee, katydid, crow, wolf, Beatles, turkey, goose, bullfrog, spring frog.

u lalu lalu lalu lalu lalu lalu lalu lalu lalu lalu lalu lalu lalu lal
atu talatu talatu talatu talatu talatu talatu talatu talatu talatu t
li tsikilili tsikilili tsikilili tsikilili tsikilili tsikilili tsikilili tsikilili
ikiki tsikiki tsikiki tsikiki tsikiki tsikiki tsikiki tsikiki tsikik
u kagu kagu kagu kagu kagu kagu kagu kagu kagu kagu kagu kagu kag
ya waya waya waya waya waya waya waya waya waya waya waya way
eah yeah yeah yeah yeah yeah yeah yeah yeah yeah yeah yeah yeah y
a guna guna guna guna guna guna guna guna guna guna guna guna gun
sasa sasa sasa sasa sasa sasa sasa sasa sasa sasa sasa sasa sasa
unu kununu kununu kununu kununu kununu kununu kununu kununu kun
tu dustu dustu dustu dustu dustu dustu dustu dustu dustu dustu dustu

EPIPHANY

A moment of epiphany is a sudden revelation or a flash of recognition when the essence or full meaning of a time, event, memory, or person is apprehended. Such realizations may also involve a *transformation*, like the change that occurs after Elizabeth's moment of recognition in "In the Waiting Room."

IN THE WAITING ROOM
(Elizabeth Bishop, 1911–1979)

In Worcester, Massachusetts,
I went with Aunt Consuelo
to keep her dentist's appointment
and sat and waited for her
in the dentist's waiting room.
It was winter. It got dark
early. The waiting room
was full of grown-up people,
arctics and overcoats,
lamps and magazines.
My aunt was inside
what seemed like a long time

and while I waited I read
the *National Geographic*
(I could read) and carefully
studied the photographs:
the inside of a volcano,
black, and full of ashes;
then it was spilling over
in rivulets of fire.

Osa and Martin Johnson
dressed in riding breeches,
laced boots, and pith helmets.
A dead man slung on a pole
—"Long Pig," the caption said.
Babies with pointed heads
wound round and round with string;
black, naked women with necks
wound round and round with wire
like the necks of light bulbs.
Their breasts were horrifying.
I read it right straight through.
I was too shy to stop.
And then I looked at the cover:
the yellow margins, the date.

Suddenly, from inside,
came an *oh!* of pain
—Aunt Consuelo's voice—
not very loud or long.
I wasn't at all surprised;
even then I knew she was
a foolish, timid woman.
I might have been embarrassed,
but wasn't. What took me
completely by surprise

was that it was *me*:
my voice, in my mouth.
Without thinking at all
I was my foolish aunt,
I — we — were falling, falling,
our eyes glued to the cover
of the *National Geographic*,
February, 1918.

I said to myself: three days
and you'll be seven years old.
I was saying it to stop
the sensation of falling off
the round, turning world
into cold, blue-black space.
But I felt: you are an *I*,
you are an *Elizabeth*,
you are one of *them*.
Why should you be one, too?
I scarcely dared to look
to see what it was I was.
I gave a sidelong glance
— I couldn't look any higher —
at shadowy gray knees,
trousers and skirts and boots
and different pairs of hands
lying under the lamps.
I knew that nothing stranger
had ever happened, that nothing
stranger could ever happen.
Why should I be my aunt,
or me, or anyone?
What similarities —
boots, hands, the family voice
I felt in my throat, or even

the *National Geographic*
and those awful hanging breasts—
held us all together
or made us all just one?
How—I didn't know any
word for it—how "unlikely"...
How had I come to be here,
like them, and overhear
a cry of pain that could have
got loud and worse but hadn't?

The waiting room was bright
and too hot. It was sliding
beneath a big black wave,
another, and another.

Then I was back in it.
The War was on. Outside,
in Worcester, Massachusetts,
were night and slush and cold,
and it was still the fifth
of February, 1918.

CATALOGUE

Many poems are simply someone's list of ideas, emotions, events, objects, or whatever. Lists—even someone else's grocery list you find in the basket of your shopping cart—are intriguing and appealing. We respond to the possibility of order. Once we list something, we name it, and naming is one of the writer's passions. As poet Richard Wilbur says "the itch to call the roll of things" almost always expresses "a longing to possess the whole world, and to praise it, or at least to feel it." "Free Union" (page 438) is a catalogue poem, as are "Saying Things" by Marilyn Krysl (page 29), "Lucky Life," and "If You Saw Me Walking" by Gerald Stern (page 192). You will come across this mode when you read the Bible's genealogical lists, Milton's list of fallen angels in *Paradise Lost,* and Vergil's hero lists in *The Aeneid.* Dip anywhere into Whitman's poetry to experience the cumulative effect of this approach to building a poem.

EXAGGERATION

Exaggeration by overstatement, **understatement,** or comparison fuels poems with humor and/or surprise. Exaggeration by overstatement is called **hyperbole.** Hyperbolic figures of speech are common: I slept for a month, I could eat a horse, he's old as the hills, it's going to snow forever. In Sonnet CXXX, Shakespeare makes fun of the conventional exaggerated comparisons made in love poems.

SONNET CXXX
(William Shakespeare, 1564–1616)

My mistress' eyes are nothing like the sun;
Coral is far more red than her lips' red;
If snow be white, why then her breasts are dun;
If hairs be wires, black wires grown on her head.
I have seen roses damasked,[1] red and white,
But no such roses see I in her cheeks;
And in some perfumes is there more delight
Than in the breath that from my mistress reeks.
I love to hear her speak, yet well I know
That music hath a far more pleasing sound;
I grant I never saw a goddess go;
My mistress, when she walks, treads on the ground.
And yet, by heaven, I think my love as rare
As any she belied with false compare.

---

[1] *damasked:* variegated.

SPECIAL KNOWLEDGE

To understand some poems, the reader needs special knowledge. The poet may use many foreign phrases or a web of allusions not commonly recognized. Some poems are written in reply to another poem, perhaps from another era, and the full effect of the one at hand is lessened without knowledge of its "ancestor." Readers gain access to these poems through research.

For the next poem to make full sense, it's necessary to know that William Blake regarded philosophers Voltaire and Rousseau as mockers of faith. Democritus, a Greek philosopher, first taught that all things are made up of atoms. Blake sees Democritus and Newton, who said light was made of particles, as materialists. Blake considers all four of these men irreligious deniers of the transcendental meaning of experience. The final image refers to the children of Israel camping along the Red Sea shore when the Egyptians were pursuing them.

MOCK ON, MOCK ON, VOLTAIRE, ROUSSEAU
(William Blake, 1757–1828)

Mock on, mock on, Voltaire, Rousseau:
Mock on, mock on: 'tis all in vain!
You throw the sand against the wind,
And the wind blows it back again.

And every sand becomes a Gem
Reflected in the beams divine;
Blown back they blind the mocking Eye,
But still in Israel's paths they shine.

The Atoms of Democritus
And Newton's particles of light
Are sands upon the Red Sea shore,
Where Israel's tents do shine so bright.

Synthesis of the poem involves putting together everything that bears on your reading. The examples above, from Thomas's gaps to Blake's complex allusions, will raise your antennae for receiving the full

In Your Notebook:

Try writing a cataloguing poem. It might be a list of qualities you like or dislike in someone, a list of reasons for not dancing or flying or moving. You might start with "It's not too late to . . ." or "If you loved me you'd . . ." or "At home, we . . ."

---

range of each poem. The creative reader responds to what is outward and what is inward, what is stated and what is intuited. "What sets this poem in motion?" is one of the best questions you can ask. Exciting poetry is never just programmatic; the poet constantly surprises our expectations or pours in a secret ingredient. We read carefully and openly if we read to see what makes each poem *that* poem and no other. Similarly, poetry can't be defined or conform to rules. A poem can be a metaphysical argument, an experience of buying aspirin, a word game, or all of these. An exception pops up as soon as you've memorized a beautiful definition.

Boustrophedon is the ancient mode of writing in which lines move from left to right then right to left. The root of the word comes from the Greek word meaning the turning of an ox while plowing a field back and forth. Trace the associations of the title through the poem. How many of the "power sources" do you pick up in "Boustrophedon?"

BOUSTROPHEDON
(Edward Mayes, 1951–)

Whereas some poems are baskets catching falling
Things, some line up for the diving board
To add twenty-five laps to their scorecards.
This is such a poem. This is the turn this poem
Has taken. If the title is misleading, it is not
Meandering. Its point, like the needle's,
Only indicates direction to the doubled

In Your Notebook:

Write a sound poem—a baby crying in traffic, the noises you hear from your window at night, the washer going through its cycles, or party music and conversation happening simultaneously.

Thread it is pulling. It might close up random
Pieces of cloth. Stitching can be satisfying
In itself. Take the anklebone broken from
Stepping in a pothole—it is mending and deserves
A crutch. When the bone ages a million years
It will be a prize for those looking. I have
Zigzagged up hills. I have read it is recommended.
Which is zig and which zag I am confused about:
How long can I zig—or zag—before zig loses
Its meaning and becomes, simply, straight line?
I would like to think I could zag all day, zag
To the mailbox, zag to the flowershop, zag home.
I have worn a furrow to the window and have three
Furrows in my forehead when I am surprised at what
I see. I do not know what the ox in the field
Is thinking, plowing on Sunday, twenty-five turns
It has memorized—better to be here than at the hecatomb[1]!
These U-turns, returns, pull the line, turn, turn the world.

---

[1] *hecatomb:* in ancient Greece, a place where offerings were made to the gods. Often the sacrifice was one hundred oxen.

In the three important poems that follow, look at craft, subject, style, voice. What other special powers (such as tension, association, or epiphany) does each have? What meanings does each have? Are there common concerns in the three?

LEDA AND THE SWAN[1]
(William Butler Yeats, 1865–1939)

A sudden blow: the great wings beating still
Above the staggering girl, her thighs caressed
By the dark webs, her nape caught in his bill,
He holds her helpless breast upon his breast.

How can those terrified vague fingers push
The feathered glory from her loosening thighs?
And how can body, laid in that white rush,
But feel the strange heart beating where it lies?

A shudder in the loins engenders there
The broken wall, the burning roof and tower
And Agamemnon dead.
                         Being so caught up,
So mastered by the brute blood of the air,
Did she put on his knowledge with his power
Before the indifferent beak could let her drop?

---

[1] *Leda and the Swan:* The Greek god Zeus took the form of a
swan and sexually assaulted Leda. The result was the birth of
Helen of Troy from an egg. Since Helen's beauty was one of the
causes of the Trojan War, her conception caused "the burning
roof and tower / And Agamemnon dead." Agamemnon, Helen's
brother-in-law and commander of the Greek army at Troy, was
murdered after the war by Helen's sister, Clytemnestra.

THE SECOND COMING
(William Butler Yeats, 1865–1939)

Turning and turning in the widening gyre
The falcon cannot hear the falconer;
Things fall apart; the center cannot hold;

Mere anarchy is loosed upon the world,
The blood-dimmed tide is loosed, and everywhere
The ceremony of innocence is drowned;
The best lack all conviction, while the worst
Are full of passionate intensity.

Surely some revelation is at hand;
Surely the Second Coming is at hand;
The Second Coming! Hardly are those words out
When a vast image out of *Spiritus Mundi*[1]
Troubles my sight: somewhere in sands of the desert
A shape with lion body and the head of a man,
A gaze blank and pitiless as the sun,
Is moving its slow thighs, while all about it
Reel shadows of the indignant desert birds.
The darkness drops again; but now I know
That twenty centuries of stony sleep
Were vexed to nightmare by a rocking cradle,
And what rough beast, its hour come round at last,
Slouches towards Bethlehem to be born?

---

[1] *Spiritus Mundi:* Latin for "The Spirit of the World."

AMONG SCHOOL CHILDREN
(William Butler Yeats, 1865–1939)

I

I walk through the long schoolroom questioning;
A kind old nun in a white hood replies;
The children learn to cipher and to sing,
To study reading-books and history,

To cut and sew, be neat in everything
In the best modern way—the children's eyes
In momentary wonder stare upon
A sixty-year-old smiling public man.

II

I dream of a Ledaean body,[1] bent
Above a sinking fire, a tale that she
Told of a harsh reproof, or trivial event
That changed some childish day to tragedy—
Told, and it seemed that our two natures blent
Into a sphere from youthful sympathy,
Or else, to alter Plato's parable,
Into the yolk and white of the one shell.[2]

III

And thinking of that fit of grief or rage
I look upon one child or t'other there
And wonder if she[3] stood so at that age—
For even daughters of the swan can share
Something of every paddler's heritage—
And had that colour upon cheek or hair,
And thereupon my heart is driven wild:
She stands before me as a living child.

---

[1] *Ledaean body:* a body like Leda's. See "Leda and the Swan."
Yeats is thinking of a woman he loved who told him stories of
her school days.
[2] *Plato's . . . shell:* In the parable, man and woman were once
inseparable and traveled about as a large egg with four legs
and arms. The gods were jealous and split them. Ever since,
each man and woman has searched for his or her other half.
[3] *she:* refers to the woman he loved.

IV

Her present image floats into the mind—
Did Quattrocento[4] finger fashion it
Hollow of cheek as though it drank the wind
And took a mess of shadows for its meat?
And I though never of Ledaean kind
Had pretty plumage once—enough of that,
Better to smile on all that smile, and show
There is a comfortable kind of old scarecrow.

V

What youthful mother, a shape upon her lap
Honey of generation had betrayed,
And that must sleep, shriek, struggle to escape
As recollection or the drug decide,
Would think her son, did she but see that shape
With sixty or more winters on its head,
A compensation for the pang of his birth,
Or the uncertainty of his setting forth?

VI

Plato thought nature but a spume that plays
Upon a ghostly paradigm of things;
Solider Aristotle placed the taws[5]
Upon the bottom of a king of kings;[6]
World-famous golden-thighed Pythagoras[7]

---

[4]*Quattrocento:* the 1400s, an era of great art in Italy.
[5]*taws:* straps.
[6]*Aristotle . . . kings:* Aristotle was the tutor of Alexander the Great.
[7]*Pythagoras:* sixth-century mathematician, musician, thinker. He
was reputed to have a golden bone in his thigh.

Fingered upon a fiddle-stick or strings
What a star sang and careless Muses heard:
Old clothes upon old sticks to scare a bird.

VII

Both nuns and mothers worship images,
But those the candles light are not as those
That animate a mother's reveries,
But keep a marble or a bronze repose.
And yet they too break hearts — O Presences
That passion, piety or affection knows,
And that all heavenly glory symbolise —
O self-born mockers of man's enterprise;

VIII

Labour is blossoming or dancing where
The body is not bruised to pleasure soul,
Nor beauty born out of its own despair,
Nor blear-eyed wisdom out of midnight oil.
O chestnut-tree, great-rooted blossomer,
Are you the leaf, the blossom or the bole?
O body swayed to music, O brightening glance,
How can we know the dancer from the dance?

Critical Discriminations

To Coleridge's ideal for poetry — "The best words in the best order" —
let's add "with the best mind and imagination writing them." Good
poems are greater than the sum of their parts. New readings continue
to reward you.

A good poem has the right craft elements working along with an energy, that mysterious X, which makes the poem a world. What works stands out immediately. We've sharpened our discrimination as readers by recognizing all that makes a poem work. It is also valuable to look at how poems fall short, become static and boring, or just grate our nerves by being sentimental or predictable.

Anyone who has read thus far probably doesn't need to hear about the inadequacy of a poem beginning, "It takes a heap o' living in a house t' make it home." Such an opening forbodes a list of clichés and homilies. If a poem verges toward greeting-card sentiment or is riddled with flaws such as love/dove–moon/June–true/blue rhymes, the one question "Is this new?" settles its worth. You may hear that "good poetry is memorable," but being memorable guarantees nothing about quality. "O retard not my motion / For I'm going to the ocean" sticks in the mind and also in the craw.

George Orwell wrote:

A good bad poem is a graceful monument to the obvious. It records in memorable form—for verse is a mnemonic device, among other things—some emotion which nearly every human being can share. The merit of a poem like "When all the World Is Young, Lad" is that, however sentimental it may be, its sentiment is "true" sentiment in the sense that you are bound to find yourself thinking the thought it expresses sooner or later.... Such poems are a kind of rhyming proverb.

The good bad poems Orwell described lack intensity or originality. The poet was too easily content. An experimental writer such as Gertrude Stein might proclaim, "If it can be done, why do it?" As readers we might say, "If it *has* been done over and over, why indeed?"

I won't waste space by reprinting much obviously terrible poetry. You can spot inappropriate forms, lame language, clichés, galloping or sing-song rhythms, weak imagery, and worn metaphors. More valuable to study are **"second-intensity"** poems—that is, poetry that could have been better.

What qualities make a poem just miss? Sometimes, we almost can hear mournful violins tuning up. Something is out of balance. Something keeps the reader from responding fully. Perhaps the poet seems to be tearing his shirt, gesturing. Drama moves just slightly over the edge into melodrama. Our red flags go up. So why do we respond strongly anyway? The force of passion may pour through. Perhaps the reader had a similar experience and wants to overlook melodrama.

Melodrama is a tempest in a teapot—a dangerous quality for a poem. (Emerson said his idea of heaven was a place with no melodrama.) We don't like to be overconvinced. In second intensity, good-bad poems we have little imaginative room to act.

The blood relative of melodrama is **sentimentality.** Because poems often deal with emotions, they constantly risk becoming sentimental. Where is the balance between good poetry and simply getting something off one's chest? Sentimentality is a kneejerk emotion. The passion goes purple. You can see that the poet may indeed feel such emotion, but *you* certainly have no reason to. James Joyce defined sentimentality as "unearned emotion." The writer assumes you agree and does not trouble to present the individual case. The sure sign of sentimentality is oversimplification. Watery nostalgia or pure corniness results. "Somebody's Darling," popular during the Civil War, batters out its one message over and over. The author manages to top melodrama with sentimentality.

SOMEBODY'S DARLING
(Marie LaCoste, 1840?–1936)

Into a ward of the whitewashed halls,
    Where the dead and dying lay,
Wounded by bayonets, shells, and balls,
    Somebody's darling was borne one day—
Somebody's darling, so young and so brave,
    Wearing yet on his pale, sweet face,
Soon to be hid by the dust of the grave,
    The lingering light of his boyhood's grace.

Matted and damp are the curls of gold
   Kissing and snow of his fair, young brow;
Pale are the lips of delicate mold,
   Somebody's darling is dying now.
Back from his beautiful blue-veined brow,
   Brush all the wandering waves of gold,
Cross his hands on his bosom now —
   Somebody's darling is stiff and cold.

Kiss him once for somebody's sake,
   Murmur a prayer soft and low;
One bright curl from its fair mates take —
   They were somebody's pride, you know.
Somebody's hand has rested there:
   Was it mother's soft and white?
Or had the lips of a sister fair
   Been baptized in their waves of light?

God knows best! He has somebody's love,
   Somebody's heart enshrined him there,
Somebody wafted his name above,
   Night and morn, on the wings of prayer.
Somebody wept when he marched away,
   Looking so handsome, brave and grand!
Somebody's kiss on his forehead lay,
   Somebody clung to his parting hand.

Somebody's watching and waiting for him,
   Yearning to hold him again to her heart;
And there he lies with is blue eyes dim,
   And his smiling, child-like lips apart.
Tenderly bury the fair young dead,
   Pausing to drop on his grave a tear;
Carve on the wooden slab at his head,
   "Somebody's darling slumbers here!"

The craft and emotion in the next two poems are more complex and developed. Are the conclusions earned by the poem or do we seem *expected* to agree? What qualities make these "second intensity" poems? Are you still moved by either? Why?

THE SECOND WIFE
(Lizette Reese, 1856–1935)

She knows, being woman, that for him she holds
The space kept for the second blossoming,
Unmixed with dreams, held tightly in the folds
Of the accepted and long-proper thing—
She, duly loved; and he, proud of her looks
Shy of her wit. And of that other she knows
She had a slim throat, a nice taste in books,
And grew petunias in squat garden rows.
Thus knowing all, she feels both safe and strange;
Safe in his life, of which she has a share;
Safe in her undisturbed, cool, equal place,
In the sweet commonness that will not change;
And strange, when, at the door, in the spring air,
She hears him sigh, old Aprils in his face.

PIANO
(D. H. Lawrence, 1885–1930)

Softly, in the dusk, a woman is singing to me;
Taking me back down the vista of years, till I see
A child sitting under the piano, in the boom of the tingling strings
And pressing the small, poised feet of a mother who smiles as she
    sings.

In spite of myself, the insidious mastery of song
Betrays me back, till the heart of me weeps to belong

To the old Sunday evenings at home, with winter outside
And hymns in the cosy parlour, the tinkling piano our guide.

So now it is vain for the singer to burst into clamour
With the great black piano appassionato. The glamour
Of childish days is upon me, my manhood is cast
Down in the flood of remembrance, I weep like a child for the past.

Sentimentality and melodrama are two of the worst offenders to creep into a poem. Watch for these more subtle problems also.

- Redundant **syntax** *can* make a poem static and monotonous. If too many sentences begin the same way—"I saw…" "I told…" "I felt…" "I went…"—the poem can begin to plod. Just as in prose, the syntax of a poem generally needs to be varied. The form of sentences has a psychological effect. If that form repeats, it should be a conscious repetition for a desired effect. For instance, choosing all declarative sentences imparts an authoritative tone. Using many modifying phrases and prepositions imparts a softness, perhaps qualifying the subject. If the writer unthinkingly uses thirteen compound sentences in a short poem about speed, the syntax is at war with the subject.

- Not enough "muscle" in the language. Too much use of nonspecific designators (*these, this, it*) blurs effect, as do too many passive verbs or strings of adjectives and adverbs. The misuse of the preposition *of* is especially "flabby." Some writers get into the habit of letting *of* name a metaphor without really *showing* the image to the reader: sea of life, mattress of the soul, river of death, crops of grief, raven of anguish, tiger of desire, moon of loss, rose of forgetfulness, or (perhaps the funniest) briefcase of sorrow. A single concrete noun can't carry an abstract word over into an image. This is a weak construction, which, if overused, can fade the language of a poem into white noise.

- Lack of movement from beginning to end. We feel the poem running in place. Not enough happens. The poet writes more than the subject warranted. Our interest ends before the poem does.

- **Overwriting** puts words out of balance with their content. Hopkins constantly *risks* this. His results dazzle us while others' runaway experiments merely daze us. To overdescribe gives a poem a top-heavy feeling: "The stark green pines against the swirling gray clouds on a late fall day." A series of double modifiers bogs down the sound as well as the sense. I wrote the following to show the detrimental overuse of imagery. Too much imagery becomes absurd. The subject gets hidden.

THE QUARREL

Rolling down the lane like waves in an angry sea
we outdistance our words in tosses of hair and chin.
Stirring the rust of misunderstanding
with large sticks of silence, we each
are prisoners in the other's eyes.
Our mouths squeezing out words like lemon pips,
lips sour with the juice of the unspoken.
Our steps
                    are distant echoes.
We pace, we stare up at the blue illusion and
only our eyes reflect sparks of expectation.

- **Decorum** can go awry. **Decorum** is the writer's instinct for appropriate form, subject, and language. Louis Bogan wrote to another poet reprimanding her for using the word *kitty* in a poem. Bogan insisted that one should say "cat." "Kitty" violated her sense of decorum. In his poem on Lord Hasting's death from smallpox, Dryden loses all sense of decorum:

Was there no milder way but the Small Pox,
The very Filth'ness of *Pandora's Box*?
So many Spots, like *naeves*,[1] our Venus soil?

---

[1] *naeves*: blemishes.

One Jewel set off with so many a Foil?
Blisters with pride swell'd; which th'row's flesh did sprout
Like Rose-buds, stuck i' th' Lily-skin about.
Each little Pimple had a Tear on it,
To wail the fault its rising did commit:
Who, Rebel-like, with their own Lord at strife,
Thus made an insurrection 'gainst his Life.
Or were these Gems sent to adorn his Skin,
The Cab'net of a richer Soul within?

- **Moralism** can run around a well-intentioned poem. Tidy moral summations tacked on the end mar the reader's sense of participation. We feel force-fed if a poem seems to say, "And the moral of this story is...." Some writers mount a soapbox. The "Take this, it's good for you" attitude produces sermons, not poetry. When the poet has a political or **didactic** purpose—that is, when the poem *teaches*—the best strategy is to show the situation rather than instruct from on high. In Randall Jarrell's "Protocols," for instance, the subject is the gassing of children in concentration camps.

PROTOCOLS
(Randall Jarrell, 1914–1965)

(BIRKENAU, ODESSA[1]; THE CHILDREN SPEAK ALTERNATELY.)

We went there on the train. *They had big barges that they towed,*
We stood up, there were so many I was squashed.
There was a smoke-stack, then they made me wash.
It was a factory, I think. *My mother held me up*
And I could see the ship that made the smoke.

When I was tired my mother carried me.
She said, "Don't be afraid." But I was only tired.

———
[1] concentration camps

Where we went there is no more Odessa.
They had water in a pipe—like rain, but hot;
The water there is deeper than the world

And I was tired and fell in in my sleep
And the water drank me. That is what I think.
And I said to my mother, "Now I'm washed and dried,"
My mother hugged me, and it smelled like hay.
And that is how you die. And that is how you die.

By letting the two children speak for themselves, Jarrell allows the reader to "overhear" them. His choice of first-person speakers gives immediacy to the situation. Probably he made this choice in order to avoid *describing* the children of the Holocaust. He might have wanted to make a moral point but knew that he had nothing new to comment on. Poets don't want to repeat. Through Jarrell's choice of speakers, we hear something new in this poem: that possibly the children regarded the journey to the camps as an adventure. Their perspective increases our awareness of their tragic deaths. We do not have Jarrell looking at the children but the children speaking for themselves. The poet knew that their voices would speak more clearly than his. Look back also at "Soldiers Bathing" (page 338) and "Dover Beach" (page 340), two poems facing moral issues.

Poems

WHAT IS POETRY
(John Ashbery, 1927–)

The medieval town, with frieze
Of boy scouts from Nagoya? The snow

That came when we wanted it to snow?
Beautiful images? Trying to avoid

Ideas, as in this poem? But we
Go back to them as to a wife, leaving

The mistress we desire? Now they
Will have to believe it

As we believe it. In school
All the thought got combed out:

What was left was like a field.
Shut your eyes, and you can feel it for miles around.

Now open them on a thin vertical path.
It might give us — what? — some flowers soon?

from NORTH CENTRAL
(Lorine Niedecker, 1903–1970)

consider at the outset:
to be thin for thought
or thick cream blossomy

Many things are better
flavored with bacon

Sweet Life, My love:
didn't you ever try
this delicacy — the marrow
in the bone?

And don't be afraid
to pour wine over cabbage

TWO YEARS LATER
(John Wieners, 1934–)

The hollow eyes of shock remain
Electric sockets burnt out in the skull.

The beauty of men never disappears
But drives a blue car through the
                                                    stars.

***

THE WORLD SO WIDE
(Anonymous, fifteenth century)

The worlde so wide, th'air so remuable.°	*changeable*
The sely° man so litel of stature,	*helpless*
The grove and ground of clothing so mutable,[1]	
The fire so hot and subtil of nature,	
The water never in oon° — what creature,	
That made is of these foure thus flitting,	
May stedfast be as here in his living?	
The more I go the ferther I am behinde,	
The ferther behinde the neer° my wayes ende;	*nearer*
The more I seche° the worse can I finde,	*seek*
The lighter leve the lother for to wende;[2]	
The bet° I serve the more al out of mende.°	*better, mind*
Is this fortune — n'ot I° — or infortune?	*I know not*
Though I go loose, tied am I with a lune.°	*leash*

---
[1] *grove . . . mutable:* trees and earth so variable in their clothing.
[2] *The lighter . . . wende:* The easier the leaving the more loathe to go.

***

Boy Riding Forward Backward
(Robert Francis, 1901–1987)

Presto, pronto! Two boys, two horses.
But the boy on backward riding forward
Is the boy to watch.

He rides the forward horse and laughs
In the face of the forward boy on the backward
Horse, and *he* laughs

Back and the horses laugh. They gallop.
The trick is the cool barefaced pretense
There is no trick.

They might be flying, face to face,
On a fast train. They might be whitecaps
Hot-cool-headed,

One curling backward, one curving forward,
Racing a rivalry of waves.
They might, they might—

Across a blue lake, through trees,
And half a mile away I caught them:
Two boys, two horses.

Through trees and through binoculars
Sweeping for birds. Oh, they were birds
All right, all right.

Swallows that weave and wave and sweep
And skim and swoop and skitter until
The last trees take them.

ADAM'S CURSE
(William Butler Yeats, 1865–1939)

We sat together at one summer's end,
That beautiful mild woman, your close friend,
And you and I, and talked of poetry.
I said, "A line will take us hours maybe;
Yet if it does not seem a moment's thought,
Our stitching and unstitching has been naught.
Better go down upon your marrow-bones
And scrub a kitchen pavement, or break stones

Like an old pauper, in all kinds of weather;
For to articulate sweet sounds together
Is to work harder than all these, and yet
Be thought an idler by the noisy set
Of bankers, schoolmasters, and clergymen
The martyrs call the world."

                              And thereupon
That beautiful mild woman for whose sake
There's many a one shall find out all heartache
On finding that her voice is sweet and low
Replied, "To be born woman is to know—
Although they do not talk of it at school—
That we must labor to be beautiful."

I said, "It's certain there is no fine thing
Since Adam's fall but needs much laboring.
There have been lovers who thought love should be
So much compounded of high courtesy
That they would sigh and quote with learned looks

Precedents out of beautiful old books;
Yet now it seems an idle trade enough."

We sat grown quiet at the name of love;
We saw the last embers of daylight die,
And in the trembling blue-green of the sky
A moon, worn as if it had been a shell
Washed by time's waters as they rose and fell
About the stars and broke in days and years.

I had a thought for no one's but your ears:
That you were beautiful, and that I strove
To love you in the old high way of love;
that it had all seemed happy, and yet we'd grown
As weary-hearted as that hollow moon.

HARLEM SWEETIES
(Langston Hughes, 1902–1967)

Have you dug the spill
Of Sugar Hill?[1]
Cast your gims
On this sepia thrill:
Brown sugar lassie,
Caramel treat,
Honey-gold baby
Sweet enough to eat.
Peach-skinned girlie,
Coffee and cream,
Chocolate darling
Out of a dream.

---

[1] *Sugar Hill:* a section of Harlem.

Walnut tinted
Or cocoa brown,
Pomegranate-lipped
Pride of the town.
Rich cream-colored
To plum-tinted black,
Feminine sweetness
In Harlem's no lack.
Glow of the quince
To blush of the rose.
Persimmon bronze
To cinnamon toes.
Blackberry cordial,
Virginia Dare wine —
All those sweet colors
Flavor Harlem of mine!
Walnut or cocoa,
Let me repeat:
Caramel, brown sugar,
A chocolate treat.
Molasses taffy,
Coffee and cream,
Licorice, clove, cinnamon
To a honey-brown dream.
Ginger, wine-gold,
Persimmon, blackberry,
All through the spectrum
Harlem girls vary —
So if you want to know beauty's
Rainbow-sweet thrill,
Stroll down luscious,
Delicious, *fine* Sugar Hill.

SILENT POEM
(Robert Francis, 1901–1987)

backroad   leafmold   stonewall   chipmunk
underbrush   grapevine   woodchuck   shadblow

woodsmoke   cowbarn   honeysuckle   woodpile
sawhorse   bucksaw   outhouse   wellsweep

backdoor   flagstone   bulkhead   buttermilk
candlestick   ragrug   firedog   brownbread

hilltop   outcrop   cowbell   buttercup
whetstone   thunderstorm   pitchfork   steeplebush

gristmill   millstone   cornmeal   waterwheel
watercress   buckwheat   firefly   jewelweed

gravestone   groundpine   windbread   bedrock
weathercock   snowfall   starlight   cockrow

IMAGE
(T. E. Hulme, 1883–1917)

Old houses were scaffolding once
　　　　　and workmen whistling.

WESTERN WIND
(Anonymous, fifteenth century)

Western wind, when will thou blow,
　　The small rain down can rain?
Christ, if my love were in my arms
　　And I in my bed again!

THE NYMPH'S REPLY TO THE SHEPHERD[1]
(Sir Walter Raleigh, 1552–1618)

If all the world and love were young,
And truth in every shepherd's tongue,
These pretty pleasures might me move
To live with thee and be thy love.

Time drives the flocks from field to fold
When rivers rage and rocks grow cold,
And Philomel[2] becometh dumb;
The rest complains of cares to come.

The flowers do fade, and wanton fields
To wayward winter reckoning yields;
A honey tongue, a heart of gall,
Is fancy's spring, but sorrow's fall.

Thy gowns, thy shoes, thy beds of roses,
Thy cap, thy kirtle,[3] and thy posies
Soon break, soon wither, soon forgotten—
In folly ripe, in reason rotten.

Thy belt of straw and ivy buds,
Thy coral clasps and amber studs,
All these in me no means can move
To come to thee and be thy love.

---

[1] *The Nymph's Reply to the Shepherd:* see "The Passionate Shepherd to His Love" by Christopher Marlowe (page 140).
[2] *Philomel:* nightingale.
[3] *kirtle:* a long undergarment.

But could youth last and love still breed,
Had joys no date[4] nor age no need,
Then these delights my mind might move
To live with thee and be thy love.

———————

[4]*date:* ending.

POEMS WE CAN UNDERSTAND
(Paul Hoover, 1946–)

If a monkey drives a car
down a colonnade facing the sea
and the palm trees to the left are tin
we don't understand it.

We want poems we can understand.
We want a god to lead us,
renaming the flowers and trees,
color-coding the scene,

doing bird calls for guests.
We want poems we can understand,
no sullen drunks making passes
next to an armadillo, no complex nothingness

amounting to a song,
no running in and out of walls
on the dry tongue of a mouse,
no bludgeoness, no girl, no sea that moves

with all deliberate speed, beside itself
and blue as water, inside itself and still,
no lizards on the table becoming absolute hands.
We want poetry we can understand,

the fingerprints on mother's dress,
pain of martyrs, scientists.
Please, no rabbit taking a rabbit
out of a yellow hat, no tattooed back

facing miles of desert, no wind.
We don't understand it.

A THEOLOGICAL DEFINITION
(George Oppen, 1908–1984)

A small room, the varnished floor
Making an L around the bed,

What is or is true as
Happiness

Windows opening on the sea,
The green painted railings of the balcony
Against the rock, the bushes and the sea running

SONNET 61
(Michael Drayton, 1563–1631)

Since there's no help, come let us kiss and part;
Nay, I have done, you get no more of me,
And I am glad, yea glad with all my heart
That thus so cleanly I myself can free;
Shake hands forever, cancel all our vows,
And when we meet at any time again,
Be it not seen in either of our brows
That we one jot of former love retain.
Now at the last gasp of love's latest breath,

When, his pulse failing, passion speechless lies,
When faith is kneeling by his bed of death,
And innocence is closing up his eyes,
    Now if thou wouldst, when all have given him over,
    From death to life thou mightest him yet recover.

A LETTER FROM THE CARIBBEAN
(Barbara Howes, 1914–)

Breezeways in the tropics winnow the air,
Are ajar to its least breath
But hold back, in a feint of architecture,
The boisterous sun
Pouring down upon

The island like a cloudburst. They
slant to loft air, they curve, they screen
The wind's wild gaiety
Which tosses palm
Branches about like a marshal's plumes.

Within the filtered, latticed
World, where spools of shadow
Form, life and change,
The triumph of incoming air
Is that it is there,

Cooling and salving us. Louvers,
Trellises, vine — music also —
Shape the arboreal wind, make skeins
Of it, and a maze
To catch shade. The days

Are all variety, blowing;
Aswirl in a perpetual current
Of wind, shadow, sun,
I marvel at the capacity
Of memory

Which, in some deep pocket
Of my mind, preserves you whole—
As wind is wind, as the lion-taking
Sun is sun, you are, you stay:
Nothing is lost, nothing has blown away.

THE LATE LATE SHOW
(Hazel Lane, 1929–)

It must be judgment day
the dead
are playing tonight
flickering through the clammy hours
while the world sleeps
just me and long gone Laurel and Hardy
watching
the piano fall
down the sad decades.

RETURN
(Fernando Alegría, 1918–)

I ask for nothing more than the old house,
those same sails of fragrant pine,
the windows tied to the green afternoon
and its whole night pounding in my pillow.

Nothing more than the calm morning,
the clatter of a horse with rubber shoes,
the clothes fluttering on suspended wires,
all those essences tumbling in white wine.

My children playing with the wheel of fortune,
the roses courting the adobe, doubtful,
the cat reading things into himself,
our grandparents resting in the shadows.

Everything still, the family sitting down,
the dead ones navigating tenderly,
you with the branch of basil reborn,
your silence filled with love and nostalgia.

It will always be too early for the shy elm,
the cherries will open their fragile parasol,
the street will keep track of the rains winter left
and new young couples will wander into oblivion.

The piano moored to its worn-out rugs,
we'll all be tangled in smiles,
I'll look in your eyes for the ring we gave away,
It will be like stroking the morning open.

The bits of glass falling out of the trees,
the letters we never read,
a fear of having said nothing
when a word was enough to light up the family.

We'll carry a little fire in our hands,
we'll set a sun in our chests
and it will be singing time.
We'll close the blinds.

—Translated by Stephen Kessler

NOTHING TO DECLARE
(C. D. Wright, 1949–)

When I lived here
the zinnias were brilliant,
spring passed in walks.
One winter I wasn't so young.
I rented a house with Ann Grey
where she wrote a book and I could not.
Cold as we were on the mountain
we wouldn't be moved to the plain.
Afternoons with no sun
a blanket is left on the line.
Hearts go bad
like something open on a shelf.
If you came to hear about roosters,
iron beds, cabinets of ruby glass—
those things are long gone;
deepscreen porches and Sunday's buffet.
This was the school
where they taught us
the Russians send their old
to be melted down for candles.
If I had a daughter I'd tell her
Go far, travel lightly.
If I had a son he'd go to war
over my hard body.
Don't tell me it isn't worth the trouble
carrying on campaigns
for the good and the dead.
The ones I would vote for
never run. I want each and every one
to rejoice in the clotheslines

of the colored peoples of the earth.
Try living where you don't have to see
the sun go down.
If the hunter turns his dogs loose
on your dreams
start early, tell no one
get rid of the scent.

DEGREES OF GRAY IN PHILIPSBURG
(Richard Hugo, 1923–1982)

You might come here Sunday on a whim.
Say your life broke down. The last good kiss
you had was years ago. You walk these streets
laid out by the insane, past hotels
that didn't last, bars that did, the tortured try
of local drivers to accelerate their lives.
Only churches are kept up. The jail
turned 70 this year. The only prisoner
is always in, not knowing what he's done.

The principal supporting business now
is rage. Hatred of the various grays
the mountain sends, hatred of the mill,
The Silver Bell repeal, the best liked girls
who leave each year for Butte. One good
restaurant and bars can't wipe the boredom out.

The 1907 boom, eight going silver mines,
a dance floor built on springs —
all memory resolves itself in gaze,
in panoramic green you know the cattle eat
or two stacks high above the town,

two dead kilns, the huge mill in collapse
for fifty years that won't fall finally down.

Isn't this your life? That ancient kiss
still burning out your eyes? Isn't this defeat
so accurate, the church bell simply seems
a pure announcement: ring and no one comes?
Don't empty houses ring? Are magnesium
and scorn sufficient to support a town,
not just Philipsburg, but towns
of towering blondes, good jazz and booze
the world will never let you have
until the town you came from dies inside?

Say no to yourself. The old man, twenty
when the jail was built, still laughs
although his lips collapse. Someday soon,
he says, I'll go to sleep and not wake up.
You tell him no. You're talking to yourself.
The car that brought you here still runs.

The money you buy lunch with,
no matter where it's mined, is silver
and the girl who serves you food
is slender and her red hair lights the wall.

THE HOUSE WAS QUIET AND THE WORLD WAS CALM
(Wallace Stevens, 1879–1955)

The house was quiet and the world was calm.
The reader became the book; and summer night

Was like the conscious being of the book.
The house was quiet and the world was calm.

The words were spoken as if there was no book,
Except that the reader leaned above the page,

Wanted to lean, wanted much most to be
The scholar to whom his book is true, to whom

The summer night is like a perfection of thought.
The house was quiet because it had to be.

The quiet was part of the meaning, part of the mind:
The access of perfection to the page.

And the world was calm. The truth in a calm world,
In which there is no other meaning, itself

Is calm, itself is summer and night, itself
Is the reader leaning late and reading there.

11

A Poet's Handbook

We do what we know before we know what we do.
—CHARLES OLSON

Invoking Your Muse

The desire to write feels something like a power surge: If you have it, you know it. Many writers say they write because they *have to*, there's no choice; the rush that runs through them simply demands to be expressed in words. This may be an occasional phenomenon or the sign of a lifelong involvement with the word.

Your own process of writing will be a long discovery. When the power surge strikes, you may or may not pick up your pen. Writers are quirky beings. Some write in the moment of intensity. Others let a thought or experience drift about in the unconscious, then calmly draw on it later. After writing, almost all new writers fear that they will never write again, especially if the work seems wonderful. An experienced writer learns to trust a process and to realize that there may be an unpredictable tide, but that the tide *will* rise again. One of the best poets I know must write in a darkened room. He starts by writing random words only on the left side of the page, meditating and freely associating for an hour. When a word or phrase suddenly takes his attention, he moves it to the right and quickly writes the whole poem. His process makes no sense to others but works for him. Another poet "writes" by speaking into a tape recorder while taking long walks, then transcribes and revises at the computer. You may be a late-night writer or one who must clear off the desk entirely. While driving, showering, bathing, when the mind is occupied but oddly free, you might get your best ideas.

Many writers keep dream journals to get closer to their unconscious lives, or record important thoughts and details in blank books. You may need blue paper, like Colette, or a cork-lined room, like Proust. Weird though these things might sound to someone else, writers find what works.

I am devoted to art sketch books. In them I keep quotes, images, observations, lists, and hundreds of phrases and single words such as "ocarina," "lithic," "pond slider turtle," and "cut out the light"—sounds I like when I come across them. When I begin a poem, I put down—only on a white legal pad—as much raw material as I can. Then I go to my great thick repository and take what I need for that particular poem. The selections I've included in my sketch book, of course, are not whimsical, even though I don't know at the time why I'm including certain definitions, phrases, quotes, or newspaper articles. Gradually, an unwieldy body of material forms, which I then shape and reshape. Sometimes I realize that the poem still wants something more. If I don't know what that is, I put the poem away until that *something* that seems right lands in my head. For a time I kept a parallel book I called an image bank. I collected old photos, art postcards, ads, and drawings. With colored pencils, I tried first to draw what I wanted to write about. Writing from a visual image intrigued me then. *Elephrasis* (description), a useful word from classical rhetoric, means a literary exercise using words to evoke a visual effect. In addition, poets want a complex of emotional, associative, intellectual, and sensual effects. I liked the process of description and sharpened my sense of imagery by practicing accurate reproductions in words of something I looked at. Gradually I stopped that approach; my process shifted.

The discovery of your own best process is helpful because once you identify it, you can recognize and create the climate in which you flourish. "Act in the little ways that encourage good fortune," as poet William Stafford put it. You also can realize what won't work—you will know if you can't write while job hunting, visiting troublesome relatives, or finishing a project at work. Forget writing for the moment; you can relax and later on find the natural time and place. There is a large, irrational aspect to writing. It's good to begin with that in mind. In an essay, Wallace Stevens writes about the "transaction between reality and the sensibility of the poet from which poetry springs." The moment you raise the pen is the moment of that transaction. You are suddenly in two worlds. Your arrival at that moment is crucial to the words that fall across that large, white expanse, the page.

Beginning with a White Page

The epigraph to this chapter—"We do what we know before we know what we do"—speaks to a mysterious subterranean level of ourselves. If you have a desire to write, even an inner sense that you *will* write, this quote invites you to trust yourself. You do know something important about who you are and what is in you that wants *saying*. Starting out, you may not yet know what works and what doesn't. Later, you will. As a writing teacher, I've been amazed at how many people have talent. Some simply let it go; they take up broadcasting or urban planning or go back to their jobs. Those who abide with their talent, who voraciously read and think about poetry, who attend readings, memorize poems, and who try out anything that will broaden the experience of writing—those are the ones who generally have the peculiar love and discipline that it takes to become a writer. You don't, however, have to sign a dotted line. You can enjoy reading and writing poetry while making your living delivering babies or pizzas.

Einstein said that the theory of relativity came to him as a "feeling." How then did he translate that vague sensation into theory? And how, once you've generated pages of notes from exercises, do you write a poem?

Suggestions for Writing and Revising

Write poems that matter very much to you, whether they are memories of childhood, meditations, or sound experiments. The quality of deep feeling, thought, or intense energy will guarantee that your poem, at least, has life.

You may not know what you're writing about as you hunt and gather in your mind for your material. Be as generous to the white page as you can; give it everything you've got at the moment. Underline all the important sounds, ideas, phrases—and ruthlessly throw away any clichés. A good rule to remember: If you've heard it before, don't use it. Start crafting and revising as soon as you have written down all the raw material you think you need. Some poets go through thirty revisions. Chances are, any poem will need work beyond the first draft, unless you've had a true gift descend upon you.

Try to push aside the censor, that demon who whispers "Not good" and "Don't dare say that" and "Who cares about your life?" Poets write about the same basic human subjects over and over. Your inner voice is one that never has been heard in the world before. Though there are thousands of love poems and death poems, your version will be new if you can catch your own sound. Give yourself a lot of leeway with writing exercises. Anne Sexton said she sometimes wanted to write but didn't know what she wanted to say: "I will fool around on the typewriter. It might take me ten pages of nothing, of terrible writing, and then I'll get a line, and I'll think, 'That's what I mean.' What you're doing is hunting for what you mean, what you're trying to say."

Try different line lengths and line breaks, searching for a natural rhythm that fits your sense of the subject. Perhaps you will want to try arranging phrases into iambic pentameter or iambic tetrameter, the two most flexible meters in English. The text, of course, will help you review the metrical patterns, if you want your poem in a particular measure. If lines don't seem necessary, perhaps your form is the prose poem. Does any line bear repeating? A repeating line, when it comes around again, needs to intensify in meaning. Invent your own forms, arranging the words so that they interact with the white space on the page (the silence).

Don't be too cryptic. This is very important. It's most characteristic in a new writer's poetry. You might have so much respect for the distilled language of poetry that you forget to give the reader enough clues. You might boil down your poem too much so that each word is incredibly important to you but not to the reader, who has no idea what you're talking about! Cut, cut, cut, you hear an inner voice saying. You sometimes need to do the opposite and add.

Write the poem, then put it aside and write what you truly wanted to say. Always push yourself to go further. Some poems are simple and some don't want to be. Ask if you have done all that the poem requires of you. Does it want more?

Polish and shine your language. See that your diction supports the tone you want the poem to have. If it's an angry poem, you don't want passive verbs and soft sounds. Fold the poem down its center axis and read all the right half's lines then all the left half's lines. Does this energy trail off on the right side? Do you want this poem to be a strong-lined poem, with energy deployed down the page? If so, work on the lines that let down the momentum. Check to see if you have the habit of ending lines with prepositional phrases or weak words (the, an, of, etc.).

Read aloud as you go. Anything that bothers your ear or trips your tongue should be reexamined. If you can, tape-record the poem and listen to it for clues to improving rhythm.

If you are in a workshop, which I recommend, ask the other members specific questions about your poem when you have them. Does this have any emotional effect? Is this hard to follow? Does this image draw too much attention to itself? Do you believe the poem? Does this word stick out? Anything you suspect is a problem needs to be clarified. Give the other writers the kind of criticism you would like to get: the hard, kind approach. What you all want is for each poem to be the best it can be. You do not want it to sound like the teacher's poetry or anyone's. Beware of criticism that comes from a dogmatic reader who knows all the answers or who wants everyone to sound like him or her. When reacting to someone's poem, remember the old saw "constructive criticism." It gives the writer more of a sense of possibility for revision if you make a definite suggestion for improvement rather than just saying what you don't like. Always think in terms of re-vision — seeing the poem anew and reworking from its original source.

Revising is also technical. I advise looking at each of these specific areas:

WORDS

What is the quality of the words in the poem? Are any overused? Are they fresh? Concrete? Vague? Abstract? If you ran your hand over the surface of the sounds, would they be smooth, rough, jagged, soft? Is this texture fitting to the subject?

VOICE

Is the poem anchored in a particular speaker's voice? Whose? What is the tone of voice? Does the tone change? Who is the listener?

IMAGES

How many senses are evoked in the poem? What are they? Is the imagery effective? Is the poem immediate or distant? In what end of the telescope does the poem take place — that is, does it seem to take place right here and now, or far away? Does the same image reappear? What is the effect of this?

MOVEMENT

What is the activity of the poem like? Look at the verbs: are they generally active or passive? Are the tenses consistent? Does the poem keep on moving? Does each stanza do different work from the previous stanza? Does the poem stay on the track? Or does the train take a side trip into other subjects?

LINE

Is the line taut like the lively tension in the string of a helium balloon? Are the end words the ones you linger on? Usually poetry is written in lines, prose in sentences. Although the lines of poetry usually add up to sentences, the construction is line to line. Cover the left half of the poem. Does the right side consistently trail off from an energetic beginning? A sure sign of this is many lines ending with prepositional phrases. Cover the right side. Are both sides of the line equally strong? Do most lines end-stop or enjamb (run over to next line)? Does the poem start immediately or does the poet need a one-minute wind-up to get to the subject? How does the poem end? A bang? A whimper? Is the end overstated, telling the reader what the conclusion is in case it wasn't clear? Generally, a slow start and a drawn-out end "frame" the poem too much, giving a blocked-in feeling.

FORM

What does the poem's shape say about the subject? Does each line start with a capital letter? Why? Are the lines irregularly placed? Why? Are the rhymes forced, or do they work for the poem? Does repetition emphasize or detract? Is there a metrical pattern?

The checklist also helps you judge the craft of poems you write.

Give yourself a chance to try various writing exercises. Good ones can do anything from warming you up to uncovering your deepest material. Gimmicky ones can be fun, but you don't learn much from them. Mechanistic ones produce lifeless work. My heart sinks when I hear teachers ask students to list the objects in their rooms. The exercises below are divided into several categories, each with a *real* purpose. You can return to ones that work for you at different stages of your writing. For some, the muse just won't be invoked this way but for many, especially when writing is hard, the objective demands set forth in an exercise prove to be freeing. Why? The odd fact is that when you are challenged from outside, you frequently do unexpected work. The other facet is crucial: play. We may bring a dampening seriousness to writing. The exercise casts it as a kind of play. Nothing rides on it, so we are at liberty. We can be wild, funny, dark, meditative all at once.

Try anything—but meanwhile also write what you normally would write on your own. There's a synergy to exercises when used in a writing group. When you have twenty minutes to complete an exercise, the pressure squeezes out writing that you didn't know you could do. Hearing others' responses to an exercise makes you more aware of your own voice and your own unique material. Varied responses can make you realize you need to dig toward the core, listen harder to yourself, or take a different perspective on the material.

Exercises

Getting Started   These exercises are for warming up, limbering the imagination, letting ideas flow through your pen, unfettering the mind. Turn off the premature editor and try to write copiously. It's better to pare down from abundance than to pad a meager beginning.

- Take the first line of a poem and write from that line. If you get stuck, take lines from other poems or texts and use them along the way. Write twenty or more lines. Later, you may want to revise the lines you've borrowed. Those lines probably are linked to issues that matter to you and the exercise opens you to those concerns.
- Cut out fifty or so phrases, words, sentences you like from a magazine. Select some as possible titles. On a large, white page, arrange these cutouts into a collage poem, without forcing the words into a preconceived subject. You may need to change your title when you're through. It's amazing how many fine poems come from this exercise. The mind is shapely even when playing; you're cutting out something of your own. The pleasure here is the discovery of the poem you didn't know you were creating.

- Freely write for twenty minutes without lifting your pen from the paper. Write anything, without trying to connect logically what you're doing. Then, underline any lines or words you like. Note recurrent ideas, images, themes. The purpose is spontaneity. List anything that strikes you as important in the free writing. Is there a poem for you?

- Keep a dream journal. Watch for patterns. Do you often dream of houses with secret rooms or attics? Are you under siege in your dreams? Who is after you in each? Read books on dream interpretation. Whatever mysteries and clues you record may be valuable in poems, though dream poems identified by "And then I woke up" are seldom interesting.

- Generate as many titles for poems as you can think of. Look for titles when reading biology texts, tax manuals, foreign language phrase books. Keep a list of possible titles. Choose one anytime and try to work from it. The mind throws out little gifts all the time. The seemingly random titles may hit an important subject just waiting to be tapped.

- Write a poem in the style of a poet you admire or despise in this book. This opens up the work further and allows you to experience the poet's modes of crafting and expressing.

- Take a poem you already have written and start a new poem with the last lines. If you *had* to continue a finished poem, where could you go with it? This pushes you to explore a subject you thought you were through with.

- Make lists. Write poems with titles like "Reasons for Not Moving," "Places I Would Not Want To Go Without You," "Why I Don't Travel Well," "Some Stars, Some Galaxies," etc. Especially for congenital list makers, this exercise can uncover real motives.

- Take one word and write everything you can from that one word — all your associations, the dictionary meaning, the etymology, the sound associations. Where does the word lead you? Flesh it out as fully as possible. This plumbs the richness of a single word and gives you a framework for constructing and imagining. The root of "trellis," for instance, connects with "page." The climbing vines can link with the scrawl of words — connections you have no way of making without probing into meanings. Spending time with word roots will make clear that every word is a fossil poem.

- This is a strange exercise that works famously for some and not at all for others. It is close to free writing in technique but far from it in material it uncovers. Ask someone to select three books from different fields (an instruction manual, guide book, history book, an art book, or philosophy text) and to read to you for fifteen minutes, switching from book to book at two- or three-minute intervals. You type while listening, typing as fast as you can. Don't edit or try to control. Type your thoughts, phrases you hear, associations from what you hear, anything, just keep typing. Use the material as you would the free-writing material described in number 3; it's guaranteed to produce raw material you could not consciously have written.
- Write opening lines to ten poems as quickly as possible. Choose one immediately and finish the poem in twenty minutes. See if time constraints inspire you. Work fast!
- Write to music, closing out all other sound. Try to follow the emotions or rhythms of the sounds.

HOME GROUND   The next exercises work from prime territory: personal experience, the "I" voice, the family matrix, memory, the heart, and the heart of the heart. Many writers have observed that you have enough material for a lifetime if you've survived a childhood. First causes, moments of change, realizations, early loves and passions, places — these are rich sources for poetry. The accepted wisdom is "Write about what you know," but I think it's important to seek what new insights and facts you can unearth about what you know. Or, to enlarge this idea, think about John Logan's statement, "It's not the skeleton in the closet we are afraid of, it's the god."

- Write out in prose, in as much detail as possible, your earliest memories. Think about why you remember these events and images and not others. What connections to emotions you now have can you make? Select the most powerful memory and work on a poem, with the object of finding meaning in the memory. Virginia Woolf remembered the pattern of her mother's dress, the Venetian blind cord trailing across the windowsill in the wind. Each memory opened her writing to her first connections with her mother and to a childhood place she loved.

- Write about a symbolic object from childhood: a ruby your aunt wore in the hollow of her throat, a pistol in your father's bedside table, your mother's stack of yellowed love letters in the hall closet, a set of trains you loved — any object that has become larger than itself. Explore the ramifications in your life then and now.

- List the sayings you heard over and over while growing up. Did this wisdom stick or did you rebel? Try a poem using the repetition of a single expression.

- Begin with the phrase, "My mother (brother, father) always..." or "My sister never...," and list as many things as you can think of. Try writing a portrait of that relative.

- Family photos are fertile ground. Write a full response to the image: all the details you see and remember, including color, smell, touch. Imagine before and after incidents of the image, stories that may or may not be true. Photos of grandparents you never knew, your parents before the divorce, your mother at sixteen, you as an infant pulling over the Christmas tree or screaming — all these are wide open to your imagination and reinterpretation.

- List the absolutes you live by. What would you always do? Never? How did you arrive at one of these standards?

- Write about the rituals, conscious or unconscious, that you practiced as a child. Did you have to have the bed turned down just so, did you torture ants, or did you get ready for school in an unalterable regimen? What family rituals were you a part of when growing up? What rituals do you practice today? What is the significance of ritual to you?

- Try to remember what it was like to be inside your six-year-old body, then your sixteen-year-old body. Think of specific moments — ice skating at night, driving too fast, the first day of school—during those two ages and write active poems using the size, muscles, point of view of yourself then. "I sing the body electric," Whitman wrote.

- List the major changes in your life and see if you can identify a moment when you realized that you were changing or that nothing would be the same after that. The changes will be vastly different—a move to a new town, the drowning of a friend, a moment of triumph or defeat. Write from within that moment.
- In your mind, walk through a significant house or apartment from your childhood. Record your memories, all the sensory details of each room, how you feel as you revisit. Why does this house still occupy you?
- Write a self-portrait.
- Write about a love relationship or event that changed your idea of love.
- When were you first aware of being *girl* or *boy*? With what emotional resonances?
- Revisit a family meal, an ordinary evening in the family circle, the smells, the atmosphere, the conversations. Or a meal at a time of celebration.
- What are the mysteries in your past? Focus on someone you never figured out or an occurrence that should have worked out otherwise.
- What lie did you tell? Why do you still remember it? Did you steal something? What attraction did the object have and how did you feel?
- In prose, write out fully a description of the landscape you can't help but call home. The red clay hills of Georgia, the broken doorways of the lower East side, the misty islands of Washington: wherever your pulse tells you *this is unmistakably home*. Describe your feelings on returning to this place after an absence.
- Is there a subject you've forbidden yourself to write about? Are you ready to look at it?
- Weddings, wakes, births, birthdays, divorces, trips, all the big occasions of life provoke powerful memories. Character and conflict tend to come to the fore in these times.

- What did you say that you would like to unsay?
- Do you have a fear or phobia? My own was explored in "Sestina for the Owl" (page 317). What do you think is the origin of your fear? What does the spider, snake, or bird remind you of?
- Record your pleasures.

The Expanded Sphere   This set of exercises focuses on encountering objective experience. Of course, your own experience often enters into poems that are not specifically about you. The work suggested below puts you in touch with an otherness, a place to perceive something about yourself, another, or the world.

- Choose a person from history or a person you are curious about and in that person's voice ("I") recount an event or an emotion. You may want to do some research. Speaking as John Kennedy en route to the hospital, Hitler in the bunker, a baker at 3 A.M., a mortician going to work, or as Madonna looking in the mirror, puts you in a new voice.
- Spend some time reading mythology. Select a myth that intrigues you and rewrite it in contemporary terms, with contemporary characters. The practice will reveal the inner archetype of the myth and its relevance to your life today.
- Observe an animal, either an exotic one at the zoo or a domestic one in your neighborhood. Spend an hour describing every detail of its appearance, personality, and actions. What is your connection with this animal? Try to recreate in words something essential of your perceptions.
- Select a painting and describe its colors and images minutely, including sensory impressions that you imagine, such as the iron smell of blood or the satiny flank of the horse. Write all your reactions to the painting: its story, impact, what it reminds you of, what you imagine the painter thought and felt. If there are people in the painting, where are they, what is going on in their minds? Finally, explore why you chose this particular painting.
- Take on a social or political issue you feel strongly about. If it's the

homeless, for instance, you might focus on a particular man who sleeps under the bridge in your neighborhood. Close attention, rather than general reactions, will keep the poem in your voice.

- Write "portraits" of someone (corner grocery clerk, dental hygienist, a neighborhood character) you encounter but don't know well, imagining his or her real and secret life. As a link to the next set of exercises, practice here the craft of the speaker. Let your subject speak as "I," then rewrite your portrait using "you" or the third-person pronoun.

CRAFT EXERCISES   The focus is on imagery, language, line use, and association. A study of these can improve your writing quickly. Throughout the text are other craft-oriented exercises. By trying out all the meters and forms, you will absorb a tremendous amount of "feel" for rhythm and for the psychological effects a form has on writer and reader. The challenge of a fixed form usually brings out something unforeseen. When writing a sonnet, don't try to sound like Shakespeare or Keats — use your own language. The life of forms depends on their rediscovery for our time, not reuse from a past time. To hone your skills, try each of these:

- Rewrite a poem you've already finished, changing *all* the nouns, verbs, and adjectives. Read the old and new versions aloud, then see if you want to revise your original poem with some of the new words. This helps you go beyond a word choice that might have been too easy and to wake up your language.
- Write a one-page poem using only one sentence. How far can you go with a stretched out sound that pulls the reader along without any stops? After this, write the same poem using extremely short sentences. How do the two approaches change the meaning of what you've written?
- Select three unrelated objects — a broken doll, a wine bottle, a hat — and place them in front of your writing table. Describe, using the most exact and literal words you can. Notice everything. Do you then see relationships among the three objects? Is there a

story involving all three? Can you, as Hopkins advised, look hard enough at any object that it begins to look back at you?

- Select a color and list ten images for that color, taking care to present the image in a context, so that a reader can experience it. For example, white: a frozen white sheet on the line, cracking in the wind. Yellow: the last tooth in an old man's mouth. Red: arterial blood spurting on a white tile floor. Putting the image in *action* or in *place* creates the reader's full sensory response. This is the first writing exercise I ever tried. My freshman teacher said a white feather from a goose's breast was not enough. I've always remembered the teacher saying, "Activate! Activate!" I made the feather slowly zigzag to the ground. Try this exercise over and over to heighten your awareness of how to form an image. The variations listed below are challenging. This writing exercise is one of the most valuable you can try.

- Try the above with softness, hardness, coldness, humidity, speed, fading, roughness, rain, snow, abrasiveness. For example, hailstones in one result of this exercise appeared in a poem as "blank eyeballs of an angel looking to heaven," "the jar of gallstones," "a soft turtle egg," "all the faraway moons of Jupiter hitting the roof," and "mothballs melting in the folded seams." One's first response is often not good enough. Hailstones falling like golf balls surprises no one, especially not the poet! Let the hailstones strike the roof of the Subaru like gunshots — something that imparts energy and meaning.

- This may seem difficult, but it's actually fun. The purpose is to let yourself make sound associations. Take a poem in a language you don't know at all and "translate" it simply by making up a version from the way the poem sounds to you. Stick to the stanza form as it is in the original. Listen carefully to each word; what does it "say" to you? For example, *sangre de pato*: sand grates the patio, song of the parrot, some day in the ghetto, the angry potato; *kindheit*: kind heart, kind heights, Clondike.

- Working on associating might seem like a contradiction in terms, but this exercise does give you access to a way of thinking that may be blocked to you by an overly literal mind. Have someone call out a list of words to you. Evocative words or phrases work best: boxcar, 1982, stairway, pocket watch, map of England, hairbrush, plum, Do Not Enter, noon, falling. With each one, try to call up an *image* of that word, something that shows the word's meaning to you. Poet Paul Hoover's image for shy: "When I go to a party I hold a picture of you, Mother, over my face." Coleman Barks's image for midnight is, "A miner buries his hands in a woman's hair." For bruises, he wrote, "paint samples." This is hard at first and the harder it is, the more valuable the exercise will be to you. Be sure to study the image chapter.

- Start with two opposing ideas in your first two lines. This opens the poem to dramatic tension.
- Keep a nature notebook. Write daily observations of weather, trees, crops, urban flower boxes, rain, snow, humidity. Write not factually but descriptively and fully. This is objective practice in noticing details and learning to convey them. Or, keep a bus notebook, describing people and events on your daily route. Your job, a person, a particular interest—all these can be part of your practice as a poet.
- Write a dramatic monologue (see page 145), one that you can imagine as a performance piece, perhaps with props, a setting, actions. Gear your monologue to an experiment with diction, trying to capture actual speech rhythms and the natural diction of your speaker.
- Revise a poem you've written so that all lines are enjambed. Then revise it so that all lines are end stopped. Compare the two versions with your original.

Your Poems out the Door

If you are interested in publishing, nothing could be simpler than the submission process. Spend some hours in the library or a good bookstore reading current literary magazines. If they are not available, ask the reference librarian for a *Literary Market Place*. If you are in an isolated area, check out books of poems and look at the acknowledgments pages to see where the poet previously published the poems. Then write to each magazine that interests you and request a copy. Always see which magazines publish poetry you like. It's a waste of time to send blindly to publications you don't know. To find out more about magazines, conferences, and organizations, visit these helpful Web sites:

Poetry Society of America   www.poetrysociety.org
Academy of American Poets   www.poets.org
The Council of Literary Magazines and Presses   www.clmp.org
Poetry Daily   www.poems.com
Associated Writing Programs   www.awpwriter.org
Poets & Writers Magazine   www.pw.org

Send three to five poems, impeccably typed, to the editor. If a poem is longer than a page, indicate whether or not there is a stanza break at the bottom of every page. Your name and address should appear on each sheet you submit. Don't send a résumé or write an involved letter, but it is nice to say something about yourself: that you work as a reading tutor or taxi driver, that you study film in Arkansas or work as a nurse, lawyer, or cook. If you admire the magazine, no one minds hearing what you especially like. If that seems awkward, just enclose the poems, list them by name, and thank the editors for reading and considering them. Always enclose a stamped, self-addressed envelope (called SASE) for return. Everyone gets rejected. It always hurts. Send the poem out again right away. If you have received an encouraging note with your poems, you might try the same magazine again soon. Usually, editors write brief responses, if any, because they are frantically busy. Some respected magazines receive a staggering 100,000 poems a year. If months go by, with no reply at all to your poems, write and inquire about their status.

To avoid many hard rejections, show your work to trusted friends. Ask if they think you're ready to publish. Of course, they may be wrong, but in general, you are operating in the dark if you just have your own opinion. We all love our own writing. Sending out work too soon often means crushing discouragement, when it would have been better to concentrate on clarifying the style and intensifying the experience of writing.

New writers often ask about copyrighting their work before they send it out. It's not necessary, and actually the circled C on a poem looks amateurish. Most poets are far too enamored of their own words to take anyone else's. Books, of course, are copyrighted, and poems that are accepted for publication are copyrighted by the magazine, usually with all rights belonging to the author, who simply acknowledges the magazine when a poem is reprinted elsewhere.

As you write more and more, you may have an urge toward more than one genre, nonfiction, fiction, or plays. If you have the opportunity, it's helpful to join a workshop or take classes in all of these, in order to explore the structures and possibilities of each. As I have found in my own writing, all the genres join at some deep taproot. More and more, writers feel the connection of all the genres, and many are reluctant now to tie themselves forever to only one. For any writing, poetry offers the most precise and, at the same time, the most imaginative training. Leafing through the chapters in this book, you'll notice how many of the topics covered carry over to the concerns of other genres. Image making or using repetition patterns or selecting a certain diction have everything to do with short stories, novels, and plays. This chapter's exercises help you search your most important material. The art can't go far without the craft. Read and reread these chapters with *writing* in mind. What you need to know as a writer of poetry is also what you need to know as a reader, and then some.

Permissions

Basho, haiku ["The silence!"] from R. H. Blyth, *Haiku Volume I: Eastern Culture* (Tokyo: Hokuseido Press, 1981). Copyright 1941, © 1981 by R. H. Blyth. Reprinted with permission.

Steven Bauer, "Intro to Poetry." Reprinted with the permission of the author.

Robin Becker, "Giacometti's Dog" from *Giacometti's Dog*. Copyright © 1990 by Robin Becker. Reprinted with the permission of the University of Pittsburgh Press.

Wendell Berry, "The Wheel" from *Collected Poems 1957–1982*. Copyright © 1985 by Wendell Berry. Reprinted with the permission of North Point Press, a division of Farrar, Straus & Giroux, LLC.

John Berryman, "Winter Landscape" from *Short Poems*. Copyright © 1967 by John Berryman. Reprinted with the permission of Farrar, Straus & Giroux, LLC.

Elizabeth Bishop, "The Fish," "Sestina," and "In the Waiting Room" from *The Collected Poems 1927–1979*. Copyright © 1979, 1983 by Alice Helen Methfessel. Reprinted with the permission of Farrar, Straus & Giroux, LLC.

Louise Bogan, "Rhyme" from *The Blue Estuaries*. Copyright © 1968 by Louise Bogan. Reprinted with the permission of Farrar, Straus & Giroux, LLC.

Neal Bowers, excerpt from "Repairs" from *Poetry* 159, no. 5 (February 1992). Reprinted with the permission of the author.

André Breton, excerpt from "Free Union" from *Poems*. Copyright 1949 by Éditions Gallimard. Reprinted with the permission of Éditions Gallimard.

Gwendolyn Brooks, "The Mother" from *Blacks* (Chicago: Third World Press, 1987). Copyright © 1987 by Gwendolyn Brooks Blakely. Reprinted with the permission of the Estate of Gwendolyn Brooks.

D. F. Brown, "Long Range Patrol" from *Returning Fire*. Reprinted with the permission of the author.

Michael Dennis Browne, excerpt ["the bulb hangs in the hot dark / like a white blood drop."]. Reprinted with the permission of the author.

Buson, three haiku ["The coolness:"; "It is deep autumn"; and "Ah, grief and sadness!"] from R. H. Blyth, *Haiku Volume I: Eastern Culture* (Tokyo: Hokuseido Press, 1981). Copyright 1941, © 1981 by R. H. Blyth. Reprinted with permission.

Billy Collins, "Tuesday, June 4th, 1991" from *The Art of Drowning*. Copyright © 1995 by Billy Collins. Reprinted with the permission of the University of Pittsburgh Press.

Cid Corman, "The Tortoise" from *Words for Each Other* (London: Rapp & Carroll, 1967). Reprinted with the permission of the author.

Robert Creeley, "I Know a Man" from *The Collected Poems of Robert Creeley, 1945–1975*. Copyright © 1983 by The Regents of the University of California. Reprinted with the permission of the University of California Press.

E. E. Cummings, "Chanson Innocente," "somewhere I have never travelled," "Buffalo Bill's," and excerpt from "Portraits" from *Complete Poems 1904–1962*, edited by George J. Firmage. Copyright 1923, 1931, 1951, © 1959, 1991 by the Trustees for the E. E. Cummings Trust. Copyright © 1976, 1979 by George James Firmage. Reprinted with the permission of Liveright Publishing Corporation.

James Dickey, "Cherrylog Road" from *Poems 1957–1967*. Copyright © 1963 by James Dickey. Reprinted with the permission of Wesleyan University Press.

Emily Dickinson, #425 ["Good Morning—Midnight—"], #754 ["My Life Had Stood—A Loaded Gun"], #986 ["A Narrow Fellow in the Grass"], and #1052 ["I Never Saw a Moor—"] from *The Poems of Emily Dickinson*, edited by Thomas H.

Yusef Komunyakaa, "Facing It" from *Dien Cai Dau*. Copyright © 1988 by Yusef Komunyakaa. Reprinted with the permission of Wesleyan University Press.

Aina Kravjiete, "In Chalk Rooms," translated by Inara Cedrins, from *Anthology of East European Poetry* (Oxford University Press). Translation copyright © 1981 by Inara Cedrins. Reprinted with the permission of the translator.

Marilyn Krysl, "Saying Things" and "Sestina: Vanishing Point" from *More Palomino, Please, More Fuschia* (Cleveland: Cleveland State University Press, 1980). Copyright © 1980 by Marilyn Krysl. Reprinted with the permission of the author.

Stanley Kunitz, "The Knot" from *The Collected Poems*. Copyright © 2000 by Stanley Kunitz. Reprinted with the permission of W. W. Norton & Company, Inc.

Kyoshi, haiku ["The snake slid away,"] from R. H. Blyth, *Haiku Volume I: Eastern Culture* (Tokyo: Hokuseido Press, 1981). Copyright 1941, © 1981 by R. H. Blyth. Reprinted with permission.

Hazel Lane, "The Late Late Show." Copyright © by Hazel Lane. Reprinted with the permission of the author.

Joseph Langland, "Hunters in the Snow: Brueghel" from *The Wheel of Summer* (New York: The Dial Press, 1963). Copyright © 1963 by Joseph Langland. Reprinted with the permission of the author.

Philip Larkin, excerpt from "Coming" from *Collected Poems*. Reprinted with the permission of The Marvell Press. "An Arundel Tomb" from *Collected Poems*. Copyright © 1988, 1989 by the Estate of Philip Larkin. Reprinted with the permission of Farrar, Straus & Giroux, LLC and Faber and Faber Ltd.

Li-Young Lee, "For a New Citizen of These United States" from *The City in Which I Love You*. Copyright © 1990 by Li-Young Lee. Reprinted with the permission of BOA Editions Ltd.

Denise Levertov, "Stepping Westward" from *Poems 1960–1967*. Copyright © 1966 by Denise Levertov. Reprinted with the permission of New Directions Publishing Corporation.

Philip Levine, "Starlight" from *New Selected Poems*. Copyright © 1991 by Philip Levine. Reprinted with the permission of Alfred A. Knopf, a division of Random House, Inc.

Robert Lowell, "Man and Wife" from *Life Studies*. Copyright © 1959 by Robert Lowell. Copyright renewed © 1987 by Harriet Lowell, Sheridan Lowell, and Caroline Lowell. Reprinted with the permission of Farrar, Straus & Giroux, LLC.

Susan MacDonald, "A Smart Dithyramb" from *A Smart Dithyramb* (Woodside, Calif.: The Heyeck Press, 1979). Reprinted with the permission of the author.

Louis MacNeice, "Snow" from *The Selected Poems of Louis MacNeice* (Winston-Salem: Wake Forest University Press, 1990). Reprinted with the permission of David Higham Associates, Ltd.

Edward Kleinschmidt Mayes, "Boustrophedon" from *First Language*. Copyright © 1990 by Ralph Kaplan. Reprinted with the permission of The University of Massachusetts Press. "University of Iowa Hospital, 1976" from *Magnetism* (Woodside, Calif.: Heyeck Press, 1987). Originally published in *Poetry* (March 1986). Copyright © 1986 by the Modern Poetry Association. Reprinted with the permission of *Poetry* and the author. "Giorni" and "Verità" from *Works and Days*. Copyright © 1999. Reprinted with the permission of the University of Pittsburgh Press.

Index of Titles

Adam's Curse (Yeats), 465
Alba (Pound), 404
Alba (Walcott), 368
Allegro (Tranströmer), 108
Among School Children (Yeats), 450
Archaic Torso of Apollo (Rilke), 426
Ars Poetica (Milosz), 366
Arundel Tomb, An (Larkin), 153
As You Like It (excerpt) (Shakespeare), 226
Atlas of the Difficult World, An (excerpt) (Rich), 6
Atomic Bride (Ellis), 202
Atomic Pantoum (Meinke), 326
Aubade (Sitwell), 182
Autobiographia Literaria (O'Hara), 147
Autumn Begins in Martins Ferry, Ohio (James Wright), 41

Badger (Clare), 83
Beauty (Cowley), 58

Best Days, The (Duval), 133
Between Walls (W. C. Williams), 268
Bitter-Sweet (Herbert), 440
Black Poet, White Critic (Randall), 420
Blackberrying (Plath), 293
Blacksmiths, The (Anonymous), 36
Blades (C. K. Williams), 282
Blessing, A (James Wright), 2
Body Poems (excerpt) (Barks), 110
Boustrophedon (E. Mayes), 447
Boy Riding Forward Backward (Francis), 464
Breakfast (Gibson), 189
Bright Star (Keats), 306

Cat & The Weather (Swenson), 289
Cataract of Lodore, The (excerpt) (Southey), 194
Chances of Rhyme, The (Tomlinson), 183
Chanson Innocente (cummings), 17

Cherrylog Road (Dickey), 44
Chorale of Cherokee Night Music as Heard Through an Open Window in Summer Long Ago, A (J. Williams), 440
Christabel (excerpt) (Coleridge), 246
Colonel, The (Forché), 346
Corinna's Going A-Maying (Herrick), 155
Counting-Out Rhyme (Millay), 4
Crystals Like Blood (MacDiarmid), 49

Dance, The (W. C. Williams), 251
Day Lady Died, The (O'Hara), 410
Deaf Poem (Gallagher), 350
Death of a Vermont Farm Woman (Howes), 321
Degrees of Gray in Philipsburg (Hugo), 476
Description of the Morning, A (Swift), 76
Do Not Go Gentle into That Good Night (Thomas), 336
Dover Beach (Arnold), 340
Dulce Et Decorum Est (Owen), 152

Early Supper (Howes), 320
Easter Wings (Herbert), 303
Effort at Speech Between Two People (Rukeyser), 342
Elder Sister, The (Olds), 274
End of Autumn, The (Ponge), 386
Envoy (Dowson), 174
Epitaph on a Hare (Cowper), 82
Epithalamium (excerpt) (Spenser), 372
Eve of St. Agnes, The (Keats), 115
Every Day You Play (Neruda), 392
Expiration, The (Donne), 413
eyeye (Saroyan), 304

Facing It (Komunyakaa), 107
Father at His Son's Baptism, A (Gerstler), 19
Fern Hill (Thomas), 50
First Photos of Flu Virus (Witt), 320
Fish, The (Bishop), 55
Fly, The (Blake), 240
Fog-Horn (Merwin), 130
Foot, The (Jones), 42

For a New Citizen of These United States (Lee), 159
For the Anniversary of My Death (Merwin), 298
Force That Through the Green Fuse Drives the Flower, The (excerpt) (Thomas), 109
Fork (Simic), 133
425 (Dickinson), 433
Free Union (excerpt) (Breton), 438

Giacometti's Dog (Becker), 418
Giorni (E. Mayes), 298
Girl (Kincaid), 361
Glistening (Gregg), xiii
Gloire De Dijon (Lawrence), 69
God's Grandeur (Hopkins), 248
Grappa in September (Pavese), 383
Great Figure, The (W. C. Williams), 276

Hamlet (excerpt) (Shakespeare), 150
Harlem Sweeties (L. Hughes), 466
He Remembers Forgotten Beauty (Yeats), 39
Heat (H.D.), 270
Her Face, Her Tongue, Her Wytt (Gorges), 239
His Running My Running (Francis), 254
House Was Quiet and the World Was Calm, The (Stevens), 477
How They Brought the Good News from Ghent to Aix (Browning), 241
Howling of Wolves, The (T. Hughes), 344
Hunters in the Snow: Brueghel (Langland), 396
Hunters in the Snow, The (W. C. Williams), 394

I Care Not for These Ladies (Campion), 411
I Hear America Singing (Whitman), 201
I Know a Man (Creeley), 291
I Think Continually of Those Who Were Truly Great (Spender), 146
I Wandered Lonely as a Cloud (Wordsworth), 15

I Will Enjoy Thee Now (Carew), 388
If I Could Tell You (Auden), 315
If You Saw Me Walking (Stern), 192
Image (Hulme), 468
In Chalk Rooms (Kraujiete), 208
In Memory of W. B. Yeats (Auden), 258
In the Bay (excerpt) (Swinburne), 40
In the Waiting Room (Bishop), 441
Infant Sorrow (Blake), 175
Ink Fish (Mirosevich), 360
Intro to Poetry (Bauer), 23
Inversnaid (Hopkins), 37
Inviting a Friend to Supper (Jonson), 163

Jabberwocky (Carroll), 26
Jubilate Agno (excerpt) (Smart), 196
Just Man, A (József), 94

Knot, The (Kunitz), 102

Lamb, The (Blake), 103
Lament While Descending a Shaft (work song), 218
Late Late Show, The (Lane), 473
Leda and the Swan (Yeats), 449
Letter from the Caribbean, A (Howes), 472
Living (C. D. Wright), 351
Long Range Patrol (Brown), 291
Long Time More, A (Wier), 24
Lord Randal (Anonymous), 188
Loveliest of Trees (Housman), xi
Lucky Life (Stern), 214
Lying in a Hammock at William Duffy's Farm in Pine Island, Minnesota (James Wright), 422

Macbeth (excerpt) (Shakespeare), 10
Madrid (Jay Wright), 62
Madrigal (Anonymous), 408
Man and Wife (Lowell), 180
Marin Headlands (Miller), 354
Meditation at Lagunitas (Hass), 292
Memory (Yeats), 302
Metaphors (Plath), 90
Michael, A Pastoral (excerpt) (Wordsworth), 364

Mnemonic (Coleridge), 254
Mock On, Mock On, Voltaire, Rousseau (Blake), 446
Mother, The (Brooks), 417
Musée des Beaux Arts (Auden), 161
Mushroom Hunting in the Jemez Mountains (Sze), 64
Mushrooms (Plath), 249
My Mother Would Be a Falconress (Duncan), 112
My Papa's Waltz (Roethke), 253
My Sweetest Lesbia (Campion), 412

Nani (Ríos), 162
Nantucket (W. C. Williams), 75
Nature's Cook (Margaret, Duchess of Newcastle), 261
Negress: Her Monologue of Dark Crêpe with Edges of Light, The (excerpt) (Dubie), 142
New Body (Miller), 391
Night Chant, The (excerpt) (Navajo song), 198
Night Feeding (Rukeyser), 416
Night Is Freezing Fast, The (Hausman), 54
Night Song (Mueller), 186
986 (Dickinson), 20
North Central (excerpt) (Niedecker), 462
Nothing Gold Can Stay (Frost), 238
Nothing to Declare (C. D. Wright), 475
Now Winter Nights Enlarge (Campion), 178
Nymph's Reply to the Shepherd, The (Raleigh), 469

Ode on a Grecian Urn (Keats), 399
Ode to a Nightingale (Keats), 378
Ode to a Watch at Night (Neruda), 401
Ode to the West Wind (Shelley), 329
Of My Lady (Hoccleve), 33
Oh, Lovely Rock (Jeffers), 48
On Donne's Poetry (Coleridge), 416
On First Looking into Chapman's Homer (Keats), 313
On My First Son (Jonson), 371
On Time (Milton), 134

Once by the Pacific (Frost), 225
1052 (Dickinson), 172

Partial Explanation, The (Simic), 148
Passionate Shepherd to His Love, The (Marlow), 140
Piano, A (Stein), 404
Piano (Lawrence), 457
Pied Beauty (Hopkins), 35
Poem (W. C. Williams), 290
Poems We Can Understand (Hoover), 470
Poppies (Oliver), 357
Portraits (excerpt) (cummings), 274
Preludes (Eliot), 78
Protocols (Jarrell), 460

Question (Swenson), 92

Red, Red Rose, A (Burns), 187
Red Wheelbarrow, The (W. C. Williams), 398
Relique, The (Donne), 415
Rendezvous (Seeger), 257
Resemblance (R. Williams), 158
Residue (Drummond de Andrade), 209
Return (Alegría), 473
Rhyme (Bogan), 265
Romeo and Juliet (excerpt) (Shakespeare), 255
Runner, The (Whitman), 85

Sailing to Byzantium (Yeats), 262
Salt (Phillips), 22
Sandy Hole, The (Kenyon), xiv
Saying Things (Krysl), 29
Scirocco (Graham), 277
Second Coming, The (Yeats), 449
Second Wife, The (Reese), 457
Sestina: Vanishing Point (Krysl), 333
Sestina (Bishop), 334
Sestina for the Owl (F. Mayes), 317
754 (Dickinson), 106
Shape of Death, The (Swenson), 305
Silent Poem (Francis), 468
Silken Tent, The (Frost), 88
Sinister (Gander), 358
Smart Dithyramb, A (MacDonald), 369
Snail (García Lorca), 190

Snow (MacNeice), 287
Snowstorm, The (Emerson), 53
Soldiers Bathing (Prince), 338
Somebody's Darling (LaCoste), 455
Somewhere I Have Never Travelled (cummings), 387
Somnambule Ballad (García Lorca), 205
Song (Donne), 179
Songs in the Garden of the House God (Navajo song), 166
Sonnet 7 from Holy Sonnets (Donne), 332
Sonnet 61 (Drayton), 471
Sonnet LXXIII (Shakespeare), 55
Sonnet LXXV (Spenser), 314
Sonnet XCVIII (Shakespeare), 312
Sonnet CXVI (Shakespeare), 328
Sonnet CXXX (Shakespeare), 445
Sonnet Reversed (Brooke), 315
Sonnet Right Off the Bat (Vega), 328
Spring and All (W. C. Williams), 16
Stanzas for Music (Byron), 265
Starlight (Levine), 288
Stepping Westward (Levertov), 13
Stirling's Hotel (work songs), 218
Study of Two Pears (Stevens), 80
Sunday Morning (Stevens), 228
Sunne Rising, The (Donne), 11

That Song (Rogers), 60
Theological Definition, A (Oppen), 471
There Was a Saviour (Thomas), 434
Thirteen Ways of Looking at a Blackbird (Stevens), 295
Those Winter Sundays (Hayden), 18
To a Chameleon (Moore), 173–4
To a Poor Old Woman (W. C. Williams), 294
To a Skylark (Shelley), 235
To Autumn (Keats), 384
To Earthward (Frost), 263
To Go to Lvov (Zagajewski), 212
To Her Againe, She Burning in a Feaver (Carew), 181
To His Coy Mistress (Marvell), 233
To the Driving Cloud (Longfellow), 244
To the Virgins, to Make Much of Time (Herrick), 368

To Toussaint L'Ouverture (Wordsworth), 371

Today (O'Hara), 65

Too Hard It Is to Sing (Dobson), 322

Tortoise, The (Corman), 436

Translations of Anakreon (Anakreon), 429

Traveling Through the Dark (Stafford), 77

Tuesday, June 4th, 1991 (Collins), xv

Tulips (Plath), 348

Two in August (Ransom), 177

Two Years Later (Wieners), 463

Tyger, The (Blake), 104

University of Iowa Hospital, 1976 (E. Mayes), 131

Untitled (King), 138

Upon His Departure Hence (Herrick), 262

Upstate (Walcott), 59

Valediction: Forbidding Mourning, A (Donne), 413

Verita (E. Mayes), 405

Very Valentine, A (Stein), 187

Village for a Wedding (Ożóg), 408

Vine, The (Thomson), 91

Waking, The (Roethke), 337

Western Wind (Anonymous), 468

What Is an Epigram? (Coleridge), 337

What Is Poetry (Ashbery), 461

What Rushes By Us (Goedicke), 135

What the Dog Perhaps Hears (Mueller), 70

Wheel, The (Berry), 168

When That I Was and a Little Tiny Boy (Shakespeare), 52

When the Ceiling Cries (Edson), 418

Wild Swans of Coole, The (Yeats), 385

Windhover, The (Hopkins), 382

Winter Landscape (Berryman), 395

Winter (Shakespeare), 71

Words (Plath), 64

World So Wide, The (Anonymous), 463

You (Stanford), 159

Index of
Authors and Titles

Alegría, Fernando
Return, 473
Anakreon
Translations of Anakreon, 429
Anonymous
The Blacksmiths, 36
The World So Wide, 463
Lord Randal, 188
Madrigal, 408
Western Wind, 468
Arnold, Matthew
Dover Beach, 340
Ashbery, John
What Is Poetry, 461
Auden, W. H.
If I Could Tell You, 315
In Memory of W. B. Yeats, 258
Musée des Beaux Arts, 161

Barks, Coleman
from Body Poems, 110

Bauer, Steven
Intro to Poetry, 23
Becker, Robin
Giacometti's Dog, 418
Berry, Wendell
The Wheel, 168
Berryman, John
Winter Landscape, 395
Bishop, Elizabeth
The Fish, 55
In the Waiting Room, 441
Sestina, 334
Blake, William
The Fly, 240
The Lamb, 103
The Tyger, 104
Infant Sorrow, 175
Mock On, Mock On, Voltaire,
Rousseau, 446
Bogan, Louise
Rhyme, 265

Breton, André
   from *Free Union*, 438
Brooke, Rupert
   Sonnet Reversed, 315
Brooks, Gwendolyn
   The Mother, 417
Brown, D. F.
   Long Range Patrol, 291
Browning, Robert
   *How They Brought the Good News
      from Ghent to Aix*, 241
Burns, Robert
   A Red, Red Rose, 187
Byron, George Gordon, Lord
   Stanzas for Music, 265

Campion, Thomas
   I Care Not for These Ladies, 411
   My Sweetest Lesbia, 412
   Now Winter Nights Enlarge, 178
Carew, Thomas
   *To Her Againe, She Burning in a
      Feaver*, 181
   I Will Enjoy Thee Now, 388
Carroll, Lewis
   Jabberwocky, 26
Clare, John
   Badger, 83
Coleridge, Samuel Taylor
   from *Christabel*, 246
   Mnemonic, 254
   On Donne's Poetry, 416
   What Is an Epigram?, 337
Collins, Billy
   Tuesday, June 4th, 1991, xv
Corman, Cid
   The Tortoise, 436
Cowley, Abraham
   Beauty, 58
Cowper, William
   Epitaph on a Hare, 82
Creeley, Robert
   I Know a Man, 291
cummings, e. e.
   from *Portraits*, 274
   Chanson Innocente, 17
   Somewhere I Have Never Travelled, 387

Dickey, James
   Cherrylog Road, 44
Dickinson, Emily
   425, 433
   754, 106
   986, 20
   1052, 172
Dobson, Auston
   Too Hard It Is to Sing, 322
Donne, John
   The Expiration, 413
   The Relique, 415
   The Sunne Rising, 11
   A Valediction: Forbidding Mourning,
      413
   Song, 179
   Sonnet 7 from *Holy Sonnets*, 332
Dowson, Ernest
   Envoy, 174
Drayton, Michael
   Sonnet 61, 471
Drummond de Andrade, Carlos
   Residue, 209
Dubie, Norman
   *The Negress: Her Monologue of Dark
      Crêpe with Edges of Light*, 142
Duncan, Robert
   My Mother Would Be a Falconress,
      112
Duval, Quinton
   The Best Days, 133

Edson, Russell
   When the Ceiling Cries, 418
Eliot, T. S.
   Preludes, 78
Ellis, Thomas Sayers
   Atomic Bride, 192
Emerson, Ralph Waldo
   The Snowstorm, 53

Forché, Carolyn
   The Colonel, 346
Francis, Robert
   Boy Riding Forward Backward, 464
   His Running My Running, 254
   Silent Poem, 468

Frost, Robert
  The Silken Tent, 88
  Nothing Gold Can Stay, 238
  Once by the Pacific, 225
  To Earthward, 263

Gallagher, Tess
  Deaf Poem, 350
Gander, Forrest
  Sinister, 358
García Lorca, Federico
  Snail, 190
  Somnambule Ballad, 205
Gerstler, Amy
  A Father at His Son's Baptism, 19
Gibson, Wilfrid
  Breakfast, 189
Goedicke, Patricia
  What Rushes By Us, 135
Gorges, Arthur
  Her Face, Her Tongue, Her Wytt, 239
Graham, Jorie
  Scirocco, 277
Gregg, Linda
  Glistening, xiii

Hass, Robert
  Meditation at Lagunitas, 292
Hausman, A. E.
  The Night Is Freezing Fast, 54
Hayden, Robert
  Those Winter Sundays, 18
H.D. (Hilda Doolittle)
  Heat, 270
Herbert, George
  Bitter-Sweet, 440
  Easter Wings, 303
Herrick, Robert
  Corinna's Going A-Maying, 155
  Upon His Departure Hence, 262
  To the Virgins, to Make Much of
    Time, 368
Hoccleve, Thomas
  Of My Lady, 33
Hoover, Paul
  Poems We Can Understand, 470
Hopkins, Gerard Manley
  The Windhover, 382

God's Grandeur, 248
  Inversnaid, 37
  Pied Beauty, 35
Housman, A. E.
  Loveliest of Trees, xi
Howes, Barbara
  A Letter from the Caribbean, 472
  Death of a Vermont Farm Woman, 321
  Early Supper, 320
Hughes, Langston
  Harlem Sweeties, 466
Hughes, Ted
  The Howling of Wolves, 344
Hugo, Richard
  Degrees of Gray in Philipsburg, 476
Hulme, T. E.
  Image, 468

Jarrell, Randall
  Protocols, 460
Jeffers, Robinson
  Oh, Lovely Rock, 48
Jones, Alice
  The Foot, 42
Jonson, Ben
  Inviting a Friend to Supper, 163
  On My First Son, 371
József, Attila
  A Just Man, 94

Keats, John
  The Eve of St. Agnes, 115
  Bright Star, 306
  Ode on a Grecian Urn, 399
  Ode to a Nightingale, 378
  On First Looking into Chapman's
    Homer, 313
  To Autumn, 384
Kenyon, Jane
  The Sandy Hole, xiv
Kincaid, Jamaica
  Girl, 361
King, Ashley
  Untitled, 138
Komunyakaa, Yusef
  Facing It, 107
Kraujiete, Aina
  In Chalk Rooms, 208

Krysl, Marilyn
  Saying Things, 29
  Sestina: Vanishing Point, 333
Kunitz, Stanley
  The Knot, 102

LaCoste, Marie
  Somebody's Darling, 455
Lane, Hazel
  The Late Late Show, 473
Langland, Joseph
  Hunters in the Snow: Brueghel, 396
Larkin, Philip
  An Arundel Tomb, 153
Lawrence, D. H.
  Gloire De Dijon, 69
  Piano, 457
Lee, Li-Young
  For a New Citizen of These United States, 159
Levertov, Denise
  Stepping Westward, 13
Levine, Philip
  Starlight, 288
Longfellow, Henry Wadsworth
  To the Driving Cloud, 244
Lowell, Robert
  Man and Wife, 180

MacDiarmid, Hugh
  Crystals Like Blood, 49
MacDonald, Susan
  A Smart Dithyramb, 369
MacNeice, Louis
  Snow, 287
Margaret, Duchess of Newcastle
  Nature's Cook, 261
Marlow, Christopher
  The Passionate Shepherd to His Love, 140
Marvell, Andrew
  To His Coy Mistress, 233
Mayes, Edward
  Boustrophedon, 447
  Giorni, 298
  University of Iowa Hospital, 1976, 131
  Verita, 405

Mayes, Francis
  Sestina for the Owl, 317
Meinke, Peter
  Atomic Pantoum, 326
Merwin, W. S.
  For the Anniversary of My Death, 298
  Fog-Horn, 130
Millay, Edna St. Vincent
  Counting-Out Rhyme, 4
Miller, Jane
  Marin Headlands, 354
  New Body, 391
Milosz, Czeslaw
  Ars Poetica, 366
Milton, John
  On Time, 134
Mirosevich, Toni
  Ink Fish, 360
Moore, Marianne
  To a Chameleon, 173–4
Mueller, Lisel
  Night Song, 186
  What the Dog Perhaps Hears, 70

Navajo songs
  from *The Night Chant*, 198
  Songs in the Garden of the House God, 166
Neruda, Pablo
  Every Day You Play, 392
  Ode to a Watch at Night, 401
Niedecker, Lorine
  from *North Central*, 462

O'Hara, Frank
  The Day Lady Died, 410
  Autobiographia Literaria, 147
  Today, 65
Olds, Sharon
  The Elder Sister, 274
Oliver, Mary
  Poppies, 357
Oppen, George
  A Theological Definition, 471
Owen, Wilfred
  Dulce Et Decorum Est, 152
Ożóg, Jan Boleslaw
  Village for a Wedding, 408

Pavese, Cesare
  Grappa in September, 383
Phillips, Frances
  Salt, 21
Plath, Sylvia
  Blackberrying, 293
  Metaphors, 90
  Mushrooms, 249
  Tulips, 348
  Words, 64
Ponge, Francis
  The End of Autumn, 386
Pound, Ezra
  Alba, 404
Prince, F. T.
  Soldiers Bathing, 338

Raleigh, Sir Walter
  The Nymph's Reply to the Shepherd,
    469
Randall, Dudley
  Black Poet, White Critic, 420
Ransom, John Crowe
  Two in August, 177
Reese, Lizette
  The Second Wife, 457
Rich, Adrienne
  from *An Atlas of the Difficult World*,
    5
Rilke, Rainer Maria
  Archaic Torso of Apollo, 426
Ríos, Alberto
  Nani, 162
Roethke, Theodore
  The Waking, 337
  My Papa's Waltz, 253
Rogers, Pattiann
  That Song, 60
Rukeyser, Muriel
  Effort at Speech Between Two People,
    342
  Night Feeding, 416

Saroyan, Aram
  eyeye, 304
Seeger, Alan
  Rendezvous, 257

Shakespeare, William
  from *As You Like It*, 226
  from *Hamlet*, 150
  from *Macbeth*, 10
  from *Romeo and Juliet*, 255
  Sonnet LXXIII, 55
  Sonnet XCVIII, 312
  Sonnet CXVI, 328
  Sonnet CXXX, 445
  *When That I Was and a Little Tiny
    Boy*, 52
  Winter, 71
Shelley, Percy Bysshe
  Ode to the West Wind, 329
  To a Skylark, 235
Simic, Charles
  The Partial Explanation, 148
  Fork, 133
Sitwell, Edith
  Aubade, 174
Smart, Christopher
  from *Jubilate Agno*, 196
Southey, Robert
  from *The Cataract of Lodore*, 194
Spender, Stephen
  *I Think Continually of Those Who
    Were Truly Great*, 146
Spenser, Edmund
  from *Epithalamium*, 372
  Sonnet LXXV, 314
Stafford, William
  Traveling Through the Dark, 77
Stanford, Frank
  You, 159
Stein, Gertrude
  A Piano, 404
  A Very Valentine, 187
Stern, Gerald
  If You Saw Me Walking, 192
  Lucky Life, 214
Stevens, Wallace
  *The House Was Quiet and the World
    Was Calm*, 477
  Study of Two Pears, 80
  Sunday Morning, 228
  *Thirteen Ways of Looking at a
    Blackbird*, 295

Swenson, May
  The Shape of Death, 305
  Cat & The Weather, 289
  Question, 92
Swift, Jonathan
  A Description of the Morning, 76
Swinburne, Algernon C.
  from *In the Bay*, 40
Sze, Arthur
  *Mushroom Hunting in the Jemez
    Mountains*, 64

Thomas, Dylan
  *The Force That Through the Green
    Fuse Drives the Flower* (excerpt), 109
  *Do Not Go Gentle into That Good
    Night*, 336
  Fern Hill, 50
  There Was a Saviour, 434
Thomson, James
  The Vine, 91
Tomlinson, Charles
  The Chances of Rhyme, 183
Tranströmer, Tomas
  Allegro, 108

Vega, Lope de
  Sonnet Right Off the Bat, 328

Walcott, Derek
  Alba, 368
  Upstate, 59
Whitman, Walt
  The Runner, 85
  I Hear America Singing, 201
Wieners, John
  Two Years Later, 463
Wier, Dara
  A Long Time More, 24
Williams, C. K.
  Blades, 282
Williams, Jonathan
  *A Chorale of Cherokee Night Music
    as Heard Through an Open Window
    in Summer Long Ago*, 440
Williams, Rena
  Resemblance, 158

Williams, William Carlos
  The Dance, 251
  The Great Figure, 276
  The Hunters in the Snow, 394
  The Red Wheelbarrow, 398
  Between Walls, 268
  Nantucket, 75
  Poem, 290
  Spring and All, 16
  To a Poor Old Woman, 294
Witt, Harold
  First Photos of Flu Virus, 320
Wordsworth, William
  from *Michael, A Pastoral*, 364
  I Wandered Lonely as a Cloud, 15
  To Toussaint L'Ouverture, 371
Work songs
  Lament While Descending a Shaft,
    218
  Stirling's Hotel, 218
Wright, C. D.
  Living, 351
  Nothing to Declare, 475
Wright, James
  A Blessing, 2
  *Autumn Begins in Martins Ferry,
    Ohio*, 41
  *Lying in a Hammock at William
    Duffy's Farm in Pine Island,
    Minnesota*, 422
Wright, Jay
  Madrid, 62

Yeats, William Butler
  The Second Coming, 449
  The Wild Swans of Coole, 385
  Adam's Curse, 465
  Among School Children, 450
  He Remembers Forgotten Beauty, 39
  Leda and the Swan, 449
  Memory, 302
  Sailing to Byzantium, 262

Zagajewski, Adam
  To Go to Lvov, 212

Index of
Terms and Topics

abstract language, 31, 67
accent, 221
accentual meter, 245
accentual-syllabic meter,
  245
alba, 368
aleatory poetry, 440
alliteration, 35, 173
allusion, 9
anapest, 222
anapestic tetrameter, 241
anaphora, 186
apocopated rhyme, 173
archetype, 101
ars poetica, 366
association, 437
assonance, 38
aubade, 13, 368

blank verse, 226

cacophony, 39

caesura, 245
carpe diem, 368
catalogue poems, 444
Chaucerian stanza, 309
cliché, 31
closing repetition, 189
combined repetition, 187
common measure, 308
conceit, 98
concrete language, 31, 67
concrete poetry, 304
connotation, 25
consonance, 38
continuous form, 276
couplet, 308

dactyl, 223
dactylic pentameter, 243
decorum, 459
denotation, 25
diction, 42
didactic poetry, 151, 460

dimeter, 222
dithyramb, 369
dramatic monologue, 145
dramatic poetry, 9

encomium, 371
elegy, 370
end rhyme, 172
end-stopped line, 273
English sonnet, 312
enjambment, 273
epic simile, 88
epigram, 325
epiphany, 441
epistle, 145
epithalamium, 372
euphony, 38
exaggeration, 445
eye rhyme, 173

falling rhyme (feminine),
  172

falling rhythm, 234
figurative image, 75, 85
foot, 220
free verse, 267

haiku, 323
half rhyme, 171
head rhyme, 173
heroic couplet, 308
heptameter, 222
hexameter, 222
homonyms, 175
hyperbole, 445

iamb, 222
iambic dimeter, 240
iambic foot, 222
iambic pentameter, 224
iambic tetrameter, 232
iambic trimeter, 238
identical rhyme, 174
image, 66
image repetition, 190
internal rhyme, 172
invisible speaker, 153

line 7, 273
linked rhyme, 173
literal image, 75
lyric, 9

madrigal, 374
meaning, 427
melodrama, 455
metaphor, 89
meter, 219
metonymy, 96
mixed metaphor, 92
monometer, 222
moralism, 460

narrative poetry, 9
nonce form, 306

octameter, 222
octave, 310
off rhyme, 171

onomatopoeia, 31
open form, 306, 341
opening repetition, 189
ottava rima, 310
overwriting, 459
oxymoron, 98

palinode, 374
pantoum, 326
paradox, 439
paraphrase, 10
pastoral, 364
pathetic fallacy, 98
pentameter, 222
persona, 142
personification, 97
Petrarchan sonnet, 313
private symbol, 102
prose poem, 345
public voice, 151
pure rhyme, 171

quatrain, 308
quintet, 309

refrain, 188
repetition, 184
rhyme, 170
rhyme scheme, 175
rhyme royal, 309
rhythm, 217
rising rhyme (masculine),
    172
rising rhythm, 234
rondeau, 321
rondel, 322
rune, 374

scansion, 221
second intensity poems,
    454
sentimentality, 455
septet, 309
sestet, 309
sestina, 317
Shakespearean sonnet, 312
sibilance, 40

simile, 86
single word repetition, 185
slant rhyme, 171
soliloquy, 149
sonnet, 306, 311
sonnet crowns, 311
sonnet sequence, 311
sound poem, 440
speaker, 138
Spenserian sonnet, 314
Spenserian stanza, 310
spondee, 222
stanza, 307
strong stress meter, 245
style, 375
surrealism, 437
syllabic meter, 249
symbol, 101
syncopation, 220
synecdoche, 96
synesthesia, 95
syntactical repetition, 191
syntax, 191, 458

tanka, 323
tercet, 308
terza rima, 308
tetrameter, 222
texture, 25
tone, 9, 44
traditional (fixed) form,
    301, 307
trimeter, 222
triolet, 320
triple rhyme, 173
triplet, 308
trochaic trimeter, 234
trochee, 222
tropes, 95

understatement, 445
unpatterned rhyme, 173

verse paragraph, 342
villanelle, 315
voice, 9, 44, 285